Peter Jackson

Peter Jackson

A Biography of the Australian Heavyweight Champion, 1860–1901

BOB PETERSEN

McFarland & Company, Inc., Publishers
Jefferson, North Carolina, and London

The present work is a revised, expanded and updated edition of *Gentleman Bruiser: A Life of the Boxer Peter Jackson*, published by Croydon Publishing Company in Sydney, Australia, in 2005.

LIBRARY OF CONGRESS CATALOGUING-IN-PUBLICATION DATA

Petersen, Bob (Robert Charles), 1937–
Peter Jackson : a biography of the Australian heavyweight champion, 1860–1901 / Bob Petersen.
      p.   cm.
Includes bibliographical references and index.

ISBN 978-0-7864-5881-3
softcover : 50# alkaline paper ∞

1. Jackson, Peter, 1861–1901. 2. Boxers (Sports)—
Australia — Bibliography. I. Title.
GV1132.J28P49   2011   796.83092 — dc22   [B]   2011008415

British Library cataloguing data are available

© 2011 R. C. Petersen. All rights reserved

No part of this book may be reproduced or transmitted in any form or by any means, electronic or mechanical, including photocopying or recording, or by any information storage and retrieval system, without permission in writing from the publisher.

Front cover: Peter Jackson, athlete, ca.1900,
a fine specimen of physical development

Manufactured in the United States of America

*McFarland & Company, Inc., Publishers
Box 611, Jefferson, North Carolina 28640
www.mcfarlandpub.com*

For Lidia,

and

In Memoriam
Charles Petersen
and
William Henry Merifield ("Will Sayers")

Table of Contents

Preface 1

1. Tropical Danish, 1860–1879   3
2. Unbleached Australian, 1879–1888   24
3. Offensive Tour, 1888–1889   55
4. Hope and Glory, 1889   83
5. Sea to Shining Sea, 1890   113
6. Diamonds and Schlenters, 1890–1892   127
7. Waiting in the Wings, 1893–1894   165
8. Corduroy Road, 1894–1900   183
9. Home from Home, 1900–1901   213

Notes 233
Bibliography 241
Index 249

Preface

Five biographies of Peter Jackson have been published, or rather six counting the earliest sketch of his life. Anonymous but probably by W.W. Naughton, it was called "Peter the Pugilist, he deserted orange groves to make his mark in a prize ring," in the *Examiner* (San Francisco), March 3, 1889, pages 12–13. This was two pages long, but Naughton got the story from Jackson himself. The second, in parts in 1901 by Will Corbett, in the Sydney sporting newspaper the *Referee*, broke off after a few episodes, then resumed in 72 parts in the *Referee* in 1918 and 1919. The third biography was a conscientious chapter in Nat Fleischer's *Black Dynamite: The Story of the Negro in the Prize Ring from 1782 to 1938*. The fourth was a small book by Tom Langley in 1976, titled *The Life of Peter Jackson: Champion of Australia*, which contained much fiction, including a totally imagined Jackson family history. The fifth was a 1985 article by David Wiggins that became a chapter in his *Glory Bound* (1997) and again in *A Question of Manhood: A Reader in U.S. Black Men's History and Masculinity* (2 volumes, 1999 and 2000), edited by D.C. Hine and E. Jenkins. An earlier edition of the present book titled *Gentleman Bruiser* was published in 2005, and in this revised volume several errors have been corrected. A novel by A.G. Hales titled *Romantic Career of Peter Jackson, His Fights Re-told* (1910, with later versions) included facts and all too many inventions which imposed them-

Peter Jackson, the Champion of Australia, the Champion of the Pacific Slope, the Colored Champion of the World. Undated studio portrait, possibly by Isaiah Taber of San Francisco in 1888 or 1889. Photograph courtesy of National Library of Australia [nla.pic-vn3060272].

selves as facts. Susan F. Clark's article in the *Drama Review* in 2000 was the first account of Jackson's playing in *Uncle Tom's Cabin*. Richard Broome, whom I thank for correspondence, wrote an entry in the *Australian Dictionary of Biography* and J.M. Carroll another in *American National Biography*. All other biographical accounts of Jackson are recyclings. The "Peter Jackson" entries at *Boxing Records* and *Cyberboxingzone* are monuments to the devotion and industry of their compilers.

Several recent books have been useful: Ward's *Unforgivable Blackness: The Rise and Fall of Jack Johnson* (2004), Pollack's *John L. Sullivan: The Career of the First Gloved Heavyweight Champion* (2006), and his *In the Ring with Bob Fitzsimmons* (2007), Donnellon's *The Irish Champion Peter Maher* (2008), Streible's *Fight Pictures* (2008), and Aycock and Scott's *The First Black Boxing Champions: Essays on Fighters of the 1800s to the 1920s* (2011). Gordon's *Master of the Ring: The Extraordinary Life of Jem Mace* (2007), was less useful than interesting. It portrayed a Jackson almost unrecognizable to me, and without footnotes its sources were hard to check.

If Peter left personal papers they may survive somewhere, but they have disappeared. Without them, the main sources for Jackson's life are newspapers. His story had to be reconstructed from press reports on microfilm in libraries and more recently on the web. I have tried to read as many newspapers as practicable where his doings were reported, though this gets more difficult by the month as digitalizing speeds up. The newspaper sources of the information are almost always linked in the text: in this way not only are innumerable endnotes avoided but the construction of sports history by the press is continually on display. The accounts of Jackson's main fights are not my impressionistic narratives but were pieced together from two or more newspaper reports of the day, carrying the reader as close as possible to the events. Only some racist language employed by the journalists has been tidied up.

Because it is derived from newspapers for the most part, this is a public life. When the *San Francisco Call* tells us on May 31, 1892, the day after Peter beat Slavin in London, that Billy Schwerin was "Peter's intimate friend, who got the last dispatch before the fight from the sable gladiator," we must regret that no private memoir about their close relationship survives. As no other newspaper mention of him with Peter has been found, Schwerin's name here makes its solitary appearance in Peter's dossier, as do so many others. We can discover only what Peter did out there in the world.

I thank a number of people for helping with this revised and renamed version of *Gentleman Bruiser*: Colleen Aycock of Albuquerque, Grahame Cumming of the NSW & ACT Masons Library, Tony DeBolfo of Melbourne, Tony Gee of London and Hazel Gee, Niklas Thode Jensen of Copenhagen, Gareth Jones of Cardiff (Wales), Chris LaForce of South Carolina, and Arnold Thomas of Melbourne. To Mark Dunn of Illinois and Mark Palmer of Cincinnati, perennial indebtedness. Mr. G. Hayes of the State Library of Victoria kindly transcribed for me entries from the Admissions Register of the Melbourne Benevolent Asylum. Philip Sampson of Copenhagen found Heering family histories and translated passages about Captain Herluf Heering.

I would also like to salute Dr. George Tyson with his team in the USVI, who has placed everybody recorded in the Danish censuses of Saint Croix onto the *ancestry.com* website so that researchers everywhere can study them.

CHAPTER 1

Tropical Danish, 1860–1879

Jack Johnson became heavyweight champion of the world by defeating Tommy Burns in Sydney, Australia, on December 26, 1908.[1] For seven weeks after the fight he wandered around Australia, and then went home. At Brisbane on February 17, 1909, early in the morning, a tug took Johnson from the Canadian-Australian Royal Mail Line's ship *Makura*, which had anchored in Moreton Bay, and conveyed him into the city. He was accompanied by Hattie McClay, the white woman whom he presented as his wife, by his new Australian trainer Duke Mullins, and by his sparring partner, 19-year-old Bobby Bryant. His former trainer-manager, Sam Fitzpatrick, the expatriate Australian who had trained Peter Jackson in his early American years, sulked aboard the *Makura* because Johnson had just sacked him.

He rode downtown in an automobile, cheered by people along the route. He was recognized because the movie of his fight with Burns had been shown in Brisbane a couple of weeks before, when the *Daily Mail* reported that Her Majesty's Theatre was "packed in every part, the audience including a large number of ladies." At the swank new Lennon's Hotel he and "Mrs. Johnson" shared a long lunch with the promoters of his Brisbane visit, A.E.J. Austin from the *Brisbane Courier*, the former boxer Harry Perry from the *Sports Observer*, Jack Dowridge, the Barbados-born black sports entrepreneur, G. Lawrence of the Brisbane Stadium, and others. It was a congenial lunch. Champion Jack had every reason to be happy, and Austin described his smile as "nailed on."

The meal was preliminary to visiting the grave of Peter Jackson, whom the *Daily Mail* frankly characterized as "an acknowledged but not actual champion of the world." The *Brisbane Courier* reported on February 18, in an article by Austin: "When lunch was over, the champion and his wife, with a couple of friends, motored to Toowong Cemetery, and there, on the quiet picturesque hillside, the living champion spent a few moments in silent contemplation of the spot where rested the mortal remains of the dead. It was an impressive sight indeed to see the splendid form of the living gladiator bending for a moment over the tomb of him who was Australia's fistic idol, and the solemnity of the occasion swept his now famous smile from Johnson's face."

Johnson did not mention his visit to Brisbane in the autobiography which appeared in 30 chapters in the *New Zealand Truth* between February 2 and July 22, 1911. The autobiography, first published somewhere in 1910, was also serialized in a French sporting magazine starting on January 21, 1911, and retranslated appeared in 2007 as *My Life and Battles*. There he wrote that "after my fight with Burns, I remained in Australia until the following February, and during that time several things happened."[2] Those things did not include any visit to Brisbane. In 1926, in *Jack Johnson Is a Dandy: An Autobiography*, he wrote merely that he "returned to the United States, having remained in Australia only a few days after the championship battle."[3] So we do not know what he felt at Jackson's graveside.

After the visit to Toowong, however, either spontaneously or prompted by his Brisbane hosts, some of whom had played a part in erecting the tomb, he "condemned as an enormity which should never have been perpetrated the alleged representation of Jackson, which the Sydney subscribers' representatives had put on the monument." Johnson had never set eyes on Peter, though he must have seen photos of him, from Fitzpatrick at least. It is not clear whether he condemned the face, which was that of a generic black, or else the portrayal of a dandified Peter. Maybe he condemned both. But his visit to Toowong was a memorable moment in boxing history, in the history of black boxing especially.

Then the party motored to the Ascot races. In the evening, Johnson performed at the Exhibition Oval lit by new electric lights. He was all smiles. The Brisbane Concert Band played him to the ring with "See, the Conquering Hero Comes." Exceptionally, accommodation was provided for ladies wishing to inspect the new champion and the woman who accompanied him. He sparred four rounds with Bobby Bryant, and three rounds with F.P. "Paddy" Corbett, an amateur from Brisbane. Then a young man from the crowd (not named by either the *Mail* or the *Courier*) wanted to "mix it," and Johnson indulged him by going two rounds as a comic finale: in effect he "rested his glove on his opponent's face and wheeled him about the ring."

Vociferous calls for Johnson to speak brought some charming utterances which were loudly applauded, among them that he was "glad to see that the people here are fair and broad-minded, and they wait to see a man and see how he acts before they judge him." He would revisit Brisbane and really show them how he could box. At midnight he returned with Mrs. Johnson to the *Makura*, boarding just before it sailed via the "All Red Route" for Vancouver, British Columbia. He never returned to Australia.

On March 27, 1901, Peter Jackson's longtime friend Will Corbett, the boxing editor of Sydney's sporting paper the *Referee*, published the first episode of his biography.[4] This is the only extant published account of Peter's childhood and youth. He had described them to Corbett while convalescing in Sydney the year before. Peter, who in 1901 was living in Queensland and reading the *Referee* every week, showed by his silence that this was his story as he wanted it told. Will published a second version of these events in the *Referee* on February 27, 1918, but the page has disappeared.

This is what Peter told Will in 1900, and what Will published, about his childhood up to about 10:

> Peter's parents, though not wealthy, were very comfortably fixed, as was the case with many of the colored folk distributed throughout the islands.
>
> Round about young Jackson's home there lived several families who had amassed sufficient of this world's goods to keep them above want for the rest of their lives — aye! and enable them in some instances to live in affluence. They had worked themselves into every branch of business, and in the majority of cases proved successful.
>
> Jackson pere was a carpenter by trade, and a tall, well-built specimen of the genus homo, as might be gathered from the appearance of his famous son. The same description fits Peter's mother, whose affection and solicitude for her favorite boy (especially when he first quitted the old home on a temporary trip abroad) is as vivid and clear in the man's mind to-day as it was in the lad's 29 years ago; but of this anon.
>
> That Jackson's father was an expert at his business is made plainly evident by the fact of

the family being so well circumstanced. Peter went to school at Frederiksted, the neighboring town to Christiansted, and during his leisure hours roamed about as fancy prompted. Thus early he gave evidence of the possession of capabilities which eventually landed him on the highest possible pinnacle of the athletic world — the absolute championship.

Boys predominated at St. Croix; in fact 'twas said that there were more boys on that particular patch than any two others of the same size in the group. Swimming was, of course, the great sport with them. How could it be otherwise in such a climate? They disported and gamboled in the briny morning, noon, and night. There were adept swimmers and divers galore among these youngsters, who were, as far as human beings may become, amphibious animals. They raced over the water and swam under it, evidencing remarkable powers of endurance and dexterity the while; but wonderfully skilled and all though the rest of them were, they had to take a back seat when Jackson was around....

Jackson had three brothers, who, strange to say, were just the opposite to him in build — short, thick-set fellows, shaped in a powerful mould, and as strong as lions. Two were older and one younger than the famous boxer. There were four sisters in the family, the elder of whom is dead, but the other three still have their homes in the West Indies, with many dusky and husky young sons and daughters round them, who never tire of telling of the doughty deeds their uncle has done out in the big world that they hear talked of and read about in their school books.

Peter left few traces in St. Croix, but he was noted in the island census of 1870, the only 10-year census for which he was present. Dr. George Tyson and his research team, the Virgin Islands Social History Associates, have now put all the individuals in all the Danish censuses from 1841 to 1911 into one consolidated list which is on the Web at ancestry.com. Other sources, including the island's newspaper, the austere *St. Croix Avis*, help to fill out the census data and Peter's own narrative.[5]

After his memories of childhood have been annotated, Peter's tale will resume and his adolescent years be commented upon.

Will Corbett gave no date at all, but Peter was born on September 23, 1860. Like Frederick Douglass and Sonny Liston, he never knew his date of birth. On his death certificate Dr. L'Estrange, his physician, who must have asked Peter, wrote that he was 39 years of age on July 13, 1901. This meant that L'Estrange believed Peter to have been born in 1861, as he always said, and on July 16, 1861, as newspapers often said. He understood therefore that Peter died three days before his 40th birthday. Newspapers gave another date of birth just as often: July 6, 1861. Peter favored July 16. Dr. George Tyson has a photocopy of the baptismal register, where Peter's name and details were entered in the clergyman's neat handwriting, his birth date being written as September 23, referring to the previous year. As he was almost a year old this was late for baptism. Because Peter always said he was born in 1861, it is evident that he did not check out the baptismal register in 1894 on the one occasion when he revisited Frederiksted. He always believed himself to be nine months younger than he was.

He was baptized in Frederiksted but supposedly born near Christiansted, the other main settlement on Saint Croix and in 1860 the capital of the Danish West Indies, otherwise known as the Danish West India Islands and the Danish Antilles. They have been since 1916 the Virgin Islands of the United States. Peter usually called the island of the Holy Cross where he was born Santa Cruz.

Will said Peter's birth was in Christiansted, because "he told me himself dozens of times." It cannot be verified. The census of 1860 shows Peter's family living in Fredriksted, not Christiansted. It is extremely unlikely that Peter's mother made the tough journey from Frederiksted in order that her sixth child should be born near Christiansted. In 1894 Peter visited an unidentified estate said to be his earliest home. Because it had not been torched, the estate must have been in the environs of Christiansted, and was almost certainly Estate Orange Grove, the Company Quarter one, not the one in West End Quarter. It probably was the estate where his father was a slave.

At times, especially in Melbourne, Australia, where fight fans were hostile to him, Peter said he was Jamaican, "a British born subject" and "born on British soil." The *Sporting Standard* of Melbourne reported quite plainly on October 21, 1890: "The stalwart heavyweight is a native of Jamaica." The *Freeman* of Indianapolis said on July 7, 1892: "He is a native of Jamaica, and he went to Australia at a very early age." The *Freeman* did not invent stories and must have been told this. Claiming to have been born in Jamaica was simpler than explaining where Santa Cruz was, especially in San Francisco where another Santa Cruz lay nearby. Peter also said he came from "near Porto Rico," which was true enough because from the peak of Bodkin's Hill near Frederiksted one could see Puerto Rico on clear days.

When he was asked how he hailed from Australia, he told a story about having been taken to Australia as a boy. He made his most explicit statement along these lines to the *Louisville Commercial*, saying on March 26, 1890: "I was born in the West Indies, at Nassau, in 1861, and I went to Australia with my parents in 1866, when I was five years old. My father and mother were respectively cook and stewardess on a sailing vessel. They carried me to Sydney, New South Wales." Most of this story was invented. But this is the only interview found where Peter himself stated his birth date to be 1861.

Along with seven other babies he was baptized by the Rev. John DuBois in the Anglican church of St. Paul in Frederiksted on August 31, 1861. His sponsors were the Jacksons' landlords, Christian and Jane Holst, living at 55 Queen Street, with John MacEvoy, a carpenter living next door, at 56 Queen Street, as the third sponsor. MacEvoy was probably his father's partner.

He was publicly christened "Peter James." But Peter may have had a secret name. In African tradition, the idea of a secret name, what in the United States was called a basket name, was to keep one from being totally known by another and so controlled.[6] If Peter had a basket name it was "Othello." This name was given him twice by the *Referee* boxing reporters, both Forder and Hales, who found it highly amusing to write pugs' names in full, like "James John Corbett" and "Francis Patrick Slavin." On September 10, 1888, and again in 1890 they humorously wrote: "Peter Othello Jackson." Peter did not demur on either occasion, so perhaps it was his secret name or at least one he fancied.

Peter's father was Joseph Jackson, born in slavery, who escaped the old plantation by learning carpentry. Many slave tradesmen could earn enough money by doing outside jobs to buy their freedom and sell their skills on the open market. At the censuses of 1857 and 1860 Joseph Jackson was called a carpenter. At Peter's baptism he called himself a porter, which meant a jack-of-all-trades, going around with a horse and cart. In 1900 Peter described him as a carpenter. He was born in either 1803 (1857 census) or 1807 (1860 census). He was an Anglican (1855 census) and, perhaps having experienced a conversion, a Moravian (1857 and 1860 censuses).

Joseph's wife was Julia, born in 1824. In 1841 she was a slave washwoman belonging to M.A. Ford of 17 Queen Street in Frederiksted, and not married. She married Joseph Jackson in the 1840s. In 1857 Julia and Joseph were living at Hospital Street 48, and in 1860 at Queen Street 55. In 1870 the widowed Julia was living at 61 Prince Street, on the property of J.C. Holst's heirs, the daughters of Peter's baptismal sponsors.

Peter's home was four streets back from the seafront. Nine households lived at this address.[7] The first household listed for 61 Prince consisted of three Holst sisters, all unmarried and all seamstresses, plus seven-year-old Lilias Holst, the daughter of one of them. The Holst family lived in a two-story house, the lower level in stone and used for storerooms, and a wooden upper level for living. Outside steps led down to the yard, where the kitchen lay for safety reasons, together with the cement rainwater cistern and the dry-earth closet. Around this yard were humbler wood-frame houses for the servants of the Holsts and their tenants. It was there the Jacksons lodged, along with another seven households totaling 33 persons or more.

No vestige of these frame buildings remains, but extant outhouses opposite Number 61 are gable-roofed sheds divided into three or four apartments, each about 12 feet square. With walls of clapboard and shingles, gables themselves of clapboard, and roofs of galvanized iron, below their eaves the sheds have wooden louvers to admit air. They resemble the dwellings built for slaves on the estates. The size of the Jackson residence itself was not stated in the census return, but it could not have been more than two rooms. Will's declaration that the Jacksons were "so well circumstanced" must therefore be read as saying simply that quality homes were nearby.

On October 10, 1870, the census taker recorded that the place was occupied by Julia Jackson, married washwoman aged 40, and four of her children. They were Samuel Jackson, unmarried fisherman aged 22; Helena Jackson, aged 10, scholar; Peter Jackson, scholar aged 8; and Felix Jackson, aged 6, scholar. The data may not all be correct. The census return contains errors which suggest that Samuel was the respondent rather than Julia, Peter for example being really 10 and Helena 9 in 1870. All of them were Anglicans.

There were three other sisters, not living with Julia in 1870. Peter was pleased when he returned to Frederiksted in 1894 to note that some of his sisters had married respectably. Peter's father Joseph was not listed in the 1870 census, presumably having died after Felix (born 1864) was conceived. The last member of the family, Peter's second eldest brother, Joseph or James, was absent. In 1876 James was in New York, and by 1870 (when he turned 19) he may have already emigrated to the United States.

Santa Cruz, which is about two and a half times the size of Manhattan, had 23,000 inhabitants in 1860 but by 1880 only 18,000. The end of slavery in 1848 had left in disarray the sugar industry of the island together with some of the social services. Many of the ex-slaves were reluctant to keep producing sugar, saying, "Cain killed Abel and cane is killing us," with the result that they were held to the land by contracts which made their work as irksome as slavery in almost every way. They were paid 10¢ a day. No effort was made by the colonial government to open up the big estates for sale and establish a class of independent black farmers. Not even a class of black sharecroppers arose. Cruzan sugar was uncompetitive because of a reluctant workforce and the slave economies in the United States until 1865 and then Cuba and Brazil until 1890. Also, in Europe sugar was being produced from beets. That Cruzan sugar and its products, molasses and rum, survived at all was due to their excellent quality. In Peter's time the best-known export of the island was "Santa Cruz" rum. This was also processed with calisaya bark and other herbal ingredients to make "Drake's Plantation Bitters, or Old Homestead Tonic," which would cure everything.

Like all the Caribbean islands, Santa Cruz was beautiful, and its peach-colored soils were fertile. The eastern half of the island was relatively flat, the other half rose into hills. By the 1860s much of the forest had been logged. The island's only animal hazards were bloodthirsty mosquitoes, some small snakes, and bold centipedes dark and large.

Among the palms and other tropical plants, fruit trees were cultivated, particularly oranges. In his advance publicity for the biographical articles, Will Corbett wrote on February 13, 1901: "Peter, the son of comfortable and indulgent parents, roamed about the orange groves of his island home in the West Indies, certainly trammeled by school discipline, but otherwise as free as the air he breathed"—a little exaggerated, but one of the charms of Santa Cruz was its oranges. Every provision ground and hut featured an orange tree. In Haiti it was traditional to bury a child's navel string and plant an orange tree on the spot, the tree with its eventual fruit belonging to the child. Maybe the tradition existed on Santa Cruz, too, for orange trees were everywhere. Still today, to say "Me nable-string bury hyah" means one is a native Cruzan. Two plantations, one near Christiansted at one end of the island, the other near Frederiksted at the other end, were named "Estate Orange Grove." Between the two towns marched a double avenue of royal palms eleven miles long, and in between the palms grew orange trees.

Frederiksted had a population of about four thousand. It had half a dozen streets running up from the seafront, and five streets running parallel with the sea: the one nearest the beach was called the Strand, then on the flat came King, then Queen, then on the lower slopes of a hill Prince, then Hospital higher, lastly New and a cemetery with the best views. The town was almost isolated, except by sea. It was only in 1878 that a mail-coach service linked Frederiksted and Christiansted going one way on one day, returning the next. Frederiksted was a sleepy colonial town, but hints of modernity could be found, like visiting American dentists and a photographer from Berlin who during his stay in 1878 took photographs for *cartes de visite*.

The only important public event in Peter's childhood was the earthquake with hurricane and tsunami of November 20, 1867.[8] There had been no hurricane in the islands since 1837 and no earthquake for a century. A huge wave came in so strongly as to pluck the United States Navy ship, the sail-and-steam *Monongahela*, from its anchorage in Frederiksted Roads and carry it almost undamaged onto the land, upright on the Strand. Fourteen sailors were drowned. The ship appeared to be sailing along the street. It was bulkier than most of the Strand's buildings, for the tallest mast was 100 feet high. The *Monongahela* dominated the town for six months. A squad of naval engineers came down from the New York Navy Yard to relaunch it, finally succeeding in May 1868. To Peter's generation, most impressive was the fact that 13-year-old Stanislaus Kostka Govern was engaged by the Americans as an apprentice and sailed away on the *Monongahela* when it was towed home to the United States. The boy would become, 20 years later, S.K. Govern, manager of the first famous black baseball team, the Cuban Giants.[9]

The population was mostly black, but included expatriate and creole Danish families like the Holsts. The police station was staffed by Danish gendarmes, the lockup at 53–54 Queen had a Danish turnkey, and the Customs House near the jetty had Danish officials. At New and Hill, overlooking the town, was Holy Trinity, built in 1792 by the established Lutheran Church and the oldest church in Frederiksted. Danish power was most obvious

1. Tropical Danish, 1860–1879

The *Monongahela* rests along the Strand, backed by houses and St. George Hill. At the extreme left of the picture is Fort Frederik with its Danish garrison. Above the stern of the ship is a steepled church, St. Paul's, where Jackson was then attending school. This engraving comes from the *Harper's Weekly* of January 11, 1868.

in dark-red Fort Frederik at the end of the Strand, with its garrison of 40 Danish soldiers. A Cruzan correspondent of the *New York Times* wrote in February 1870 that, "The principal use of the Danish soldiers is to keep in subordination the negroes, whose awe for uniformed soldiers and steel bayonets is very great," and indeed a fixed bayonet does awe many people. The garrison did little except polish their Minié rifles menacingly. The men could look forward only to their weekly issue of young rum, called "kill-devil," and to an early death — for the mortality of European soldiers in the West Indies was horrendous. If young Peter ever visited Christiansted he saw Government House and the governor and such pomps as the Danish West Indies could afford, but in 1871 the capital was removed to Charlotte Amalie on St. Thomas.[10]

By the time Peter was born, over two generations of interbreeding had erased distinctions between old African nations, had created a homogenized population of blacks in the Danish West Indies: on his island, the Cruzans. In his novel about Peter, the inventive A.G. Hales wrote: "He came of a stock that at one time had been great and powerful, a fighting breed, and a ruling family; but the family had fallen upon evil days, poverty and loss of power had come upon him as a heritage, but his breeding made him a brave fellow, and a straightforward, manly fellow as well."[11] Whether this statement transmits Peter's own tale about his being of royal descent or whether it is a rhetorical flourish by Hales is impossible to determine. Certainly Peter's ancestry had no admixture of white. When a bout between him and John L. Sullivan was first talked of, the matchmakers told Sullivan that Peter was a mulatto like George Godfrey, as if that would make him more acceptable. It didn't; and such talk ceased when he arrived in San Francisco black as anthracite or, in the words of the *Brooklyn Eagle* when he first showed in New York, "as black as midnight."

Julia being a washwoman, the money coming into the house came from her work apart from Joseph's earnings while he lived, and Samuel's sales of fish while he lived. Women could find little paid work other than washing and sewing, but these provided plentiful occupation because, before Singer sewing machines appeared after 1850, everything from napkins through crinolines to quilts had to be sewn by hand.

The Jacksons ate when they could, and fasted when they had no food. Cooking was done over charcoal, destroying the island's forests, which by Peter's time were disappearing fast. Breakfast was usually tea or coffee plus some bread or corn pone. The staple food of the poor was *fungee*, corn-meal mush with okra or banana in it. Millet was slave food, but they might sometimes be forced to it. Many kinds of fruit flourished. The Jacksons had one advantage, that as a fisherman's family they could eat fresh seafood, unlike many families whose protein was dried cod and salted herrings. However, they had to dream about eating flying fish, caught only in the open Atlantic. As to meat, the most they could afford was goat because even meat from the hogs, black and lanky beasts that roamed the streets, was expensive. But at least the Jacksons were above the field hands, whose rations during the cutting season were sugar canes and whose only meat ever might be sweet-fleshed cane rats.

The clothing of the poor was as cheap as was compatible with decency. Males wore khaki drill, or a linen coarse as mattress ticking. Females wore an apron over a long dress with one petticoat. Both sexes wore hats, some women a bandanna or turban. The most notable deficiency in Cruzan attire was shoes; bare feet were liable to be invaded by chiggers. A tiny knife was used to extract these from under the toenails. Peter was always particularly careful about his feet.

Diseases from poor diet and sordid housing were common, but were treated by folkloric medicines. Many babies died of tetanus. Tuberculosis was endemic. A number of other maladies, vaguely described as marasmus, low fever, etc., might have been diagnosed as forms of tuberculosis or kwashiorkor. Tropical diseases like yaws and elephantiasis flourished. Before 1848 the Danish authorities had imposed inoculation for smallpox on all slaves, but once the blacks no longer counted as property the imposition faded away.[12]

The Cruzans had folkloric ways to handle their illnesses. The fearful believed that even visiting a doctor led to hospitalization and death. People treated themselves until they were close to dying. At that point they entered the hospital where, as if by a self-fulfilling prophecy, they indeed died. One hospital was at Richmond, a suburb of Christiansted. There too was the island's jail, along with a leprosarium and an insane asylum. The other hospital, on the Strand at Frederiksted, had 40 beds for males, two to a room, and 30 for female patients. The blacks went into the hospital as willingly as into a prison. Not 100 yards round the corner from 61 Prince was an apothecary's, but it is unlikely that the Jacksons used its medicines, because they were imported, expensive, and suspect. Over the centuries the slaves had placed little faith in white medicine. Like the Chinese, the Africans had their own, and consulted knowledgeable weed-women. Peter probably never saw a doctor when a youngster, he disliked the idea of white doctors, and he was reluctant to admit he was ill.

Peter grew up speaking Cruzan English, which went something like this: "Dat night A could'n sleep. A was thinkin' ahl de time 'pon de shoes, an' hoping dem fit noice. Sebben o'clock nex' mahrnin' be toime me mek me hot-watah. A cahl me woife, Sue, foo come help me git ahn me shoes." This is a text dating from 1880 which being translated says: "That night I couldn't sleep. I was thinking all the time about the shoes and hoping they would fit nicely. At seven o'clock the next morning it was time for me to make my hot water. I called my wife, Sue, to come and help me get my shoes on." Peter obviously had a long and uphill road to speaking standard English. The "noice," however, and the "toime" and the "woife" in the transcript suggest he would have found few difficulties with Australian vowels. While he jogged at Sausalito in 1888 Peter used to sing what the *San Francisco Examiner* was told were "quaint Maori ballads," but they had to be songs in Cruzan.[13]

He was very good at picking up accents. Early accounts of him in Sydney which call him an American convey his accent after some months aboard an American ship. When he first reached San Francisco after nine years in Sydney he was described as speaking with a slight lisp and "a colonial accent," that is with an Australian one. Californians laughed at his pronouncing his name with no American "r," as "Petah" in the Australian (and Cruzan) way. Back in New York after three years in Britain his accent was called purely English. His first recorded words, spoken in Sydney on November 22, 1880, to Larry Foley and George Hill, two strangers to him, make him sound like a true Englishman. They were: "Never mind, gents, I only want you to see fair play."

Most of the culture brought from Africa was verbal culture, since so little else could be carried across the Atlantic by the slaves. Old people asked the old riddles, repeated the old proverbs like: "When dags have money dey buy cheese, when deir money done, dey eat bones," explained as: "When a man have a dollar he buy meat, det money done he turn right back an' he eat pickle' herring." They told venerable animal stories. In the 1920s the former slave driver Michael Richards, who was some 80 years old and therefore about 17 when Peter was born, told stories he had heard on Estate Mannings Bay, about the doings of Bo Rabbit, and about Ahnancy the cunning spider. These stories were told to youngsters and at wakes where a company was passing the time. When his tale began to fray at the edges, Richards would conclude the rambling story with a little saying which meant: "I could use a drink." Richards would say to end his tales: "The wheel bend and the story end," alternatively "An' den de wheel ben' an' den de story end."[14]

In the 1860s and 1870s African religion survived in the Danish West Indies. If one reads behind the words of insensitive white observers, in Peter's youth Santa Cruz had an African religious culture which was flourishing almost as vigorously as it does today in Salvador de Bahia. The blacks had a carnival every New Year's Day with "their barbarous music and their still more barbarous songs," according to the *New York Times* of February 15, 1870. The carnival culminated in the crowning of a Queen and a King and ended with "dancing to the most hideous music," forming a kind of conga-line that weaved its serpentine course through the town. At night in the countryside, in groves, under silk-cotton trees and at crossroads, other ceremonies were enacted. Belief in the old gods survived, and the Moravians were perennially accusing the slaves of snake worship. Though condemned by the authorities, the *bamboula*, a solo-and-chorus song and dance performance to drumming, which resembled the *bambelô* of Brazil, was performed. Shango, the virile and passionate god of thunder brandishing his two-headed ax, his colors red and white, his food the flesh of male animals, was well remembered. Slaves must have been surprised at the flag of Denmark flying from the forts, a red ground (for war) bearing a white cross (for religion): the *Dannebrog*. Red and white were the colors of Denmark, but also of Shango. The slaves took such consolation as they could from the coincidence. In San Francisco, the Danes had their Dannebrog Society. Throughout his career, Peter favored Shango's colors.

Asked in 1900 about his boyhood activities, he talked about his leisure. Though he knew everybody in town, the Jackson clan itself numbering many "cousins," and though festival days, butchering days, wedding days, wakes, funeral days with the brass band, and market days filled the year, Peter remembered playing. He hung with a large band of buddies. The boys dove off the rocks, raced each other on the sand, enlaced swimmers and dragged them under. They dueled with singlesticks; they head-butted each other in the old West African style. West African traditions of wrestling, boxing, and overarm swimming had survived on Santa Cruz in some form. They were wharf rats without a wharf: they paddled half a mile in dinghies and coracles from the short wooden jetty near Fort Frederik out to where the big ships anchored, and dove for the coins that passengers tossed into the depths. The water was transparent for fathoms down. In 1900 this leisure was the aspect of his island life that Peter remembered most fondly.

The memoir of March 27, 1901, says merely that he attended school in Frederiksted, but in July 1901 Will Corbett said Peter was "educated in a British school, under British law." The school which Peter and his siblings attended was called the "National School" or "English Church School" because it was an annex of St. Paul's Church. It was along Prince, a five minutes' walk for a boy if he didn't get distracted. It was controlled by the rector, the Rev. John Clarkson DuBois, one of the most important persons in Peter's history. DuBois baptized him, oversaw his schooling, and cultivated his tastes and his manners.

DuBois, a white of Huguenot descent, grandson of a Coldstream Guardsman and born in Tortola in 1829, had been schooled in Antigua by a clergyman. DuBois never visited England, but "he was himself, like most West Indian gentlemen, thoroughly English, never being made to swerve in his loyalty even by his education and ordination in the United States." Unlike most of his confreres in the Diocese of Antigua, who were from Codrington College in Barbados, DuBois trained for the priesthood at Trinity College in Hartford, Connecticut. He makes an uncredited appearance in its history. Trinity College instituted the first Anglican liturgical and church architecture society in America, as well as one of its first missions to the laboring classes. DuBois ever afterwards paid great attention to St. Paul's fabric and its ritual, as well as to his poorest parishioners. He was ordained in 1855, and for the next 29 years ministered at St. Paul's. DuBois also founded the St. Croix lodge of Freemasons, "Eureka" No. 605 (Grand Lodge of Scotland), which attracted many of the island's councilors as members, and to the end of his life continued as its chaplain.[15]

His parishioners praised him also as "champion of the right and friend of the oppressed." He was described as "a very handsome man, of commanding presence, and of refined manners." His father, Francis B. DuBois, born in London, became British Vice-consul in Frederiksted in 1853, and when he died in 1877 the son succeeded him. A British flag may have flown over the consulate, church, and school. If so, then Peter could properly claim that he was "educated in a British school, under British law."

In November 1884 DuBois died while on a visit to Antigua and was buried there. Charles Branch wrote an obituary, published in the *St. Croix Avis* on December 10, 1884. Bishop Branch, quoting from memory and incorrectly, concluded with lines about Hamlet's father from Act 1, Scene 2 of *Hamlet*, thus:

> He was a man — take him for all in all —
> We ne'er shall look upon his like again.

DuBois's parishioners wanted him in Frederiksted, but the body was not buried in St. Paul's graveyard. Instead, a marble pillar bearing an urn was placed there with the inscription: "Great Is Your Reward in Heaven."

DuBois's school was conducted according to the Bell system of mutual instruction used in Episcopalian or "National" schools. The beginning pupils were instructed by brighter and older pupils, usually called monitors, who were in turn prepared for their graded lessons by the schoolmaster, so that in a descending series like a pyramid it was theoretically possible for one salaried adult teacher to teach the same lesson simultaneously to 1000 children. The pupils sat at long desks and learned to read from printed primers, learning their letters step by step: a-b-c, then ab-ac and ba-ca and so on, as with a hornbook. Writing was done step by step by the little inky strugglers in paper copybooks. The language of instruction was English, here as everywhere else on Santa Cruz, and this meant the books could be bought in gross from the National School supplier in London. The Bell schools were inexpensive to maintain, incurring only recurrent costs for primers and copybooks.[16]

How many attended DuBois's school is uncertain, but the 40 or so schools on Santa Cruz in the 1870s counted about 50 pupils each, on average. The curriculum consisted of the "Four Rs," the fourth R being taught by a catechism, a simple book about Christianity in the form of questions and answers. The girls were taught the elements of plain sewing, probably by Mrs. DuBois. Older pupils got extra lessons in geography and history.

Certainly it was from DuBois that Peter learned to manage "shall" and "will" and "should" and "would" as few Australians and Americans have ever learned to manage them, and where all traces of Cruzan pronunciation, though not of Cruzan cadences, were eradicated. Though a half-joking Joe Choynski said some years after Peter's death that "it took Peter Jackson half a day to write his name," he was adept and quick in language. The reporter from the *San Francisco Examiner* heard Peter say to Godfrey during their fight in 1888: "See here, Godfrey; does you want me to kill yer? You wants to remember you've got a fam'ly to support." This was the only time ever when Peter was reported talking less than perfect English, though it was also the only time Peter was reported talking personally to another black. Maybe he did slip into his old Cruzan patois when not in the company of whites, or maybe the *Examiner* reporter invented the speech. In 1913 Neville Forder made Peter talk in the mid–1880s to his patron George Hill like an Alabama field hand. 'No, Suh,' answered Pete. 'Ah'm not goin' to fight dis Dooley, Suh. Ah'm goin' to mow him right off de stage, Suh.'" Forder was only told about this incident. But Forder reports that after a fight in March 1887, which he did see, "Peter said, in his velvetty voice, full of deep regret, 'I'm really sorry he was so headstrong, and more so that I hit him so hard.'" So maybe George Hill liked Peter to talk slave-boy to him.

DuBois's emphasis on pure English, with Shakespeare as its exemplar, was later reinforced by Peter's friendship with the sports journalist W.W. Naughton, whose hobby was writing notes on Shakespeare's works. Peter was no snob, however. The *Sporting Standard* told its readers in September 1890: "Jackson, it will be interesting to know, is a close student of the poets. He reads Shakespeare, but his favourite author in verse is Adam Lindsay Gordon. He says he is never tired reading, 'How we beat the favourite.' Having been the favourite so often himself, it is a kindred feeling." Gordon's lines tell about a horse race, and Peter patronized the racetrack. Eugene Corri wrote: "Peter could quote very freely from Longfellow's 'Hiawatha,' from Emerson, Edgar Allan Poe, Tennyson, and, marvellous to relate, Ruskin and Carlyle." The *Boston Sunday Globe* of May 6, 1894, was moved to tell its readers: "Peter is also a fine Shakespearean reader, and many times has corrected persons who were rated high in that line while they were giving quotations from the bard's immortal works. He carries a large volume of the plays with him, and during his leisure moments, when not playing checkers, he reads them." The *San Francisco Morning Call* said Peter was a great admirer of Shakespeare and could recite whole pages of Shakespeare offhand. All this surprised those who knew the generality of boxers.

In DuBois's school geography and history were taught to the older and brighter pupils, the lessons being about the Bible lands and Europe. It was from them that Peter derived his political notions about Denmark.

It was a small kingdom, ruled by King Christian IX from 1863 to 1906 with Queen Louisa, but the Danes had a small empire. They owned Greenland and the Faroes as well as the West Indies, and formerly they had outposts in India and slaving forts in West Africa. A small nation and recently halved in territory by a war with Prussia, Denmark was still well-connected by dynastic marriages. The eldest son, who became King Frederik VIII, married Louise, only child of the King of Sweden and Norway. In 1863 the elder daughter Alexandra married the Prince of Wales, becoming in 1901 Queen of England and Empress of India. In 1866 the younger daughter Dagmar married the Tsarovitch Alexander becoming in 1881 Tsarina Maria Fedorovna, Empress of All the Russias. The second son, William, became in 1863 King George I of the Hellenes and married a Grand Duchess of Russia. The youngest son, Waldemar, became an admiral in the Danish navy and married only a shade less brilliantly, to a Bourbon princess. These were creditable liaisons for a small imperial power. In the early 1860s the impoverished Danes began to negotiate with the United States to sell them the Danish West Indies. The transaction was not concluded, however, until President Wilson signed the accord in 1916.[17]

In Peter's mind, the mind of a colonized black boy, the school lessons about the Danish metropolis must have linked up, in some fuzzy fashion, with the British culture otherwise prevailing in the National School. The Cruzans were characterized as pro–British by Charles Taylor, who called them "an English speaking people, imbued with English traditions." But Taylor tells us that in 1879, when Prince Waldemar visited the island, the first Danish royal ever to do so, he "was received with such demonstrations of loyalty and affection as had never been tended to anyone before." Queen Louisa's birthday was celebrated "by a display of all the flags, both public and private, that our little island can muster," and similar occasions produced similar demonstrations. It is hard to accept that the general Cruzan population was "imbued with English traditions," but certainly Peter's own education in boyhood was strongly English.[18]

However, he never renounced his Danish allegiance. The New South Wales archives do not show that he got naturalized while in Sydney, although he often fought abroad with a display of the Australian insignia and sporting colors. Like many other boxers, he was criticized in the United States for making money there while not taking on American citizenship. He let the British assume that he was legally an Australian, and they praised him as one of their own talented colonials. But he remained all his life a subject of King Christian IX, who died in 1906. Often when fighting he wore the red-and-white of Shango and Denmark.

From DuBois's school there was no progression. Any further education on Santa Cruz, such as that provided by Johann Ripperger at the Burgher School, was aimed at university studies in Denmark and conducted in Danish. It was therefore patronized by the sons of the expatriates.

Being enrolled at the English School meant Peter attended church services often, both as one of the scholars and as a Jackson family member. St. Paul's was by far the most impressive place Peter could see in Frederiksted, with its neo–Gothic building and its Puginesque furbishments, its tray ceiling painted sky-blue and hung with chandeliers, its organ loft whence music floated down on the singing congregation. When Bishop Jackson came to Frederiksted on his biennial visit in 1870, Peter was probably confirmed by his Lordship, but he soon discarded all traces of Episcopalian religion. When Peter was able to read, he could peruse the tablet on the wall between the entrance doors of St. Paul's, in memory of William Henry Bard of the City of New York, who died on April 16, 1834, aged 18. The tablet read: "Attacked with Consumption, he was brought to this Island by his mother accompanied by her daughter and niece, in the anxious hope that a milder climate would restore health to her beloved child." But the end of William's story was sad, because "the first to feel there was no hope of recovery, he resigned himself to the will of GOD with Christian submission."[19]

The annotations to Peter's memoirs of 1901 have been carried through to about 1871. He recalled his youth in the following words:

> The subject of this story had barely passed his tenth year when Captain Hearing, master of a Danish merchantman, who had previously taken a great fancy to Peter, besought his father to let him take the youngster for a trip or two in the role of an apprentice, and as the lad, in common with most of his age, had long felt a keen desire to see what the rest of the universe was like, and Captain Hearing occupied a high position in the estimation of Peter's parents, the matter was soon arranged, with the result that Peter one fine morning found himself leaving father, mother, brothers, sisters and home for the first time.
>
> The vessel had hardly thrown off from the wharf before he felt that if he owned the great world so often pictured in his mind he would give it to get back amongst his people again. Indeed, once or twice he was on the verge of jumping overboard and swimming to the fast receding shore; but friendly counsel prevailed. "See how you like it for one trip," said the good-natured skipper. "That won't be long, and if you wish I will leave you on the Islands when we come back." So far, however, from desiring to stay behind when they returned, Peter made several journeys to and from Denmark, and remained for two or three years on an island near Copenhagen. Subsequently he joined the Danish corvette *Dagmar*— again as an apprentice — and was there for close upon two years.
>
> At this period Peter had reached his fifteenth or sixteenth year, and feeling homesick, got his indentures cancelled, and visited the parental roof once more, only to find that one of his brothers had died, and the other was in New York, whither our friend turned his steps, but the one sought for had left a few days before.

Peter was at school until July 1871, and was thinking of becoming a sailor. Many ships called at Frederiksted and their crews made merry on shore as best they could in that little town. The local rum was famous. He would have liked to become an apprentice sailor on the Danish naval training-ship *Dagmar*, which every couple of years did a tour of duty in the West Indies, alternating with tours in the Mediterranean. It was in the Caribbean for a year in 1867–1868, and visited St. Croix at the time of the earthquake and tsunami. He had seen the *Dagmar*, its funnels and three masts and red-and-white swallow-tailed flags, had seen its smart young crewmen strolling round Frederiksted.[20]

On July 6, 1872, the *St. Croix Avis* noted anchored in Frederiksted Roads the bark *Svanen* (that is, "Swan") from Copenhagen. Captain Herluf Heering had been its master, but had died. Two days later, on July 8, the brig *Frode*, commanded by Captain Christian Heering, arrived at Frederiksted — and left the same day. Herluf had been Christian's brother, born in 1838 and unmarried, carefree and merry, according to his family. He sailed his ship to St. Croix in August 1871, anchored in Rio de Janeiro in late October 1871, and died at Pernambuco (now Recife) in Brazil on May 10, 1872. In those years Pernambuco suffered five epidemics of yellow fever and five of smallpox, and maybe Heering died in one of these. Lacking formaldehyde, the crew could have put the body into a barrel of rum to ship it to Denmark. According to the *Veritas International Register of Shipping* for 1872, the *Svanen* was captained by C.W. Ebsen, who in 1852 had been Herluf Heering's first commander. It seems likely that Ebsen was dropped off by the *Frode* in Frederiksted while Captain Christian picked up his brother's body. Three weeks later the *Avis* announced that, presumably under Ebsen, the *Svanen* had left for Denmark on July 26 carrying a cargo of sugar and rum. If Peter's tale has any truth, he must have sailed with Herluf Heering aboard the *Svanen* from September to May, and then continued on his own before being deposited back at Frederiksted in July.

The *Svanen* and the *Frode* belonged to Peter F.S. Heering, the inventor in 1818 of "Heering's Copenhagen Cherry Brandy," often marketed as "Cherry Heering" and still an ingredient of High Hat cocktails. It was "purveyed by appointment to the Royal Danish and Imperial Russian Courts, and H.R.H. The Prince of Wales," an example of capitalizing on dynastic connections. Herluf and Christian were two of Peter Heering's sons. In October 1872, the *Svanen* was sold to a Captain C.S. Sorenson. This fatal voyage to Brazil had been its last under the Heering flag.[21]

When Will's account was published, Peter did not correct the misspelling of "Heering." Besides this, in 1901 when Peter was among the most famous men in the world, it was prudent to glide over the reality that Heering, who "had previously taken a great fancy to Peter," effectively bought the boy from his hard-pressed mother. Julia must have been glad that Peter would henceforth be fed by somebody else, and not pleased when he returned so soon. The reference to Joseph's as well as Julia's welcoming Heering's offer was fantasy, because Joseph had died before 1870.

As Will conveys Peter's story, Captain Herluf's idea was that Peter would become a seafarer, either in the Danish navy or in the merchant marine. But the Danish navy did not enlist black colonials, so that "apprenticeship" meant learning to be a merchant seaman. A few years later Peter claimed to be an A.B., that is a trained sailor, and perhaps he was. No evidence has been found supporting Peter's claim that he lived in Denmark working aboard the *Dagmar*. This tale is no more substantial than the born-in-Nassau one. The Heering story would seem to be a reaction to Joseph's death, when Peter lost his protective father. Thus Peter said the dead Joseph sanctioned the *Svanen* adventure, as if Herluf was a father substitute upon whom were projected all Peter's youthful dreams. But everything came to grief in Pernambuco. However, his nine months on the *Svanen* as ship's boy, interacting with Captain Herluf Heering and the Danish crew, had provided a marvelous opportunity for building up his basic Danish.

Peter's fisherman brother Samuel died in the early 1870s. James was in the United States and Felix only eleven. Peter was now the breadwinner, supporting his mother and Helen and Felix, but he found no ready work. He could try being a trimmer at the recoaling station, shoveling coal into bunkers for 5c a ton. Carrying on one's head 80-pound baskets of coal to the ships was a job for women at 6¢ an hour — and out of that the women paid commissions to the ganger. This was in the years when rich Cruzans were paying 10¢ to 50¢ a pound for ice imported from New York. Peter could convey hogsheads in a moses-boat out to the ships. Longshoremen were getting 20¢ an hour when they could get work, a youngster 10¢. He was handy, he could whittle, he could help the town's shoemaker with his cobbling and reheeling, learning what made a good shoe and boot. But the money earned in a week from his jobs would scarcely buy him a finger of cherry brandy. Besides, such jobs were not careers. Was he to ferry hogsheads for the rest of his manhood?

The island's economy was in the doldrums. In June 1871 there had been a tornado and another earthquake. Drought marked the early 1870s. The sugar fell from 16 million pounds produced in 1860–61 to 9½ million in 1872, and to only 4½ million pounds in 1874. Cruzan production had sunk to a quarter of the normal. At the same time the production of beet sugar soared in Europe, and only Cruzan rum could endure the competition forced on the sugar industry by the last two sugar-and-slave economies, Cuba and Brazil. Alarmed Cruzans turned hopefully to tourism. The island was proclaimed an ideal resort for invalids, especially consumptives like William Bard. Some grand houses offered accommodation to paying guests at $10 to $14 a week. Planters who had produced only sugar for two centuries now talked about diversifying into bananas and bay oil from the bay-rum trees and kapok from the silk-cotton trees. These desperate plans had small results.

On January 3, 1876, a hurricane, one of the worst ever to visit the West Indies, assaulted Santa Cruz all afternoon. The damage was frightful. Santa Cruz seemed to be doomed. Peter had found no secure job, had no money coming in, no prospects. The winter of 1877–78 brought extremely dry weather and the crops failed. Peter gathered his things together and early in 1878 went north to join his brother James in New York City. It was 16 years before he saw Santa Cruz again. In 1901 he told a clergyman, "I have very few memories of my parents, and I was out upon the world when I was only a youth, and I have never known much of the comforts of a real home." In short, aged 40 and close to death, he still resented his growing years.

The thing in his homeland that lingered longest with Peter was the scent of the oranges. He referred to this in memoirs he supplied to Bill Naughton in 1889, and in those for Will in 1900 for the *Referee*. Indeed, the latter memoirs were clumsily titled *From Orange Groves to the World's Pugilistic Championship*.

A few months after he left St. Croix, the situation had gotten so bad that workers revolted against their conditions. Smoldering resentment burst into flames in October 1878. The workers were unhappy with the labor laws which still, 30 years after slavery was abolished, kept many of them tied to the old estates. Moreover, they were protesting the introduction of farm machinery.[22]

Among the riots, looting, and destruction, John DuBois found himself living the most exciting hours of his life. A rabble armed with cutlasses and clubs made a tumult outside St. Paul's Church. He calmed the rioters and persuaded them to quit the town. But it was too late even for British diplomacy. The rioting surged up, unstoppable. DuBois, however, and his church and school went unmolested, almost the sole things untouched in the town. The insurgents tried several times to capture Fort Frederik. Foiled, they took possession of a rum store, and having drunk it dry they set it on fire. The few green-uniformed firemen were helpless. The police force took refuge in the fort with its cannons pointing seaward. The old Minié rifles were beautifully polished, but when the armory was broken out, proved to have defects, which was why the English army had replaced them with Enfields in 1854. The town was pillaged by the mob. Almost all the buildings in Frederiksted were torched.

The Strand blazed along with the streets behind it. Prince Street burned, with the Holst house. Its upper floor was never rebuilt. As well, the estates from Frederiksted out to the suburbs of Christiansted were destroyed. The rampage ended only when a pitched battle took place at Estate Anna's Hope and many blacks were shot down. The colonial government, which had not had the slightest inkling of the coming revolt, thereafter prudently reformed the labor laws. The British government gave its brave vice-consul a gratuity of £200, that is $1000, and contemporaries of DuBois at Trinity College sent down by the bark *Carib* an affectionate testimonial: "Expressing to Mr. DuBois the admiration here felt for his steadfast service in that island; and, notably, for his personal bravery and influence during the lamentable insurrection and riot of last October."

But by the time of the great Fireburn, Peter had left the Danish West Indies and become a sailor. He was on the other side of the world in the Dutch East Indies. And by the time of the labor reforms Peter had settled down in Sydney, Australia.

In 1878, sailing north from Santa Cruz, he started his life as a rolling stone. James had written Peter telling him where he lived, but when he arrived in New York, James had moved to another address. He asked around but James had vanished into the vast United States. Peter found himself on his own in New York, which was nothing like Frederiksted, gaping up at the skyscraping buildings, wandering the lighted streets with their incessant traffic, past illuminated store windows displaying inconceivable goods, past opulent bars all mahogany and plush, peeping into luxurious theaters where white prostitutes sauntered,

Seamen's Names.	Station.	Age.	Of what Nation.
H. W. Bucknam	Mate	25	Maine
Peter Johnson	2nd	28	New York
Isaac Winter	Cook & Stewd	22	West Indies
Ernest Cazavas	AB	27	Nassau
Robert Glenner	AB	24	—
Peter Jackson	AB	22	West India
John Bush	AB	22	Washington
Marvis Brown	AB	21	Charleston
Henry Slaughter	AB	28	Buttimore

Crew list, completed in Sydney on February 19, 1879, by an agent of the Harbor authority, records the sailors of the *H.J. Libby* arrived from Samarang under "Captain Charles Henry Bucknam of Portland USA, Master." It can be noted that the agent heard Slaughter's home town as Buttimore.

incredulously noting the brazen black prostitutes along "African Broadway," as Seventh Avenue from 23rd to 40th was called.[23]

If he was sorely tempted by New York's ready sex, he had no money to pay for such relief, even in the sailors' brothels at Corlears Hook. In fact he had almost no money to eat with. Fulton eateries served buckwheat cakes and cheap Souchong black tea, but even that cost a few cents. A foreign black youth in Gotham, broke and friendless, he reached the depths of despair, but only for a little while. Hardhearted though it could be, New York showed him another world entirely from the one he had known, a most exciting world. He never wanted to return to Santa Cruz. So his realism led him to take the one job that was almost always on offer. He became a merchant seaman. He signed aboard a Yankee bark leaving New York, bound for India and points east. He bought, as a sailor commonly did using his advance money of two months' pay, a few items at the Catherine Market: pea-jacket, sweater, knitted cap, eating utensils and other things.

The 621-ton *H.J. Libby* hailed from Portland, Maine, and was owned by Benjamin Webster and Company of Portland. Being a four-masted bark it was, in American parlance, a shipentine. It was relatively new, having been launched into the Kennebec River in 1873. Built after Nebraska became a state in 1867 and before Colorado in 1876, the *H.J. Libby* displayed a flag with 37 stars. It was commanded by Captain Charles Henry Bucknam of Providence, Maine, born around 1825, with as mate Henry W. Bucknam, aged 25, of Maine, almost certainly the Captain's son. The Bucknams were from a Maine family established at Yarmouth and thereabouts since before 1700. Among many Samuels, Abigails and Ichabods, Captain Charles was a seventh-generation Yankee. It was one of Bucknam's earliest voyages in command, if not the first, because until late 1877 its master had been Captain J. Brooks.

The crew totaled seven, and they were most likely all blacks. It was easier with an all-black crew, who came cheaper anyway. The tensions between a black crew and a white command, however, were in this case not lessened by the unlikelihood of ever playing the mate off against the captain. The second mate, Peter Johnson of New York, was in a more difficult position than second mates usually were.[24]

To get the job, Peter could have simply hunted out the ships' mates who drank in the lower East side, at bars like Orrin Nickerson's opposite Pier 19. Or another crewman, the cook Isaac Winter, himself from the Danish West Indies, could have brought Peter to Johnson or the younger Bucknam.

The crew were aged between 21 and 28, according to their statements in the "Arrivals" entry in the Sydney Harbormaster's log in the New South Wales State Archives. Peter was paid an adult wage, being big enough physically to put his age up from 17 to 22 without arousing suspicion. He must have reached almost his final height of six feet and half an inch, and though he was skinny he was sinewy and strong. The qualifications of American seamen, even American captains, were indeterminate in that period. Peter could call himself an Able Seaman, which perhaps he was, at a higher rate of pay than an ordinary seaman. Most of the other crewmen, all declaring themselves Able Seamen, were about Peter's stated age. If they were all of them blacks, they came cheap from Nassau, Washington, Charleston and Baltimore. In this period a sailor's pay was around $15 a month, that is 50c a day. A black crew were almost certainly paid less, probably in the order of $10 a month or 30c a day, to be paid at the end of the voyage after any advances and all costs for kit purchased on board had been deducted.[25]

If a seaman left his ship ahead of the date he had signed on for, he was paid nothing.

Because the owners of the ship and cargo appreciated even the slightest savings, it was therefore in their interest that conditions aboard be made so unpleasant that the crew would desert. This practice of terrorizing was known as "running a crew out of a ship." Many captains took pride in their efficiency in getting rid of their outward-bound crew and hiring new sailors for the voyage home. If it had a bucko mate with no recourse to the old man, the *H.J. Libby* was very likely a hell-hole. But a sailor's life was not for everyone. Regardless of bucko mates who ran crews out, in the half-century after 1860 of sailors reaching New York, 49 percent deserted. At San Francisco the desertion rate was 45 percent, but San Francisco was called the capital of shanghaiing.[26]

American ships raised the anchor on outward voyages to the shanty *Rio*, so Peter sang it with the rest as they turned the capstans in the East River, near where the Brooklyn Bridge was starting to take shape. Then they headed out through the Narrows and past Sandy Hook, southeast into the Atlantic. He would not see America again for 10 years.

The *H.J. Libby* had visited Australia in 1875, direct from Boston with a mixed cargo of 500 cases of kerosene, furniture, sewing machines and fish. This 1878 trip was via Calcutta, and it was probably carrying a mixed cargo of the usual American exports to India: kerosene, cotton goods, tobacco, Baldwin apples, and ice. It was not a regular trader between the same two ports. That year, 1878–1879, was a year of depressed freights across the world, and ships found themselves seeking cargoes wherever they could. Tea firms could not rustle up a cargo in Shanghai and the tea clippers had to carry wool on the Melbourne-Liverpool run. That year the ship took very likely a cargo mostly of ice to India, from Calcutta a miscellaneous cargo to Java, from there a full cargo of sugar to Sydney. A downturn in the world economic cycle determined Peter's life.

For something like 50 years there had been a brisk trade in ice between America and India and, though the trade would end a few years later, it was still strong in 1878. The ice was extracted from Wenham Lake near Boston, sawn into blocks in Boston, and loaded at Boston. And a smaller trade in ice came from the Kennebec River in Maine, the *H.J. Libby*'s home. The ship carried Baldwin apples because India mysteriously produced no apples either. Captain Bucknam tried to sail fast because the ice melted every day during the voyage and they had to cross the equator twice, working the trade winds. But it was difficult to sail from New York to Calcutta in under 100 days. Though pumps kept working, less than half the ice packed in Boston usually survived to be off-loaded in India, where it fetched $800 to $900 a ton.[27]

About the end of October the sea turned red and the coast of Bengal was reached. They arrived at the mouth of the Hooghly, from where the news of an ice-ship's arrival was always telegraphed to Calcutta. A tug guided them up the river and deposited them at the bottom of Hare Street, close to the opium go-downs and the monumental statue of Kali at No. 32 the Strand.

From there it was only a short stretch to the Ice House and Ice Depôt at 10 Hare, where an American "Ice Agent" and his assistants took charge of the cargo. The Ice House stood until 1882 next to the General Post Office, which suggests how important ice was. Like the Strand back in Frederiksted, this Strand was the street on the waterfront, in this case the corniche road along the Hooghly. The river was full of drifting garbage, torn trees, belly-up sheep and human corpses. Vultures circled above. The ice unloaded, the ship could be tied up further out in the stream and serviced by bumboats and sampans. Divers had to go down into the filthy water to anchor the ship by chain cables to an enormous buoy. It was after the equinox, but still storms and bore tides were possible and the Hooghly might sweep everything away as it had done 15 Octobers earlier.[28]

They stayed in Calcutta probably about a week. The river air was steamy and heavy, miasmic, and hard to breathe. The only open space was the great park called the Maidan. Coolies briskly moved the ice into the Ice House before it melted entirely, each with a great block on his head. The crates of apples were also moved out, and then coolies stowed the new cargo on board. The usual Calcutta cargo destined for Europe and America consisted of indigo, rice, jute in bales, linseed, cowhides, and bags of saltpeter. Proceeding to Java, Peter's ship could have taken some of these on board, but it is more likely that it took textiles to feed the insatiable appetite for cloth in the East Indies, along with well-known Bengal cheroots. This miscellaneous cargo could be offloaded in Java, the hold thus made available for its cargo of sugar to Australia.

About the start of November, they sailed down the Hooghly and steered southeast. But there had been at least one change of personnel. Peter was now the cook and steward, and had been told to buy the coat he would need. Unlike the galleys below deck of the English and American navies, on ships like the *H.J. Libby* the caboose was on deck, a seven-foot cube located right behind the foremast and near the forecastle. Inside was a charcoal stove, a range of utensils, and a bench on which the cook could sit or sleep. It could be cold up on deck at four in the morning. Cooks had to bundle up.

When told he was the replacement cook, Peter hunted up a coat. That quarter of Calcutta, between the Strand and Dalhousie Square, contained a mixture of important edifices like the Police Headquarters, the General Post Office and the Great Eastern Hotel, with lesser commercial buildings and the Lal Bazaar where sailors lodged. In the teeming maze around the Lal Bazaar, Peter bought his coat.

It was a greatcoat or ulster of an old-fashioned cut, in brown self-checked material, which must have belonged to a very tall man because it came down almost to Peter's ankles. And a big man, because although Peter bulked up a lot between 18 and 30, it was still roomy. "When Peter encases his elongated form in this ancient garment," said the *Referee* on March 6, 1890, "he looks like the cook of a 'lime-juicer' out of a job. His counterparts can be seen any day on the Liverpool docks or in other English seaports where culinary artists of sable hue are found in abundance seeking marine engagements." In 1878 it was already old-fashioned. The Lal Bazaar vendor would have been glad to move a coat so big and so old. But it was of excellent quality, and must have been brought to Calcutta by a rich goliath who refused to believe that India was hot. It was exactly what Peter needed in his new job.

They sailed down the Bay of Bengal and out onto the Indian Ocean heading for the Dutch East Indies. This part of the voyage would take a month. As the new "doctor," Peter worked hard mastering a sea cook's routines, helped by Isaac Winter's instructions from his sickbed.

The menu conventional on merchant ships was monotonous and repulsive, only varied when some fresh food could be procured. Salt meat was the staple, as well as hardtack. This was crackers four inches square by one inch thick, harder than wood to the teeth. Worms lived in them which had white bodies and black heads. At first one broke the cracker and shook the worms out; later one became less fastidious. "Danderfunk" was soaked hardtack baked with salt pork and molasses. "Duff" was flour boiled in a bag and served with molasses as dessert. If any dried fruit existed, it was "plum duff." On this farinaceous and salt meat diet American merchant seamen subsisted for up to six months. The salt left them thirsty, but the drinking water often went slimy. Mutinies were more often provoked by bad food than by any other feature of ship life.

At meal times, the crew sat in the forecastle, their dormitory. Peter came out of his caboose with a kind of metal tub, and handed it down the hatch to the crew, who each filled his trencher from it. The captain and mates were served by Peter individually in their cabin. He doubled as steward. In other words, on the *H.J. Libby* he performed both of the functions which 12 years later he attributed to his father and to his mother on that mythical 1866 voyage from Nassau to Australia.

Their first sight of land was Java Head, at the Sunda Straits, then the green pyramid of Krakatoa with its fishing huts. Then came the hills rising to high peaks behind Anjer, at the end of Java. Here were low swampy foreshores, praus moving on the water, small brown people in bright clothes and their Dutch colonizers in white. Here began the railroad that ran the length of the island, here was the whitewashed Dutch East Indies Post and Telegraph Office where Captain Bucknam could wire ahead to shipping agents in Batavia and Samarang, and to Sydney. Peter, who loved birds, could have bought one of the famous caged swallows from a bumboat. (On August 27, 1883, Krakatoa erupted with the loudest noise ever heard on earth, and sent a tsunami to destroy Anjer and all those pretty towns beside the Sunda Strait, killing some 40,000 people. Sunsets over the next few years were the finest that have ever been seen.[29])

They sailed through the Sunda Straits, past the little settlements on their shores, and turned right to sail the length of Java. The *H.J. Libby* went to Samarang (now Semarang), where in early December it took on its cargo. It had to stand in Samarang Roads. The sugar was loaded by lighters coming from vessels moored in the roadstead because Samarang had no port, just the swampy coast with a meandering river. The loading took some days.

From Samarang were exported salt, opium, pepper, tapioca, tobacco, kapok and edible bird-nests, but they sailed east from Samarang on December 6, 1878, with a cargo of some 750 tons of sugar. They called at the most easterly port in Java, Banjoewangie, spectacularly situated below volcanic peaks 8000 or 9000 feet high and four miles over the sea from Bali. Here was the last overseas station of the telegraph cable to Port Darwin and the rest of Australia, sharing a building with the local telegraph office. Half a dozen Javanese operators handled the cables 24 hours a day.[30] The mail steamers called at Banjoewangie for pilots and any telegrams, and probably the *H.J. Libby* did too, because Bucknam had no intention of landing before Sydney. Isaac having resumed his cook's duties, Peter rejoined the crew.

The ship sailed from Banjoewangie into the Indian Ocean again, sailing immediately east towards New Guinea. The heavily laden ship was battered by foul weather in the Arafura Sea. When it reached Cape York it turned south and made its way down the east coast of Australia through heavy weather, outside the Great Barrier Reef, sailing on to Port Jackson with the city of Sydney. Since seeing the outline of Timor, for 10 weeks the crew had been practically out of sight of land. The tempers and the violence on board, after they had all been seven months cooped up together and eating danderfunk, would have been high. The two mates must have been disciplining the men ferociously.

So on February 19, 1879, the *H.J. Libby* sailed through Sydney Heads into Port Jackson, its southern side with bays edged with charming cottages, its northern side after Manly sparsely settled, showing dark bush and elephantine rocks. The bark proceeded up the sinuous harbor of Sydney, vista after vista opening before the crew's eyes. The bark passed islets and scurrying ferryboats, passed Woolloomooloo, went by the Botanical Gardens where the main building for the Sydney International Exhibition — the Garden Palace, 700 feet long with a great dome and towers — was fast rising on the waterfront. It passed Circular Quay with its backdrop of business district and churches, passed the point called the Rocks with its verminous slums, rounded into White Bay, and dropped anchor at Pyrmont. The Colonial Sugar Refining Company had built its brand new sugar-works with a towering smokestack close to downtown. This city looked nothing like Calcutta and Samarang. It was bright and sparkling and looked almost as rich as New York. And every person the sailors could see on the shore was white.

Will Corbett prefaced the first episode of Peter's memoirs by writing: "Christiansted (St. Croix) in the West Indies gave the man to the world; Australia supplied the boxer." Sydney became Peter's home for the next nine years, and there he learned to fight.

CHAPTER 2

Unbleached Australian, 1879–1888

The *H.J. Libby* sailed out of Port Jackson for Java on Tuesday, May 29, 1879, with six cases of preserved meats and 854 tons of coal. In 1885 it returned to Australia direct from New York carrying kerosene and barrels of white herrings, and again in 1892 with 11,000 cases of kerosene. It tramped the world until March 2, 1896, when, with a cargo of salt, it was wrecked off Long Island near Jones Beach.

But Peter Jackson did not leave aboard the *H.J. Libby*. It had arrived with nine crew and it left with nine, but at least two of them were replacements because Peter and 28-year-old Harry Slaughter had quit the hated ship weeks before. Captain Bucknam did not notify the police of them, because every vamoosed sailor saved Benjamin Webster and Company some money.

Harry and Peter deserted in late February. Their ship was out in the stream at the time but it was easy to reach shore at Pyrmont. Apart from advance money, they had earned nothing for their months on the ship. They had no money and nothing they could pawn. Peter decided to earn them some cash using his cobbler's skills. Pyrmont was a respectable working-class area, with its main economic activities being shipbuilding and cutting sandstone in three quarries owned by Robert Saunders: Paradise, Hell-Hole, and Purgatory. Peter whittled little boats and other toys and went round Pyrmont peddling them to children's mothers for tiny sums. Soon he had collected enough pennies to pay for their ferry fares across the harbor to the North Shore. They set off manfully to walk to Newcastle some 100 miles to the north. Newcastle did a huge trade in coal with San Francisco, since its local coal from Mount Diabolo burned dirty. Ships in abundance could take them from the Hunter River right to the Golden Gate, eight thousand miles and a 60 days' voyage away.

Peter and Harry did not get far on foot. In the summer twilight they were trudging up McMillan's Hill when along came Tom Watson driving his four-horse bus. He was on his 6:20 P.M. run, the last for the day on the new route from North Sydney up to Pearce's Corner at Wahroonga. Tom was surprised to see two black men walking along the track. When he found they had no money to pay him and had satisfied himself that they were not "turnpike sailors," that is beggars tricked out as sailors, he offered them a lift. After hearing their story, on his way home he took them to the Greengate Hotel, where he explained their plight to Tom Waterhouse, the licensee. Waterhouse promised to do something for them. Watson then generously gave them food and a hut to sleep near his own place on Fidden's Wharf Road.[1]

Apparently through Tom Waterhouse's kindly offices, Harry was placed with George Pockley in one orchard near the Greengate Hotel and Fidden's Road, while Peter worked in another orchard at first. It was owned by the Waterhouses, and its overseer was a black called Liege. In 1918, the boxer Owen McMahon told Will it was a family tradition that his grandfather from Stony Creek corner had hired Peter to dig a water tank in his orchard. William Baker, writing his memoirs in 1967 when he was in his 90s, said that his father employed Peter on his peach orchard, but if this was a true memory he was employed by Baker for only a short while. Harry Slaughter thereafter disappeared from Peter's story. Hopefully he did get to Newcastle and San Francisco and finally home to Baltimore.[2]

Tom Watson and Billy Waterhouse, one of Tom Waterhouse's 13 children, got Peter a job as a lumberjack down Fuller's Bridge Road, which led into the Lane Cove bush and mangroves where only a corduroy road of logs was viable. Peter, who now at 18 was a strong young fellow, was handed an ax and put to chopping down trees and chopping them up into billets, which were used for stoking the boats the Waterhouses owned. They dressed him in regulation moleskins, Scotch-twill shirt and cabbage-tree hat, and they called him "Big Jack." His pay was 10 shillings a week with food and tobacco, about $125 a year, so that Peter was now doing better than he had as a sailor.

Peter worked at his timber, felling and hewing tree trunks for some weeks, but one day he chopped into his foot. An accident to his pampered feet? To tell the truth, he saw no long-term future for himself as Big Jack the lumberjack. Mrs. Tom Watson nursed him while his foot healed, and after three weeks of convalescence and discussion everybody decided that the time had come to utilize Peter's nautical experience.

"Captain" Billy Waterhouse, who was launching a luxury pleasure boat for hire, took Peter to work on it as a fireman, under Captain Tom Clayton and with H. Clayton as engineer. Peter told the *London Sportsman* in November 1889 that "by trade he was a machinist," having learned his trade from the Claytons. The *Prince of Wales,* launched in 1877, had been refurbished. A steamboat, it was 100 feet long with a draft of 8 feet. It could carry 300 passengers and had sleeping accommodation for 42 persons. The dashing *Prince of Wales,* however, led a double life, for being very powerful it could also be hired to do a tug's work. It returned to the water in August 1879.

Thus Peter was rescued from the Lane Cove bushlands, but had not just found two jobs through the Waterhouses. He had also found boxing.

The Waterhouses, the parents and their 13 children, were part of a network of families in the Lane Cove district. They had married with the Bakers, the Butchers, the Browns, and the Smiths. Scattered though the population was, the Lane Cove district made a small community. These families were mostly orchardists and they were very much a drinking and sporting set. John Waterhouse, who had married into the Baker family, was into horseracing and boxing. They all had a great interest in cockfighting, Tommy Waterhouse being a prominent promoter of this illegal game. After several cockfights at the Greengate, a bit of sparring or a fight usually ensued. Victors and vanquished often ended up sleeping over in a large bark shed, which was dubbed "The Casualty Ward."

The McMahons, from Stony Creek corner, and the "Fighting Bakers" were renowned for their scrapping. Tom Waterhouse (1810–1884) had himself been an exponent of bareknuckle boxing, and on August 14, 1861, fought "One-Eyed" Burke, the champion of Victoria, for the championship of Australia: 28 rounds, a draw. Then in March 1866 he fought 49 rounds with James Kelly, three hours. He is also said to have fought Billy McMahon for over four hours in Boyd's Forest at Turramurra. Boxing was seen and much talked about in and around the Greengate Hotel. One of the Waterhouse sons, Billy, opened in the 1880s the Waterhouse Hall in North Sydney for dances and boxing matches.

The best of the local pugs, George Swarzas, who had married another of the Baker daughters, used to spar with Peter on Saturday afternoons. In 1918 Owen McMahon told another family story, this one about his uncle, Jim McMahon, and Peter, who were together at the Greengate one day playing euchre. "A dispute arose. The players argued and became hot. Each said things not at all pleasant to the other. Coats were thrown off and a desperate battle ensued, which resulted in the downfall of the negro."[3] Whether this story is any truer than the one about the water tank, apparently Jim McMahon boasted for the rest of his life of being the only man ever to have defeated Peter Jackson. He wasn't.

Having decided to stay, Peter found it easy to enjoy the delights of Sydney. In 1879 Sydney was 90 years old and had a population of about 220,000.

He did not find extreme racist discrimination because Sydneysiders, like San Franciscans, were less concerned about the few blacks in their city than about the influx of Chinese. A crewman off the liner *Mariposa*, Will McKnight from Ohio, 27 years old and the Second Baker, wrote a letter home that appeared in the *Cleveland Gazette*, the black newspaper, in October 1886. He was writing in July from Sydney and promised more Australian news, but nothing further was published. McKnight wrote: "The colored people here occupy a different position in the social scale to what they hold in America. They occupy here a position equal to that of any other nationality. The population of colored people is 1,000, and they are holding good situations, and are respectable citizens and have the welfare of their adopted land at heart as much as any other race." In 1880–81 the School of Arts on Pitt showed the *Colossal Mirror of the War in Zululand*, an immensely popular diorama in nine or ten sections with moving figures and *son et lumière* effects. The *H.J. Libby* had not called in at Delagoa Bay, so Peter had not encountered the black warrior nation which was so severely taxing the British army. Various blackface and black minstrel shows toured Australia. In his early time in Sydney, Peter was able to see the Georgia Minstrels and meet one of the stars, Charles "Judge" Cruso, who played Mr. Bones and did humorous stump speeches which were so up-to-date that after the Brisbane season he composed a Queensland stump speech for the amusement of southern audiences.[4]

After his few months on the *Prince of Wales*, Peter became a longshoreman. Then he became the stoker and threw the ropes on the *Emu*, a paddle steamer owned by the Port Jackson Steamboat Company and ferrying six times a day between Circular Quay and Manly, "the Brighton of Australia," with a stop at Woolloomooloo. It was skippered by an associate of the Waterhouse family, Matthew Byrnes.

In an obituary of Peter, hastily thrown together in 1901, purporting to have been published on May 4 (prematurely) in an American magazine called *California Turf* (which didn't exist), and excerpted in two Sydney papers in July, Neville Forder wrote that, after Peter got to Sydney, "his first employment there was as a deck hand on the harbor steamers of the late Captain Byrnes, a good old sport, who, when he saw Peter put upon by big, full-grown men, his shipmates, encouraged the lathy young black to take his own part, and in a very short time there arose among those hard-drinking, hard-swearing, gritty and grimy, coal-dusty and crapulous water-fountains a strong feeling that the young Peter was very good sort of chap to leave alone." There may be some truth in what Forder wrote twenty years afterwards.

Then he was employed as an oiler on another Waterhouse boat, the *Manly*, skippered by Captain Richard Taplin, which plied up the coast to the Bellinger River. Taplin, bluff and hearty, was something of a boxer himself.

The Bellinger, some 300 miles north of Sydney, was served by other boats, but the difference was that the SS *Manly* was a steamboat, and advertisements for its sailings stressed that.

The service started off briskly enough but soon stalled. The *Manly* left on June 10 for the Bellinger via Newcastle. It arrived back on June 17 with 700 bags of maize and turned round that day. It left the Bellinger on June 22 and arrived back on the 24th. It carried one passenger. The venture was not successful. Peter crossed the bar at the mouth of the Bellinger for the last time on November 30, and was back in Sydney on December 1.

Though his trips on the *Manly* were only half a dozen, nevertheless they provided anecdotes that were retold over the years. The happenings, recounted in Will's biography, can be dated between June 1880 and the end of November.

One anecdote concerns an accident to the ship's propeller, which occurred as it was crossing the Bellinger bar, from the river into the open sea. A rope got coiled around the screw. Taplin was frantic, as he recalled, because they had no diving equipment, and who would be prepared to go down into a sea where sharks were likely cruising? Then: "'I'll go down, Mr. Taplin,' spoke the athletic young colored chap with a smile playing on his lips, and in a modest kind of way, and do my best to free the rope, if you don't mind.'" So Peter stripped off "in a twinkling," and went underwater until he had unwound the rope. The operation took Peter an hour, and showed what skills could be acquired during summers in Frederiksted.

During the 18 months from joining the *Prince of Wales* to leaving the *Manly*, that is from mid–1879 to the end of 1880, Peter lived in a boarding house on Market, down towards the harbor from Sydney's covered markets. A fellow-boarder was Harry Blundell, and the two of them, together with Fred Thelwell, a sailor from the *Manly*, decided to build on the introduction to boxing that Peter had already gained. They started to hang out at Mick Dooley's and Jack Seymour's Athletic Hall at 103 Engine, off Sussex and near their boarding house. There Peter fought Jack Gregory, dubbed "Cigarette Kelly," with gloves. Until his death in 1916, Gregory enjoyed his reputation as Peter Jackson' first opponent. Seymour was enterprising. Handing over the business to his brother Ed, about 1882 he followed Harry Maynard and Dick Matthews in moving from Sydney to San Francisco. Seymour with Matthews founded the California Athletic Club, at first in the former Deutsche Verein rooms at 214 Dupont, then at 216 Grant Avenue. Matthews taught wrestling and his brother Richard taught boxing. Afterwards Maynard ran a saloon and drop-in center for San Francisco messenger boys called the West End Athletic Club.

When he was on the *Prince of Wales*, Peter worked alongside John Feneley, who wrote after Peter died: "I claim to be Peter's first acquaintance in Sydney. No one had better opportunities of knowing the deceased in life, before he entered the fistic arena, than I had, and on his departure from here to America by the steamer *Alameda*, he wished very hard for me to accompany him in the capacity of manager."[5] Feneley was not Peter's first acquaintance in Sydney unless he bought a toy ship in Pyrmont; more likely they met aboard the *Prince of Wales*. But they hung out together and he proved a great friend to Peter.

In March 1894 Peter told a reporter from the *Decatur Morning Herald Dispatch* that: "I have been in the ring for ten years. I began in Australia, where I was learning the machinist's trade. I just drifted into fighting." But if it was drifting, it was purposeful drifting.

Peter wanted to improve his boxing, so he bought one of the most recently published boxing instruction manuals. Donnelly's *Self-Defence; or, The Art of Boxing* had appeared in

London and New York in 1879 with an Irish green cover showing a gilt man (Donnelly himself?) who had just thrown off his shirt and stood in his undershirt with his dukes up. The instructions were illustrated with 40 engravings showing the various blows, stops, and guards. It begins unceremoniously with two *Useful Hints for Sparring*: "Keep your eyes open. Abstain from biting your lips, or putting your tongue between your teeth. Very serious accidents may occur from so doing." Donnelly's description of techniques was equally direct and informative. For example, Plate XXXIV on page 91 illustrates the Left-Hand Upper Cut; the text reads: "This blow, which in reality is a counter, should be given when a man in leading off at your head with his left hand holds his head down. Guard your face with your right arm, step in about twelve inches, and hit upwards with the left. The arm should be bent and elbow turned down. The force of the blow must come in a great measure from the body." The other pages were plain like this.[6]

London-born Ned Donnelly was a disciple of Nat Langham's, and he taught boxing at the London Athletic Club on Panton Street. Like Jem Mace, he was illiterate, so his book was put on paper by Charles Blacklock and edited by John Waite. It was a popular success: it had five editions and was being sold at the *Mirror of Life* office as late as 1902. George Bernard Shaw, who took Jack Burke as the model for the hero of his novel *Cashel Byron's Profession* (1885–6), gave a portrait of Donnelly as "Ned Skene," ex-champion of England and the colonies, in whose "Gymnasium and School of Arms" in Melbourne the exiled Byron learned pugilism.[7] Peter and his buddies practiced what Donnelly's little book preached, sparring with one another and even shadow-boxing before retiring for the night, but what even the most cunning book could teach had limits. Peter wanted a mentor who would take the time to study him and adapt the teaching to his particular talents.

While reading Donnelly's book and visiting Dooley and Seymour's boxing hall he met Harry Sallars, a black pugilist. Asked in 1900 about Sallars, Peter said, "He looked the picture of rude health and the personification of lissomeness and athletic strength. He sort of hypnotised me whenever we were together." Sallars was the father figure that Peter had apparently been searching for since Joseph and Captain Heering died.

Harry Sallars *circa* 1880, from F. Hayes, *Champions of the Ring* (Melbourne, 1910?).

2. Unbleached Australian, 1879–1888

Sallars was in his 60s when Peter met him, having been born in Baltimore, Maryland, in 1817. He was a bare-knuckle fighter who had worked in the Boston gym of the black trainer John Bailey, and also at "Professor Molineaux' Sparring and Athletic Academy" in Worcester. Sallars became a seasoned boxer in the States, said to have fought Bob Fisher and Metta Frank and others. By trade he was a cook and steward. He arrived in Melbourne in 1858, having quit his ship like Harry Slaughter and Peter. In Melbourne he started boxing with the *nom-de-ring* of "The American Stranger" and with a neat black-and-white check for his colors.

His glory days were past by 1880 when Sallars moved to Sydney with a view to opening a boxing hall. He was living with a buddy close by Peter's lodgings, possibly Albert Chamberlain, born in Jamaica about 1835, a former soldier in a West Indian regiment, now a boxer and trainer. It was easy for two black pugilists to make acquaintance in Sydney. Its population had not climbed to 400,000 by 1888, its established boxing venues were only three or four in number, and any black was as visible as a bromeliad in a rose-bed.

Peter met Sallars probably at Dooley and Seymour's. His account of their friendship was curiously vague. They met and hung out together. They played poker. Sallars gave him lessons on fighting, teaching him all he knew. They went to Dooley and Seymour's together and Sallars encouraged Peter to fight and criticized his performances afterwards. One of these practice battles was against "Black Charlie," an aboriginal fighter. A few years later Peter sparred formally with "Black Charlie" at Dooley and Seymour's. And then Sallars and Peter and their black buddies socialized, playing cards, eating in cafes and drinking in bars, of course when Peter was off the *Manly*.

Peter's explanation of why he ceased hanging around Sallars was that his notions failed to supply the something that Peter was conscious of lacking. His ideas were more about slugging than boxing, and quite different from the scientific methods exposed in Donnelly's book. The way to stand and to hold the arms which Sallars taught just wouldn't go together with Donnelly's instructions. Peter had known all that from the start, of course, and his gradual disenchantment had less to do with Sallars the pug and more to do with Sallars the man. He was disappointed at his mentor's old-fashioned technique, but it seems he outgrew the fascination.

Sallars saw that Peter was growing cooler. One night at a poker game matters came to a head. As Peter told Naughton of the *Examiner* in March 1889, something occurred that he did not like and, taking his money, he quit the table. "Sellars [*sic*] became enraged and he placed his back against the door, telling Jackson in threatening tones that he would either have to play or fight. Jackson's eyes blazed and, seizing a chair, he said: 'I know that I am no match for you with my fists, but I am going to get out of here if I have to bring you down with this chair.' Peter's vehemence and grit took the champion aback and he, though never a craven, mollified his tones and strove to conciliate Jackson. The latter, however, was filled with resentment and as he left the room he said: 'The day will come when I'll occupy the position you do now.'" They made up, but things were never the same. Sallars advised Peter to apply for tuition to Larry Foley, the real Australian champion. Peter had not raised his eyes so high as Foley before, but he did eventually take this parting advice. After Sallars he didn't look for a father figure again. Instead, from then on his own relationships with younger men became fatherly.

Sallars returned to Melbourne and eventually was admitted to the enormous Melbourne Benevolent Asylum at Hotham. The details from the admissions book show Sallars a widower with no children, no relatives, and no friends who would take him in. He was admitted on November 27, 1884, with defective vision. He had lost most sight in one eye years before, but now had cataracts, which must have been affecting him already in Sydney. He discharged himself soon afterwards, probably unable to endure sharing his life with 1500 other indigent people, but was readmitted in July the next year for reasons of "old age and general debility."

Sallars died in the Melbourne Benevolent Asylum on Saturday, October 2, 1886, less than a week after Peter became champion of Australia. Peter's portrait graced the first page of the *Melbourne Sportsman* on September 29, 1886, and an account of his victory was on page 8, so that hopefully Sallars had the news read out to him before he died.

While Peter was still with the *Manly* he met Foley, and not by going up to him as Sallars had suggested. Foley discovered Peter brawling in the park in Wynyard Square on Saturday November 20, 1880.[8] It was the evening of election day in the West Sydney electorate. Foley and his patron George Hill went to the hustings to hear the results and were in Wynyard Square Reserve, between Margaret and Wynyard, near the Freemasons' Hall and the Freemasons' Hotel, when they noticed a lively scuffle.

A black stripling was in combat with larrikins or hoodlums, seven or eight youngsters led by "Long Alf," who was a disciple of "Dixon the Dog Hanger," and used to make mayhem after midnight, and assault and rob in bars and streets. The assailants were vigorously and viciously attacking the black youth, hitting him from all sides and fighting dirty, but he held his ground. Foley was going to intervene, but the black youth called out, "Never mind, gents, I only want you to see fair play," and he proceeded to knock Long Alf and six other larrikins down. The waiting crowd cheered him. "Of course," Foley recalled in 1897, "we all complimented him upon his prowess and I was asked by several to take him in hand, Mr. George Hill particularly urging me to do so, as Peter seemed a really first-class natural fighter. A few days I had Jackson at my place, and took to him very much indeed, because of his smart, intelligent manner, and thorough good nature."

Foley could appreciate Peter's prowess against the larrikins, not only because he was champion of Australia but because he knew the tough Rocks area well. He was 31 years old in December 1880, and was the licensee of the Queen's Theater and Hotel at 149 York between King and Market which belonged to George Hill. In 1882 it was renamed Foley's Hotel. In February 1885 he transferred to Nissen's cafe, an old tavern on George which also was owned by George Hill, and after considerable refurbishment it reopened as the White Horse Hotel.

As soon as Peter got back from his next trip to the Bellinger River, on Wednesday, December 1, 1880, he called on Foley, accompanied for moral support by Jack McCarthy. He was following the earlier advice of Sallars, but he gave Jack all credit for having talked him into going along when he hesitated about taking up Foley's off hand invitation. Foley decided that he would match Peter and evaluate his prospects. He thought of putting on the gloves with Peter himself, but instead used Jack Hayes, a seasoned fighter who was conveniently in the hotel. Peter proved to Foley by this fight that he was indeed a natural. Foley undertook to teach him lessons about boxing that went far beyond Donnelly's, because Foley himself had been taught by Mace, the English boxer and former champion of the world.

Mace was in Australia from March 1877 to the start of 1882, and he introduced the Queensberry rules of boxing to the colonies.[9] This was well before the Americans, urged on by Richard Fox, adopted them, calling them at first the "National Police Gazette" rules. From those Mace years on, Foley and the Australians generally discarded bare-knuckle fighting and the old London rules of prizefighting.

Peter never fought with his bare fists. In 1886 a pug from Bourke, Alfred "Stonewall" Jackson, who had fought Dick Hunt in 1867, challenged him to a bare-knuckle fight. Peter replied, according to the *Melbourne Sportsman* of October 27, 1886, that "I decline to meet you with naked hands in the prize ring; not that I fear the result, but simply because it is illegal, and no good would come of it. I wish to abide by the law as far as possible, and I don't want to run the risk of getting into trouble by meeting you. I am prepared to box to a finish under the Marquis of Queensberry's rules." On July 25, 1889, the *Detroit Free Press* interviewed him and stated: "All Jackson's fights have been with gloves, he never having fought under London rules." The next year he confirmed his attitude to bare-knuckle fighting, when in Kentucky on March 26, 1890, he told the *Louisville Courier Journal*: "I will not myself fight with bare fists; I never did and never expect to." And during the weeks before his death in Roma, people who met Peter for the first time remarked on his hands being unblemished, and he told them he had always worn gloves when he fought. Foley was the last of Australia's bare-knuckle champions; Peter was the first of the gloved champions.

He entered Foley's employ, quitting the *Manly* that day. He acted as roustabout and kitchen hand in Foley's hotel. Foley taught him to box until the day when he admitted he had nothing more to give his pupil.[10] Foley was not a born teacher. He gave the standard instructions: "Eye, hand, foot should be in line," etc., but one observer recalled in the *Referee* for March 9, 1932: "Larry, teaching a boy to fight, was an entertainment. 'D'ye understan',' he'd say to a pupil. 'D'ye get 'ut,' and execute such a brilliant move of defence and attack, that the poor lad would be bewildered with science." Peter rose above Foley's teaching.

Peter frequently acted as Foley's substitute, fighting men who wanted to have a go with Australia's champion. Peter fought and beat, on an average, three men every week. Foley recalled that at eleven in the morning somebody would want a fight. Upstairs Peter and the man would go to the gymnasium with its boxing ring, accompanied by half a dozen spectators. They would fight, have a shower, come downstairs, swallow two or three drinks, chat for five or ten minutes or sometimes an hour, and separate good friends. At midday, in the afternoon, and at midnight often enough, the same thing would occur. It went on day after day, month after month, for several years. Peter handled the violent end of the hotel's business while Foley looked after the other, smoking Havana cigars and quaffing wine. Peter called Foley "the boss," but without idealizing him.

Foley then explained to his interviewer that no reports of these impromptu upstairs bouts, with nothing hanging on the result but "the honor of the thing," ever saw the light of day in a newspaper. Newspapermen were not always within hailing distance, and anyway they might not have been allowed to give the public the benefit of what they saw, for reasons, Foley said mysteriously, which it was superfluous to go into. It was in one of these bouts that Peter beat "Dubbo," the renowned aboriginal boxer from Victoria, in one and a half rounds.

Paddy Slavin, a year younger than Peter, who came to Foley for instruction in 1882, was another challenger. Thus Peter encountered Francis Patrick Slavin, the man with whose destiny his own was so curiously entwined. Slavin was born to Michael and Julia, Irish immigrants, at Vacy, a hamlet near Maitland north of Sydney, on December 18, 1861. As well as an older sister, Mary Ann, he had two brothers, Bill, born in 1859, and Jack, born in 1865. The parents registered the births of none of their children, but did have them baptized.[11] His family left Vacy to look for gold and lived in several places. His father died when he was nine, and after some years of irregular schooling Paddy found an apprenticeship with a Muswellbrook blacksmith and wheelwright, and for the next decade hunted gold, made horseshoes, walked competitively, and got into fights. Somewhere in there he learned to play piano. Unlike almost everybody else, Peter never called him Paddy but always Frank, and Frank always called him Pete. Paddy was basically a pedestrian at that time and had not a great taste for boxing. In between fights they hung out together until Paddy went back north.

In early February 1882, Mace passed through Sydney, leaving (in steerage) on February 14 aboard the *Wakatipu* for Wellington, New Zealand. While he was visiting Foley at the Queen's Hotel, the shy Peter was introduced to him and may have sparred for him. It was from Mace he learned his first lessons in boxing, "not by actually putting on the gloves with him, but by watching Mace spar," or so Peter used to say. Peter meant his first real lessons.

Another anecdote about the Foley's hotel years survives. It can be dated to 1882. The *San Francisco Chronicle* printed it on June 11, 1888, as told by Peter. He was making a point about savagery and civilization. He pretended to be from Fiji. To be a Fijian meant one was dark and cannibal. People simply couldn't tell a Fijian from a Bengali from a Jamaican. In that period Barnum was exhibiting a quartet of "Fijian cannibals," one of whom was an African American and the others look to have been so, too, behind the nose bones and the fright wigs. They were presented as cannibals, or ex-cannibals, or reformed cannibals, for nobody cared what else Fijians were capable of being.

George Hill, Foley and others were in the bar at Foley's gymnasium, with Peter sitting on the ice chest and gazing abstractedly at the fly-catcher hanging from the ceiling. Presently a young fellow entered and joined in the general conversation, which turned on sparring partners. "I used to spar," said the newcomer, "and without wishing to blow my own horn, I will say that I can hold my own with the best of them."

"This may be a good man to try the Fijian with," said Hill to Foley, who caught on, replying: "Oh, what's the good of knocking the nigger around; he doesn't know anything of the game yet."

When the newcomer asked for an explanation, Hill said: "You see that colored lad behind the bar. Well, I've just got him here from Fiji. He can't speak a word of English, but as he is strong and active I was thinking of having him taught boxing. When you spoke just now I thought it wouldn't be a bad idea for you to put on the gloves with him, but you mustn't hurt him. As I said before, he can't speak English, and he is as sensitive as can be."

Peter gazed up at the flies and the stranger promised not to hurt him. Hill then signed to Peter to put the gloves on, and he arose with a full-sized smile on his face and went into the gymnasium. The mittens were donned and the attitude Peter struck made the stranger roar with laughter. His legs were set wide apart and he held his arms in much the same manner as the mother in the drama does in welcoming her long-lost son.

The stranger tried with his left, and by a seeming "fluke" Peter crossed him on the ear with the heel of his right hand and sent him staggering. "Good shot," cried the stranger, as he tried again and reeled back from Peter's right. Turning to Hill, the stranger remarked: "He's infernally awkward, but he gets there."

The stranger sailed in again, whereupon he sailed out on his back. When he had been resuscitated, he was asked to try another round, but he pleaded "out of practice," and invited the crowd to drink. Nodding his head toward Peter, who was once more sitting on the ice chest, he told Hill to "make signs to him to come and have a drink." The stranger's face was a study when Peter slid off the chest and, in a deep, sonorous voice and English undefiled, cried out: "Certainly, I'll have a drink. Give me some whisky and soda." So Peter recounted this story in 1888, stressing to San Franciscans that though he was black he was not a savage.[12]

As for Peter studying the flies on the ceiling, it was a folkloric recipe for hand-and-eye alacrity to catch flies on the wing, or to put out sugar and catch them as they buzzed about it.

Several times Peter's early fights were set down for the record, but their dates and places were not. He fought Dubbo, who was a middleweight. Therefore, if Peter fought Dubbo in a fair fight, it must have been early on, when he was slighter in build.

In 1883 he twice fought Jack Hayes, the heavyweight country boy from Goulburn who had tried him out for Foley in 1880, the reports specifying that it was according to Queensberry rules. Their first fight, at the Queen's Hotel, was declared a draw. In their second fight, described as a private match for a small stake, Peter knocked Hayes out in the seventh. Hayes died in 1919 without ever fighting again, but famous for his encounter with Peter. Sam Britten, a country boy from Bega, also got beaten in a private match lasting 18 minutes. It was in these early fights that Peter's Calcutta greatcoat assumed importance in his career.

In the words of the *Referee*, looking back on March 6, 1890: "After his noviciate in a boxing gymnasium in Sydney the colored hercules made his debut as a professional fighter in an unimportant match arranged to test his quality." This was presumably his first formal match with Jack Hayes. "He wore on entering the ring for the first time the old weather-beaten overcoat, and he won with ease." However, the ulster became his good luck charm only after the Farnan match, when he omitted to wear it and attributed the disaster to that fact. Thereafter he carried it with him on all his travels. "After that Peter's threadbare ulster became a familiar sight to the patrons of the prize-ring, and is now as well-known on three continents as John L. Sullivan's portrait."

Peter's earliest fighting career is obscure not only because reporters were absent, as Foley said, or because a fight was held *sub rosa* for some reason. It was also because in Sydney no sporting paper like Melbourne's *Sportsman* (1881–1904) was published. Most reporting of sport was left to the daily newspapers but, if they gave space to sports, they gave little to boxing, which their proprietors considered low and dangerous. The *Sydney Morning Herald* refused to report the weekly boxing, though it would accept money to advertise matches. Therefore if Peter's fights were mentioned at all in the press, they were dealt with perfunctorily. The *Evening News* was one of the few papers in the early 1880s that regularly noticed boxing.

But all sport was becoming increasingly fashionable, with a great interest in sculling, in which Australia possessed world champions. A replacement for *Bell's Life in Sydney*, which had ceased publication in 1872, was clearly needed. The weekly *Bulletin*, founded in 1880, had a sports column that expanded to a page, under the rubric of "The Referee." Then a weekly paper called the *Referee* started up in 1886, edited by Edward Ellis, who had been connected with G.R. Sims on the *London Referee* and in San Francisco with the *Chronicle* under Charles and Michael de Young. He began Sydney's first Sunday paper, the *Sunday*

Times, as well as the new sporting paper. Even the *Sydney Morning Herald* now began to report boxing.

The *Referee* ran for 53 years, until 1939. It quickly became one of the most respected sporting papers in the world, and through its foreign contacts it got news items from everywhere and published them, often extracts from overseas papers. Every month, too, it published a substantial "American Letter," written until his death in 1914 by a New Zealander, W.W. "Bill" Naughton, son of the Auckland Commissioner of Police. Naughton was based in San Francisco, at first working for the *Chronicle* and then as sports editor for Hearst's *Examiner*. The first boxing editor was E. Neville Forder, another New Zealander and schoolmate of Naughton's, who wrote as "Boxer Major," then moved to *Truth*. The second (briefly) was A.G. Hales (1860–1936), who wrote as "Smiler." The third, casually from 1892 and permanently from 1896, was Will Corbett, who with one break continued as boxing editor until his death in 1923. In September 1891, in a city with about 100,000 adult males, the *Referee* was selling 22,777 copies, 4500 more per week than 12 months before, and it could be read in every barbershop. Ellis had created a success.

Ellis started a cheaper sporting paper. It began in 1889 as the *Dead Bird*, which was banned for obscenity but was resurrected as *Bird O' Freedom* (1891–1896), thereafter being the *Arrow* until 1933 when it merged with the *Referee*. The same journalists worked on both papers, using alternative pseudonyms. Will Corbett, for example, was "The Amateur" in the *Referee,* and in the *Arrow* was "Right-Cross." He apportioned his budget of boxing news and commentary between the papers, though important items were reserved for the more expensive *Referee*.

Peter enjoyed the support of Forder, Hales and Will, and of the *Referee* and *Arrow* editors themselves, while Naughton was Peter's friend and sponsor in the United States. The papers covered his Australian career, then culled news about his doings from the numerous overseas sporting papers to which they subscribed, and republished it for their readers. Also living in Sydney was Frederick Egerton Diamond, who was for some 30 years the Australian correspondent of Fox's *National Police Gazette*. He was friendly to Peter and they wrote letters to each other over the years.[13] On September 10, 1887, the *Gazette* claimed to be mailing 50,000 copies weekly to Australia and New Zealand.

The papers retrospectively recorded Peter's early fights, but a bare list of a few is all that they could compile. Most of these fights were undated and remain undatable. At Foley's he fought Mick Dooley, his old inspirer, over six rounds. It was a draw. He was supposed to fight a heavyweight sailor visiting aboard the *City of Sydney*. The man could not leave his ship and so Peter and Dooley boxed four rounds to keep the crowd happy. He fought a lot of men from all over.

Starting on Anniversary Weekend 1884, nightly from Monday, January 26, until Saturday, January 31, Larry with William Miller from Melbourne put on a sporting entertainment, with wrestling, boxing, Indian clubs, etc. Miller brought with him some of his pupils, including Jack King, the champion featherweight of Victoria, and James Lawson, a mulatto of about 5 feet 4 inches in height who had arrived recently from California. In 1900 Peter described him to Will as "a living, moving bronze statue, clean-limbed, lithe, sturdy, and bountifully muscled from neck to heel." Lawson *versus* King was called by the *Evening News* a Lilliputian battle.

Peter fought an artilleryman, George Cave, who was so out of condition that Peter was able to win punching only with his left. The *Evening News* gave Peter his title of "Professor," but felt it necessary to tell its readers he was "a colored man." Clearly he was almost unknown in early 1884. This Cave fight may be the germ of the legend that Peter often boxed using his left hand only. Told for the first time in W.W. Naughton's *Kings of the Queensberry Realm* (1902), the story was retold by Nat Fleischer in his *Black Dynamite* (1938) and repeated by Rex Lardner in his *Legendary Champions* (1972). If ever again Peter fought solely with his left, or with some form of handicapping, newspapers failed to report it.

Peter also exhibited with his pupil Tom Lees, originally from New Zealand, who was two years older than he. Lees, said the *Evening News*, "evidently has a lot to learn before he can take his place in the first flight of boxers." On the last evening, Peter and Lees sparred for a silver cup.

Miller and Foley were trying to get together enough money to go to the United States. According to the *New York Clipper* of March 8, 1884, Miller had already signed to fight John L. Sullivan and Foley had issued a challenge to Charles Mitchell. Peter was supposed to go to Melbourne and fight Miller. Unfortunately Miller hurt himself wrestling, and the American project fell through.

Jackson's first important fight, and for many years his only disaster, took place in Melbourne in July 1884. Until 1883 Foley did not defend the Australian title he had won bareknuckled from Abe Hicken in 1879. When he did defend it with gloves he effectively lost it, giving in a fight between him and Miller in Sydney on May 26, 1883, a pathetic performance. It was only because the ring was invaded by toughs, in the characteristic Sydney fashion, that the referee, amid catcalls and groans, called it a draw. But then he awarded all the prize money to Miller without objections from anyone. The *National Police Gazette* reported the bout on November 4, 1883. The news had been sent presumably by Fred Diamond, who minced no words in calling it "one of the most remarkable glove fights on record," and saying that "a more thoroughly un–British, unsportsmanlike finish to a game contest we never knew."[14]

Miller and Foley toured together, raising funds. On March 1, 1884, they opened at the Victoria Hall in Melbourne together with Billy Farnan, advertised as "the well-known Emerald Hill boxer." So little known was he, however, that his name was misspelled "Farnam" in the advertisement. Moreover, the *Sportsman*, in its report of the night, also misspelled his name. He had little reputation beyond Emerald Hill. Foley and Farnan had a quarrel and Farnan challenged him to fight. Foley refused, and Farnan at once declared himself the Australian champion on the grounds that Foley declined to defend his title. Foley disregarded the challenge on the grounds that Farnan had not a record that entitled him mount a challenge. Though to a limited extent a pupil of Mace's, he had only fought nonentities; not Miller nor Abe Hicken, for example. But Farnan declared that Foley had forfeited the title and he wrote two letters, one in late April 1884 to the Athletic Editor of the *Sportsman* thus: "I now claim the championship of Australia, under the Marquis of Queensberry rules, and am prepared to uphold my claims against any man for £100 a-side." The second went to New York, to the *National Police Gazette,* announcing that he was the Australian champion. Fox published the letter on August 30, 1884, with a caption, "Champion Pugilist of Australia," under a steel engraving of Farnan from a photograph. He was accepted in the United States as the new Australian champion.

Fox was always keen to see Sullivan beaten, and he bruited Farnan. He was going to sponsor a visit by Farnan to America in late 1884. Sullivan for his part roared that not only could he lick Farnan, but that he was going to do so. When Pat Sheedy, Sullivan's manager, announced in early 1885 that, after his visit to England, Sullivan would be coming down to Australia expressly to fight Farnan for the championship of the world, he commented: "If everything works satisfactorily, it will be the biggest fight in the history of pugilism, having the two best men in the world pitted against each other." Even the *Sportsman* was disconcerted by Sheedy's news, but Farnan was not, because it was now definite: he was the acknowledged contender for the championship of the world.

Foley deputed Jackson to meet Farnan, and to put him in his place. Peter was given $100 for expenses. He arrived in Melbourne about the end of June 1884, training at the Flagstaff Hotel in West Melbourne. He did his roadwork under the admiring eyes of young Bill Doherty, the future middleweight champion of South Africa and champion heavyweight of Australia.[15]

The fight took place on July 26, in the Victoria Hall. Farnan wore a sash in his old football club's colors, South Melbourne's white and red, which were Shango's colors. The first round was all Jackson's. In the second round, however, Jackson lost control of his body, flinging his arms around Farnan's neck, dashing his arms about wildly. Farnan almost knocked him out; in the third round he knocked him down for the count. The Melbourne crowd, and even Jackson's Melbourne seconds, had no idea that this was not Jackson's usual style, and the fight was awarded to Farnan amid jeers of "Fake! Fraud!" aimed at Jackson for throwing the fight. During the rounds the crowd had taken to yelling out "Schlenter! Schlenter!" at Peter. The *Sportsman* didn't report that, but Peter remembered it. A schlenter was a false diamond, often made from a lemonade-bottle glass marble, used in South Africa to test the trustworthiness of the blacks who mined the diamonds. The word was used then in South Africa and Australia to mean a sham, and crowds shouted it when any sporting contest seemed fraudulent. That first Farnan fight and those "Schlenters!" would return to haunt Peter's final days.

For his part, when he recovered his wits Peter decided that his water had been spiked with something, probably laudanum or morphine. John L. Sullivan claimed in 1905 that Joe Goss, his second at the Paddy Ryan title fight in 1882, "was offered $4500 in cold cash — not stage money or promises — to drug me enough so that I couldn't win." The practice may have been common enough.

Peter's stomach was painful for some time. A few days later he angrily chased one of his seconds down Swanston Street. This was probably Peter Newton, whom afterwards Farnan himself accused of shady doings. But Farnan had won, with his red and white sash. Moreover Peter partly blamed himself for not wearing his Calcutta overcoat.

Peter returned to Sydney. The second bout came off there on September 4, 1884. On this occasion, all the participants from July were present again, except Newton. This time there was no extraordinary behavior from Peter, but still he could not overcome the rock that was Farnan. He was never at his best against unscientific sluggers who just soaked up his punches. It seemed clear that he was losing, and in the traditional Sydney fashion, toughs invaded the ring and broke up the fight. The police were called.

An hour later, after a conference with the Athletic Editor of the *Melbourne Sportsman*, Jack Thompson ordered the men to meet again at the hotel at Marrickville where Farnan was staying. But when Peter refused to enter what he called "a rat pit," a decision was taken. The second Farnan fight was declared a draw.

Farnan hoped for glory, but he never visited the States. He had only two fights with Lees and another with Slavin on October 29, 1887, which Paddy won easily. In 1891 Farnan displayed signs of religious mania, and was committed to Kew Asylum where he died aged 39. And when Sullivan did come to Australia he fought nobody.

As well as working in Foley's hotels and boxing all comers, Peter joined the Port Jackson Swimming Club, formed in 1880 at G.T. Foley's Baths on Sydney Harbor, and there he gave free (and occasionally paid) lessons in swimming and diving. The regular instructor was a Dane in his fifties, Lieutenant Ferdinand Von Hammer, who according to the *Sydney Morning Herald* of December 21, 1871, used "a system similar to that used in all the swimming schools of Northern Germany, Denmark, Sweden, &c.," evidently the J.C. GutsMuths (1798) system. Peter attracted paying pupils, who called him "Ton of Coal." This was how he met Will Corbett, his elder by four years, the secretary of the club and the champion swimmer of New South Wales. Will, then a post office telegraphist with a talent for writing, became Peter's most faithful friend. Will competed in April 1882 for the championship of Australia but was beaten by the Victorian champion Walter McIndoe. He must have found Peter's West Indian swimming skills exceptional, to pay for them.

Will Lawless (one of Will Corbett's successors at the *Referee*) told Nat Fleischer that Peter "was a master of the Australian trudgen stroke." It is unclear what Lawless meant by that. In 1873 John Trudgen introduced into English swimming a new stroke, overarm swimming with scissor kick. Trudgen had sojourned in Buenos Aires, where he saw unidentified Indios, and perhaps blacks, using it. In the 1860s perhaps ten thousand persons of African descent lived in Buenos Aires. F.J. Lawton, visiting Grand Bassam on the Côte d'Ivoire in 1891, was bewildered by finding the locals all using the trudgen stroke, having no idea that the stroke was traditional outside Europe. The trudgen stroke was superseded by the Australian crawl, overarm swimming with flutter kick.[16] Historians seem to agree on its invention in Sydney in the late 1890s, but it is not impossible that in the 1880s Peter was teaching some Cruzan swimming techniques, themselves ultimately derived from West Africa, which anticipated the development of the "Australian trudgen" stroke.

Corbett had an anecdote about Arthur Clampett coming to the Domain Baths for the first time. Peter spun him a yarn about giant octopuses that slithered out of the harbor and over into the baths. Then, when Clampett was swimming the pool, Peter played one of his childhood pranks on him, by enlacing his legs with sucker-like fingers from underwater and dragging him down. It was simple wharf-rat fun! But Clampett passed out from fright and had to be resuscitated. Nat Fleischer utilized the anecdote in 1938. Clampett was the buddy of Clarence Whistler, the American wrestler, and the incident occurred about October 1885. Clampett had visited the White Horse with Whistler the previous July, then gone with him to Melbourne, returning in August to Sydney, where he found a job running the gymnasium at the new YMCA. In San Francisco he claimed to be the champion roughwater swimmer of Ireland and to have been awarded a Royal Humane Society medal. In Auckland the *Observer* on July 4 reported him as "the champion swimmer of America." The *Sydney Morning Herald* reported on September 1 that "Professor Clampett has the distinction of being champion long distance swimmer of the world." Clampett was an Irish imposter, and his boasted crossing of the Golden Gate was only a swim at Seal Rocks from which he had to be rescued. It is possible that the octopus prank was punishment for Clampett's lies.[17]

Peter also taught boxing, being known as "Professor" Jackson from 1883, and had many pupils, several of whom had flourishing careers. His pupils included Billy McCarthy, a former sailor who fought Jack "Nonpareil" Dempsey for the middleweight championship in February 1890, and Steve O'Donnell, who became chief boxing coach at Harvard. He taught Dan Hickey, who ended up as chief boxing instructor at the New York Athletic Club, and Tom Meadows, who became the lightweight champion of Australia and California. Another pupil was Bill Smith, who fought in the USA as "Australian Billy Smith," and who was reputedly Peter's favorite pupil. Jerry Marshall, the New York colored man, was attracted from Newcastle. Jim Hall had a good career in America while Paddy Slavin was considered as an opponent for Sullivan. The blacksmith and hotelier Tom Taylor was one of the few without a ring career, but he taught new generations of pupils on Peter's lines. Will remembered Peter encouraging Taylor and McCarthy to punch at his stomach and ribs until they tired of it, his way of proving that blacks were not congenitally weak in the stomach, or *bingey* as he called it, using an aboriginal word. This exercise probably brought on a hernia.

His most famous pupil was Bob Fitzsimmons, who arrived from New Zealand in 1883 and for a time studied under Peter.[18] Fitzsimmons was not regarded highly in Sydney and called a freak, though he had arrived with the personal recommendation of Mace himself. Even Peter misunderstood his talent. The two never fought. Towards the end of his life Fitzsimmons denied Peter ever gave him a formal lesson and claimed to have learned from watching him fight, but he was distancing himself from his early years. His departure for the United States on the *Zealandia* in April 1890 went almost unnoticed. Those who had known and dismissed him in Sydney were astonished and embarrassed when "Kangaroo Bob," as he was sometimes called in America, became middleweight champion of the world in 1891 by defeating "Nonpareil" Dempsey, then heavyweight champion of the world by defeating J.J. Corbett in 1897, lastly light-heavyweight champion of the world by defeating George Gardner in 1903, when he was 40 years old. No other boxer had ever achieved such a cluster of honors. The *St. Louis Post-Dispatch* of March 10, 1894, said that Fitzsimmons "offers to fight any man in the world, bar Peter Jackson," and on March 15 said Bob told the crowd at Armory Hall that he regarded Peter, his old teacher, as the greatest living fighter. After defeating Corbett, Fitzsimmons said, according to the *Cleveland Gazette,* the black newspaper: "He is the greatest fighter that ever breathed. He's the daddy of them all, and for that reason I don't care to meet him." Fitzsimmons was consistent. He seems to have been stating the true reason and not drawing the color line. The *Arrow* said in April 1897: "It is not likely that Rufus-headed Robert will measure skills with his tutor." This was Will's understanding. He reiterated in 1914 that Fitzsimmons refrained "out of friendship for his old tutor."

Peter's way with his pupils was not Foley's slapdash.[19] He took them along a carefully structured course of lessons, explaining each step with great clarity and allowing no progression before every step had been mastered. Beginners were taught, for example, to stand with the eye, the arm, and the foot in line, all pointing directly to the opposing boxer. The toes of the left foot had to be absolutely straight in front of their owner, turned neither to right nor left in the slightest degree. Will, who took some lessons from Peter and knew all his pupils, said he had a goose-step in his method of instruction. Will meant, in 1918, that he was a bit of a Prussian, but in fact this was the way Peter was taught back in Frederiksted. The difference was that in the monitorial schools like DuBois's each graded lesson was taught to 20 at a time, whereas Peter was able to both teach a small class and teach individual pupils one-on-one, and could take infinite care of each one of them.

The course of lessons taught the Mace technique, and Peter would allow no improvisations and innovations within the system that Mace had taught Foley and Foley had taught him. For instance, he insisted that his pupils hit straight from the shoulder. Someone asked him to demonstrate a left-hand uppercut. "'Never heard of such a thing', replied Jackson disdainfully, and he cast a withering glance at the person voicing the request." This story was told by Joe Choynski, but the man who had feverishly studied Donnelly's manual 10 years before must have been having a little joke. Peter taught them to conserve their energy, to wait for their opponent's lead or, by feinting, to make him lead. He even taught them, unusually for the period, how to feint. Will said: "Feinting was an important part of boxing to which Peter Jackson gave a good deal of time and consideration, and taught in a way that the dullest pupil must have understood." He taught them all that he knew, or rather all of what he knew which was capable of being reduced to a system. In short, he tried to be the mentor to his pupils that Sallars and Foley had been.

Larry Foley (1849–1917) with Jack Thompson (born Solomon, 1845?–1894), celebrating their becoming business partners in 1886. Photograph courtesy National Library of Australia [nla.pic-vn3797456].0

Most of the promising men of the day came to Peter because Foley had almost entirely given up teaching, and in 1886 his gymnasium was rebuilt as Foley's Athletic Hall, in which Jack Thompson (born Solomon) was the silent partner. The activities were run by a manager and instructor, Harry Maundrell Cansdell, who was basically a strongman, not a boxer, though he played many roles on the Sydney sports scene. Peter often sold the tickets and acted as M.C. on fight nights.

Nothing hints of Peter's having any relationship with a woman when he was in his 20s, except for enjoying meaningful talks with a barmaid at the White Horse who was Paddy Slavin's sister Mary Ann. But in 1913 Neville Forder, in his *Reminiscences and Records by Boxer-Major*, wrote this: "After his defeat of Lees, Jackson married and took, or was put into, the Lighthouse Hotel, Sussex-street. But he was not a success as a boniface, being a man very reserved with strangers; while it was not long before he was made to understand that it was not well for black and white to wed. He found it impossible to continue in business with his wife; so he sold out, they parted, and the lady dropped right out of the story of the life of Peter Jackson. It was a sad chapter, and Peter would never willingly turn back the pages to recall it, or discuss it in any way." Forder arrived in Sydney from Auckland after October 1887, and over a year after Peter exchanged the United States Family Hotel for the Lighthouse. Forder was gossiping; he may have heard tell about a common-law wife. His story founders on the fact that no Peter Jackson was married in Sydney before Peter left for San Francisco.

In his 30s he was accused by his detractors of destroying himself with prostitutes, and perhaps he had always patronized them. In September 1890, after Paddy had married in London, a daring reporter from the *Sporting Standard* of Melbourne put it direct to Peter: "'And the ladies?' we asked. 'Why didn't you follow Slavin's example?' 'Ah,' said Peter, evidently in doubt as how he should turn the joke, 'they're a fine lot of girls in England, very nice, indeed; but I'm not a marrying man.' He was on delicate ground, and wished to get on to something more congenial. Woman was not his forte," the *Sporting Standard* decided.

Around the same time "Smiler" Hales asked him: "Where did you see the prettiest women you ever saw?" and got an odd reply. Peter said, suavely but evasively: "Well now, I feel like a whisky bottle that's being sucked clean dry. Of course I have seen some lovely ladies; there are plenty of them in Australia and in America. If a man took his hat off to each he met he'd be bald-headed in a day. Why, pretty women in America are as plentiful as snow-flakes in winter, but if I've got to tell the truth I must confess that Brighton Beach, in England, beats the world."[20] Hales was not a trustworthy reporter, but those discreet remarks sound genuine. References in 1956 by Deghy to Peter's "Missus" in Putney in 1892 quite clearly concern Paddy and Edith, who at the time were expecting their first child, Frank Slavin, Jr., and living in "a very pretty little terraced house" in Putney.[21]

With two exceptions, these were the only times he was reported as having spoken about women and marriage. Peter moved more confidently in the world of men. He apparently made the not uncommon psychological distinction between physical sex, which he may have engaged in with prostitutes, the gay ladies who were so numerous in Sydney and other cities, and emotional warmth, which he mostly directed toward men friends. In that period, quite intense bonding between buddies, and even affectionate gestures, were not reprimanded. It was an innocent age.[22] It was common for unmarried boxers and trainers to share a bed. In his *Life and Reminiscences of a Nineteenth-Century Gladiator* (1892), John L. Sullivan's discussion of training started off with these remarks: "I do not believe in having a trainer sleep in the same bed with the person training. My reasons are that a man can sleep better alone and will not be obliged to inhale the breath of the other man." Sullivan's criticism was simply hygienic.

Once during these years Peter made the papers for reasons other than his career. On April 17, 1884, a 26-year-old shoemaker from Melbourne, Alexander Agar, was killed in a fight near Randwick racetrack. The *Evening News*, which was first with the story, headed it: "Fatal Prize Fight, A White Man Killed by a Nigger."

Agar's opponent was Jimmy Lawson, whom Agar had pursued from Melbourne five weeks earlier in order to settle some score. Peter and Lawson had become firm friends in the 10 weeks since the Anniversary Weekend show. Peter was present at the fight, and after Agar died he took Lawson back to the Lighthouse Hotel, where apparently Peter lived, his challenge to Farnan on May 23 being issued from there. Peter was trying to comfort the terrified Lawson in the bar of the Lighthouse when they were both arrested by Sub-Inspector James Bremner, who "asked Jackson if he had been out at the prize fight that morning; he said he was out at a fight, which was half over when he got there, that he did not know it was a prize fight, and he had not taken part in it." Peter's was an ingenious excuse, for it had been not a prizefight but a grudge match. Still he was charged with being an accessory to murder. At the police station that he met John C. Dunlop, a detective policeman with whom he became friends. The *Evening News* still didn't know who Peter was, for it wrote of "Peter Jackson, 24, labourer, of America," and said "Jackson is a tall, powerful black man, fully six feet high." He was described as "a countryman of Lawson's." The age was incorrect, for in April 1884 Peter was 22, the age he had claimed when he joined the *H.J. Libby* five years before.

After the police investigation, Peter appeared at the coronial inquiry but was dismissed by Coroner Shiell as not involved. Several of the accused were described as "colored," but this seems to have meant "too dark to be white" in 1884 Sydney. Peter and Lawson were the only ones referred to as blacks. At the trial itself on May 28 the five accused were found guilty of manslaughter, and the four of them with records sentenced to 15 months or two years. Lawson, who had no record, was sentenced to a year's hard labor in Darlinghurst jail. By June 1885 he was out and boxing again. He went to Queensland, where he fought under Jack Dowridge's management in 1887, and back to California. His last fight was in Brooklyn in 1898. In Australia one positive thing emerged from Agar's death, that laws were passed banning bare-knuckle prizefights.

Peter was described as a laborer, but in time he decided to be his own boss and no longer simply employed by Foley. At about the time that Foley was moving into the White Horse, Peter used George Hill, Frank Smith and Ted Belisario to procure the license of the United States Family Hotel. He was authorized as a publican for one year, from July 1885 until June 1886.[23]

The records of ratepayers in the City of Sydney are sparse for the 1880s, while the records of liquor licenses issued in the late 1880s are missing from the New South Wales State Archives. The documents which survive suggest that Peter Jackson was the licensee of the United States Hotel, though during the 1880s the rates for it were paid by Lucius O'Brien, the owner of the property.[24] In early 1880, before he took on the Queen's Hotel, the licensee had been Foley.

The United States Family Hotel was downtown at 256–258 Sussex, at Sussex and Druitt. It had three floors and nine rooms. Peter needed a hotel for income, he needed it for his post-boxing career, and if he failed abroad there he would need it as a refuge. His time at the United States Family Hotel was half a success, half a failure. As a popular host he had to socialize with all comers

The earliest portrait of Peter Jackson found. It is on page 64 of "Vigilant" (ed.), *Australian Sporting Celebrities with Biographical Sketches of their Careers* (1887), and shows him dressed for his position as bartender and host of the United States Family Hotel.

and talk with them about their interests, and he grew immensely in confidence and became a good talker after previously being shy and tongue-tied. But as an organizer and manager of a commercial enterprise he was poor. This had become so painfully obvious that the Sydney *Bulletin* could publish a little verse about it in April 1887:

> *The Professor can fight, the Professor can spar,*
> *And draw forth the claret the while,*
> *But he can't run a pub, or sit still in a bar,*
> *Because he ain't built in that style.*

Everyone knew the enterprise was faltering. Foley and Hill, in connivance with their buddy Charles Ricketts, conceived an ingenious plan, that somebody else should run the hotel—should be the legal licensee—while Peter would work the bar and teach his young boxers. Peter contacted his brother James, the brother whom he lost in New York in 1878 but who evidently had resurfaced in his life. James had gone to Boston. Peter asked James to come to Australia and to manage the hotel for him. At the appropriate time James applied for a publican's license, but not for the license of the United States Hotel. He was granted the license of the Lighthouse Hotel, to take effect from July 1, 1887. Peter continued to run the United States Family Hotel until March 1887, when the *Referee* announced: "Professor Jackson has disposed of his public house, and is willing to fight any man in Australia for £200 and the belt." He then proceeded, in the second half of 1887, to run the Lighthouse Hotel, at least its social side, with James as its commercial manager. James was the official licensee for two years, from July 1, 1887, until June 30, 1889.

This was a legal device to keep the Lighthouse business going in Sydney in case the California venture failed. James was Peter's insurance against shipwreck in the United States. James stayed in Sydney for three years, until the brothers must have deemed Peter such a success overseas that he would never need a Sydney hotel to retreat to. After Peter had conquered America and Britain and made his triumphant return to America, James left for home. Ever after, he was known in America as "Kangaroo Jackson."

In the Lighthouse the dining-room on the second floor was gutted and refurbished for training purposes, with a punching bag and a roped ring. Large mirrors permitted self-observation while practicing moves; people spoke of shadow-boxing improved. Men came to train, men came to spar, men came to unload their aggression onto Peter. Dick Matthews, who had fought in California and would become the champion of New Zealand, was downed by Peter in a four-round bout which was described as "a quiet trial in Sussex street, when Jackson soon proved himself master of the situation." Matthews told the *National Police Gazette* of April 17, 1886 that on his antipodean tour he had "won victory after victory," with the next week's issue, April 24, calling him "Champion of Australia." He hadn't told Fox about Peter. On September 10 the following year his "false representations" in New Zealand about having trained Jack "Nonpareil" Dempsey were exposed by Fox.

Many such visitors came. In March 1894, speaking to a *Decatur Morning Herald Dispatch* reporter in Decatur, Illinois, Peter admitted: "I do not remember all the men I have fought with and probably would not know them on the street if I met them. Fighting is my business. I never see the man with whom I am to fight until we get into the ring. They are dressed different on the street and I wouldn't know them."

After Farnan lost to Lees, Sullivan said that when in Australia he would now fight Lees. When Peter beat Lees, some people, Gillies of the *Maitland Mercury* for one, expected that

Sullivan would then fight Peter, but in Boston that particular scenario was not contemplated, at least not yet.

Eight months after the second Farnan fight, on Saturday, May 2, 1885, the final night of the season of Giuseppe Chiarini's Royal Italian Circus and Menagerie of Trained Animals at Belmore Park, Peter sparred four rounds with Miller. This was in conjunction with a "Great Boxing Tournament" for the championships of New South Wales. Foley had decided to promote this to bring some order to the chaos the New South Wales titles were in.

Every night the prelude to the boxing was some circus acts including a horse called Black Prince, bought in the Hunter Valley and trained by Signor Chiarini, which went through its paces. On the first night, after Chiarini had withdrawn, "Professor William Miller stepped into the ring and announced that it was the wish of Mr. Laurence Foley and himself to promote the art of boxing and place it on a respectable footing, and to that end they had hit on upon this idea. He was quite certain that if the large audience would remain quiet and keep their feelings within bounds, everything would pass off in the most satisfactory manner." The *Town and Country Journal*'s athletics columnist, "Nimrod," remarked that "such, indeed, was the case," and from then on the *Town and Country Journal* ungrudgingly gave space to boxing. The first night concluded with Foley and Miller boxing and the next night with Foley and Peter. The Saturday night ended with Peter boxing Miller for four rounds before 3000 spectators. The "Great Boxing Tournament" was declared a great success.

Shortly after the tournament Chiarini took Black Prince and his circus on to South America, planning to make his way home to Italy. He never arrived. When Chiarini died a few years he was chief riding master and equerry to Pedro II, the Emperor of Brazil.[25]

Since he had not lost, Farnan still claimed the championship of Australia, and in Melbourne he found strong support for his claim. Peter's pupil Tom Lees was living in Victoria and fought Farnan in Melbourne on May 20, 1885, knocking him out in twelve. On April 19, 1886 Lees again defeated Farnan and claimed the Australian title. At this point Foley had had enough and decided to abdicate all his titles so that Lees, whom he considered only the Victorian champion, should fight Jackson, considered the champion of New South Wales, and thus determine the national championship.

The fight was advertised in the *Sydney Morning Herald* as "A Grand Boxing Contest between Tom Lees and Professor Jackson for the Championship of Australia, £400, a trophy valued at £50, and the Champion Belt, kindly thrown in by L. Foley." The fight took place on September 25, 1886.

The crowd included politicians past and present, and apparently every black in Sydney. The *Sydney Bulletin* of October 2 noticed: "White predominated, but darkies attended so largely as to give the hall a sort of piebald appearance." This was the first indication that Peter would become the Great Black Hope. A posse of police attended, and Foley posted pugs round the ring as bouncers. At one point, they had to subdue "one excited individual of the larrikin type" who tried to enter the ring.

Jackson weighed 198 pounds, Lees 172 pounds. The gloves weighed four ounces and were made of reddish leather padded with horsehair. But each glove had a red and white leather wrist trim, presumably so that the spectators could note every movement. At the end of the match Danny Hehir, an associate of Foley's, souvenired them and carried them off to Western Australia, where they remained until 2002 to emerge at a Christie's auction.

The fight was farcical but the crowd did not laugh. Lees ran around the ring and

Jackson chased him. Lees punched feebly for the most part while he fled, but Jackson thumped Lees unmercifully when he caught him.

By round 30 Lees could scarcely stand. Twice he was hit in the face, and when Jackson's left came a third time he crumpled, falling into his opponent's arms. The *Sportsman* reported that when Lees proved a bit "groggy," Jackson was averse to punishing him. Not only did he call to Newton and Taylor to take him off but he supported the beaten man, holding him for a moment while he looked inquiringly at the referee. Told by the referee to finish it, he knocked the dazed Lees down. Newton then lost no time in throwing up the sponge. Jackson was declared the winner and therefore Champion of Australia.

On October 30, Gillies of the *Maitland Mercury* said that champion Lees had been supposed to fight Sullivan, and now that Peter was champion, "I have heard a suggestion that Lees' sable conqueror should be given an opportunity to meet J.L. Sullivan." Whose suggestion this was is unknown. Certainly Boston was silent, and the Sullivan-Jackson story had several episodes yet to be enacted.

A week after the fight, on Saturday, October 2, 1886, in a little ceremony at Foley's Athletic Hall, Jack Thompson presented Peter with a championship belt. Jackson "replied in suitable terms" and Foley buckled it on him. Originally Foley intended to award a facsimile of his own belt, but he acquired a second one. After Foley defeated Abe Hicken, in October 1880 he was presented with a gold and silver belt made by Evan Jones, the esteemed Sydney jeweler, and paid for by admirers. Foley now referred to this as the "Knuckle Champion Belt." The one he procured was in silver, 12 inches wide and weighing 24 ounces troy, and Foley referred to it as the "Glove Championship Belt."

But it was not that. It was the champion belt of New South Wales, presented to Ike Reid in commemoration of the his victory over George Hough on April 6, 1847. "The plates are appropriately engraved," the *Bulletin* continued, "and the trophy was speedily recognised by Bill Sparks, Dave Ingram, and other old-time bruisers, as it lay alongside Foley's silver and gold belt." It was appraised as worth 100 guineas.[26]

The belt was of dark-blue silk plush edged with silver braid, and on the back of the belt, presumably as a clasp, was the word "Champion" in large silver letters. The silver plates formed a triptych, the two side ones blank. The central plate showed a *nike* or victory holding a laurel wreath above the head of Ike Reid posing in knee-breeches and long sideburns, while her other hand displayed a scroll bearing the words "Champion of New South Wales." In the week between Peter's victory and the presentation, Foley had taken the belt to a silversmith's to have a lower inscription containing Reid's name erased and one with Peter's engraved in its place. It now read:

This picture of the silver portion of Jackson's Australian championship belt appeared in the *Australasian Antique Collector* in 1979.

2. Unbleached Australian, 1879–1888

This Belt is Presented
by
L. Foley
to Peter Jackson
Champion Boxer of Australia
2nd October 1886.

For the rest of his life Peter carried his belt with him everywhere, as he did his greatcoat, depositing it with a bank wherever he was based. *Sporting Life* on August 30, 1889, when he arrived at Liverpool in England for the first time, reported: "Whilst Jackson's trunks were being overhauled by the Customs officers a large number of spectators lined the docks and showed much enthusiasm at the powerful-looking Australian, who appeared to enjoy the situation, and was much amused when the Customs officers found his silver championship belt (presented to him by Larry Foley, of Sydney), which was detained for the present, but, of course, will be forwarded in due course to its owner." He was scrupulous about retrieving it whenever it had been inspected. He was always unwrapping it for favored journalists and others. Only in January 1901, going to Brisbane on his last journey, did he leave it behind, and then in Will's care.

Against a studio backdrop of saplings he posed glumly, with dukes up and wearing the belt, to be photographed by W.C. Norman of the Electric Photo Engraving Company at 8 Bridge. Such photographs were regularly sold to fans by the photographers. And the next year he appeared, a pen sketch by Samuel Calvert on one page and a paragraph about him opposite it, in a book by "Vigilant" titled *Australian Sporting Celebrities with Biographical Sketches of Their Career.* Calvert sketched a dapper Peter in a suit, vest, and tie held by a horseshoe stick-pin, with his hair parted in the middle. It was Peter "mine host" of the Lighthouse Hotel, with little resemblance to the photograph of the champion. Precisely because it was a line drawing, however, and not a photograph requiring the new technology of half-tone printing, newspapers in Australia and America often reproduced this portrait.

It was decided the champion of New South Wales should capitalize on his victory. About 900 men watched him defeat Lees, but now thousands wanted to see him. Foley had exhibited around Queensland after he became champion. Peter heeded this lesson, and persuaded opponents whom he had just pummeled into submission to go touring with him. That was where the money was and all boxers did it. The *New York Herald* estimated in 1918 that between 1881 and 1898 Sullivan had earned close to $125,000 from his ring battles and about $885,000 from his tours.[27] Lees was not involved. Neville Forder ("Boxer-Major") wrote in 1913 that Lees "never got another fight in Australia, and the fame of that wretched performance followed him round the world." He fled to England to the source, apprenticing himself to Jem Mace.[28]

Peter put together a boxing troupe in mid–1886: himself, his buddy Jimmy Lawson, Ned Powell, and others. They and their tent and their transport composed a boxing booth. The booth toured south of Sydney through coastal towns like Wollongong, Minnamurra, Unanderra, and Gerringong, where the spruiker or barker would invite local guys to take a glove from him and so accept the challenge to fight a few rounds, usually four, with one of the troupe. He who accepted was called a take.

They arrived in the seaside town of Kiama, which boasted two stone quarries.[29] The first horse-drawn streetcar ran in Sydney in September 1879, and the network extended rapidly. The rails ran on a bed of crushed rock, along which the horse walked. Bluestone was needed for the tracks. Ahead of this, through his family's access to Parliamentary information, George Hill shrewdly leased the Bombo Point quarry at Kiama where cubes of basalt could be mined and shipped up to Sydney to be crushed. He made a fortune out of this venture. In the mid–1880s, when Peter visited Kiama, some 70 to 80 men were employed at Bombo Point, living in tents and huts and with nowhere to go for recreation except a dive called "The Club."

One of the quarrymen who offered himself as a take was Paddy Slavin, now 26 years old. In the four years since he and Peter contended at Foley's hotel, Paddy, like his two brothers Jack and Bill, had gained a reputation as a fighter up north. In fact he was now the heavyweight champion of Queensland. He fought with Peter in the tent, cheered on by the quarrymen. Paddy was by now a fine figure of a man, six feet tall with piercing blue eyes, and strong from having been breaking bluestone with a sledgehammer. Though he was largely a self-taught boxer he impressed the visitors sufficiently for Peter to invite him up to Sydney to learn more about boxing scientifically. Another Kiama man, Joe Goddard, was also invited up.

After learning boxing in Sydney, Paddy had crossed to Western Australia and fought there, winning a 75-round bout in Kalgoorlie in 1884. Back east, and aged about 23, he joined a boxing booth like the one Peter was bringing to Kiama, and went north and across the border with it, into Queensland. In 1885 he tried his luck as a digger on the Queensland gold fields, at Charters Towers. Bill and Jack joined him. They had no luck. They all three turned back to boxing, mostly with bare knuckles. In Paddy's Queensland career in 1885 he knocked out the Charters Towers veteran Martin Power in the 13th round and won £50; beat Tim Shanahan of Gympie in 2 rounds, winning £10 and a medal; and eliminated Sam Burke of Rockhampton in 10 seconds. Early in 1886 he fought James Burke, the champion of Queensland, and won £200 and the title in four rounds. His last victory in Queensland was over "Professor" Babbs from Geelong at the Australian Gardens in Brisbane, after which he offered to fight any man for a sum between £200 and £500. This challenge was not answered and, probably accompanied by Bill and Jack, Paddy returned to New South Wales, where he found work as a lumberjack and then at Kiama in the Bombo quarry.

Paddy did take up the invitation to Sydney, and took more lessons from Peter on how to fight Mace-wise and Foley-wise, though he was never converted completely to glove fighting. He had absorbed too well the old back-country ways of doing things. In September 1892 the *St. Louis Post-Dispatch* reported on Peter, saying: "He gave Frank P. Slavin his first lessons in the rudiments of the manly art. Slavin, under Jackson's tuition, became very clever in the short period of six months." Paddy never denied this. He had a good heart, but he was naive and suggestible.

They were supposed to have a fight in January 1887 but the arrangements fell through. Paddy claimed to have become an instructor at Foley's, and inside of six months to have beaten Ivo Bligh in one round, Tom Taylor in two rounds, and Jim Fogarty in three. With Dooley he took longer: eight rounds. But he didn't fight Peter, only unofficially.

About March 1887 their friendly relationship suffered an eclipse. The pair had a quarrel behind Foley's bar, with some scuffling. Foley made them adjourn to the boxing room, where they fought two or three rounds. Peter cowed Paddy in ten seconds, according to Forder, who was there, knocking him down "with a badly-slit lip and an eye that filled while you looked." Foley's opinion (in 1889) was that they would never meet in an official fight if Paddy could help it. The *St. Louis Post-Dispatch* of January 3, 1892, before the

London fight, reported from New York: "Speaking of meeting Peter Jackson, says he met the darky only once in a fight and that was in a hotel in Melbourne five years ago, when they were separated by friends." As the English *Sporting Life* reported on May 31, 1892, when asked about his fight with Peter, Paddy said the story "had no foundation in substance or fact. All that occurred was a little bar-room scrimmage, which was stopped soon after it commenced." After the punch-up Slavin quit the Foley entourage and went along to Peter Newton in Melbourne where, according to "Smiler" Hales in 1892, Paddy "learned from him what he knows about the fighting game." Years later the *Referee* journalist Will "Solar Plexus" Lawless joked that the men claiming to have been in the White Horse and seen Paddy battle Peter would fill Sydney Stadium.

Paddy drew with Costello on May 14, 1887. But he was reluctant to fight Peter. The *Chicago Herald* reported from London on Christmas Day, 1889, that in an interview, Paddy explained why he had never fought Peter: "His backers drew him out of one match with Peter Jackson, and he was compelled to forfeit another because of a sprained wrist." Any such action by his backers is a mystery, but on February 15, 1888, the *Melbourne Sportsman* did report, belatedly, that he had sprained his wrist fighting Costello two weeks before the scheduled fight with Peter, that is on May 14. If that was so, for 14 days he failed to tell anybody about it.

Early in February 1887 Peter met the man who became his best buddy, John L. Herget, who was the lightweight champion of California. Herget and Martin "Buffalo" Costello, styling himself "Champion of California," visited from San Francisco to get some experience fighting around Australia. "I went over there with Buffalo Costello," Herget recalled in 1901, "and about the first person we met was Peter. We found him very congenial, and he treated us beautifully." Costello liked Australia, brought his brother Jack over, ran the Lounge Hotel on Bourke in Melbourne, and stayed for six years. Herget stayed for eight months. Both coming and going he had fights in New Zealand, as Peter never did.

Born in 1867 and of Swiss descent, Herget used in Australia the name "Charles Mitchell," the name of the British middleweight. Herget had been trained by Maynard and Seymour. Later, back in San Francisco, when Charley Mitchell had taken to visiting America, he was known in the game as "Young Mitchell." He met Peter when he had just turned 20 and had been fighting for two years. On February 26, 1885, the *National Police Gazette* had published a picture of him at 18, without letterpress but with the caption: "San Francisco's Youthful Contribution to the Celebrities of the American Ring." He was five feet six inches tall and weighed 150 pounds. The *Bulletin* described him as "a splendidly built youngster" and "a picture of symmetry," as Costello's "sturdily-built little chum," and as "the perfectly-built and conditioned Mitchell." He fought "Torpedo" Billy Murphy at Foley's on March 14 and won by knockout in five, Murphy becoming featherweight champion of the world two years later. He traveled the countryside with Cannon's Athletic Company, and in Albury drew with Peter Boland after 40 rounds fought on private land, the stakes being $1000 a side. They fought in a rainstorm. On the same occasion, Costello fought Paddy. Herget departed for San Francisco aboard the *Alameda* on October 26, 1887.

According to the story which Peter told to Naughton, he decided to go to America during the winter of 1887. Although he told a different story in 1911, Naughton gave Peter's account thus in the *San Francisco Examiner* on March 3, 1889: "While acting as trainer Jackson usually had his headquarters at Foley and Thompson's Athletic Club, an extensive sporting institution o'ertopping the cliffs of Bondi, one of the most picturesque marine suburbs of Sydney, and it was while listening to the war of the surf on the beach below and watching the huge waves combing white locks on the bar that the dusky champion first conceived the idea of seeking fame and fortune in other lands." Naughton sometimes called Peter the "Marquis of Bondi."

Peter had given Naughton an idealistic version of his decision, to accept the invitations that everybody was pressing upon him and to recognize that simply nobody was left in Australasia to fight except for Paddy, who was eluding him. Peter made up his mind on pragmatic grounds, and not by pondering the wintry surf at Bondi. "Once having taken root in his mind," the *Examiner* biography continued, "the desire for travel grew apace, and in 1887 the champion made up his mind to cross the broad Pacific and try to obtain fresh heights in pugilism." As late as September 1887 the fancy talked of George Godfrey's being brought out to Australia to fight Peter. Godfrey was a fine boxer and matching him with Peter would have made the biggest fight held in Sydney until then. But Godfrey, who lived in Boston with his large family, did not want to travel down under. Let the bachelor Peter come to him. It was reported that, if Godfrey refused, "Peter Jackson says he is under a year's engagement to a couple of sports, and will make tracks for the States."

The sports center where Peter hung out in 1887 was on the heights immediately south of the beach. Foley and Thompson purchased the Mercantile and Marine Club in March 1887, intending it to be another grand athletic venue. Opposite Foley's club was the Cliff House, a hotel named after Adolph Sutro's famous Cliff House in San Francisco. The licensee from 1887 to 1890 was John Dunlop, the former detective with whom Peter had become acquainted when Jimmy Lawson was arrested. Dunlop must have encouraged Peter when the latter unveiled his plans. Dunlop became licensee of the Castlereagh Hotel in Woollahra, and it was there in 1892, after the fight with Paddy in London, that Peter mailed an 18" × 15" photograph of himself clearly labeled "CHAMPION," a gift to the man opposite whose hotel he had conceived his grand ambition.

News of Paddy finally came. He was in Melbourne, where he fought Miller. In September, because of police interference, he fought Costello away from Melbourne, on "Bungowannah" station, nine miles out of Albury on the New South Wales border. The *Evening News* said that Paddy was calling himself the "Champion of Queensland," which was a perfectly correct presentation of himself. They fought for thirty rounds and Paddy won. Gillies of the *Maitland Mercury*, who had a disabused view of Paddy, said in September 1892 that, before his London fight with Peter, Costello was the only scientific fighter Paddy had ever met.

When Paddy got to Melbourne he was romanced by a section of the fancy, headed by John Daugherty, Patrick Reynolds and Joe Harris, with associates of George C. Piesse from the big London perfumery house Piesse & Lubin, nicknamed "Rats" and Paddy's backer. They resented Peter for being from Sydney, for being a foreigner, and for being black. Even Miller favored Paddy. With champagne and flattery they persuaded him that he was the real champion boxer of Australia. He believed it even when sober, but when in Sydney he thought it prudent to conceal his belief. "An atrociously vain man" was the *Maitland Mercury's* uncharitable description of Paddy.

After Melbourne, Paddy went to New Zealand, where he fought Harry Laing at the Wanganui racetrack. Paddy was unreservedly claiming to be champion of Australia. The *Referee* said sarcastically:

Answering a question which evidently emanates from its own office, a Melbourne paper tells its mythical correspondent that Slavin, and not Jackson, is the champion of Australia. The thing is so absurdly ridiculous that it is a wonder the paper in question is not ashamed of the absurdity it endeavors to promulgate and uphold. First, Slavin ran away from Sydney to avoid meeting Jackson. Then when at a safe distance he started growling and barking. He and his party were offered every possible chance for a meeting, and would never come to terms, and when at last terms are arranged and his backers turn round to look for their man, lo! there he is in New Zealand, fifteen hundred miles away.

The Sydney *Bulletin* commented on Paddy's wrigglings:

> Sure the darkies are finally freed,
> And Liberty's banners are waven,
> For Jackson, stout champion indeed,
> Can't meet an opponent *enslaven*.

Not deathless poetry, yet it made its point. In desperation, in October 1887 Foley promised to give Jackson and Slavin £200 if they would fight in his hall, and as the men had been talking over a match for £300 a side, this would have made a substantial prize of £500 for the winner. The offer did not entice Paddy. In February 1888 Peter was still making offers. Messages flew back and forth about a fight at Sydney or Melbourne; then when Albury was agreed on, messages flew to and fro about whether the fight would be on boards, as Peter preferred, or on the grass, which was Paddy's preference. Apparently because he would not agree to all their little conditions Paddy's Melbourne backers cried that Peter had forfeited the championship. Fox, in the *National Police Gazette* of October 29, 1892, said it as clearly as anyone ever has: "it has always been the rule that a champion must defend his title against all challenges that are legitimate." Here this principle was being reduced to absurdity. When to silence them Peter agreed to any conditions whatsoever, the wires from Melbourne ceased. Paddy was not doing these negotiations, being himself still in New Zealand and incommunicado at the time. Peter was never able to defend his Australian title before he left for overseas, nor obliged to.

Peter having left for America, Paddy's Melbourne supporters invoked a principle never mentioned before: that the champion of Australia must be not merely a resident of Australia but physically present in the country. They did not demand that the champion of Australia should be an Australian by birth or naturalization, though this might have occurred to them, since in fact the Archives of New South Wales do not record that Peter ever got naturalized there. They claimed that by going to California Peter had forfeited the title and that Paddy was now by default the champion. On July 6, 1888, Paddy drew with the "Irish Lad." A fight between Paddy and Dooley was then arranged and Paddy won. Paddy's supporters claimed that this fight on December 10, 1888, clinched Paddy's right to the title. Ingenuous Paddy was told it did and seems to have believed them, even though they gave him not a belt worth 500 guineas but only the promise of one. Not until he lost to Peter in London in 1892, in the only fight the two ever did have, was he forced to admit to himself that Peter had been Australia's champion all along.

On July 30, 1887, at Foley's, Billy Williams lost to "Young Fitz," a repetition of their match back in January. "Young Fitz" was Samuel Fitch, born in 1866 in Maitland, that seedbed of boxers. When Sam's father died in 1882 he left wife and seven children so desperately poor that his grave remained unmarked. Sam wanted out of Maitland poverty. Having moved to Sydney, he was calling himself Fitzpatrick and was saying that he was born in Sydney, in Balmain near Pyrmont. Though a regular English name, Fitch is also, in parts of Ireland, taken to be an abbreviated form of Fitzsimmons and Fitzpatrick. His change of name made Sam sound more Irish, and by 1890 he was even claiming to have been born in County Queens in 1864 and taken to Maitland as an infant. But he didn't persevere with the Irish pretense. In the *New York Globe* in 1914, speaking of Griffo, Sam said: "Griffo was born in Australia. So was I. That's why I am so familiar with his history, though he was never directly under my management." The night Fitzpatrick fought Williams again, Peter and Dooley were there to give a three-round exhibition. So Peter met Fitzpatrick that night, even if he hadn't earlier.

Fitzpatrick joined Hall and other boxers in the exodus for California, arriving in San Francisco on Christmas Eve 1887. Gillies of the *Maitland Mercury* remembered him with short legs and an inability to punch from the shoulder, calling him a slogging round-arm hitter, and for years he put ironic quotation marks around "Fitzpatrick." Briefly dubbed the "Australian Wonder," he had some victories over the likes of Jack Norton and Dan Slattery, whereupon Gillies remarked how dreadful Californian boxers must be. Naughton did the best he could for Fitzpatrick, who was better known by now as the "Australian Comet," but as a boxer he resembled a meteor. In February 1888, after another defeat, he gave himself three more months before quitting San Francisco for Sydney. But luckily he stayed. It was not boxing that Fitzpatrick was born to do.

Over the next 10 months Peter fought regularly at Foley's, trying to get funds together. He was supposed to fight Jim Stewart from Glasgow on February 7, 1887, for $1000 and his title—but he could not get his money up, at least according to the *Maitland Mercury* of January 15. In April 1887 he fought with Mick O'Brien from Victoria, in June with Jim Nolan. In July it was with O'Donnell. In August, it was Stormo Smith. In September it was Nolan again. Nobody could stand up to him. He ran through all his possible opponents in Sydney and recycled them. He sparred with Dooley yet again. He decided on trips away from Sydney. The *Referee* said he would be plundering the country to pay for his trip, saying that England was his destination.

Peter set off for Newcastle and planned a visit to Brisbane, and another to Adelaide in South Australia. He couldn't organize the boxing exhibitions in Brisbane because he was at Newcastle, so he sent agents ahead to set them up. This involved, to the disapproval of the *Brisbane Telegraph* of August 29, "large coloured bills pasted all over town during last week." Wall posters were a novelty in Queensland.

At the Victoria Theater in Newcastle on August 15, Harry "Dummy" Mace fought George Mulholland, after which Miller and Peter gave an exhibition. Then Peter fought four rounds with a terrified Hugh Healy, who ran about the ring to the amusement of the crowd. The theater was packed and great enthusiasm reigned. The show was advertised as: "Peter Jackson's *Farewell Exhibition* in Newcastle, previous to leaving for America to fight for the championship of the World."

After Newcastle he took a boat up to Brisbane. There he made the significant acquaintance of Jack Dowridge, who knew Foley well from the time Foley had stayed in Brisbane. John Edward Dowridge, born on Barbados in 1848 and living in London during the 1860s, had been, like Ned Donnelly, a disciple of Nat Langham's, and had mixed with Donnelly at Langham's Mitre tavern in St. Martin's Lane. Langham's greatest pride was that he had trained Mace. It was in those years that Dowridge started boxing as a lightweight, and like the Englishmen Tom Cribb and Jem Ward, and like his American contemporary Harry

Woodson, Dowridge was dubbed "The Black Diamond." The nickname stuck. Until he died in 1871, Langham managed a boxing booth that toured Britain, and Dowridge served his apprenticeship in it.

Arriving in Brisbane in 1872 he took over the "Hole in the Wall," a tobacco and candy store on Queen, from Foley, who was returning to Sydney. Dowridge invested in Brisbane property. He became the owner of a sweepstake which he shifted to Tasmania when Queensland banned sweepstakes, and commuted to Hobart. He opened restaurants, a barber's and tobacconist's shop, a gymnasium and boxing school, and ended up owning the Theater Royal and the Theater Royal Hotel on Elizabeth. All these activities made him very rich. He married Julia Yeats about 1877 and they had a daughter who died in infancy and two sons born in 1879 and 1882 who themselves became boxers. For decades Dowridge was Brisbane's fight promoter and trainer, his most famous products being George Dawson, the champion lightweight of Australia, and dashing Charles "Kangaroo" Armstrong, a former pupil of Foley's, who briefly in the 1880s was the husband of Nellie Melba.[30] Dowridge and Peter became friends, even though they saw little of each other during the next 13 years.

On Friday, August 26, Peter appeared at Dowridge's Variety Hall (which doubled as Dowridge's Athletic Hall) at Turbot and George in downtown Brisbane, with "a host of well-known athletes" which included Miller, Billy Smith, Paddy Gorman, Dave "Stranger" Ingram, who was Harry Sallars's old acquaintance, and Bill Slavin. Also in the lineup was Edward "Starlight" Rollins, a black from British Guiana, who had been shanghaied in London and jumped ship in Sydney, had been taught and promoted by Dowridge in Brisbane, and after this appearance with Peter would become himself a pupil of Foley's. It was announced that Peter, "previous to sailing for America, will give an athletic exhibition." In the *Evening Observer* the notice read that Peter would give the exhibition "previous to sailing to Europe to meet Kilrain and Smith," which assumed that Jake Kilrain would stay on there after his fight with Jem Smith in France. Alternatively, it was said that he "will give in Brisbane his farewell exhibition of boxing." The *Telegraph* said: "Very exorbitant charges were made, but the hall was crowded, the spectators including members of Parliament, squatters, and some of the leading professional and business men of the town." But prices were 2, 3 and 5 shillings, with stage chairs at 10 shillings. Such prices were normal for Sydney, but in Brisbane at the time a large bottle of beer cost only sixpence. "The Champion," said the advertisement in the *Courier* on Saturday morning, "will wager £50 to nothing that he will stop any man in four rounds who likes to oppose him."

The Brisbane visit turned nasty when police harassed the troupe by ingeniously prosecuting Smith for assaulting Bill Slavin, and Slavin for assaulting Smith during their bout on Saturday, August 27. On the Monday, therefore, it was announced before the bouts that, contrary to the advertised fights to a finish, only friendly sparring would take place. The audience muttered, but there was no more police harassment. The case was heard by Police Magistrate Pinnock on August 30 and the dual charge dismissed.

Peter was back in Sydney by Thursday, September 2, and was said to be leaving for New Zealand within a few days en route to America. The excursion to Adelaide was shelved until 1890. But he didn't sail yet.

On November 26 at the Sydney Gymnasium, Alf "Stonewall" Jackson finally had the satisfaction of boxing Peter Jackson for four rounds, according to the Queensberry rules and with gloves. The *Bulletin* said his wind gave out in the second or third round. Peter dealt gently with the veteran. Peter met up with Paddy's brother Bill again on Boxing Day 1887, when Peter's pupil Billy McCarthy boxed him.

On November 21, Jack "Irish Lad" Burke, who had boxed Kilrain and Charley Mitchell, and Sullivan when he was only 23, arrived with Jack Hall in Sydney from San Francisco. In California he left bad impressions and many unpaid bills. He brought with him a novelty in the shape of a punching ball suspended from the ceiling. In Sydney everyone had punched at leather mail-bags stuffed with kapok. People now visited Sturt's Palace Hotel at Mortlake to see Burke punching his ball. Using a strung-up football, Paddy Slavin followed suit.

As soon as Burke arrived he told the newspapers that he would not fight a black. He claimed that he must draw the color line or be ostracized in America. The Sydney fancy poured scorn on this, pointing to all the white boxers who had fought blacks without harm to their careers, naming Costello for a nearby example. An anonymous Australian correspondent of the *New Zealand Southland Times* said that Jackson should retaliate by drawing a color line against redheads. Burke's determination not to fight a black man was irrevocable. He would only fight the champion of Australia, by which he meant Foley in spite of Foley's retirement and Peter's defeat of Lees. In recent years, apparently since his defeat by Peter Nolan, Burke had avoided fighting big men. Peter put up £500 that he would stop Burke in seven rounds; or his £1,000 to Burke's £700 that he would beat him to a finish at Foley's in public, or in private if Burke so wished it. Burke ignored Peter's offers, though he was money-hungry, a gambler, and returned to Britain broke.

The *Bulletin* said: "Peter Jackson was howling out at the top of his voice for any white trash from any part of the globe, but Burke apparently did not hear him." This was not the first time in his life that Peter had been discriminated against because he was black, but it was the first time in his boxing career. And it was by no means the last.

On Monday, January 9, 1888, Foley, who was 38 years old and painfully out of condition, fought six rounds with 26-year-old Burke for the gate (minus expenses) and a Centennial Boxing Cup. The match was held in the open at the Carrington Grounds. It was adjudged a draw, and the crowd left disgusted. Burke's timekeeper was Naughton, then still with the *San Francisco Chronicle*, who was back in Sydney on a visit. Peter, wearing a guernsey in "centenary blue," seconded Foley.

Burke stayed in Australia for months. On July 10, 1888, after Peter had left for America in March and Paddy had returned from New Zealand in May, he was matched in Melbourne with Paddy, who was claiming to be the champion of Australia. Their bout was refereed by none other than Queensberry himself, who had arrived in Melbourne by the *Liguria* the month before. They drew. Paddy fought again with Burke on February 4, 1889, and won. Encouraged by the fact that Burke had once stood up for five rounds against Sullivan, Paddy got ready to leave for England.

In May 1889, when in the course of his farewell tour of the colonies he returned to the town of his childhood, Paddy was billed as "Native of Maitland, Champion Boxer of Australia, and Challenger of the World." In 1890 the *St. Louis Post-Dispatch* charitably called him "the white champion of Australia." Piesse supported him. Some news from London in 1893 was that "Charles Parsons is backing Slavin, so it is said, but the general opinion here is that it is George Piesse's money." Paddy sailed away to Britain on the *Carthage* in July 1889. Nothing was ever said in Melbourne about his thereby forfeiting a title, though in the next 40 years he never once revisited Australia.

On February 4, 1888, Peter sparred with a "very fleshy" Dooley for three rounds, "the last being really ding-dong." On February 11 he fought Taylor. It was all money for California. On February 20 and 21 Peter was in Newcastle again with a boxing troupe including Bill Slavin and Paddy Gorman and some Newcastle boxers. He refereed.

Peter kept a surprise to finish his Australian years, a surprise for those who knew him only as a boxer and even for those who were aware of how good a swimmer he was. The next week, on Saturday, February 25, 1888, he went to the Corporation Baths for a swimming carnival, in celebration of the founding of the Port Jackson Swimming Club eight years before. A band played numerous selections; everybody was jolly. Called by the advertisers "Professor Jackson, the well-known athlete," Peter with five others had entered the distance diving competition in which, the advertisers promised, "the world's record will be broken." Peter's dive was an eye-opener to the Sydney swimming fraternity. He crossed the baths as straight as an arrow, but having turned and sticking one foot out of the water to show he had done so, he swam back, steering a crooked course and emerging in the shallows with a snort like a walrus. He had won. He had swum 240 feet and lasted 58 seconds under the water, which may have been the world record. Peter had usefully spent his boyhood around ships, diving deep down for tourists' dimes! Sydney had never seen anything like this feat, and it became legendary. He was awarded a medal which he showed in San Francisco as the "medal for the swimming championship of New South Wales." Years later Snowy Baker, desperate himself to become legendary, falsely claimed he saw Peter swim under water in 1901.[31]

Peter told a reporter in Chicago the following year: "I follow fighting and sports in general purely as a business and not to satisfy a brutal nature. I can row, swim and run as well as box, and whatever I do I try to be a gentleman. I make it a point of my fights never to administer a knock-out blow unless I am compelled to do so. It is no satisfaction to me to render an opponent insensible with a blow when he is whipped and at my mercy." In short, out of all the sports he practiced he had coolly chosen to box professionally because boxers were paid the most.

On April 18, in the centenary year of the arrival of the first white settlers at Botany Bay, Peter stood on the deck of the Spreckles' Pacific Mail Line ship, the *Alameda*. The night before, Foley had organized a big benefit or farewell night. Four of Peter's pupils, McCarthy, Taylor, Hickey, and O'Donnell, who inherited Peter's training job under Foley, gave him a medal with lovelocks, a heart, and his initials — all worked in diamonds — and engraved with the words: *To A Man*. When he arrived in San Francisco he showed off the medal, and two days later was robbed of both his medal and his watch. Their recovery was never reported. However, the *Australasian* of July 20, 1901, said: "One of the gifts which Peter cherished above all others, and one of the few he retained of the many he received during his pugilistic career, was a heart-shaped locket with a diamond in the center. It bears the inscription, 'To Peter Jackson, a man,' and was given him by a number of his particular friends in the heyday of his success." The two objects are described so differently that Peter must have procured a replacement for the stolen medal.

The *Dead Bird* said in 1889: "Jackson left our shores, quietly and unostentatiously, and with a small flour-bag full of Australian sovereigns, freshly handed to him by benefit-treasurer W.F. Corbett, grasped carefully in his strong right hand." He had never been naturalized as a British subject, but he always fought calling himself Australian and he often wore the white and sky-blue that were Australia's sporting colors then.

The *Alameda* made its way down Port Jackson, through the Heads, and out onto the

Pacific Ocean. Tom Meadows and Paddy Gorman the Queenslander were going with Peter, all three under the "fatherly interest" of Captain Charles Morse, whose main claim to fame was that his ship had conveyed Spalding's baseball team to Australia on its world tour. Morse had a little gym with a punching ball, and Peter was expert at it by the time he reached San Francisco.

It was nine years since a frightened sailor boy arrived in Sydney, and now the champion of Australia was sailing through the Heads again, bound for Auckland, Apia and Honolulu, and for the Paris of the Pacific, golden San Francisco. When Naughton greeted him on his arrival there, he noticed that in just one year the devil-may-care Peter had developed into a far-seeing, level-headed and ambitious man.

Australia had made a boxer and Peter the boxer knew what he wanted. Just before he left, he wired a challenge to Jem Smith, the bare-knuckle champion of England, for a glove fight at $5000 a side. Smith's acceptance was wired to Honolulu. John Gillies wrote in the *Maitland Mercury*[32]: "Australia's boxing champion, Professor Peter Jackson, has left our shores on what may properly be called an offensive tour, for he intends, I learn, on challenging each and everybody in the land of the stars and stripes on his arrival."

And so it was.

CHAPTER 3

Offensive Tour, 1888–1889

The *Alameda* left Sydney on April 18 and Auckland on the 23rd, where George Harting, later a famous timekeeper, embarked. He and Peter became fast friends. The ship paused for mail off Pago Pago in German Samoa on the 27th and left Honolulu on May 5. The voyage was uneventful. Off Monterey they sighted California. About 9:00 A.M. the *Alameda* reached the Farallones, rock pinnacles where a fog bell tolled. At 10 A.M. they took on the pilot. At 1:00 P.M. one of the tugs *Neptune* or *Rescue* took them through the sandbars into the Golden Gate, passing on the right the cliffs above Seal Rocks and the heights of the Presidio, passing on the left the Sausalito Peninsula, with directly ahead Oakland and Alameda. At 3:00 P.M. on Sunday, May 12, 1888, the *Alameda* swung right to San Francisco and tied up to the Spreckles' dock at Brannan and First.

Before Peter was a city not unlike the one he had left, though not half its age, with many fine buildings but far more in wood than in Sydney, altogether hillier.[1] No restriction on entry to the United States operated, unless it was for pauperism, a known criminal record, or a disease like tuberculosis. All the homeless and tempest-tossed were still allowed in. Peter entered the United States without difficulty, and his comings and goings thereafter were never questioned.

San Francisco was smaller than Sydney, having a population of 300,000—but when Oakland and Alameda and other settlements around the Bay were added, it was more like 400,000. Los Angeles counted 50,000 and Sacramento 26,000, while the only other considerable cities along the West Coast, Seattle and Portland, did not hold 90,000 between them in 1888. San Francisco was one of the few places in the United States where boxing was allowed in a fashion, in private clubs for their members, though police raids were not unknown and temporary bannings of the sport a matter of fits and starts.[2] This was the city of Jack London and Bert Williams, of Frank Norris, of Isadora Duncan and William Randolph Hearst. It was Peter's city for conquest.

Peter was 27 in May 1888, and he had no time to lose. He needed money, brass. His bag of sovereigns given him in Sydney was shrinking; indeed, he was almost broke. One dollar was worth 4 shillings and 2 pence in sterling, the currency based on gold. Probably his little flour-bag had held 100 gold sovereigns, and so equaled $500. San Francisco was a tremendously expensive city because many things, especially manufactured wares, were brought from the East. So he had to start his offensive tour at once. In June the following year the *London Sportsman* said: "It is safe to say that Peter Jackson will not fight to a finish with anyone for three years or more, during which time he will, it is to be hoped, gather enough of this world's goods to face any contingency." It was not that Peter had a lust for gold, it was that he hoped he would never want as Joseph and Julia's little son had wanted, ever again. This dog would be eating cheese.

Though new in town, he had contacts. Already so many Australians were in town that an Australian Club was organized, with rooms at 1320 Market. It had 80 members in 1892. Until then, many Australians used to hang out at the Gaiety Saloon on Ellis, near the Baldwin Hotel and kept by Con Marshall, a Britisher. All the Australian boxers used to drop in at Con's for a beer. And naturally, everyone dropping in at the Gaiety had their contacts in the sporting world, in the pool-rooms and other saloons and at the clubs. For example, when William McClellan fought Mike Donovan in San Francisco in April 1878 he was photographed with Harry Maynard, Arthur Chambers, and Billy Edwards, men who each played a part in Peter's career. Donovan wrote an article for the *Brooklyn Eagle* on January 12, 1890, which showed him familiar with all the boxers and the fancy in New York, San Francisco, and New Orleans. He knew Queensberry personally. Boxers across the world knew or knew of one another.

Peter used every resource he had. His name had appeared in local papers the year before, and the *Examiner* and the *Chronicle* covered his arrival. He had the support of Morse and Naughton. The point was to show himself, to let people see him, see his footwork, see him move, see him feint and weave, and hopefully take him up. He succeeded at once. He arrived on a Sunday and already on Wednesday night he was sparring at the Cremorne Theater.

This venue, often referred to as the "old Cremorne," was owned by Jack Hallinan. An Australian, he was a boxer and wrestler and a strong supporter of the Golden Gate Athletic Club on Stevenson, according to the *National Police Gazette*, which profiled him on December 15, 1888. The first night Hallinan himself did a turn with Peter, but thereafter his exhibition partner was Cornelius Riordan, known as Con. Riodan was brought as a child from County Tipperary to Melbourne, where his father opened a grocery store in Carlton. Riordan had been a pupil of Professor Miller's at his Olympic Club gymnasium in Melbourne, then left for San Francisco in 1886. Peter already knew him through Miller. He was the boxing coach and teacher at the Golden Gate Athletic Club and therefore a buddy of Hallinan's. In 1888 Riordan was 26 years old, almost six feet tall, and weighed 170 pounds. He had the reputation of being a clever boxer though faint-hearted boxer, and he was also an incipient lush.

Peter boxed Riordan at the Cremorne nightly for two weeks, before ever larger and more excited crowds. They said Peter's boxing was the best ever seen in San Francisco. The *National Police Gazette* of July 14 reported one of the audience as saying on June 4, "the white fighters will draw the color line tighter than ever now," and another as saying, "fear, alone, will prevent them from meeting him."

The boxing was governed by the new *Police Gazette* rules, which were the Queensberry rules renamed to make them readily acceptable in the United States. They were used in the match between Patsy Cardiff and Pat Killen in Minneapolis the previous August, for the title of champion of the Northwest, which Killen won. Peter, of course, had always used these rules.

Captain Morse, for his part, had gone to Lamartine R. Fulda, the president of the California Athletic Club, and asked him to help Peter. Fulda got Peter onto the program of sparring preliminary to the Tom Cleary–Young Mitchell fight on June 26. In this, Herget knocked out Cleary in the 30th and won the middleweight championship of the Pacific

3. Offensive Tour, 1888–1889

Coast. Somewhat earlier, Fulda offered to pay for a month's boxing lessons from Peter, to ask friends of his also to take lessons from him, and to allow Peter to do his teaching in the boxing-room. This was a privilege never given anyone before, and it caused some muttering about "upstart darkies," but Fulda's committee endorsed his offer, and Peter began his teaching at the California Athletic Club before June 18. He was made what was called a "salaried attache" of the club, starting on January 1, 1889.

On May 28 a letter was left at the *Chronicle* office for Sam "Australian Comet" Fitzpatrick, who then contacted Peter and became his trainer. Fitzpatrick was only a mediocre boxer, but he proved to be such an excellent a trainer that he brought two of the greatest black boxers in history up to their perfection.

Peter signed a contact with the California Athletic Club, by which he became an instructor there and they managed his fights program. Over at the Olympic Club at 424 Post was James J. Corbett on much the same deal. This contract lasted generally for his career over the next four years — or at least he took refuge in it when it suited him — to the extent that he would fight only when directed by the California Club. It should be noted that, as President Fulda expressed it in June 1891, "none but persons of the Caucasian race are admitted to membership" of the club, although the club was prepared to employ a black.

So it was all professional success in his first months in America, though Peter was not perfectly happy in San Francisco. He developed what the *Chronicle* of July 7 called "a lame back" caused by his changing weather, from "a roasting Australian climate" to the "chilly evening winds and many sudden changes" in San Francisco. And he was robbed of his "To a Man" medal, which he had shown off to reporters. But, being not in the least puritanical, he found time to enjoy the pleasures of San Francisco.

Six general newspapers issued daily editions: the *Chronicle*, the *Call*, the *Examiner*, the *Evening Post*, the *San Francisco Bulletin* and the *Daily Alta California*. These would cover Peter's career. Two black newspapers issued in 1888: the *Elevator*, published since 1865, and the *Vindicator*, since 1884. These seem, from what is left of them, to have covered it too.

Where he lived is unknown. He might have found lodging with a white family, but it is more likely that in these early days he lodged with blacks. The blacks were concentrated on the Barbary Coast and along Mission, a society within a society: a Union Bethel Church (African Methodist) on Powell, two other churches, Masonic lodges, bathhouses where one could wash up for 12c, dressmakers, barber shops, brothels, shoe stores, tobacconists, boarding houses, herb-doctors, etc. Like the many white sex workers, a few black prostitutes worked on the Barbary Coast, in so-called cribs, little houses or sties they rented. They catered mostly to black men and Mexicans. The practicing herb-doctors showed that many blacks still trusted the African pharmacopeia.[3] Ten percent of the 2,000 blacks in San Francisco were immigrants from the West Indies or the children of immigrants. Bert Williams was from the Bahamas. There had been a West Indian welfare organization since 1854, and on Pacific in the heart of the Barbary Coast stood its West Indian Benevolent Society Hall. West Indian Emancipation Day was celebrated annually. But it is hard to say how much warmth Peter felt for his fellow West Indians. It seems that he never spoke, to reporters at least, about his life in Santa Cruz, about his family, or about James, who was holding the fort for him back at the Lighthouse Hotel.

Peter joined a couple of black clubs. Connected with the Acme Saloon, at 668 Mission near Third, described as a favorite resort of colored sports, was the Acme Club, run by the proprietor, Charles A. Jamieson. Peter joined the Lotus Club at 24 Third, which had "gentlemen's private club rooms." The Unique Club had a saloon and rooms at 189 Jessie between Mission and Market. Another club, the Lorraine Club, conducted intellectual debates. Through members of these clubs Peter may have found bed and board with respectable black families. One of his managers was told that in those early San Francisco years he had lodged with a black woman whose daughter died of consumption, but the story got garbled in the reporting. Later, when he was richer, he lived in hotels.

He continued his sparring. He did exhibitions with Riordan at "a well-known sporting resort on Market street" and "a Market-street place of amusement," Hallinan's Cremorne. They both wore what the *Chronicle* called "sleeveless shirts." It was only a four-round exhibition, but the *Chronicle* said on June 5 that "there was not a man who saw Jackson play with Riordan last night but who said that the colored champion was one of the best, if not the very best boxer who has appeared in the city." Local boxers were going along night after night hoping to glean more technique. The *Chronicle* concluded its coverage by saying: "The exhibition showed that Jackson has well earned his reputation. The man who knocks him out, if such a man there is, will be one of the best men the world has known."

He fought Mike Sullivan, one of the city's deputy sheriffs, on June 15, 1888, in the San Francisco Athletic Club at 431 Sixth. Peter realized that the husky Sullivan was expected to humiliate him before an audience stacked with Sullivan supporters. He had not as yet shown in San Francisco that he could punch, having so far only sparred, so Sullivan was supposed to prove that he could not fight. The first two rounds consisted of Sullivan swinging and Jackson dodging and tapping him, but in the third round Sullivan got rough and Peter hammered him until he went down. Sullivan then stepped to the footlights, pulled off his gloves, and told the spectators that he had understood it would be a friendly spar. "I didn't come here to fight!" he said. Jackson cried that he was a champion and would do whatever it took to maintain that position. They then sparred the last two rounds, and essentially Jackson toyed with Sullivan.[4] The color bar was now being lowered bit by bit.

It was now agreed that it was time for Peter to make his American debut with a real fight. Norton suggested reviving the idea of a fight with Godfrey by inviting him to come over from Boston. Godfrey was the best black heavyweight, and would provide a conclusive test of Peter's quality. He held the title, conceived for him some 13 years before, of "Colored Champion of the World."

He had repeatedly challenged John L. Sullivan. The champion was reported as having said, "If any man on earth can beat me it is George Godfrey." Interviewed by the *Examiner* at Benicia on July 30, 1888, Godfrey told his story of how he was matched to fight Sullivan on September 21, 1881, in Boston, at the rooms of Professor Bailey, for the entire gate receipts. About 200 were present and both men had stripped for the fight when the police broke into the room and declared any fight off. Billy Brady referred to this story in 1916, adding, "To my certain knowledge Sullivan had boxed with a negro at San Bernardino, California, during one of his exhibition tours."[5] Later Godfrey tried several times for a match with Sullivan, but once he became champion he refused to meet Godfrey on account of his color. Godfrey appealed in vain, once even offering him 50 percent of the take to spar for four rounds, but Boston's Pride refused. Godfrey was well regarded by the fancy, and wildly popular with blacks.

Naughton wired Godfrey. He grumbled a little, saying: "I don't want to go to California to fight the Australian champion. I'd rather fight here, but I'm not in this business for fun; I'm in it for a living. I have a family of six children to provide for." Moreover, the previous

January he had traveled out to Colorado to fight McHenry "Black Star" Johnson. However, Godfrey's trip to San Francisco was being subsidized with $400, and San Francisco, though far from Boston, was not the bottom of the world like Sydney. Godfrey agreed to fight Peter on August 24, 1888, for his title and a prize of $1,200, with $300 for the loser. The *Examiner* said that if Peter beat Godfrey he would "come pretty near being the champion of the United States as well as champion of Australia," though of course the final step was to defeat John L. Sullivan.

On July 14 the secretary of the California Athletic Club announced that the fight for the heavyweight colored championship of the world had been arranged. The fight would be according to the *Police Gazette* rules, and with two-ounce gloves. The announcement was wired to key individuals, for example to Fox in New York.

On July 2 Peter went into training at Sausalito under Fitzpatrick, who "has the reputation at least of being a competent trainer." Originally he was to have trained under Herget's trainer, "Doctor" Geohegan, but must have preferred Fitzpatrick when they met up. Peter complained once again that in San Francisco itself he had developed a bad back from the weather, which was like Sydney's but deceptively so, with the days pleasant and the evenings chilly and foggy. He claimed the climate on the Sausalito Peninsula agreed with him more.

And he could swim there. The *Chronicle* said he had a gold medal for swimming and he swam every morning. The *Examiner* published an article on him and Godfrey on August 12, with a sketch of Peter diving about ten feet from a platform into the bay, at the back of Ryan's hotel. He was shown wearing red-and-white striped trunks like those in Winslow Homer's painting *Undertow* (1886), and more chic than Australian swimwear. The article described him as "an elegant and fast overhanded swimmer," that is he used an early kind of Australian crawl. He had sweated during his brisk walk of several miles, and Fitzpatrick helped him out of his clothes — a peaked, tight-fitting silk cap, neckerchief, light coat, singlet, thin trousers, canvas shoes — gave him a dry rub, and helped him into the hip-hugging trunks. Then he dived underwater a long way. He submerged and re-emerged and swam briskly around, then: "He ran up to the cabin, and Fitz received his dripping form in the immense Turkish towel. The bronze fighter was soon thoroughly dry, and Fitz began his hard rubbing and slapping to stimulate the circulation of the blood. As Jackson stood, one foot on a stool and the other on a bench, to submit himself to Fitz's attentions, his magnificent physique was more noticeable than at other times." Fitzpatrick used two thickly woven worsted mittens to rub him down with. The *Examiner* remarked on his slender waist, and then, as if to show that the *Chronicle* had no monopoly of turning Australian into Cockney, it reproduced Fitzpatrick's rejoinder: "That's Jackson's weak point, hand 'e knows it. The bloomin' marks on the hother side knows it too, and they halways goes for hit, but 'e knocks 'em out before they gets there, you know." During one of his swims, Fitzpatrick, always the joker, yelled out "Shark, shark!" and had then to run away from a furious Peter.

The California Athletic Club had quarters with a frontage of 160 feet at New Montgomery and Mission, near Howard and "within three blocks from the Palace Hotel," as the *Chicago Tribune* said in an article titled "Richest Club on Earth," republished on May 1, 1890, from the *New York Herald*. (Sporting news was now being syndicated across the United States and indeed the world.) President Fulda, the head of Fulda Brothers, proprietors of extensive cooperage and planing mills, had married into the de Young family of the *Chronicle*. Overall the California Athletic Club lacked the prestige of the older Olympic Club, but it excelled with its boxing. In 1888 it cost $10 to join but by 1890 it cost $25. The dues were

$2.50 a month. In 1888 it had 1,000 paying members. In 1892 the superintendent of Branch A of the San Francisco post office and a director of the Tammany Democratic Club was a prominent member, the sheriff was a member, and the chief of police an ex-officio member.

The events at the California Athletic Club were never called fights but always contests. The referee for all the big contests was Hiram B. Cook, "a moneyed man, a gentleman, and a true lover of sport," and chief deputy auditor or controller of the City and County of San Francisco. He had once been prominent in the Olympic Club but had left to be the first president of the California Athletic Club, thus being Fulda's predecessor.

As early as June 1888, according to the *Chronicle*: "The relations between James J. Corbett of the Olympic Club and Peter Jackson are somewhat strained. They were to have boxed at the benefit given for the widow of the assistant professor of athletics at the Olympic Club, but Jackson, learning that Corbett had spoken disparagingly of him, refused to show with him. Jackson is willing, however, to meet Corbett in a set-to of four rounds for points, or a go of ten rounds, in which case he guarantees to stop Corbett in that time." Instead, at Mrs. Stohm's benefit in the Grand Opera House at 737 Mission on June 29, Peter boxed the vice-president R. Dick, assistant boxing instructor at the Olympic Club and weekdays the manager of the California Sugar Refinery. Corbett was still an amateur. He boxed six rounds with Professor William Miller, who was visiting from Melbourne, on November 15. Peter was not present. Corbett had his first professional bout on December 11 that year, fighting Peter's old pupil Billy Smith in Portland, Oregon.

On June 29 Godfrey arrived from Boston. He was met at Benicia by the California Athletic Club officials and an *Examiner* reporter, who said Godfrey remarked, "I have yet to see my first defeat." In San Francisco, Godfrey signed the articles in the club rooms. He was shown a picture of Peter. "He's a big man," he exclaimed. The *Chronicle* described Godfrey as "a sedate-looking mulatto."

Godfrey trained at Joseph Dieves's place on San Leandro Road under Tom Cleary. Six miles from Oakland, this later became Peter's own favorite training ground. Dewitt Van Court recalled that "Joe had several fine trotters and Peter spent a good part of his time exercising them."[6]

Jackson's seconds were Fitzpatrick and Herget, aka "Young Mitchell," champion middleweight of the Pacific Coast. Godfrey's were a slightly more impressive pair: Tom Cleary, ex-middleweight champion of the Pacific Coast, and Arthur Chambers, the retired lightweight champion of the world. His chosen timekeeper was Corbett, the young bank clerk from the Olympic Club. Naughton acted as Jackson's timekeeper, while Dave Eisman held the watch for the Club. Hiram B. Cook as usual was referee.

Pressmen were admitted to the dressing rooms before the match and saw Peter standing up naked astride two chairs for Herget to swab him over with bay rum. Its perfume recalled the Caribbean. He had the beginnings of a headache. When a reporter asked why he wore porous sticking-plaster on the small of his back he answered, "If it doesn't do me good it certainly won't hurt." These plasters, usually made of sheepskin stiffened with pitch and beeswax, were worn by many boxers.

Godfrey was first in the ring at 9:30, dressed in a heavy overcoat, white knee pants, and canvas bicycle shoes worn without stockings. He wore the American colors. He had shaved his head but kept his stubby black mustache. At that time newspapers described boxers, especially their clothing, to help their readers visualize the action.

Jackson appeared a few minutes later. "He was clad in his historic Sydney ulster, which served to elongate his form, so that he towered in the air. His face, black as ebony, shone like a lump of anthracite coal, and his white teeth and eyeballs glistened as he grinned good humoredly in response to the hearty cheer that greeted him." The *Chronicle*, as usual fascinated by their accents, told how Australians in the audience hailed Peter on his way to the ring with: "'Ow hare you, Peter," with "'Ello, Peter, hold man," etc. One is reported as saying with "a pronounced cockney accent" that : "'E must 'ave won the toss." This never happened with Peter's accent. All the papers ever picked up on was his pronunciation of his name as "Petah." This was Australian, but it could equally well have been Cruzan.

He wore white tights with a blue belt and sky-blue stockings — that is, Australia's sporting colors — and black-laced shoes that he had designed himself. He looked four times darker than the mulatto Godfrey. Throughout the match Godfrey sparred with his legs apart and well braced, while Jackson ambled about in the deceiving loose-jointed style that had become well known. Jackson stood up to his full height, having very little span of legs, while Godfrey, who was much smaller, spread his feet out widely.

First Round

After the customary friendly salutation at the scratch, each man drew back and threw himself into position. Jackson held his left well balanced, ready for a shot, his right across his breast. Godfrey held his left rather low, with his right in a position that, to the eye of an expert, meant mischief when sent on its mission. The feeling for an opening was short, and ended with Jackson driving his left into Godfrey's neck. The latter landed a return on the shoulder, and then both men forgot about the noble art and went in for a two-handed slog. It was give and take for nearly half a minute. Jackson appeared more awkward and less straight in his hitting than he did when boxing at the Cremorne, but the knowing ones noticed that he had a right, and that it reached Godfrey's wind very often. There was considerable infighting. In the latter part of the round there was some clean work, Godfrey scoring two clean clean hits on Jackson's ribs and Jackson scoring two on Godfrey's nose in return. Another short wild slog was on the program, which Jackson ended by driving Godfrey away with a terrific left in the stomach. He followed it up with both hands, and was hammering Godfrey on the ropes when time was called. The action was so intense that the spectators feared that the fight wouldn't last long enough to give them their money's worth.

Round Two

Godfrey made a short left lead on coming up, and Jackson got away with the easy back skip he had shown already in sparring bouts; but when Godfrey tried it again he followed him up and led with his left. It was a tremendously long reach, straight from the shoulder, and Godfrey stopped it from going further with his chin. Godfrey started to bleed from the mouth. Godfrey was astonished, it seemed, and tried to play even with a swinging right which only hit Jackson's left elbow. Jackson then pitched the weight of his body forward, his left fist out. The blow fell just above Godfrey's chin, not quite low enough to prove a knockout blow, but powerful and dazing enough to send him to the floor. It was the first and only knockdown of the fight. Godfrey did not mind it much, and while the cheering was subsiding he got to his feet again without taking his 10 seconds' allowance. Jackson had stepped back, although he might have remained over his prostrate opponent as the fall had been made in Jackson's corner. When Godfrey was fairly on his feet Jackson came forward quickly to press any advantage. Both men rushed in at the same moment, Godfrey making a wild lead with his right, but striking only wind. Jackson led four times in rapid succession with his left, fetching Godfrey's head each time, and parrying with his right fist as many blows as Godfrey returned. Godfrey's swinging blows with either hand were exceedingly dangerous. There was an interim to the hard fighting for a moment or two and both men looked smiling, but Godfrey was blowing hard whereas Jackson was cool and easy.

Round Three

Jackson opened up with a left drive into Godfrey's wind, which made the champion grunt. Then there was some more windmill work, but hotter than the last. Godfrey tried to be a rusher after the breakaway, but Jackson simply straightened out his long arm and popped Godfrey in the throat with staggering force. The next exchange was quite even, each man getting in right and left on neck and ribs. Jackson was driving him hard, and Godfrey was grunting from numerous rib-roasters when time was called. The *Police Gazette* reporter concluded that Godfrey could not understand Jackson's style of fighting.

Between the third and fourth rounds Chambers passed a yellow baby sponge over Godfrey's lips while whispering instructions. Jackson's back and chest were bathed in lots of cool water.

Round Four

Jackson's left lead this time was well parried, and Godfrey rushed in. The short-arm fighting lasted but a second or two, with evenly distributed punishment. As soon as the standoff positions were assumed again Jackson saluted with his left, Godfrey's arms rose above his waist and the Australian got in one of his terrific wind-jammers with his right. It struck just below the left nipple and the thud sounded like that of a baseball bat fetching a side of beef. Godfrey stood it astonishingly well, and in another second returned it with interest, his right hand with a swing reaching Jackson under the right ear and sending him sideways nearly to the ropes. It was a staggerer, and from one end of the hall one of Godfrey's friends shouted: "$100 on Godfrey!" But they were at it hot again. Like two gamecocks they pounced in at each other, each getting in a left that acted to counter the other. Godfrey tried to get in a wicked right-arm swing, which is his great blow, but Jackson's wonderful lightning duck saved him. The pass was not cold when Godfrey got in again very cleverly under Jackson's neck, pushing his head back between his shoulders. Jackson was retreating at the time or else that lead might have done him serious damage. Godfrey did not hold the advantage long, for Jackson fetched him a left poke in return, drawing a copious rivulet of the crimson from Godfrey's left eye.

Round Five

Both were shy at the start. A rally gave Godfrey the worst of it, with many punches to his nose, and thinking that his man was dazed Jackson went in with both hands to wind him up. Drive, smash, bang, his manters landed, knocking Godfrey back and back until he had made half a circuit of the ring. Blood came streaming down in torrents, and he was about done to all appearances. He was drenched in his own blood, and Jackson's tights were smeared with it. But suddenly he made a stand, and got back at Jackson in a way that made the non-chance-taker give a wonderful exhibition of his ducking powers and ability to get his stomach out of the way. Jackson said he would give Godfrey a settler in a minute, but the bell rang right then.

Round Six

They both stepped up nimbly and smiled as good-naturedly as two old friends passing each other in the street. Godfrey played cunning by looking down toward Jackson's generous foot. He expected to get Jackson to look there too and strike him high. The blow fell short, and Jackson followed up the miss with a belly-whacker, under which Godfrey doubled up in time to get a left hander also on the jaw. Jackson pressed his man again, lots of blows on the eye. Godfrey did his best with a left drive which passed aside of Jackson's head, and Jackson got in his right again over Godfrey's heart. He followed it with two straight left-handers to the jaw. Godfrey returned a rib-roaster with the left and a right-hander on the left ear. This retaliation was greeted with deafening cheers. but Godfrey's eye was bad; he bled all over his tights.

Round Seven

At the start of the round, Godfrey pluckily shaped up, but Jackson, with that peculiar glide of his, got close and slap, bang on mouth and body. Jackson worked his long arms pretty lively but when Godfrey merely grunted and kept on fighting after a clean right-hander in the stomach, Jackson stood off for a second looking thoughtful. Godfrey surprised him by assuming the offensive and planking him in the throat with his left and smashing a few short ribs with his right. He was speedily well punished for his temerity, for as he recovered himself, Jackson put a fresh swell on his nose and an extra shade of rise on his eye. The long rest that followed was only broken by three leads from Godfrey, all short.

Round Eight

Jackson continued his work on Godfrey's ribs, and reached there most unmercifully twice in quick succession with his right. Then he slammed into his nose. Godfrey gamely took the blows and watched sharply to get in his right for a knockout blow. Jackson's head seemed to be anywhere but in the place where Godfrey's fists went. His failure to reach gave Jackson a good chance. His left started out and reached the stomach, and his right with a downward movement at half arm fetched Godfrey on the jaw. It staggered him, but Jackson, who had jumped back after striking, was a little too far to get in again.

Round Nine

Both commenced as though anxious for a fight at close quarters, but Jackson's weight was too much, and soon Godfrey was being chased about the ring, receiving a clout wherever

Jackson could land one. Godfrey tried to stand his ground but couldn't, and could only arouse admiration by exhibiting an ability to stand punishment that was marvelous. Jackson tired of hammering his poor nose and neck, and making a duck and a feint he drove his right into Godfrey's wind. A grunt and a blinking of the eyes were the only manifestations, and Jackson looked disgusted. Peter is reported by the *Examiner* as speaking to Godfrey in this manner: "See here, Godfrey; does you want me to kill yer? You wants to remember you've got a fam'ly to support." (The *Police Gazette* did not hear this.) Godfrey's smile broadened and he improved the opportunity afforded by Jackson's speech to smash the orator on the ear and again in the ribs, receiving no return for either. A rally and a clinch followed. The referee told them to break and they did just as the bell rang.

Round Ten

Jackson stayed silent. He started in immediately with his left, having Godfrey's left nipple as a bullseye. He got there and got there once more, and Godfrey for the fiftieth time swiping the wind left himself open for a righthander which shook up his vitals. The usual thing then occurred: Godfrey winced and drew back, and Jackson kept close to him, measuring off the distance by banging Godfrey in the jaw with the left. These blows drove Godfrey to the ropes, where he succeeded in landing a short blow on Jackson and caused the latter to haul himself off. The round wound up with Godfrey receiving a stinging blow on the left ear.

Round Eleven

There was a good deal of close fighting and cautious sparring. Godfrey was unable to land a left on Jackson's neck but did land a right on Jackson's broad expanse of nose. Jackson chased him round the ring with his two fists going. He returned the blow to the nose, which was swelling enormously. Time was called when Godfrey like he was looked about to drop to the floor.

A big lump of ice was pressed over and around Jackson's head during the intermission, to do away with his worsening headache. Godfrey was sucking a wet sponge meanwhile.

Round Twelve

Godfrey started with a right and a left, then Jackson started punching. One of Godfrey's terrible right-hand swinging blows spent its force on Jackson's left elbow. Jackson gave him a battering right and a left. He then stood back and said, "You're a tough little man," whereupon Godfrey smashed Jackson in the mouth. Jackson revenged by lefts to the jaw and neck. They were very stiff blows from the shoulder and Godfrey was sinking under them but was able to duck the right that came next. Then the bell rang.

Round Thirteen

The round was quiet. Both were tired. Godfrey ducked and Jackson upper-cut him with a right that rattled his teeth and caused him to spit out a small bucket of gore. His cheek became enormously swelled.

Again between rounds Jackson got ice on his head. Godfrey's eye would have closed had not the blood been squeezed out by Chambers.

Round Fourteen

Godfrey was not anxious to pitch in and made Jackson follow him round the ring. Godfrey hit Jackson on the right eye and caused a swelling. Jackson caught him and pummeled his stomach. Godfrey clinched. At the call of "Break away!" the men separated but Godfrey was back in a twinkle and Jackson made one of his wonderful dips. In ducking, Jackson's right again fetched Godfrey over the heart and then at close quarters battered Godfrey's face. Three times Jackson punched his ribs. The spectators wondered why Jackson did not finish Godfrey with a right to the jaw.

Round Fifteen

Jackson went at Godfrey with both fists, chasing him into a corner. Godfrey ducked and clinched, lolling on Jackson or running when he could escape the rain of blows. Godfrey looked very sick, and was so dazed that he tried to sit down in his chair. He broke for his corner as though he wanted to quit three or four times, but each time was chased out by his seconds. He was tired, but Jackson himself had not the strength to put the following touches. Both men were panting. Time was called when Godfrey was about to drop to the floor.

Round Sixteen

Jackson it seemed was determined to knock Godfrey out, but Godfrey would not go down. Godfrey gave one smasher in Jackson's face but received a dozen in return. Jackson backed Godfrey onto the ropes and gave him right and left regardless. Godfrey tried to lead but each time left himself open. He had blood all over his face and his chest.

Round Seventeen

Godfrey came up briskly and made a bluff at being strong, but a left-hander on his poor ribs turned him back to dodging and clinching. Jackson resumed his two-fisted driving and beat Godfrey, bleeding and staggering, from one end of the ring to the other. On the ropes and in the open, ferocious upper-cuts, drives and swings, but he wouldn't go down. He scarcely made it back to his corner

Round Eighteen

Jackson's eye looked as if it was closing but he let out his left bunch of fives again, and Godfrey's weakness became more apparent. He wanted to clinch. He certainly could not hit, and a clinch was his safest position. He nearly went under when Jackson's half-arm blow from the right fetched him on the neck. His knees wavered, but he stood his ground. Another left-hander sent his head backward and Jackson's terrible driver brought up over his heart. Godfrey could not hold up his hands to guard. That blow wound up the round with Jackson a sure winner, but very tired. Godfrey was gone.

Round Nineteen and Last

Godfrey staggered into position but Jackson knocked him out of it and then went at him in the old-time two-handed way. Godfrey tried to clinch and use his short-arm blows, but Jackson held him up with his right and swung that terrible left into Godfrey's stomach. One, twice, thrice he got there, and then a fourth one landed just over the heart. Godfrey doubled up in pain. He was still standing, but he had no desire to be killed, and faintly murmuring: "I'm licked. You can claim the fight," he extended his right hand and threw up the sponge.

The new colored champion of the world said: "My God, what a head that man has got! I hit him there enough to knock his nob off, but, my golly, he surprised me. He is a good fellow, and I think he can whip any man of his size in the world. Such a taker of punishment I have never met, and I don't think there is another man living today who could stand up to some of the blows I gave him. He fought game, and I think he showed his good judgment in giving up the fight when he did." Everyone agreed with Peter except Chambers, who was reported as saying, in a stage-Lancashire accent (or was it a mega version of the Cockney so beloved by the *Chronicle*?), "Has long has ha man 'as got 'e's heyes hopen han' can stand hon 'e's feet 'e 'as no right to call 'imself licked."

After the fight Godfrey spent the night and next day at the Hammam Baths on Dupont, in Chinatown. Dupont was a continuation of Grant beyond Vallejo, later all called Grant. He was dreadfully cut about, and his pectorals severely bruised; whereas Peter had only a mouse that had closed his right eye, a swelled lip bleeding a little, and a swelled nose from Godfrey's solid right in the 11th.

A Professor Joe Graves from Trinidad, a resident of Colon in Colombia (Panama), wrote to the *Police Gazette* on October 24 saying that he was the undisputed heavyweight champion of the West Indies and of the Isthmus of Panama and therefore he would not allow Peter to be called the colored champion of the world until Peter had defeated him. Graves turned up in New York in April the next year, after the Cardiff bout, still wanting to fight Peter. Peter and others thought Graves' challenges to be merely amusing; but he was asking, as Peter himself and a good many others did, why a title should be described as "of the world" when it was purely a United States one.

On Saturday, August 25, Peter and Fitzpatrick collected the $2,000 prize at the CAA clubrooms. Barney Farley was present and suggested a fight with McAuliffe for $3,000. Peter said any prize would do. On Sunday, August 26, Farley announced that McAuliffe, champion of the Pacific Coast, said he *would* fight Peter. The *Chronicle* said: "It will, therefore, be seen that McAuliffe has changed his mind in reference to the color line." The black employees at the Palace Hotel had backed Godfrey and were really put out. They would never do such a thing again! Thereafter all their bets were on Peter. Neville Forder wrote in 1914 that, with the win over Godfrey, "Peter Jackson became a 'lion' and was treated almost as well as a victorious white, while 'Coontown' made a hero of him, and would have made him its idol, but for the fact that Peter never could fraternize with the melon and chicken-eating men of his color. He was an Australian and a boxer—not a pugilist, and he was admired all the more by the whites for this attitude." It is hard to see what point Forder was making, but it seems true that Peter preferred the company of educated people.

Peter and Godfrey posed for Isaiah Taber, the society photographer. They were in dress suits with top hats. Peter as victor was enthroned in a tasseled arm chair, with a cane negligently in right hand and left hand resting on thigh. The mustachioed Godfrey was standing behind him, at his left shoulder. Both boxers looked away to the right of the camera. Their trainers were dressed much less smartly, in street clothes and bowler hats: Gorman in a cutaway coat and Fitzpatrick, looking older than 23, in a three-quarters coat, leaning slightly on his umbrella with his left hand behind his back. They did look into the camera. The group gave an impression of friendliness mixed with a little embarrassment.[7] Forder said that Peter's new outfit was "the gift from an admirer, who had won over him, of a £20 suit of clothes that took the shape of immense-skirted frock coat, long vest cut low, wide, light-colored pants, and the whole surmounted with a gleaming, silk bell-topper." Maybe this "admirer" was the doctor who urged him to get photographed nude. Ever after this he wore a top hat in public, making him look very tall.

It was announced on September 18, 1888, that Peter and Godfrey would start an eight-week sparring tour, under contract with Lew Johnson the minstrel, and then Peter would become a boxing instructor at the California A.C. They were to tour to Portland, Oregon, to Astoria, to Seattle, to Tacoma, and to Spokane. They were supposed to go on to Boston, but Godfrey returned home alone. The advertising, for example in the *Oregonian* of Portland, stated that fans would see "a friendly set-to" between Peter, champion colored heavyweight of Australia, and Godfrey, champion colored heavyweight of America. Paddy Gorman and Fitzpatrick (both late of Australia) would also appear, as well as the wonderful Eclipse Quartet. In Portland, A.P. Butler, a local boxing identity, acted as M.C. and sparred with Gorman and Fitzpatrick. And so it went.

The tour pleased many, but it was a financial flop. Peter lost a lot of money, and it is not certain that the team ever reached Spokane. He hastened back to San Francisco to train for his fight with McAuliffe.

Peter found that the racial system in America was different from Australia's. The *Chicago Tribune* of December 19, 1888, said: "He has been greatly disheartened while here by the ardent prejudice against him on account of his color. He was refused admittance to several baths and other places, an experience which he said he never met with in the Australian colonies."

The matter of the baths made the pages of the *San Francisco Vindicator*, the black paper. In late November 1888 he made a deal to race over 50 yards against California's champion swimmer, "Professor" Ed Pinkham of Oakland. Pinkham had recently been beaten by Albert Sundstrom for the world swimming championship, and hoped to restore his pride by challenging the New South Wales champion. Peter was backed for $200 by George Harting, "a young Australian sporting man." Being in training for McAuliffe, Peter wished to swim the race in a covered pool because the water out in San Francisco Bay, and in the ocean (presumably near Cliff House), was too cold in November, He went to both the new Palace Baths (on Filbert near Powell) and the Crystal Baths (on Powell near Bay) for practice swims, but was denied admittance. These were indoor pools using pumped sea water. No proprietor would permit a black in his pool. Harting and Pinkham had to give up the project. Peter took to swimming in the open bay.

The next day the *Chronicle* reported Peter saying: "Oh, that is only another drop in my cup for having a black skin. When I first arrived here I was ordered out of one of the restaurants in a public market where I had dared to sit at a table and call for a meal. On another occasion a bartender in a Kearny-street saloon told me that it was more than his position was worth to serve me. I told him that while in the company of Mr. So-and-so I had been served there before, and he replied, 'Yes; and the young fellow who served you lost his billet for doing so.'"

Yet California was one of the most tolerant states in the union. On November 22, 1889, in the black newspaper from Kansas City, the *American Citizen,* George Gears, a black man who had been a couple of times to San Francisco, wrote of California "I love its healthful and delightful climate, its noble and generous hearted people, I love its freedom, and I love its gold."[8]

In an interview published in the *London Sporting Life* in 1914, Davies told an anecdote about how Peter dealt with prejudice in 1888: "Peter went into a cafe in San Francisco and asked for a drink. Beer constituted Peter's simple wish. 'That'll cost you $20," said the bartender sneeringly. Without batting an eye, Peter went down in his pocket, put two $20 gold pieces on the bar, and said pleasantly, 'Have a drink yourself.'" Davies had polished the anecdote to a sheen during the intervening 25 years, but it was the sort of thing Peter might have done once the money started to flow. He had a careless attitude towards wealth.[9]

He was waiting to become boxing instructor at the California A.C. The *San Francisco Illustrated World* gave the wages at the California Athletic Club in 1890. Of the five boxing instructors, "Nonpareil" Dempsey was in 1890 making $160 a month, Billy McCarthy $150, Jimmy Carroll $125, and Frank Aiken, junior instructor and janitor, $100—while from the start Peter made $200 a month. Joe Acton, the wrestling instructor, earned $150. For comparison, the bartender and billiard-room keeper took home $75 a month. Peter's salary was much better than that of a machinist or sailor, but it began with 1890. Meanwhile he was poor.

He saw McAuliffe and begged that the loser be given $500 from the purse of $3,500. "Joe, I'm a stranger in the country, far from home," he said, "and I have no money. If I lose this fight I will be 'broke.' Let's agree that that the loser shall get $500." McAuliffe would not agree, his manager Barney Farley insisting that all the prize money should go to the winner. "Jackson had to give in." McAuliffe added insult to injury by saying, according to Naughton, "I didn't want to make this match at all, and intended to bar colored fighters as long as I remained in the business. I've been goaded into it and I want to fight for everything in sight."

Peter trained in Oakland, and came over to Frank Craig's establishment at 130 Fourth on December 28. That evening 2,000 crowded into the California club, where tiers of seats had been added, and New Montgomery outside was thronged. The queue of members stretched up the sidewalk towards Mission. Latecomers were obliged to squat on the floor near the ring.

Two electric lights now hung over the ring and as well, for the first time, a bell was used. A bell the size of a bucket hung in the north end of the gymnasium, and a man stood on a raised platform to make it peal at the beginning and termination of the rounds, by ringing one when a round began, two when a round ended. Dave Eisman was the timekeeper on the night. Hiram Cook as usual was chosen to referee.

The champion of the Pacific Slope, McAuliffe, appeared first, with Farley and Joe Bowers, and with his younger brother as bottle-carrier. He was in a short grey coat under which he wore pink fighting drawers, with a red, white, and blue sash, pink socks and brown canvas shoes. He had his mustache waxed, and a strengthening plaster on his right wrist. Jackson "appeared wearing a long dark overcoat," alternatively "an immense checkered ulster," obviously his brown mascot. "He had on white knee pantaloons and wore a sash and stockings of light blue, the national colors of Australia. Black laceup fighting shoes completed his costume." The ulster covered him up; when he took it off, there was a murmur of admiration, not only for his physique but for his get-up. Clearly if Peter was going to defeat a white, he was going to do it as an Australian. He also wore his perennial smile. He had Meadows and Fitzpatrick for his seconds.

Before the fight, President Fulda said from the ring: "We propose to show that any man, whether black or white, can get fair play in this club. When the reputation that Mr. Jackson has attained in his profession is taken into consideration, the question of color is lost sight of." Cook then lectured on the Queensberry rules to the spectators and the boxers who "stood in careless positions, pictures of strength and easy grace."

At the warning, "Shake hands," the men advanced and gave each other a warm grip with both hands. Jackson smiled benignly on McAuliffe and the good-natured Californian returned the compliment. "May the best man win, Pete," said McAuliffe, and Peter responded, "Those are my sentiments, Joe."

The fight began at 9:25 P.M.

First Round

The men sparred cautiously at first, until McAuliffe led off with his right and caught Jackson lightly just behind the ear. This was followed by an interchange of sharp blows. McAuliffe made several heavy lunges and got one good one on Jackson's neck, which the latter countered. Then Jackson put in two or three right-hand body blows, and a right overhander that puffed up McAuliffe's left eye. And before the round closed Jackson gave McAuliffe a right-hander on the nose.

Round Two

McAuliffe led with his left but fell short. Jackson returned with his right bunch of fives and caught McAuliffe well in the breast. Some hot fighting and several clinches followed. McAuliffe tried for Jackson's ribs, but Jackson drew back out of danger. Jackson next struck McAuliffe on the ear and caused blood to stream down his shoulder and chest. The Jacksonians yelled "Good boy, Pete." Then Jackson followed McAuliffe round the ring, stabbing into his stomach.

Round Three

Jackson at first feinted repeatedly and tried to make McAuliffe lead, but he kept on falling short and Jackson eluded. There was some heavy hitting by both at close range and

Jackson was pounded more severely but retaliated, opening McAuliffe's ear again. McAuliffe caught him once on the side of the head and caused him to stagger across the ring. Jackson struck out terrifically but fell short. Jackson's eye swelled, while McAuliffe's nose looked decidedly bulby.

Round Four

The men sparred cautiously for a full minute, whereupon McAuliffe let out savagely, but Jackson escaped by jumping aside. Jackson planted a light one on McAuliffe's ear, which the latter returned on Jackson's ear.

Round Five

Jackson opened the round by getting a light blow on McAuliffe's forehead. He followed this up quickly with three directly to the nose, and forced McAuliffe against the ropes. McAuliffe spat a mouthful of blood. He then forced McAuliffe around the ring at a lively rate, but did little visible damage; however, word spread that McAuliffe's nose had been broken.

Round Six

Jackson had so far displayed wonderful quickness. In this round he struck McAuliffe several staggering blows on the head, and forced him against the ropes. Showing all his teeth in a broad grin, he also succeeded in jumping back quick enough to avoid several powerful blows which were aimed at his head.

Round Seven

At first Jackson ducked all of McAuliffe's heavy punches. The men retained the utmost good humor and would smile every time at an advantage gained by either. Then McAuliffe got one swinging blow on Jackson's chin, which sent his head back with a jerk. It did no damage. Jackson retaliated by pushing McAuliffe back onto the ropes. But little was done during the round.

Round Eight

The previous light round had rested the men some, and they opened lively. Jackson ducked and weaved, avoiding McAuliffe's blows, and the spectators broke out laughing at his clever movements. He caught McAuliffe in the wind twice, and was apparently directing his blows to that spot. Jackson continued to force his adversary around the ring and had by far the best of the round.

Round Nine

McAuliffe was not leading at all. No particular damage was done by either, but Jackson continued to drive his right at McAuliffe's head or at his wind, as he chose. But the blows were light.

Round Ten

Jackson again forced the fighting and pounded McAuliffe several times in the face. Returned them and caught Jackson on the neck. Jackson was advancing when he slipped and fell to the floor, landing squarely on his back. He got up and coolly squatted on his haunches for a few seconds, watching the timekeeper, then started in again on McAuliffe.

Round Eleven

McAuliffe's eyes were beginning to puff up slightly and his ear was still bleeding. Jackson appeared none the worse than at the start. He pounded McAuliffe in the ribs but the latter was not much annoyed by it. McAuliffe could never get one of his good punches to land. But he returned one of Jackson's hard blows in the face just before the bell.

Round Twelve

The round was a kind of interlude. Both men were evidently getting tired, and hardly a pass was made by either throughout the round.

Round Thirteen

This round was a repetition of the twelfth—nothing was done in this one, either, except a couple of half-hearted punches.

Round Fourteen

Jackson caught McAuliffe lightly on the chin and again in the throat, the latter blow knocking him against the ropes. McAuliffe looked for an opening, but "the scientific Australian" was not inclined to give him one. The round ended with McAuliffe being battered on the ropes.

Round Fifteen

Jackson forced the fighting, pounded McAuliffe on the ribs, and gave him one hard one on the nose, which he followed up by several others. McAuliffe laid his heaviest punch on Jackson's chin, but he only shook his head and grinned. Jackson appeared to think he had McAuliffe whipped, and continued to force him round the ring. A punch on the nose made McAuliffe totter, but he was saved by the bell.

Round Sixteen

Jackson opened with two right-handers on McAuliffe's hugely swollen nose, which he followed up well. McAuliffe led out savagely several times, but Jackson jumped aside quickly and escaped the blows. McAuliffe was by now just waiting for Jackson to hit him.

Round Seventeen

McAuliffe caught Jackson lightly on the jaw, but the latter returned it well and rained a half-dozen hard ones on McAuliffe's head, which seemed to daze the latter a little. He punched his nose again and again, one blow sending him into a post. McAuliffe's left eye was now closing.

Round Eighteen

Jackson gave McAuliffe a terrific one in the ribs, which sent him lightly to the floor. When he rose Jackson forced him in the corner and pounded him in the head unmercifully. McAuliffe hung on the ropes. It looked as if he would have to go down, but he managed to stand up under the blows until the call of time saved him from a fall.

Round Nineteen

McAuliffe tried to elude Jackson, but was followed in remorseless fashion, left-handers to ribs and stomach, blows banging him on his bulby nose. Jackson then commenced his tantalizing tactics of making a number of rapid feints. With McAuliffe on the ropes there was heavy infighting, Jackson fighting like a tiger at close range. He kept too close to McAuliffe to be hurt by his swipes. At the end McAuliffe walked to his chair, chin sunk on breast. Farley lifted his head and gave him a sip of brandy. Jackson danced back to his seat.

Round Twenty

Jackson hammered McAuliffe's nose, holding him bailed up in a corner. As McAuliffe put his foot back he stepped on his water bottle, which rolled and lost its cork, water going all over the floor and making McAuliffe slip. Jackson's arms with lightning-like rapidity flew back and forth, each time giving punishment. McAuliffe did almost nothing.

Round Twenty-One

The left side of McAuliffe's face swelled, his nose bulged and his left eye nearly closed. Both fighters swung, and Jackson's right staggered McAuliffe. He followed it by a straight left. Then McAuliffe's ribs were pummeled. McAuliffe clinched and got a left-hander onto Jackson's chin.

Round Twenty-Two

The best and most telling blow was a straight left from Jackson, McAuliffe's head going back between his shoulders. Not a second passed before Jackson's right went in straight to the stomach, followed by the left to the jaw. McAuliffe went flabbily against the ropes, little being between him and defeat. Only time saved him.

Round Twenty-Three

Jackson opened with some left-handed prods at McAuliffe's jaw that were only teasers for an opening for a right-hander in the wind. In the middle of the round McAuliffe went down in his own corner from a poke in the stomach, and when he got up he showed considerable claret about the mouth and nose. He was pretty well battered up.

Round Twenty-Four and Last

Jackson was forcing the contest, edging his man to an off corner where his left came into play as it already had scores of times before. Jackson's work was evidently to worry his man above while with his right he would strike in on the ribs above the heart. It was virtually a repetition of the punishment he administered to Godfrey. McAuliffe was considerably dazed with the couple of preliminary left-handers he stopped with his chin, but instinctively he edged out of the corner into which he had been forced. His greatest care seemed to be to protect his left side — above the heart — from another blow, and in doing so he found himself worked in the opposite corner from which he had just escaped. Jackson, as light as a two-year-old, danced in and out, to and from his more ponderous opponent. McAuliffe's energy, his vim and power, were all gone. Jackson feinted with his left, McAuliffe's arms parried, and Jackson landed him as squarely as a straight right-arm blow could, right on the nose. No man could ever have come up for another round after such a blow. California's idol's knees went from under him. His big white form rolled up in the corner, the ropes which he unconsciously essayed to reach for support being the only preventive to his falling prone to the floor.

Jackson danced back to his chair. Fitzpatrick was praised by all for his fine work in training him. McAuliffe had a broken nose, a face like raw hamburger, torn ears and a bruised stomach, whereas Peter had a slightly swollen left hand, a slight lump near the left eye and a slightly fattened lower lip.

The new champion of the Pacific Coast said, holding a levee in his dressing-room:

> Joe is a noble boy and he is a game fighter. I was lucky enough to do him, but that was no more than I expected, or else I never would have fought him. Contrary to intimations that were given me, the members of the club gave me, a colored man, a good and fair chance with McAuliffe, and I hardly think it necessary for me to say that it was nothing more than I expected of gentlemen who have already treated me as they have. I thank them. My contest with McAuliffe was the hardest I ever have had, and my defeating a man as good as he is gives me renewed hope that I may do better yet. At any rate, I will try hard to work myself to the top.

It was an admirable and adroit speech, and the 27-year-old Peter's calling a 24-year-old white man a "boy" brought no comment from the *Examiner*. Peter also had a suave word for the Californians: "There are no people in the world like them."

Many bettors were rueful after McAuliffe's defeat, but in the black quarter around Jessie Street there was amazing rejoicing, which spread throughout the black communities of America.

They sang a song which must have been composed and circulated in advance, since so many knew it:

> *Peter Jackson found a snow-white lamb,*
> *Snow-white lamb,*
> *Snow white lamb;*
> *Peter Jackson found a snow-white lamb,*
> *Astray in Frisco town,*
> *Hoo-da! Hoo-da!*
> *Astray in Frisco town.*
> *McAuliffe found a big black ram,*
> *Big black ram,*
> *Big black ram;*
> *McAuliffe found a big black ram,*
> *And tried dat ram to down,*
> *Hoo-da! Hoo-da!*
> *And tried dat ram to down.*
> *Whar am now dat color line,*
> *Dat color line,*
> *Dat color line?*
> *Whar am now dat color line*
> *Set up in Frisco town?*
> *Hoo-da! Hoo-da!*
> *Dat line in Frisco town.*

In the small hours, every saloon that admitted blacks was full. They were still singing. The *Examiner* reported one excited individual in a huge ulster, smoking a cigar eight inches long, who shouted out: "Peter Jackson can lick John L. Sullivan!" and was answered with something like: "No, sah. No, sah. I corrects you, sah. Pete Jackson can jis' lick de world. You h'yar me?"

A month later, on the evening of January 21, 1889, in Lacoste's "Frank's Rotisserie" at 419 Pine Street, the "leading colored people of this city" tendered Peter a banquet.[10]

After Peter collected his money, he had Hallinan go round to McAuliffe's and offer him $500 of it. Joe would not accept the money, "remarking in a manly fashion," said the *St. Louis Post-Dispatch* on January 31, "that he was content to abide by his own terms." His feelings were not obviously hurt. On February 9, 1889, a benefit was held for McAuliffe in

Woodward's Pavilion. He and Peter sparred four lively rounds in front of 8,000 fans. Fulda and Hiram Cook were upset about the advertising for the fight, claiming that McAuliffe and Jackson had plastered San Francisco with big bills portraying them "in fighting costume and with bare fists," when everybody knew the California Athletic Club had never permitted bare-knuckle bouts and never would.

The *Chicago Tribune* said on December 30 that Sullivan's backer decreed that Peter could not challenge Sullivan, "as he had long ago declined to meet any colored man in the ring or any man who stands up with a colored fighter." He had boxed a dark man, Mace's discovery Herbert Slade, the half-Maori New Zealander, but drew the line at black men. And though Kilrain said in a letter to Herget he would fight whoever won, nobody believed that any longer. Ten years later, Fitzpatrick would remember Kilrain's phantom promise.

A couple of months after he defeated McAuliffe, on March 10, 1889, Peter was interviewed by the *Chronicle*, and on that occasion made his professional position explicit. A certain M.M. Brown of Deadwood, Colorado, said to be a well-known mine owner, had contacted Patsy Hogan, the San Francisco correspondent of the *National Police Gazette*, saying that he (Brown) was challenging any man in America to a fight to the finish—on behalf of Peter Jackson. Hogan had sent Brown's vicarious challenge to New York and Fox had printed it.

Shown the text during the interview, Peter told the *Chronicle* reporter: "I have no idea where Hogan got his information from, but if he had taken the trouble to call on me I could have told him that I have not authorized any individual to challenge the world in my behalf. The whole thing reads like other fictitious telegrams that have been sent East from this city from time to time."

The reporter asked who Mr. Brown was.

"I haven't the slightest idea," Peter replied, "but he is evidently some one who is looking for cheap notoriety. While on this subject I would like the *Chronicle* to state that as long as I am in this country the only medium through which I will arrange contests to a finish is the California Athletic Club. I have placed myself entirely in its hands as far as orthodox ring contests are concerned, and I am compelled to make this public through seeing my name mentioned in connection with all sorts of schemes of which I am totally ignorant." He could hardly have spoken more plainly. Then he gave the reporter a little scoop.

"You might further mention," he said, "that after my match with Cardiff, win or lose, I will rest a few months. I have been in almost constant training since I have been in San Francisco, and I feel that I want to lay off for a while. I may take a trip while I am out of harness, but as I said before I will only enter into contracts to fight to a finish under the auspices of the California Athletic Club. I am advised to this course by my friends, both in Australia and San Francisco. I intend to adhere to my determination."

He did not adhere to his plan of resting for a couple of months, but after the Cardiff fight he had no big bout until the end of the year.

During the first year of his residence in San Francisco, Peter became famous for things other than his boxing. His swimming was publicized, and he may have been the first man in the United States to use the Australian crawl.

He was known for his dressing, not only for stylish clothes and his brown ulster but for his boots and his singlets or sleeveless undershirts. He designed a boxing boot in soft leather and without heel, and had a pair made to his specifications. Again his quasi-appren-

Jackson sparring with Joe Choynski at Alameda in 1889, one of a series of photographs by Worthington and Knight of San Francisco. This picture is from M. Howell *et al.*, *The Sporting Image: A Pictorial History of Queenslanders at Play* (1989), the original being among the collections of the Mitchell Library, Sydney.

ticeship to the cobbler in Frederiksted paid off, because the boots proved successful and during his career he had them duplicated when needed. They were copied by other boxers.

It seems that Peter introduced the singlet to the United States. Before the Young Mitchell-Tom Cleary match on June 26, 1888, he sparred with Choynski, and it was remarked that "Jackson appeared in his by this time well known 'singlet' as the Australians have it, and which, interpreted into United States, means a sleeveless shirt. Choynski appeared in regular ring costume, stripped to the waist." The word "singlet" was used in Sydney as early as the 1840s. Again in Chicago in 1889 Peter fought in "a black armless shirt" embroidered with the initials C.A.C. "Sailor" Brown too wore "a sleeveless shirt." It is plausible that Peter adapted for boxing a garment worn by scullers on Sydney Harbor. If this is so, then he thus started the singlet's American vogue, which lasted until 1934 when Clark Gable appeared minus singlet in *It Happened One Night*.

He was known not only for his clothing but for the lack of it. Isaiah Taber's photographic studio and store were at Post and Montgomery. Peter patronized Taber, who in turn sold Peter's images to his fans and others. A photograph of him with arms folded over his bare torso and in full-face showing his turning left eye was reproduced, round about the end of 1888, on a card in the series for S.F. Hess and Co.'s "Creole" cigarettes from Rochester, New York. If squint he had, it dated either from childhood and his vision had adapted, or from adulthood and perhaps after a head punch — in which case Peter would have had double vision, which seems unlikely. One of Peter's female fans used to buy every new photograph that Taber produced.

In May 1889, after the McAuliffe fight, Peter was measured by a doctor who (for some reason) urged him to get photographed stripped. Taber took one shot of him in profile looking quite Egyptian in a token loincloth, then posed him naked for a three-quarters rear shot. The nude photograph was widely distributed and long remembered, but it is not recorded what his female fan thought of this one.

In Sydney the photo in half-tone graced the fifth page of the first issue of the *Dead Bird*, the naughty-sporty paper, two months later on July 20, 1889. The *Dead Bird* accompanied Peter's picture with: "The portrait which adorns our fifth page will be readily recognized, even without the name on the pedestal, as that of our champion boxer, Peter Jackson, and we venture to assert that never has there been given to the world a more beautiful sample of reproduced living statuary.... The marble man should blush to hear himself called a fine shapely man after seeing it, and Australia should be proud to have fed and reared such a model as our champion."

The following week, in its second issue, the *Dead Bird* published a daring cartoon showing a young woman, coded as a prostitute by her pet-

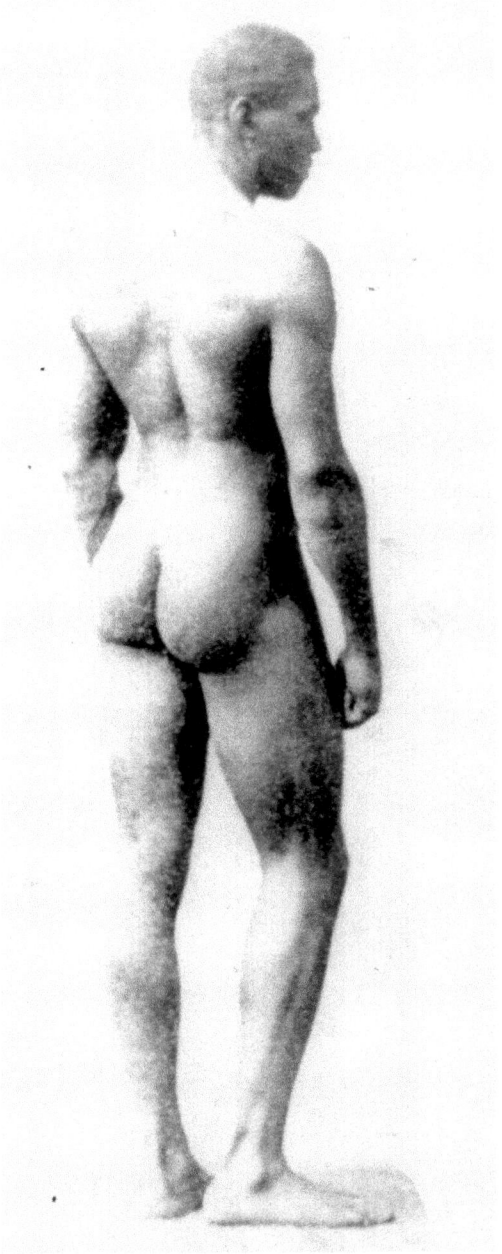

Jackson as one of the earliest "Nubian" nudes photographed by Isaiah Taber in San Francisco in 1889 and published in the first issue of *The Dead Bird* (Sydney), on July 20, 1889. This picture comes from M. Howell et al. (eds.), *The Sporting Image: A Pictorial History of Queenslanders at Play* (1989), the original being among the collections of the Mitchell Library, Sydney.

"MISS INQUISITIVE."

This cartoon of a shady lady was published in the second number of the *Dead Bird* on July 27, 1889.

ticoat and her unbound hair, holding Peter's photograph up to a mirror in a vain effort to see the man from the front. She was portrayed as lascivious and dumb. When Peter revisited Australia in 1890 the half-tone nude was printed again, though without any letterpress or cartoon, in the September 16 issue of the *Bird o' Freedom*, and captioned: "The Daddy of Them All." In May 1894 the picture made a reappearance in the San Francisco *Examiner*, alongside one of Eugen Sandow.

Taber's photographs of Jackson nude are some seven or eight years earlier than the famous "Nubian Series" by F. Holland Day, shown and discussed in *Race Men* by Carby and conventionally called the first "artistic" photographs of black men.[11] In his book on Carl Van Vechten's photography, Smalls says that after the Civil War the dangerous and threatening black body was domesticated by sexualizing, classicizing, eroticizing, primitivizing and feminizing it.[12] Six feet and half an inch tall, and weighing 200 pounds in 1889, Jackson's pugilist's body was threatening and dangerous, but Taber's portraits did not domesticate it in any of those ways.

After the McAuliffe fight and in the run-up to the Cardiff fight, Peter had become a person so interesting to San Franciscans that the *Examiner* on March 3, 1889, published a biography of him, spread over pages 12–13. It was merely a long article, but it was the first comprehensive life, going from Peter's birth in Santa Cruz, through his Australian years, to his defeat of McAuliffe. From internal evidence it was written by Naughton from information provided by Peter himself, and titled "Peter the Pugilist: he deserted orange groves to make his mark in a prize ring." It was illustrated with line drawings of Peter and Choynski sparring, from photographs taken at Alameda by "Eclipse" of 5 Stockton, that is, by H.W. Worthington and Edward Kraft — not by Taber. At about the same time H.S. Crocker's of 215–219 Bush, the publishers and legal stationers, produced a 16 ¥ 28-inch lithograph of Peter posed in fighting gear with fists up, and titled "Peter Jackson, Champion Heavy Weight Pugilist."

Peter's last fight in California during his first residence was with Patsy Cardiff on April 26, 1889. The deal was $2500 for the winner, $500 for the loser. The California A.C., in order to accommodate the large audience expected, extended the gallery above the regular tier of seats on the south end of the hall. More than 2000 could be squeezed in.

At 9:15 P.M. Jackson appeared in his long, dark overcoat and jumped over the ropes. He wore white breeches, olive stockings and black shoes. He had a plaster on his back like the one he had in the Godfrey fight, though none was mentioned at the McAuliffe fight. Fitzpatrick and Jack Haines were his seconds, and his bottle-holder Alf Kerr, a visitor from Sydney. Cardiff then dipped between the ropes, Professor John Donaldson, Tommy Warren and a bottle-holder following. Cardiff was clad in navy-blue breeches with purple trunks over them, short brown socks and black shoes. Peter was 6 feet and ½ inch and weighed 200 pounds, while the 26-year-old Cardiff was 5 feet 10½ inches tall and weighed 185 pounds. He gave the impression of being "short, round, and white as a lily." He looked nervous while Peter sat there with his perennial smile, lolling in his brown ulster. George Harting kept time for Jackson, M. Gooding for Cardiff, and Dave Eisman was club timekeeper. Hiram B. Cook was referee.

The fight started at 9:23 P.M.

After a little circling in the first round, Jackson commenced by shooting his left into the pit of Cardiff's stomach. He then drove his right in on the ribs and there was a clinch,

Cardiff getting his right home on Jackson's ear in the breakaway. Jackson led with his left and Cardiff clinched again, even thus early in the game evincing a desire to clasp Jackson round the legs and upset him. He even grabbed Jackson by the neck and forced him against the ropes, trying to push him over. There were loud cries of foul at Cardiff's crooked work; and some thought Cardiff was trying to anger Jackson, but in vain. Jackson landed a heavy left on Cardiff's face, but in return he was hit on the nose, which started to bleed. When Jackson went to his chair he complained of having been butted in the mouth.

Jackson sent in a clear left hand at the start of the second round. Cardiff slipped a second one and hugged, and the men pummeled each other on the ribs before they separated. Jackson then scored another left-hand body blow and then they fought close, the exchanges being about equal. Toward the end of the round Cardiff cross-countered Jackson rather heavily on the jaw with his right bunch of fives, and there was considerable cheering.

Jackson opened the third round with a clean left-hander on Cardiff's chin, following up the blow with a right-hand "heart warmer." Cardiff's leads passed harmlessly over Jackson's shoulder, and a cross-counter was delivered by Jackson every time. Cardiff hugged Jackson as if he were trying to break his back, and then endeavored to throw him, bringing upon himself several cries of foul and yells of disapproval. When they stood away, Jackson got his right home heavily on Cardiff's nose and as he tried to repeat the blow Cardiff ducked, went in, and hugged like a catamount. There was plenty of clinching and some good spells of infighting during this round, Cardiff sending in some good blows and being cheered by his admirers.

When Cardiff toed the scratch for the fourth round, he showed several strawberry patches in the region of the heart, the effect of Jackson's handiwork. Jackson, as usual, made the paces, sending his left in alternately on Cardiff's stomach and face. Cardiff stood up well and made some vicious right-hand swings, which, however, missed their effect. Towards the end of the round the fast work told on both, and they sparred for breath. Cardiff gave a good account of himself during the close work in this round.

In the fifth round Jackson started at a lively clip. He got home on Cardiff's face and Cardiff rushed in and hugged, bearing his man to the ropes and trying by catching him around the legs to upset him. He pushed Jackson back over the ropes. There was considerable hooting at Cardiff's foul fighting, but Jackson made no complaint. He simply disengaged himself whenever hugged as speedily as possible and resumed fighting. Cardiff showed the effect of the heavy work in this round. His left cheek was bleeding and the eye puffed, but he faced the music boldly, and occasionally countered Jackson in a solid manner both on ribs and neck. Cardiff did considerable ducking during this round and was always on the alert to swing his right when breaking away. Jackson was "onto him," however, and smothered many a well-meant right-hander with his shoulder.

Jackson opened the sixth round with a double-handed visitation of Cardiff's body. Cardiff, as usual, hugged at the first opportunity and seemed to have all he could do to keep himself from wrestling. The warning yells frequently reminded him of his shortcoming, and he desisted only to err again in a few seconds. Jackson administered some heavy punishment in this round. At one stage he sent Cardiff down on his knees, but stood away. Jackson taxed his wind reserve considerably. Towards the end of the round he was sparring and resting his lungs while Cardiff was making wild left- and right-hand sweeps in the hope of further damaging Jackson's breathing apparatus. Jackson smiled derisively, however, and kept out of danger.

CHAPTER 4

Hope and Glory, 1889

The Cardiff fight was attended by men from San Jose, Alameda, and Los Angeles and by many local sports including Joe McAuliffe and Jack Hallinan, who bet $2,000 on Peter. But among them was one sport who would play a greater part than Hallinan in Peter's career. This was Hugh Lowther, the Earl of Lonsdale, of Lonsdale belts fame, who was a dashing 32-year-old, 6 feet tall and athletic, an amateur boxer who had taken lessons from Jem Mace and claimed to have beaten John L. Sullivan in a friendly punch-up. He had arrived in San Francisco just two days earlier from the Canadian Arctic, where he had been exploring since February 1888 for the North Pole or the Northwest Passage or anything, and had (not just once) been given up for lost. Having arrived, Lonsdale had himself photographed in a fetching Eskimo outfit and the next evening saw the boxing at the California Club. He was blown away, not by the bouts but by Peter.[1]

In his memoirs, published in the lurid pages of *The People*, in the episode titled "The Greatest Fight I Ever Saw" on November 7, 1937, Lonsdale wrote: "Every man in his life has one special moment that he loves to look back on. Maybe not the greatest moment of his life, maybe not the proudest — but one when something pleased him greatly, when his heart beat strong and gladly in his breast, when life seemed good indeed. In such a manner I look back to the hour of my discovery of Peter Jackson. I think of it with pride, for somehow I felt when I found him rather like that fellow who brought his statue to life — Pygmalion, wasn't it?" He went to Peter's dressing room, they talked, Lonsdale made a proposition, Peter accepted. "Well, I wasn't a sculptor," continued Lonsdale's reminiscences, "who had carved the perfect physical shape of a steel-muscled negro youth and then watched it come to life; but I came upon this living man who seemed to me as near to physical perfection as could be; whom I saw to have a lion-like heart, a gentle nature, and all the equipment of the champion fighter. I took him home and he fulfilled my every dream." Lonsdale's unguarded language could not be used nowadays; for example, by "home" he seems to have meant Britain. Peter had been talking of Europe after doing the eastern states, and had already confirmed his match with Jem Smith at an unstated date and place. The day after meeting Lonsdale he announced that he was now going to England. Lonsdale said that he paid for Peter's Atlantic crossing, and as one of the richest men in England, Lonsdale could have easily afforded it. What is certain, however, is that it was Lord Lonsdale's invitation that convinced Peter to head for England and Lord Lonsdale's patronage that opened doors for him once he got there.

But Lonsdale did not take Peter along with him when he left San Francisco for home in late May 1889. Peter followed a few months later after another important meeting. The

Chronicle gave him its blessing for a holiday trip to Europe, saying: "This he both deserves and needs. Three hard-fought battles in eight months, resulting in three victories over men of world-wide reputation, comprise rather an enviable record, and the strain of constant training has been enough to remind the Australian champion that a few months 'out of harness' will do him good and not in any way militate against his chances of success when next he is called upon to face some worthy opponent in the magic circle." There had been a plan for Peter to leave San Francisco for Europe on April 24, 1889, with Naughton "and a number of Australian gentlemen who are on their way to Paris," where the Exposition Universelle of 1889 would begin its six-month season on May 6. But Peter stayed on for the Cardiff match on April 26.

He did leave on May 9, 1889, but for Nevada with the intention of sparring nightly in the large western towns and returning in early June. This tour was managed by Jack Hallinan. The *Daily Territorial Enterprise* of Virginia City, Nevada, explained on May 8 that Hallinan was making his debut as a manager, saying: "Jack has all the capital necessary to carry his scheme through like a prince, even if he does not take in a nickel."

But Peter's tour of Nevada lasted less than a week and was only the trip to Virginia City. On May 11, in Piper's Opera House, Peter met Fred Kaufman, a German who was slated to fight Pat Kehoe. Kaufman, who fought as "Shorty Kinkaid," had been a pupil of Walter Watson's. The fight was for six rounds but Kinkaid quit in the fourth. The fans were delighted to see Peter prove his reputation: "He was simply a baby in Jackson's hands." Advance publicity had trains from Carson and townships like Sutro, Silver and Dayton coming in force, with Reno "coming in rockaways," but in the event the attendance was disappointing and the 1,200-seat theater no way full.[2] As for Kehoe, he would not fight Peter, so the tourists returned to San Francisco. In Sacramento a reporter from the *Daily Record* interviewed Peter on May 24 and asked: "Is it true that you were refused admission to the Virginia City hotels?" Some gossip had drifted from the north. Peter replied firmly: "I was quartered at the International Hotel there, which is the best in the city, and will stop at the Gilman House in Portland."

The *Daily Alta California* reported on May 19, "On Thursday evening Peter Jackson entertained the friends he has made since his arrival in San Francisco at a banquet served in first-class style at Joe Dieves' place on the San Leandro road. The banqueting board was laden most generously and was done ample justice to by thirty couples, the Antipodean giant showing his good sense as well as good taste in not excluding the fair sex. The rooms were decorated with masses of flowers, and amid their perfume the party spent a happy time, an impromptu dance closing the entertainment." The *Daily Alta California* had possibly disapproved Peter's male companionships.

On May 25 Peter and Hallinan left for Portland, Oregon. Naughton went ahead as advance-publicity man. Peter took Tom Lees. They exhibited in Portland on the 28th and then traveled on the Northern Pacific railroad up to Spokane in Washington.

In Spokane on Friday, May 31, Peter's offer of $20 for standing four rounds with him was accepted by a local man, Jerry Flowers, who was a huge black with no science. The crowd screamed at him to "Hit him, Jerry," but Flowers could only reply, "God damn it, I can't find him." They moved on into Montana, to Missoula, where some black soldiers were desperately bored guarding white settlers against the Native Americans. Peter and Lees went out to their camp to exhibit for them, and quite a few of them pressed into Missoula for the show on June 3. They moved on to Helena, and then they gave an exhibition in Butte.

It was then back in the train, over into Minnesota and to Minneapolis, where they gave an exhibition on June 15. "His trip from San Francisco to New York will be governed by a contract with Hallinan," the *Chronicle* had said, but Hallinan soon returned to San Francisco, leaving the tour for Peter to manage.

While he had a contract or an understanding with Hallinan, Peter was under written contract to the California club, which allowed him when away to enter into matches for a fixed four, six, or eight rounds, apparently trusting him to decide. When he wanted to fight more rounds than eight he had to ask the club for permission. And he did so, for Peter was scrupulous in fulfilling his contractual obligations. Also, as a black boxer he found it convenient to load responsibility onto the club. He never challenged, he said; rather, he was directed by the club to accept challenges.

After Minneapolis they visited Grand Rapids, Michigan. They performed before what was described as a top-heavy house, meaning that only the cheap upper tiers were filled — by blacks. Some of the supporting boxers didn't turn up, and Fitzpatrick was obliged to don the gloves for an exhibition. Peter boxed three rounds with Lees. Chicago was reached on June 18, 1889. Herget was already there, preparing for his bout with Johnnie Reagan. Asked in May about Herget, Peter had said: "I regard him as the best man in the world at his weight, and I don't think that anybody can whip him."

By the time Peter reached Chicago his tour was $1,500 in the red. To add to his woes, he managed to lose his wallet containing $800 in cash and a letter of credit for $300 more. He recognized that he needed expert management. He looked through his letters of recommendation, asked at the *Chicago Tribune* office, and was directed to Charles Davies.

In February 1910, Davies was interviewed by a *Chicago Tribune* reporter. What he said was not necessarily correct in detail, but he remembered truly overall:

> I was standing in my brother's place, 93 Clark street, one afternoon when a big, tall colored man stepped up and handed me a letter. It was from Mose Gunst of San Francisco. It introduced the colored man as Peter Jackson. He wore a tall hat, and he looked at least seven feet high. The letter said Jackson was all right and was anxious to get on some fights in the East. "You can make no mistake with this fellow," read Gunst's letter. Just then someone asked Jackson to have a drink. In a manner which nearly won me because of his cleverness, Jackson refused, saying he did not drink. I did not like the idea of handling a darky but I read the letter again and looked Jackson over. I finally said I would take him and handle him for half; Jackson accepted and I became the manager of the greatest fighter the world has ever seen.

It would prove an alliance both pleasurable and profitable. For Peter, to take even half the profits was better than to lose money. As Peter told Hales in 1891: "Davies was very cute, and could make money for his show where all other managers would fail."

Charles Edward Davies was born in County Antrim, Ireland, in July 1851. His mother died when he was seven. In 1863 his father took his family to New York, only to die four years later, leaving Davies and his siblings orphans. He grew up on the lower East Side, in that rough and tough New York which Peter encountered in 1878. His father had worked for Pinkerton and one of his brothers became a Pinkerton agent in Chicago. Another brother, George, also drifted to Chicago and opened a saloon on Clark. Davies joined him in Chicago after the fire of 1871 and thereafter made Chicago his base. In the 1870s he sported a full black beard and a high collar of the kind affected by clergymen, in the style of David

A poster printed in 1889 by the Chicago Bank Note Company for Charles E. Davies, who here calls himself "The Parson."

Belasco. He shaved off his beard when beards lost fashion, and thereafter looked like a spoiled Jesuit. In 1879 William K. Vanderbilt saw him at a pedestrian meet in Madison Square Garden where one of Davies's hopefuls was competing. Vanderbilt noticed Davies conferring with another trainee pedestrian and remarked that "it must be his spiritual adviser." He alluded to him as "the Parson." The nickname stuck because of his sober clothes and deliberate manner. Davies hated being called "Parson," though he used it when needed, as on the poster he immediately put out to publicize Jackson. Peter called him Charles.

The Chicago Bank Note Company produced a lithograph from a photograph taken by "Pl. Photo. Eng. Co." (in San Francisco or more likely in Chicago). It showed Peter in white pants, presumably his red stockings and his heel-less shoes. The left foot is at forty-five degrees from the body, the right shoe points straight at the camera. His face is in three-quarter profile, his torso is bare, his left fist is up and his right fist points to the left elbow. He wears no gloves. Whether from the lithograph or the photograph, this image was reproduced many times, for example on the front page of the *Melbourne Sportsman* on June 7, 1892, where it had superimposed on it an Australian coat-of-arms.[3]

Davies moved with the times. He imported Matsada Sorakichi, the Japanese wrestler, but when hoodlums moved in on wrestling, Davies moved out and got into the fight game. He was in San Francisco in 1883, where he met many sports including Mose Gunst, owner of a cigar store on Kearney. He arranged Burke's fights in Chicago in early 1885, and he became Burke's manager, returning to California with him in late 1885. He organized matches for him involving Charley Mitchell, Alf Greenfield and the "Nonpareil," and even the one with Sullivan. He had managed many other pugilists, including Cardiff. Davies had a Speciality Company of reputable athletic performers: wrestlers like William Muldoon, and Ed "Strangler" Lewis (whose nickname was given him by Davies), and boxers like Harry Gilmore and Reddy Gallagher. Davies had himself never worked with any blacks.

Davies was organizing a benefit show for victims of the Braidwood mining disaster and persuaded Peter to become involved by fighting Charles "Sailor" Brown on July 1, six rounds to see if Brown could last. "The 'Parson' is confident of a big house. Jackson alone should be card enough to fill the Armory," said the *Chicago Tribune*. The Armory or Battery D was near the lake front at the corner of Michigan Avenue and Monroe. It was huge, and was used for religious conventions, political meetings, etc.

Davies went to New Orleans to see the Sullivan-Kilrain fight on July 8 and invited Peter along but Peter declined. In Louisiana, Governor Lawry forbade the fight, and so did the governor of Mississippi, but they still fought at Richburg on July 8. They then tried to elude the police but were jailed, faced charges, and were fined. The aftermath stretched out till June 1890. Corbett fought Kilrain, however, in New Orleans on February 18, 1890, without controversy, winning in six.[4]

In a sweltering Chicago on July 11, Peter was matched with 26-year-old Charles "Sailor" Brown for six rounds with four-ounce gloves, in front of 4,000 spectators. Before the fight, a black presented Peter with flowers, ostensibly from the citizens of Chicago. Addressing the crowd, wrote the *Chicago Herald* on July 12: "Jackson replied in a voice that sounded as if it came from the cellar. He said he was delighted at the reception and the courteous treatment he had received since his advent in the great city by the lake and would try to keep the friends he had made." Peter did not knock out Brown. The fight was stopped in the fourth by the M.C. because Brown was clearly whipped.

"Sailor" Brown had fought Herget, Tom Sharkey, and Peter Maher. But on the evening of July 14, according to the *Chicago Herald*, he was introduced in a bar to the fugitive Sullivan, who asked him, "You are the man who fights niggers, ain't you?" And when Brown admitted to having fought Peter, Sullivan punched him in the face, yelling, "Take that, you nigger fighter!" The *Herald* said that Mr. Brown left on the 9:10 P.M. train for New York.

The next day two white men, one of whom may have been Davies, accompanied Peter to the Park View House in Garfield Park, a suburb of Chicago, to see Sullivan, who was recuperating there after his fight with Kilrain and his escape from Mississippi. They asked to bring Peter upstairs to be introduced to the champion, as a kind of gift for what they supposed to be Peter's 28th birthday on July 16. Sullivan refused to see him.

In the lobby Peter commented to a reporter:

> I am not struck on seeing anybody who doesn't want to see me. I thought I would like to meet Sullivan, having heard so much about him, but if he doesn't desire my acquaintance I will not force it on him. Since I came to the United States I have met a great many men of education, wealth, and high social and political position, and all have treated me most agreeably. I have no objection to Sullivan drawing the color line on me. That is his privilege. So long as the California Athletic Club is behind me I can be as independent as anybody, and I know the gentlemen who compose that club will be my friends while I behave myself, no matter whether I win or lose. It is something of a pleasure for me to feel that I have friends whose friendship does not depend on my ability as a fighter.

It is unlikely that Sullivan felt chastened when he read this polished speech. The *Boston Police News*, in a garbled version of the story, ended Peter's statement with: "or the color of my skin."

Peter had to fulfil the last of those engagements he had organized himself. He arrived in Cincinnati with Lees on July 20, but when they got to the People's Theater it was darkened. Mayor Moseby and the police would not permit sparring. They returned to their hotel followed by 1,500 disappointed fans. The *Dead Bird* back in Sydney commented, "What sort of a white dove of

PETER JACKSON,
Australia's Representative for the World's Championship.

This heroic nationalistic sketch was published in the Melbourne *Sportsman* on June 7, 1892, when Jackson had defeated Slavin in London. Its caption, "Australia's Representative for the World's Championship," meant that John L. Sullivan must surely now fight Jackson.

purity have the pig stickers got for a mayor?" Cincinnati was always blowing hot and cold over boxing. They left Cincinnati at once. In 1895 the mayor said that because boxing attracted "a very undesirable element," he would not permit any thumping in his city.

Under his new manager Peter opened in Detroit, where he cleared one grand in one evening. Davies certainly had the Midas touch. Naughton arrived in Detroit from San Francisco on July 23, bringing with him the "Champion of Australia" belt, which was put on show in the store of Gillman & Barnes. Fitzpatrick, Lees, Davies and Peter arrived the next day and registered like Naughton at the Plankinton, a hotel frequented by the racing set. The *Detroit Journal* said Peter was "a splendid specimen of physical beauty," while his physique was described by the *Detroit Evening News* as "by all odds a lulu," and it expressed the hope that even if he couldn't defeat the insolent Sullivan he might give him an unforgettable lesson. Otherwise, the public would reject Sullivan, "even if they have to hire the Clan-na-Gael or some other one-horse secret Irish society to remove him." According to the *Detroit Evening News*, Peter was immediately recognized "from lithographs" by the "horsey crowd" at the Plankinton. These were either *National Police Gazette* illustrations or the posters put out by Davies, and the incident shows well the power of the illustrated press in constructing celebrity.

On July 25 he fought a local black, George C. Peters, "Detroit's colored champion," at Whitney's Grand Opera House filled with more than 2,000 fans. The preliminaries involved local black boxers. Finally Peter, wearing "a black shirt with the letters 'C.A.C.' embroidered thereon," his singlet, fought four rounds with a bare-chested Peters, or more like fooled with him. Davies had sized up Peters and told Jackson not to slug him. The crowd "hissed at Jackson because he would not at first hit Peters. Prompted, however, by the popular demand, he did hit Peters twice in the third bout, and the latter wanted to take off the gloves right away, but finished the match on the promise that he should not be hit again," according to the *Detroit Journal*. Peters had beaten McHenry Johnson, the "Colored Hercules," in 1886 and knocked out Mervine "Cleveland Thunderbolt" Thompson the year before, and had been keen to meet Jackson. Thompson and Johnson would figure in Fox's *Lives and Battles of Famous Black Pugilists* the following year, but not Peters. The *Detroit Free Press* reported dryly that Peters had been overmatched, and that his nose had been bloodied.

On July 27 the band arrived in Cleveland: Peter, Fitzpatrick, Lees, and Charles Daly, probably the lightweight who would box Jack McAuliffe in St. Louis in 1893. Peter and Lees exhibited in the 1,900-seat Euclid Avenue Theater. Surprisingly the *Cleveland Gazette*, the black newspaper, did not notice Peter's visit to the city. At the Lyceum in Buffalo on July 29, which held 2,200, Peter fought Billy Baker, winning on points in four. Peter must have approved of sandy-haired Baker, because he used him for an exhibition on August 6, and in Hoboken on August 8 he fought him again.

In Erie City the following evening, July 30, 1889, Peter fought Tom Lynch, an Irishman from Buffalo, 180 pounds to Jackson's 200, the usual deal of $100 if Lynch could last four rounds. It was the last episode in a typical Davies evening with a few bouts including one with Sam Fitzpatrick, described as "a finely built fellow and a fearful hitter"—something to tell the *Maitland Mercury* about. As usual the performances were on the stage of a theater, in this case Genessee Hall. The *Buffalo Express* said that Lynch toed the mark gamely but then shut his eyes when Jackson hit him in the stomach. Suddenly galvanized, Lynch rushed upon Jackson and clinched. The referee, Ed Higgins, yelled: "Break away!" Lynch, however,

THE LIVES AND BATTLES
OF THE
COLORED CHAMPIONS
OF THE PRIZE RING.

From the time of Thos. Molineaux to Peter Jackson.

★

Price, - - 25 Cents.

★

With Numerous Illustrations and Authentic Portraits of

Peter Jackson,
Tom Cribb,
Harris Martin (the Black Pearl),
Arthur Frazier,
Bill Richmond,
McHenry Johnson,
Master Kendrick,
Bob Smith,
Geo. Dixon,

Mervine Thompson,
Thos. Molineaux,
Viro Small,
Geo. Taylor,
"Sambo" Sutton,
Prof. Charles Hadley,
Harry Woodson,
Geo. Godfrey,
Bob Travers,
C. A. C. Smith.

This book is a history of the careers of American and English Colored Pugilists from 1810. It narrates, in detail, many famous battles, such as Molineaux's fights with Tom Cribb, Geo. Dixon's fight with Nunc Wallace, etc., etc.

Sent by mail to any address on receipt of price, 25 cents. Send all orders to

RICHARD K. FOX,
Franklin Square,   New York City.

Known also as *Lives and Battles of Famous Black Pugilists* and as *Black Champions of the Prize Ring from Molineaux to Jackson*, this book, with introduction by Richard K. Fox, was published in 1890. Extremely rare nowadays, it was being advertised in the *National Police Gazette* as late as December 1894.

clung to Jackson, and it took the combined effort of four men, the seconds and the timekeepers, to pull him away. No sooner were they separated than Lynch clinched again. They were tugged apart.

Jackson got mad, and blazed away furiously at Lynch, dealing him a couple of nasty blows in the stomach and face, while Lynch hit Jackson a stinger in the nose. Some quick fighting followed, Jackson smashing Lynch hard. Lynch lost his head, grabbed Jackson by the neck, and tried to throw him. In the scrimmage Lynch sank his teeth into Jackson's shoulder. In short, Lynch descended to the most primitive of all modes of aggression: like other boxers before and after, he began biting.

When they had been forced back into their corners, Captain Kraft of the Fourth Precinct announced he would end the match unless the men behaved themselves. Lynch's seconds told him to cool it, but Lynch was deaf. At the second call of "time" Lynch rushed in madly and received a couple of stingers that set him wild. He closed in on Jackson, bit him again, and kicked him vigorously. He was pried off.

"Is there kicking in this?" demanded Jackson as he set out to paralyze Lynch. Amid a wild sea of brandishing arms, Lynch clinched again, grabbing Jackson by the legs and dumping him headfirst through a piece of scenery. The referee, seconds, timekeepers and Captain Kraft couldn't get Lynch off. He stuck fast to Jackson, but he was finally detached and Jackson could jump to his feet. They were both in fury. And they struggled madly to get at each other.

"The black nigger," shrieked Lynch, "Let me get at him. I'll kill him." Jackson sprang from the arms of his captors for another go at Lynch but was held back.

"Come out here and fight," yelled Lynch. "Let the black son of a gun come out here." Probably in place of "son of a gun" he used a stronger term. Kraft ordered the fight stopped and told the stagehands to ring down the curtain. "The cops hauled Lynch away, but not till Peter had shaken every bone in his body and loosened every tooth in his head." By this time Lynch's friends had cooled him down somewhat and he was induced to walk over to Jackson's quarters and ask him to shake hands. "No," muttered Jackson, "God forbid that I should shake hands with a low, contemptible cur like you." Lynch retorted, "You ought to be proud to touch the hand of a white man."

Referee Higgins awarded Jackson the victory because Lynch had fouled him twice by biting him.

On August 5 Peter fought Paddy Brennan, a local man, in Genessee Hall. The terms were that Brennan should win $200, twice the usual offer, if he stayed four rounds. Brennan had fought Mervine Thompson in 1884 and would fight Mike Queenan in 1892. Jackson knocked him about, cut a gash above his right eye, broke his nose. This was all in the first round. At the end of the round the police stopped the fight, and Brennan was stretchered off. Jackson fought him in so savage a manner, and one so uncharacteristic of him, that Brennan may be suspected of having made disparaging *sotto voce* remarks about his race when they shook hands.

From Buffalo the band crossed into Canada. Peter, with his hair parted down the middle and called the champion of the Pacific Slope and Australia, appeared in Toronto on August 6. Some gentlemen from Toronto who were visiting Chicago for footracing had seen Peter fight Sailor Brown on July 11 and were so impressed that they "closed with him to give an exhibition in the Mutual Street rink" in their city. Peter was presented to the crowd of some 2,500 by Ned Hanlan, the champion sculler, who had returned to Toronto that morning after two years of rowing abroad, including Australia. The two could have met in the Australian summer of 1887–88 when Hanlan twice rowed in Sydney, though neither the Sydney papers nor the *Toronto Globe* mentioned it. Peter punched a ball and then sparred with "sandy-complexioned" Billy Baker, having been warned by Police Inspector Ward not to knock anyone out. The spectators found it a tame event.

They went from Buffalo to New York City. Peter was much taken with his second arrival in Gotham. In 1900 he compared it with his first in 1878, as a friendless boy lost on the Lower East Side. Now, in 1889, "he was the conquering hero who had marched triumphantly from distant Australia to 'Frisco, and thence through all the intervening states of the land of Uncle Sam," Will wrote in 1900. Peter said New York was eager to see him and greeted him enthusiastically. "America," said Peter, or more probably Will, "which had previously looked upon the black man with contempt as a something immeasurably beneath her, marveled at the doings of this one." His reception by New Yorkers in 1889 erased all the pain of 11 years before.

At Hoboken on August 8, 1889, he sparred with Billy Baker, billed as the "Champion of New York." They went four rounds in Cronheim's Theater which, with 2,000 seats, was packed with sports from New York, Brooklyn and New Jersey. Peter had grown a natty little mustache. The *New York World* announced that "the Australian is a big, strong, clever boxer," and noted with pleasure: "Jackson's boxing was varied, too—something that can be said of but few of the present run of pugilists." The *World* published the names of sportsmen who "thoroughly endorsed" Peter: Harry Maynard of California, Mike Donovan (the inventor of the punching ball), Ed Conners, Billy Madden, "Old Sport" Campana, Mike Boyle, Jack Hopper, "Greek George" (perhaps John Hatzopoulos, the wrestler who toured Australia in 1895), and Ed Dillon of Fishkill-on-Hudson. These names either constitute a simple list of endorsers or reveal Peter's backers at this time.

The next night, August 9, at the end of a variety show, Peter defeated Jim "Ginger" McCormick with four-ounce gloves in two rounds. According to the *National Police Gazette*, Peter did not use his right hand, just short arm jabs with his left; though the New York correspondent of the *St. Louis Post-Dispatch* wrote of "left and right-handers on his opponent's face and body in short order, countering and cross-countering like lightning." The dazed McCormick kept wandering over to the stage scenery, "sheltering himself by hugging the wings," and Jackson kept leading him back to center stage where they could be seen. Toward the end of the second round either Jackson knocked McCormick out or "Ginger" took his time getting up, the *World* intimating that he "decided to remain on the stage floor longer than the ten seconds permitted by the rules."

They played Boston on August 17, when Chief of Police Goodrich would not allow any boxing between Peter and Joe Lannon, so that Peter and Lannon, with Ike "Spider" Weir and the local boy George Godfrey, entertained the 2,000 spectators by punching a bag.

On August 19 Peter fought four rounds with the 21-year-old Jack Fallon of Brooklyn in Mike Shine's New York Circus, at Fourth Avenue and 14th, in an 18-foot ring. Fallon disappointed the crowd. The *Brooklyn Eagle*, Fallon's ally, said the next day: "Jack was fat and he could not do much with Jackson." The *World* said: "In the first round he struck out a few times for his man, but came no nearer to landing than if he struck for the Bartholdi statue." The Statue of Liberty had been unveiled for less than three years. Fallon was beaten in two rounds, "red and puffing and considerably astonished at the end," said the *Brooklyn*

Eagle. But all the same Davies decided to take Fallon to Britain to be used, in his words, as Peter's punching bag.

Peter congratulated himself upon contracting with Davies, even if he was paying him 50 percent. This first eastern venture under his management had earned a profit of $8,500. Presumably after paying off supernumeraries, Peter and Davies split the profit. Any money he made abroad he would invest in government bonds.

Peter made useful acquaintances in New York City, for instance the Considines, John and George, who owned, at Broadway and 42nd across from the Knickerbocker Hotel, a cafe much frequented by racing men and pugilists. It was a place where boxing contracts were signed. And he met the Nail brothers, whom some blacks in San Francisco had wired after his victories. Jack and his brother Fred ran a restaurant and liquor business at 461 Sixth Avenue, near 28th. At this time Black Harlem's growth was mostly in the future. The Nails moved their establishment uptown and became important Harlem real estate agents. They also became Peter's backers.[5]

In New York Peter posed for two photographs which, along with the Parson's poster, largely created and for years froze his image. He was photographed in the Bowery by John Wood, who specialized in shots of boxers and whom everyone from Jem Mace to Mike Leonard patronized. Fox sold Wood's photographs through the *National Police Gazette* at 10c each. This picture was used on a cigarette card issued in 1895 by Mayo's Cut Plug tobacco "for chewing and smoking," and then again on the "Mecca" cigarette card of 1909.

The other picture was taken in the Union Square studio of Napoleon Sarony, the celebrated theatrical photographer. This photograph was reproduced almost instantly in the series of over 500 cabinet portraits published by Newsboy Plug Tobacco. Peter was photographed on many other occasions, and often in practically the same outfit, but the Wood photo and the Sarony photo were, with the Chicago poster, the three most widely circulated of Peter's images. His photographs almost always showed the right side of his face, the rare ones of his left side or of him full-face seeming to show a slight inward turn of the left eye.

Peter, Fitzpatrick, Naughton and Davies, together with Fallon and Christine, his wife of three days, left New York on the steamer *City of Rome* on Wednesday, August 21, 1889. They reached Queenstown in Ireland on the August 28, where Peter was interviewed at 2 am by a *Sporting Life* reporter who arrived on the mail tender. Peter told the reporter that he was 34 years old. He also said that he believed his height to be six feet and one inch. Then, asked how many fights he had had, he said: "Eleven, I think — eight in Australia and three in America." Peter was being deliberately obtuse.

The party was met by an immense crowd at Liverpool, and arrived in London on Thursday, August 29. Met at the Euston depot by Richard Moyle, Robert Watson (who was "Paul Pry" from *Sporting Life*), J.T. Hulls, George W. Atkinson, Jack Harper, Charley Bates from the White Swan Hotel, and C.W. Blake, the editor of *Sporting Life*, they were driven in a coach and four to the well-known Anderson's Hotel on Fleet street.

Moyle was a Sydney friend of Peter's now living in England. A year before, when it was announced that Peter wanted a match against Jem Smith, it was reported by the *London Sportsman*: "His agent in advance, James R. Moyle, Esq., a wealthy Australian, now of Garland Villa, James's Road, Tunbridge Wells — and the Conservative Club — has come here to arrange a match." Moyle became a small-time boxing entrepreneur in England. That night he provided the coach and four, and paid for an evening at a theater of varieties. How

This photograph of Jackson was taken in New York City in 1889. Napoleon Sarony was the fashionable portraitist of theatrical stars. His studio was in Union Square. Courtesy of Special Collections, Fine Arts Library, Harvard College Library [119.1976.4788].

John Wood's photographic studio was in the Bowery. His photographs of athletes sold steadily because they were issued by the *National Police Gazette* as "Fox" pictures. This photograph of Jackson, carte de visite with "Fox" overlay, was taken in 1889 when he reached New York. Photograph courtesy of Harvard Art Museum, Fine Arts Library [119.1976.2369].

wealthy he was is debatable. He may have been a son of Charles Moyle the grocer and fruiterer at 347 Sussex, in Sydney, a couple of city blocks from the United States Hotel and the Lighthouse, who after Charles Moyle died in 1885 took his inheritance and headed for England.

On Saturday August 31 the *Sporting Life* office was visited and the travelers interviewed. That evening Moyle took Peter to his home, no longer at Tunbridge Wells but at Much Hadham near Ware in Hertfordshire, and entertained him for a couple of days.

On September 2 Peter was back in London enjoying a warm reception at the Pelican Club, which was the forerunner of the National Sporting Club and which would be promoting his fight with Smith. The president of the club, Sir John Astley, commonly called "The Mate," welcomed him and introduced him to Lord de Clifford, Lord Esmé Gordon, Lord Charles Ker, Major Hope-Johnstone, and others who figured only as *Messrs* but were nonetheless rich. Queensberry the vice-president saw Peter later. He met many other members, but especially those constituting the Boxing Committee of which Queensberry and Lonsdale were the most prominent: Lord Churston, Lord Esmé Gordon, George W. Atkinson, Charles W. Blacklock, a businessman and sports patron, Arthur Wells the owner of the club building, and the rest.[6]

At the club he met Hugh Lowther, Earl of Lonsdale, again. As they had arranged, Lonsdale carried him off to Rutland, to Oakham, to Barley Thorpe Hall, his palatial "hunting box" where he had his own gymnasium. Oakham, 17 miles east of Leicester, boasted a 1584 grammar school, a 14th-century church, and a 12th-century castle. The Earl's mother, Countess of Lonsdale, lived at Cottesmore Hall nearby, and Lonsdale's brother the Hon. Lancelot Lowther (who succeeded to the title), and his aunt Lady Augusta Noel also lived in Oakham. Peter had not before been amid so much history and among so many nobles.

"When I brought him to England and down to my place at Barley Thorpe in Rutland, all who saw him were speechless with admiration," Lonsdale wrote many years afterwards. He found Peter fascinating. "Why, I have seen him in my own drawing room with his gloved fist quench five candles one after the other, simply hitting at the flame and scarcely touching the wick. He never missed." It was more genteel than snatching flies on the wing, but one fears that the Earl's guests must soon have been smothering their yawns. However, Peter's parlor tricks may indeed have diverted Lonsdale's crowd, who thought cutting off a military man's waxed mustaches (Major Hope-Johnstone's) and mounting them on purple plush under glass was a damned amusing thing. Lonsdale said that Peter spent most of his time at Barley Thorpe working out. It was a way to avoid any awkward moments. But Davies said he remained idle from August 29 until October 2, simply regrouping his inner forces for the rest of the offensive campaign ahead. And he socialized. "Everyone who was anyone among sportsmen came to see Jackson," recalled Lonsdale in 1937, "either at my place or in London."

Davies told New York reporters: "Lord Lonsdale promised to give Jackson a good reception after his arrival in Great Britain, and he did so in a right hearty fashion. We visited his mansion, where we had a splendid time of it. He invited Jackson to train at his shooting lodge at Penrith, and volunteered to pay all his expenses, but we declined the generous offer." Peter stayed briefly in Rutland, perhaps not wanting to become too much indebted to Lonsdale and perhaps because he heard news of the Prince of Wales' annual visit to shoot in Lonsdale's "splendid pheasant coverts." Before September 14 they were back in London getting ready for Jem Smith.

At 26, Smith was pink and white like a sugar pig. He had been employed as a laborer in a lumberyard. He had the build of a piano mover. In a picture of him seated on the thigh of his kneeling second, Jack Harper, a common enough pose at the time, he looked like a robust baby. He had won his title in the fight with Jack Davis in 1885, but people always murmured about his being a bogus champion. The *Sport* said that "he took upon himself the title of the champion of England" over the protests of other men like Alf Greenfield, although Henning's *Fights for the Championship* (1902) says that his having licked Davis "entitled Jem Smith to enrol his name amongst the champions of England." He was 5 feet and 8½ inches tall with a weight in September of well over 200 pounds, which he brought down to 189 pounds by the night. He had himself photographed at Brighton by W. and A.H. Fry looking ponderous.

At first, Smith had expected Peter to fight under the London Prize Ring rules, but "Peter in reply said knuckle fights had no charm for him, and if any one wanted a match it would have to be with the gloves." John Corlett of the *Sporting Times* heard Peter say apropos: "Why should I spend my time in running away or hiding from the police, as Sullivan and Kilrain have been doing, when I can get so much money by showing what I can do with the gloves, and not breaking any law rules?" Now Smith wanted a fight to the finish, but Davies was insistent that Peter could fight no more than 8 rounds by virtue of his contract with the California Athletic Club. The Smith party then demanded 12 rounds. Davies wired Fulda for instructions. Fulda wired back: "You can make match for 10 rounds; no more."

The contract was drawn up accordingly and signed at the *Sporting Life* office on September 26, Davies signing for Peter, who was in Much Hadham staying with Moyle. Davies and Fitzpatrick, and Smith with his manager John Fleming and trainer Jem Howes, were there, plus other sports including Charley Bates and Bob Habbijam of the West End School of Arms. After the signing, they all adjourned to Anderson's hotel for drinks, and then to Bates's White Swan, Salisbury Court, "where they had a jolly time of it."

On October 2, Peter started in the Royal Aquarium Theater the sparring and boxing season that Davies had organized for him. The Royal Aquarium Summer and Winter Garden was built at Westminster in 1876 and demolished in 1903. Of red bricks, it was huge: it covered three acres, its central hall was 340 feet by 160 feet, it had tanks for freshwater animals and saltwater animals, it had palm trees, a reading room, picture and sculpture galleries, a swimming pool and a skating rink. In the western part of the complex stood the Royal Aquarium Theater. The whole Aquarium constituted an entertainment barn and, far from being a temple of high culture as its builders had hoped, was known for its free nonstop music-hall entertainments ("over 400 artistes and 150 turns"), its flower shows, its aquatic shows, its prostitutes, eventually for its being a venue for projected movies, most famously the film of the Corbett-Fitzsimmons fight in 1897.[7]

Davies realized the importance of this season and appeared in a dress suit. Lonsdale credited Davies with introducing the silk topper into English boxing. He said that Davies, because he scorned the old red or green sweater, had changed boxing officials' attire forever. For his part, Peter dressed carefully so as to be clearly visible from anywhere in the whole enormous room, which could hold 5,000 spectators. He wore his brown ulster, and doffed it to reveal a white leotard, black pants with a white stripe down each side, a black and white belt, red stockings and black shoes. Because Charley Mitchell had abruptly asked for too much money, he sparred with Fallon, billed as "The Strong Boy of Brooklyn," at 10:30

P.M. It made a sensation, though Fallon was lack-luster. Peter had made sure he was called "the Australian," but almost at once he was being billed as "Peter the Great."

Everyone was there. The *Sportsman* gave a list of more than 30 important sports whom it noted in attendance the first night. Only a few need be mentioned: Moyle, Pooley Mace (Jem's half-Gypsy cousin), and Bob Habbijam. Eugene Stratton, dubbed "The Whistling Coon," the minstrel-show star, born in Buffalo in 1861 but domiciled in London since 1880, a blackface song-and-dance man, attended the Jackson-Smith fight, too.[8]

Also there to see him box that night was Ned Donnelly. Ned was stout by now, but was now the Royal Professor of Boxing and two years before had seconded Kilrain in his fight with Smith. Did they introduce themselves, and did Peter thank Donnelly for the encouragement his little green-and-gold boxing manual had given him in 1879? Did he remember Jack Dowridge to Donnelly? It would be pleasant to think so.

As reported in *Sporting Life* on October 3, Davies spoke before the spar:

> Ladies and Gentlemen, I appear before you a stranger in a strange land. Since I have been in this country I have received the kindest treatment and courtesy. I am Jackson's manager, and I wish to state that in his travels every pugilist he has met he has defeated. This is the first time he has appeared before an English audience, and he will spar tonight with Jack Fallon, the Strong Boy of Brooklyn, and I hope they will both please you. In conclusion, I wish to state that Jackson is matched to box Jem Smith for 10 rounds, for £1,000, given by the Pelican Club, and if defeated I shall be satisfied that the best man has won.

After the next night Fallon was dropped ("shunted" was the expression used) because, it was said, he had exhausted himself performing his honeymoon duties. He set about preparing to fight Jack Wannop, a former opponent of Smith's. Thereafter Peter sparred with Jem Hook of Billingsgate, with William "Coddy" Meddings, and with a colored man named Jack Watson. Three nights into the season, Queensberry attended. On Saturday, October 5, an exhibition between Peter and Alf Mitchell from Cardiff was refereed by Mace himself. So Peter met Foley's teacher again after eight years. In a letter to the *Referee*, Naughton referred to Peter's opponents as "the flower of England's fistocracy"—and they were that, sad to say.

On Monday, October 7, the immense hall was full when Peter boxed Jack "Bully" Partridge. Sir John Astley and his large aristocratic entourage were there from the Pelican Club to see "the Australian Black Diamond," alternatively "the Antipodean champion," in action. He boxed with both Alf Mitchell and Alf Ball the next day, October 15.

The *Sportsman* said Peter "sauntered into the building," shaking hands with friends and well-wishers of "the dusky Cornstalk." On October 13 Queensberry was there again at the ringside and the place was simply crammed, according to the *Sportsman*. He boxed Jem Young on October 14 and Davies engaged him for exhibitions. The next night Mace returned, just to watch him handle Alf Mitchell and then Alf Ball. All of these bouts were exhibitions, none of them prizefights, which were illegal in England in public places. The season at the Aquarium was a professional triumph, and profitable. Paddy did three rounds a night at the Aquarium at this time, and earned $450 a week. Peter probably earned the same or a little more. In those years leading actors in London earned around £40 a week, and music-hall stars around £60 a week. Boxing certainly paid well.

The *Sportsman* wrote enthusiastically on Wednesday, October 9, saying:

> Gentleman Jackson, sometime Champion of England, the conqueror of Mendoza, the friend and intimate of George IV, Lord Byron, and other celebrities of that era, was considered the handsomest man in England, and the greatest athlete of the period in which he lived. Another Jackson of equal, if not greater proportions, from the Antipodes is now in our midst, making a bold bid to rival the fame of his illustrious predecessor in the art of fisticuffs and other accomplishments. Peter, as he stalks among the crowd nightly at the Aquarium, like "Saul among the people," comports himself like a prince of the blood, and might easily be mistaken for some foreign potentate on a mere visit to the Old Country for the purpose of studying man and manners, so regal and easy is Peter's style of action in his ordinary attire.

The following night Paddy Slavin, dubbed the "Sydney Cornstalk" in England since arriving by the *Carthage* in August, boxed in the Aquarium with Bill "Chesterfield" Goode. Peter and Davies attended. Peter offered to fight Paddy for 10 rounds under Queensberry rules. Richard Fox had arrived in London. The three had a confabulation at the *Sporting Life* office on October 22. Paddy said he wanted to fight Peter, yes indeed, but not for a year or so yet. Peter said it had to be within four weeks or forget it. Davies actually drew up the articles for a match on November 25 between Peter Jackson of Sydney and Frank P. Slavin of Maitland and left them at the *Sporting Life* office for Paddy's signature, but Paddy never signed them. He preferred to forget it, because he was interested in fighting Jem Smith bare-knuckled.

For the earlier part of this first Aquarium season Peter stayed at Barnes, near Richmond, but afterwards he and Fitzpatrick, with Davies and some friends including Moyle, settled in Brighton, "Queen of Watering Places," in order to train for his fight with Smith. They stayed at first in the Sea House Hotel and then in an apartment over an oyster shop on Ship. He was finally able to swim again to his heart's content in a saltwater bath, at the famous Brill's Baths on the esplanade. Smith, who also chose to train at Brighton, patronized Hobden's Baths. Brighton had a Turkish bath, too, which Smith needed for his slimming campaign. Moyle busied himself organizing a "boxing entertainment" for November 2 at Ginnett's Circus. On October 25, *Sporting Life* reported that "the members of the Jackson-Davies combination were photographed yesterday on the beach in the presence of a large and admiring crowd of marines, fishermen, and beach loungers."[9]

When interviewed at Brighton for the *Sportsman* on November 5, Peter ignored the prospective match, instead discussing the sensational strongman contest at the Royal Aquarium between Samson the veteran and Eugen Sandow the debutant. He let Davies carry most of the shoptalk while, humming a tune, he changed into flannels and worked out with a punching ball, to the admiration of the interviewer. He seemed relaxed. Davies said: "We can take defeat in a proper manner, but, confident in our own resources, we expect to win."

Peter and Smith encountered each other only once, at a swimming contest at Brill's Baths on November 3. It is not clear why Peter attended, for he did not swim himself. Smith was in the company of his manager, Jack Fleming, and his trainer Jem Howes. Peter had Moyle and Joe Fallows in tow. At this point, Moyle dropped out of Peter's story.

When asked the following year about his love life, Peter spoke enthusiastically but generally about the girls at Brighton. The New York correspondent of the *San Francisco Chronicle* quizzed Peter, saying: "Is it true, as has been stated, Mr. Jackson, that you have become engaged to a pretty English girl in Brighton, where you trained?" Seizing on one word, Peter adroitly replied: "That talk is all rubbish. My only engagement is with the California Athletic Club." Undeterred, the reporter pursued him with: "Did you have much

Francis Patrick (Paddy) Slavin, possibly photographed in London in 1892. Photograph courtesy of National Library of Australia [nla.pic-vn3060289].

attention from English women as well as men?" Peter's reply deserves applause for its finesse: "I got some letters that would make very rich reading, but of course they have been destroyed."

Whatever the facts about Peter's sentimental involvements, an article written by Naughton for the *Indianapolis Freeman* three years later, and reflecting Peter's experiences in 1889 and 1892, said: "For example, in London it is no unusual thing to see a gentleman of color arm in arm with some white young lady escorting her to church, theatre or elsewhere, and vice versa, a white gentleman and colored lady, and these little interchanges of white and colored courtesy while evidently satisfactory to the ladies and gentlemen engaged therein, are carried on with perfect freedom from the stare of ignorant and impertinent curiosity, ridicule or insulting comments." Whatever the case, in between admiring the ladies on the Chain Pier or escorting them to the Alhambra Theater, Peter found time at Brighton to acquire a jaybird and a bulldog.

On November 11 he returned to London for what *Sporting Life* called a fight between the Champions of the Old World and of Australasia. "Both men have issued their colors, and they can be obtained at the *Sporting Life* office on the usual terms." Peter's colors were of white Japanese silk with sky-blue border, and showed in the center the Australian coat of arms, its shield supported by an emu and a kangaroo and surmounted by a rising sun. In the corners were a badge for New South Wales made up of a Union Jack and a Southern Cross; the motto: "Advance Australia"; a badge for the United States consisting of stars above stripes; and a monogram of the California A.C., with the club's motto: "Fair Field and No Favor." Smith's colors showed his torso in the middle, with crossed flags and a heraldic lion below, and an English rose in each corner. Before the match Dick Roberts and Smith's brother Tom hawked Peter's and Smith's colors from the ring at £1 each. Customers complained that not many of Peter's colors were for sale. Fitzpatrick mailed one to Gillies of the *Maitland Mercury*.

An early arrival was Barney Thompson the bookmaker, Jack Thompson's brother, who had formerly lived in Sydney. Mace was there. Numerous titled personages attended and many officers of the household brigade, guardsmen, and officers of the army and navy. Eugene Stratton was there and 21-year-old Coningsby Disraeli, nephew of the novelist and statesman. Queensberry, Bernard Angle, Charley Mitchell, and Bat Masterson attended, as well as the editor of the *Sportsman*, not just his reporters. Everybody in the room was, of course, a member of the Pelican Club, whether of long standing or hastily signed up. They had a while to wait.

As soon as Smith and Jackson arrived they disputed about judges. At last Arthur Bettinson, the English amateur, and W.J. King, an American and a former amateur champion, were agreed on. Captain A.S. Drummond of the Boxing Committee was made timekeeper and George Vize the referee.

The fight started at 1:20 A.M., when most spectators had been waiting for three hours and more, some for six hours as they had arrived early to get a seat. To amuse the audience, Tom Smith stopped selling colors and sparred with Tom Lees as a preliminary. The former champion of Victoria had not notably improved under Mace's tuition, the *Sportsman* saying: "There was little to choose between the pair." It got late. The audience had grown restless and looked forward to 10 rounds of sparkling action. They did not get them.

Finally Smith appeared wearing a white flannel jersey. Under this he wore, "as provided by the conditions," white spring-side boots and white breeches. The contract only said "light" boots or shoes, and must have been referring to weight rather than color. Appearing in his black boots and wrapped in his old brown ulster, upon stripping Peter showed he was wearing his white and blue, the Australian colors that he had donned for the Godfrey fight: white flannel knee breeches with a narrow blue stripe running down the outer side, and light blue stockings. He "looked like an Achilles in black marble; his physical beauty was perfect, and his flesh as hard as stone," the *Sportsman* said, with a nod toward Westmacott's strapping bronze Achilles in Hyde Park. The *Sportsman* called him "the Australian" and "the West Indian," the *Sporting Life* just "Jackson." Fitzpatrick and Fallon were Peter's seconds, and Smith's were Jack Harper and Jack Baldock.

Astley, the president of the Pelican Club, entered the ring and "pointed out that the judges were excellent; and that perfect fairness would be shown both men. He said they had come there to see a fair match. There would be no draw. Englishmen were tired of draws. He announced that the winner would receive £800 and the loser £200, but they must have a good rattling fight or not a penny would be paid. This was to be a fair stand-up match; there would be hard hitting, and the best man would win." The *Sportsman* said it was a sensible little speech.

After the referee instructed the boxers, Baldock formally objected to Peter's wearing a belt, which Peter asserted he must wear. Half an hour was spent squabbling over this. It was proven to be a suspensory bandage as used for scrotal hernias, and the judges denied the objection. Then in his turn Peter objected to his gloves, which had been made by Feltham's of the Barbican under the supervision of Mace himself, saying that they were too small. Vize said they were not, and Peter complained that "the referee has not my hands!" but was ordered to force the gloves on. They split, so another pair was produced. The audience chafed under these delays.

At 1:21, finally, Jackson and Smith retreated to their corners. "Time!" was called, and they walked to the center.

Round One

Sparring for an opening, Jackson appeared the more anxious and made several feints to lead off. After a little finessing Smith stepped in and got the left home in the region of the stomach, but failed to effect much mischief. A good deal of vain attempts were now made, and Smith raised the hopes of his partisans by punching Jackson about the body with his left. At this stage Jackson commenced fighting at a great pace, and both put in good work up to the call of "Time!" Jackson said some of Smith's punches went so low that he considered crying foul.

Round Two

Both men were fresh, eager, and ready for the fray when "Time!" was called for the second meeting. The loud cries of "Smith wins for a hundred," instead of disconcerting Jackson, only seemed to give him more nerve, as he at once assumed the offensive, and with excellent effect, as the first time he led off, he got home with a long, straight shot with the left which sent Smith staggering to the ropes. Back to the fray Smith rushed impetuously, and driving his left with tremendous force into the pit of his opponent's stomach he once more caused his admirers to go into ecstasies. A second the pair were at close quarters, the exchanges being of a particularly heavy nature, both fighting for the body. Obeying the order of the referee to break away, the pair were soon in close quarters again, Smith evidently determined to find a weak spot in the anatomy of his opponent. But even at half-arm fighting Jackson was as good as his rival, and even before the spectators were aware of the fact the real coup de grace had been administered, for just as the pair were getting practically "out of holds" Jackson administered a terrific upper-cut with the right, which fairly staggered his opponent. This was at once evident, for Jackson fell with the recoil, and when he rose to his feet Smith was unable to go after him. Then followed a scene of the wildest excitement, for as Jackson returned to the charge Smith retreated to the ropes, and his condition was evidenced by the fact that he had to cling to the ropes with his right hand for support. The *Licensed Victualler's Gazette* said: "He held on to the ropes with his right hand, and used his left in a deprecatingly protesting way as a seal uses his flipper."

Jackson was too much blown to settle the fight at this point, but again and again he smashed his left hand on Smith's face without the latter's being able to offer the faintest semblance of resistance. Smith made an occasional feeble endeavor to show fight; but back he had to go to the ropes for assistance. At length Smith tried desperately to retrieve his fast-waning fortunes, but it was his last. Rousing himself for a heroic effort, he faced his opponent in the middle of the ring and, clasping Jackson round the body, gave him a back-heel and thus threw him heavily. The second round had lasted two minutes.

At this, Fitzpatrick, Fallon, and Davies invaded the ring and shouted foul. After volleys of "Shame!" on all sides, the referee, at last making his voice heard, gave his decision: "We declare the match in favour of Jackson." Smith ripped off his gloves and went for Jackson, crying, "I'll fight him with my fists!" Held back, he tried it again. Peter said to him: "You know you lost the fight in the first round when you hit me low." Smith retorted, "I didn't, you jumped in the air when I delivered." Smith had to be removed. Smith's fans were so shocked that they did not start any brawl. If they had, the police outside, hired by the club, would have intervened.

The whole fight had lasted five minutes. The 951 members of the Pelican Club present therefore had paid £5 (or $25) a minute to view a shambles. They were disgruntled about the waste of money, and disgusted with Smith. They were further upset upon learning that Smith and Peter were about to begin a season sparring together at the Royal Aquarium.

This had not been a championship match. Smith's title was for bare-knuckle fighting, and he had not hazarded it by fighting Peter with gloves. Strictly, Peter claimed only that he had defeated the bare-knuckle champion of England when wearing gloves. According to the report received by the *Chicago Tribune* on November 11, "Smith declared his intention of challenging Jackson to fight with bare knuckles, but Jackson's manager will not permit him to accept." Jack Fallon's Brooklynese imitation of Smith's London accent was rendered by a *Brooklyn Eagle* reporter on January 12, 1890 as: "I dunno 'ow to use them blarsted pillows. I con beat ony mon breathin' with the raw uns."

Peter received many congratulations, three of them by telegram. The first was from President Fulda: "Club congratulates you. Banquet on your return. Surprise." This was intriguing. The second was from New York, and read: "We sincerely congratulate you on your success.—Messrs Nail Brothers." His people were rejoicing. The third read: "Accept our heartiest congratulations.—Jack Thompson, Larry Foley, Sydney, Nov. 12." That was fast: obviously the cable through Banjoewangie was working efficiently.

Smith was an awful man, but Peter knew perfectly well where the big money was, and he had Davies employ Smith to exhibit with him during the rest of November. The *Chicago Herald* of December 5, 1889, said that the arrangement with Smith at Royal Aquarium had been profitable, and mentioned the sum of $100 for four rounds. It was good money. One newspaper said that as boxing instructor at California Athletic Club, Peter's salary, more of a retaining fee while he was abroad, was $125 for a month.

They boxed on the central stage of the Aquarium on Thursday, Friday, and Saturday, November 14, 15, and 16. The free list was entirely suspended and to reserve a seat £1 was charged for the first two rows and 10 shillings for the rest of the rows. At 6:00 P.M. the unreserved seats were sold for 2 shillings to anyone ready to wait for the 9:30 start. The seats on stage could "only be gained by payment of a special fee." Davies was clearly expecting to clean up with this second Aquarium season. He introduced the show thus: "Ladies and Gentlemen, Mr. Jem Smith, Champion of England, and Mr. Peter Jackson, the Colored Champion Boxer of the World, will engage in a scientific and friendly set-to." It is not clear how many ladies were in the hall.

"When Smith was introduced as the Champion of England," wrote John Corlett of the *Sporting Times*, "he was received with hisses by a considerable section of the audience, who appeared to think that the pugilistic reputation of the country had suffered in his hands at the Pelican Club." Peter meanwhile "sat in his corner, with his coat thrown carelessly over him." He had the gratification of again seeing Mace in the audience. It was remarked, however, that people would not put their hands deeper into their pockets. "During the minute's rest Jackson's colors were passed round the stalls, but little trade was done." These men were not rich Pelican Club members. For fear of brawling, a squad of police were on duty near the Aquarium, but they were not required.

The Smith-Jackson season was extended to November 25, after which Peter left for Plymouth. Here he boxed Wolf Bendoff on three evenings in St. James' Hall. Bendoff had visited in Australia in 1888, after Peter left, and had fought Jack Burke there. On Tuesday their exhibition was badly received: the fans had been expecting a fight, and complained that they were given "a tired exhibition." Their other Plymouth exhibitions were in the Royal Amphitheater.

On the second-last evening Davies read out from the ring a telegram he had received: "Luke Short, Fort Worth Texas, to Charles E. Davies. For fight between Jackson and Sullivan, to take place here, will guarantee 20,000 dols. Our State license permits." The audience showed a more lively interest on Saturday night, for now they were watching the contender for the heavyweight championship of the world. On November 23, the *London Graphic* said correctly: "It is needless to add that the match is likely to come off— on the Greek Kalends." Finally in Plymouth, on Sunday, December 1, Peter exhibited three rounds with the Royal Navy's boxing champion "Sailor" White, off the ship *Excelsior*, then two rounds with Bendoff and two with Jem Young from East London, the 160-pound champion.

On December 2 he appeared at Brighton in an Alhambra that was packed out. He boxed four rounds with "Scotchy" Gunn the champion of Sussex in a "purely scientific" demonstration. Peter then threw out his usual challenge: win £20 if you could last four rounds with him under Queensberry rules. A local named Woodham accepted, a ring was set up on the stage for the purpose, Peter scarcely threw a punch, just ducked and danced away and wore Woodham out in three rounds.

At the end of the evening the referee handed him a silver cup inscribed:

> *Presented*
> *to*
> *Peter Jackson,*
> *Colored Champion of the World,*
> *at*
> *the Alhambra, Brighton, England,*
> *Monday, December 2,*
> *by*
> *a few admirers in Brighton*
> *of*
> *his sterling qualities*
> *as*
> *a man and a boxer.*

The troupe returned to London and exhibitions at the South London Gymnastic School. The *Chicago Herald* of December 10, 1889, had Davies say about Peter: "Recently, on visiting one of the large London markets, the market men all received him with cheers, and as he passed through sang 'He's a Jolly Good Fellow.'"

But it was not all camaraderie with the working classes. American papers reported: "While Peter demonstrated his superiority over the British boxers, established himself as an attraction, and drew big houses, the 'Parson' hob-nobbed with gentry, nobility, and even royalty itself." Davies, however, was careful not to lose his American manners, insisting: "I said 'Yes, sir' and 'No, sir' to everybody alike and ignored titles. Nobody got 'your Highness' or 'your Lordship' from me."

Peter was less ostentatiously democratic than Davies. Lonsdale recalled: "I myself had the gloves on with Jackson several times, but, of course, our encounters were never anything other than friendly sparring. 'Cover up, my Lord—cover up!' he would say to me, telling me that I was inclined to leave my chin open. '*That's* better, my Lord,' he would murmur when I managed to land one on his glistening body." It was not for nothing that Peter had spent years as a pupil of John DuBois.

In mid–December Lonsdale presented Peter with a stickpin, in the shape of a pair of dumbbells with a fly perched on them, set with diamonds and sapphires. Lonsdale said with glee that it meant: "There are no flies on you," a phrase he had heard in the United States. He left the dumbbells unexplained. Peter graciously stuck the pin into his scarf. Davies for his part was given a pin set with rubies.

Gentry and nobility were largely in evidence during their tour, but royalty raises a question. On January 18 Davies told the *Chronicle*'s representative in New York: "We had a high old time with Albert, Prince of Wales. His Royal Highness was exceptionally friendly with Jackson, and actually made a pump-handle of his arm. He shook hands with him again and again." Just when and where this meeting occurred is uncertain, because Davies did not say and the *Sportsman* did not report it. It must have been when the prince was in England, perhaps at Newmarket race track on September 24. Ned Donnelly, with his Buckingham Palace connections, could have introduced them.

Later on, this story had Peter being presented to the Prince of Wales as Sullivan had been in December 1887. However, it was not the Prince of Wales, Albert or "Bertie," whom Peter met, but his elder son, Prince Albert Victor Christian Edward. He was Queen Victoria's grandson, the 25-year-old second in line to the throne: the Heir Presumptive. He was being groomed to assume the leadership of the Freemasons of England. He was Prince Eddy, who died an early death. From the start of September until the 22nd, Prince Eddy was with the royal family in Scotland, at Balmoral and other great houses. He then rejoined his regiment in England and may have attended the races, limping from falling while deerstalking. Then he went on September 27 first to Denmark, afterwards to Athens for the wedding of his cousins, Constantine, Duke of Sparta, and Princess Sophia of Prussia.[10]

Just why he greeted Peter so warmly, giving him no doubt the Masonic handshake, is uncertain. One explanation is that Peter was a black subject of Prince Eddy's grandfather, the King of Denmark, and so far the only famous one. Besides that, Peter and Prince Eddy were two of the few people in the world who knew the Danish West Indies and Sydney, Prince Eddie having visited them both during his cruise on the *Bacchante* seven years before. They may have exchanged travel reminiscences between their pumpings.[11] Prince Eddy was major royalty in 1889, and Peter and Davies (in spite of his demurs) were truly gratified by his noticing them.

One of the outcomes of the Smith fight had been an offer for Peter to show in Paris for a fortnight in December. The offer was not taken up, but on December 6, Peter, Fitzpatrick, and Davies, accompanied by Robert "Paul Pry" Watson, crossed to Paris for a few days. The Universal Exposition of 1889 had closed on November 6 but the Eiffel Tower was still shiny.

Peter was interviewed by the *Galignani*, a Paris newspaper in English, the equivalent of the *Daily American*, and said: "One of the things they will ask me, when I get back, will be whether I have seen Paris; and I feel that I ought not to let the opportunity slip." But he had been learning French in view of this trip. Davies was disappointed by the coverage given them. "The French press," he recalled for the *Chicago Tribune* in October 1899, "published what purported to be a pictorial reproduction of the contest between Jackson and Smith, but it was the most barbarous attempt at newspaper illustration I ever encountered." It showed Peter fighting Smith down in what looked like a wooden ratting-pit. They exhibited for three nights at a music hall, poorly advertised. "The big black pugilist created a tremendous sensation," Davies said, but the vogue for "la boxe anglaise" had yet to come to France.[12]

Peter told the *Galignani* reporter, who asked about Paddy: "In regard to the championship of Australia, I am the holder of the only championship belt issued with that title. The belt is now in my possession, and neither Slavin nor anybody else can claim that which has never belonged to them."

Little else about his Paris trip appeared in print at the time, but when Peter returned to London in 1892 there was hilarious insider talk about memorable events in 1889: about Davies's "spoofing" a waiter in a restaurant near the Madeleine, that is playing a practical joke on him, about an incident with Paul Pry's luggage and Davies's "brace of jacks," whatever that was; and about "the *cabinet particulaire* on a boulevard," a discreet reference to some spoofing in a *vespasienne*, a public convenience of a kind that these travelers would never have encountered before.

Peter's French was good. In Boston the following January, interviewed by "Uppercut" of the *Boston Daily Globe*, he told how he had asked the the elevator-man in the Hotel Metropole what powered it. "Uppercut" himself was literate in French and reproduced Peter's words: "Qu'est ce que fait monter le lift, le vapeur ou l'eau?" Peter said the elevator man's reply "nearly paralysed me, for he shrugged and said: 'Ni l'un ni l'autre: le vin.'"

Fitzpatrick then exploded with: "Well, say, Pete, what in the name of the Australian kangaroo are you giving us? Spit it out in God's own language so we can all laugh." Obviously the *Boston Globe* did not consider that Australians spoke Cockney. "Why," returned Jackson, brimming over with good nature, "I asked the Frenchman how the elevator was run — by steam or water." "And what did he say?" Fitzpatrick demanded. Peter replied: "He said 'Wine.'" Undoubtedly he had worked hard at his teach-yourself-French manual.[13]

Peter contracted influenza in Paris, and back in London he was sick for a week, missing dates at Leeds and elsewhere and losing money, maybe $3,000, but he considered Paris worth a few misses. A year later back in Australia, on September 3, 1890, Peter told the *Referee* about the trip: "We went to Paris, and it is the most marvellous place on earth. We did not show there, as the Frenchmen are not fond of boxing. We stayed four days, and when we got back you could hardly understand a word Sam Fitzpatrick said, he spoke with such a strong French accent." When Peter returned to Paris five years later, the boxing vogue was intense.

One result of the influenza was that Peter's nose began to bleed. All his snuffling and blowing must have opened a vein weakened by punches. Peter's nosebleeds were reported in the papers as hemorrhages. Tom Allen, the former bare-knuckle champion of America, leapt to the conclusion that Peter had tuberculosis. Allen's was not an outrageous speculation, because nose-bleeding was thought to be a forerunner of tuberculosis and because so many boxers became consumptive. At the end of November, 1891, the *Examiner* reported that "Nonpareil" Dempsey was consumptive, whereupon Professor Whitney, described as "one of the resident physicians of Bellevue Hospital and a man learned in pulmonary complaints," who had treated many boxers, told the *New York Morning Journal*: "There is not the slightest doubt the majority of pugilists that have come under my notice have died from inflammation of the lungs. Blows may create inflammation unknown to the patient, and they are so robust that in most cases they look forward to another course of training to drive away all traces of a trouble that may have become chronic." In 1891 this was the sum of medical wisdom on the subject.

It was popularly believed that tuberculosis had a particular affinity for blacks in the Americas, for Kanakas in Australia, and for Jewish immigrants in New York City, but it is obvious that these people were the most afflicted because they were poor, their work exhausting, their housing substandard, and their food the least nourishing. Tuberculosis could scarcely be attributed to the profession of boxing itself. All that was required was to breathe dried sputum, or to drink milk from diseased cows or eat tubercular meat, to sleep within range of a tubercular patient, or to be in a sunless and badly aired house. Whitney had not considered the life boxers led outside the ring, in the cheap hotels and boarding houses, in the boxing arenas with crowds of onlookers, in the poolrooms and smoky bars with spittoons everywhere. Made of boards, the raised sidewalks in San Francisco were perfect incubatory devices and everybody, not only the chewers of tobacco, spat onto and through them.[14]

Peter's lifestyle was such that he could have caught tuberculosis on any day. Thus Allen's leaping to the conclusion that Peter had tuberculosis was not unwarranted. However, what Peter suffered from in London in 1889 was just epistaxis or nosebleeds. When he had recovered he exhibited with Jem Young at the South London Palace in London Road and at the Paragon Theater of Varieties.

Three weeks later the party were on the move again, crossing to Dublin on Monday morning, December 23, and booking into Morrison's Hotel on Dawson. Fred Gallagher from the *Sport* office acted as cicerone. The *Irish Times* predicted that boxing would flourish again in Ireland after Peter's visit. "The appearance of Jackson," it said, "is certain to arouse a considerable amount of enthusiasm in Ireland, as, not even excepting Sullivan, the West Indian may be regarded as THE PUGILIST OF THE CENTURY."

It was reported by the *Freeman's Journal* that back in Australia Peter had promised that on a certain date, at a certain hour, he would ascend Nelson's Pillar in Sackville Street, indeed that he had bet $1,000 on himself. This monument, erected in 1815, was one of the most conspicuous and most hated objects in Dublin, being described in 1891 in James Dignam's *Dublin Guide* as nothing but a "mode to Englify us." It was some 120 feet high, with a 13-foot statue of Admiral Nelson on top. Although it afforded a grand panorama of the city, in 1889 it was largely the resort of English sailors who sat on Nelson's head. It is hard to guess what rumors raced around that day, but thousands of people turned out to see Peter go up Nelson's Pillar at 1:30 P.M. The *Sportsman*, exaggerating a little, reported a gathering of 20,000. If the crowd expected him to ascend it on the outside like King Kong climbing the Empire State Building, then they were disappointed when Peter entered the doorway, presumably at the appointed time, and climbed the 167 internal steps to the viewing platform like any other human.[15]

The main business of the Irish visit, the sparring exhibitions with Young and Bendoff on Monday night, was successful. The *Sportsman* reported: "Jackson's reception in Dublin yesterday even rivals that accorded to the great John L. Sullivan himself." Leinster Hall, new and grandiose and holding 4,000, was packed. "Among the patrons who came to see the black boxer," said the *Freeman's Journal*, "were all classes and conditions of people. Queen's counsels enough to make a very big bar; Castle officials, members of the medical profession, Crown prosecutors, journalists, members of the Corporation, military men, and a large multitude of the great unwashed." Peter was introduced by the editor of *Sport*, H. Gallaher. He boxed three rounds with Young.

The next evening, Christmas Eve, he made the acquaintance of a boxer who became famous in America. Peter offered 20 guineas to anyone, amateur or professional, who could stand before him for four rounds. Harvey du Cross, the heavyweight champion of Ireland, was not in evidence and the offer was taken up by the 20-year-old Peter Maher, who, though he had had several bouts including one against John Seenan the year before in which he won the Irish middleweight championship, was described by the *Freeman's Journal* as "an amateur" and by the *Sportsman* as no more than "a promising young Irishman." Maher would cross Peter Jackson's path many times during the years ahead. *Sport* called their match "one of the most humiliating spectacles that any Dubliner could well witness," saying: "Maher was altogether out of that 'condition' which would afford him any chance in such a contest at the best of times. He hardly made an effort, and Jackson, judiciously directing his attention to his weakest point, had him internally sick as soon as he desired." Maher stood up for one round, but the referee stopped it in the second. Later, Maher preferred to call this bout: "1889 Exhibition with Peter Jackson." The *Chicago Tribune* of July 30, 1893, would say of Maher that "he is a big, stout Irishman, slow as a man possibly could be and as afraid of a punch as the average woman is of a mouse. He simply missed his vocation." But Maher fought on, until 1913.[16]

Davies had dinner on Christmas Day with his two sisters in Belfast, whom he had not seen for 28 years. On Boxing Day the party visited Blarney Castle, and Peter was held upside down and lowered to kiss the famous stone, thus notionally increasing his eloquence.

The *Freeman's Journal* said: "Jackson has certainly one great point to recommend him, and that is that he is a thorough gentleman, with all the quietness of conscious strength, and all the native nobility of a big man. He talks very little, and that in a most musical whisper, and his conversation seldom savours of 'shop.' His intonation is delightful, his grammar perfect, and his vocabulary apparently voluminous. He is purely an amiable 'nature's gentleman,' and if the 'noble savage' was anything like Jackson the sooner the Caucasian is 'played out' the better." The *Freeman's Journal* was paying compliments. Peter's gentlemanliness, moreover, was not a natural phenomenon but had been carefully constructed over the years.

After a short and hectic visit to Dublin, by December 28 Peter and Young were sparring in the Drill Hall at Bristol, and by New Year's Eve in the Varieties Music Hall in Leeds, where they would have been three weeks before only for Peter's Parisian influenza. Three nights later they were in Hull.

On January 3, 1890, the *Watertown New York Times* printed a syndicated news item from London, which said that "Peter Jackson, the colored Australian pugilist, has sent a despatch to the United States, announcing his acceptance of the challenge of John L. Sullivan to fight for $1,000 a side. He will sail for New York on January 15." This was possibly a misprint for $10,000.

Reporters asked Davies why he missed Paddy fighting Jem Smith in Bruges. He replied testily that he hadn't gone to Belgium because he had been busy managing Peter in Ireland. The bare-knuckle champion of England had fought Paddy in the only way he knew how. The illegal fight was held on a grass tennis court in the private house belonging to Atkinson Grimshaw, a retired Cameron Highlander. Smith arrived with Fleming and with a squad of his Birmingham bully-boys. Paddy, tempting fate, had "Australian Champion" printed on his colors. But then, the *Sporting Clipper* of December 8 had said that the fight was for "The Championship of England and Australia," which if a true report meant Paddy was extraordinarily reckless. After 13 rounds, the outclassed Smith was bundled out of the ring by his cronies and off the premises. In a letter to "a British Columbia paper" reproduced by "Tad's Tid Bits" in the *Niagara Falls Gazette* of May 18, 1921, Paddy remembered Smith with spikes one inch long on his boots. Paddy was then set upon with sticks and knuckle-dusters and half-bricks. After a quarter of an hour Smith returned for the 14th, but Paddy was held by the bully-boys and bashed again. One of the Pelican Club members, Lord Mandeville, pulled out a bowie knife which he happened to have on him and menaced the thugs, while another member drew a pistol. Paddy himself had two guns in his overcoat pockets hanging on a cherry tree outside the ring, but could not reach them. The scared referee, saying to Paddy: "I do not want to stay here to see you killed," nor himself either, declared a draw.

The Bruges affair caused a great scandal, and almost undid the work the Pelican Club had been doing to make boxing respectable. In the event, the Pelican Club reprimanded Fleming and stood him down for a time. It expressed its disapproval of Smith. He was the last bare-knuckle champion, because the Bruges affair sounded the death-knell of bare-fisted pugilism.

Thereafter Smith was treated like a pariah, and found his acquaintance shrunk to "a few of the bullies who still condescend to drink with him at obscene doggeries," as the London correspondent of the *Chicago Herald* put it. But Smith claimed truly enough that the match was a draw, so that Paddy had not won and he had not lost, whatever moralists might say. Therefore he continued to style himself "Champion of England" at least as late as 1900. Some thought him shameless, but this was a dubious area because Mace had felt able to still sign himself "Champion of the World" in 1897.

The short-lived *Sporting Review*, in its final issue on December 21, 1889, contained a boxed notice which read thus :

> *Sacred to the Memory of*
> BRITISH FAIR PLAY,
> which expired at
> BRUGES
> on
> MONDAY LAST,
> after a long and honourable career.
> R. I. P.

Peter for his part took the Bruges disgrace as the subject for some preaching in Boston.[17] "A boxer can be a gentleman," he said,

> and there is no reason why he should not be as courteous and kind as if he were engaged in some other occupation. I don't like the word "fighter," and I am opposed to bare knuckle and skin-glove encounters. Contests governed by the rules of the London prize ring are growing less. For that I am thankful, and all who love fair play and clean sport should feel glad that turf fighting in the old style is staggering around on its last legs. The late mill [fist fight] between Slavin and Smith has almost killed it in London, and Sullivan's declaration against it in this country ought to wipe mills with the "raws" completely out. I contend that contests under the Queensberry rules, when protected by reputable organizations such as the California Athletic Club and the new Union Athletic Association of Boston, are livelier, more interesting, and the work accomplished in one round could not be duplicated in an hour under the old rules.
>
> And here is another thing I would like to say, and that is that boxers of today should act in a way to command the respect of the public. Generations will come and generations will follow the thousands gone before, and there will be boxers. The sport is cleaner today than it ever was. The Greek cestus has seen its day, and has taken the course said to have been taken by the song-celebrated McGinty. The bare fist as a weapon in competitions for lucre is losing prestige and will soon be no more, and as the sport grows whiter under repeated washings, those who engage in it should endeavor to elevate themselves.

Down Went McGinty was a popular song in which McGinty fell to the bottom of walls, and of holes, of the sea.

The Blarney Stone had worked its magic, it seems. With this kind of polished speech, its impeccable propositions and its quotable quotes, it is no surprise that Peter had become one of the darlings of the new, "progressive" sports journalism. Peter himself had misgivings about this role. On May 23, 1891, immediately after the Corbett fight, he told a reporter from the *Examiner*, the paper always favorable to him, "I don't want to be interviewed and I won't be. I have tried to avoid interviews, but on several occasions have forgotten myself and talked too much." In 1891 the first press agents and the first minders for celebrities were just appearing.[18]

The travelers' English sojourn was drawing to its end. On December 29 Peter was said to be sailing for New York on January 15, next that he would be leaving England on January 20 and spending two months in the eastern United States, then beginning five months of training for his fight with Sullivan for $1,000, which on January 3 he had confirmed. The

Graphic, which had announced Peter as a "cullered pusson" back in July, and thereafter scarcely mentioned him, reported on January 18 that plans for a swimming race against "a well-known journalist," perhaps Robert Watson, had been abandoned.

Davies left Liverpool for America on the *Britannic*. He said in a last interview that Peter would fight Sullivan in May at the earliest, probably in June. In San Francisco, he said, a fair fight was assured. After seeing all Sullivan's fights except the one with Charley Mitchell, he could not predict the winner: "John is a great man, and so is Jackson, that's all I can say." The *Chronicle* had reported Sullivan as saying: "I will meet Jackson at the California Athletic Club with gloves, providing that organization will make it an object. If the club fails to put up a suitable purse then I shall quit the business anyhow." It was about "making it an object" that Sullivan and Fulda were telegraphing back and forth. Davies arrived in New York on January 19, 1890.

Peter was given his London farewell banquet on Wednesday, January 15. It had to be transferred from the Colosseum Hotel where Peter was staying and held at the Albert Academy in Tottenham Court Road. Paddy (called the Champion of Australia by the *Sportsman*) was there with his manager Jack Lewis, Ambrose Preece came from the Pelican Club, Jack Fallows and Tom Fallows were there, and a trio came from Ware: Messrs. Sharp, Tidy and Hammond. These were Peter's buddies rather than his patrons.

Peter was presented with an oil painting and "a handsome gold signet ring, suitably engraved." The chairman, Arthur Bettinson of the National Sporting Club and the Belsize Amateur Boxing Club, toasted him. He said many nice things about Peter, and hoped Peter would not judge the English by the scandal at Bruges.

The *Sportsman* described Peter's response:

> During his stay in England he had been extremely successful, owing principally to the many friends he had found in the British Isles. They said, "Nothing succeeds like success," but he believed that if he had not had the good luck that he had, he thought so much of British fair play that he was certain he would have found quite as many friends. He had been one of the most fortunate men in the world, and since the time that he first landed in California a lucky star had been with him. He never thought at that time he would have traveled over 16,000 miles to receive such a welcome as he had, and especially the gathering there that night. He could not possibly express his feelings for the kind treatment he had received from all classes of Englishmen. He did not judge them by what had occurred lately at Bruges, because 20 blackguards could not speak for 20 million Englishmen. He was an English subject, bred, born, and brought up as such. The ring they had given him he would prize for life. He was going to fight a man that as yet had never been defeated. Of course he didn't know whether he would win, but he would try with all his might. If he went down he would shake hands with and say, "You are the better man." If he won he would sooner be the victor than be a king. He thanked all Englishmen a million times over.

Peter also said he and Paddy "knew each other as well as any two men living, and appreciated each other as much." He was heartily cheered.

Fitzpatrick in turn was given "a handsome Malacca walking-stick, beautifully mounted," and Bettinson said that "as a trainer he had never met a more genial and nicer young fellow." Fitzpatrick advised everybody that when the Sullivan fight took place they should bet on Peter.

In the course of responding to the toast of "The Visitors," Paddy said about his relationship with Peter that "of course they were antagonists, but still they were the very best of friends." He said he knew that what happened in Bruges did not make the English people guilty. Naughton responded to the toast of "The Press." Musical items and comic turns followed. Ambrose Preece rendered "Anchored" and "All Hail, Australia," while Fred Cash not only sang "He Won't Be Happy," but extemporized a song about Peter and Paddy. Also, "a couple of capital songs" were sung by Peter himself, to Paddy's piano accompaniment. Peter sang an "Irish" ditty "I Owe Ten Dollars To O'Grady," and Paul Dresser's song, "Mother Told Me So," a choice which must have struck as odd anybody listening closely to its lyrics. These ran:

> *There's a little maxim that was told to me by mother dear,*
> *When in childhood I was seated on her knee.*
> *She told me that a rolling stone would gather little moss.*
> *Many lessons of advice she gave to me.*
> *She told me that the Father watched o'er me from above,*
> *She bade me pray to him with head bowed low,*
> *She said if I'd take her advice, some day I'd be with him.*
> *I believe it, for my mother told me so.*
>
> *She told me never turn my back on sorrow or distress,*
> *But give whate'er I could to help the poor.*
> *You'll never know what poverty is, lad,*
> *Until you find the wolf of hunger knocking at your door.*
> *So try and love your neighbor as you always love yourself,*
> *Your deeds will make you known wheree'er you go.*
> *A man who's honest needs no monument when he is gone.*
> *I believe it, for my mother told me so.*
>
> *Chorus:*
> *She told me that in manhood temptations I would meet,*
> *And that very few true friends in life I'd know.*
> *She also said the world was full of falsehood and deceit,*
> *I believe it, for my mother told me so.*[19]

The evening at the Albert Academy ended with Frank and Pete engaged in deep talk over a bottle of champagne. A fortnight later, in St. John the Evangelist Church (Episcopalian) on Charlotte at Fitzroy Square, Paddy married Edith Slater from the Nayland Rock Hotel at Margate, and honeymooned in Monte Carlo.

After the banquet Peter and Fitzpatrick threw an all-night party back at their hotel, the Colosseum. At 7:15 A.M. they were farewelled at Euston by the few people left standing, including Bettinson and Frank Tarbeaux, an old American friend of Davies' and a shady character revealed in his 1930 *Autobiography of Frank Tarbeaux*. "Just as the train was steaming out of the station, Mr. Tarbeaux went to shake hands with Jackson, and amidst the laughter of the crowd he was pulled into the reserved compartment by the dusky warrior, and he, perforce, had to make the journey to Liverpool, where the party arrived about noon." Tarbeaux had been submitted to a variant of Peter's octopus joke.

CHAPTER 5

Sea to Shining Sea, 1890

The *Adriatic* sailed that evening, with Peter, Fitzpatrick, Naughton and the livestock. The one bulldog and the single jaybird of October had multiplied into Scotch terriers and bull-pups and cages of singing birds that were all going to America.

In Queenstown on January 17 they went off the ship and into town. Peter, who had traces of his influenza, bought himself some sprigs of shamrock and a blackthorn walking stick. This was in addition to the half-dozen gold-headed canes presented to him by admirers, who had also given him a signet ring and another tie pin. Through a reporter he expressed his gratitude to all, but especially to Lonsdale.

He was informed that Sullivan was now asking not $1,000 to fight him, not even $10,000. He had sent Fulda a telegram that said: "White men 10,000 dol. apiece; niggers double price." That was Fulda's surprise. Fulda was highly amused by Sullivan's message and in 1917 he quoted it to show Sullivan did not draw the color line on Peter. Fulda had Sullivan's telegram framed and hung up on the club's wall. Peter told the reporter in Queenstown: "To be candid with you, if I did not think that I was going to obtain a victory over Sullivan I would not meet him. I always fight to win."

On January 26 the *Adriatic* reached New York, and there Peter was presented by a testimonial signed by 29 fellow passengers. "We the undersigned, cabin passengers per steamship Adriatic from Liverpool to New York," it read, "desire, at the termination of the trip, to convey to you our thorough appreciation of your modest, gentlemanly deportment while crossing the Atlantic in our company. We beg to assure you of our earnest wishes for your future success in your profession, and we have every confidence that your uniform courtesy and modest bearing will be at all times a passport for you into the society of gentlemen." Peter gave a copy of this to the *National Police Gazette*, so he could not have detected anything patronizing in it.

The *Chicago Tribune* on January 27 quoted a letter from Davies which said that Peter and he would be dividing $40,000. Fallon told the *Brooklyn Eagle* upon his return to the States that Peter had made $10,000 out of his English tour, Fitzpatrick $900, Naughton $750, and that he himself took $1,800 and a diamond ring worth $500 (given by Davies to Christine Fallon). Somebody who claimed to have seen Davies's accounts book said that the takings were just over $30,000 and the expenses $10,000, explaining that "the expenses were heavy because Davies had to do the 'elegant' for numbers of the nobility who patronized the dusky Australian." Davies himself reckoned takings of $32,000 and expenses of $15,000. In May 1890 the *Chicago Tribune* estimated Peter's own earnings from the tour at $10,000. Whatever the final figures, it was commonly held that "Charles E. Davies and his great boxer are coining money."

On March 22, 1890, the *National Police Gazette* published a large engraving of Peter, very stylish in a topcoat with a wide astrakhan collar, holding his ivory-headed cane in his right hand and a soft hat in his left. His hair was longer. He sported a thick mustache and wore in his cravat what looked very much like a fly and dumbbell stickpin. The photograph from which the artist made the engraving was taken in New York by Benjamin Falk in February. Peter appeared supremely self-possessed, masterful. He could well anticipate that his victories in Britain, victories of several kinds, would be followed by more victories back in America, and indeed he prospered for the next three years.

Peter stepped off the *Adriatic* in New York on January 27, 1890. Davies had booked his star to show that very afternoon, so with the matinee performance on January 27 Peter began a season at Hyde & Behman's in Brooklyn, appearing with Jack Ashton from Providence, R.I. On the same bill were the "Irish" duo of Sheadon and Flynn, famous for their "McGinty" songs. Recently licked by Godfrey, Ashton had been Sullivan's sparring partner since November 1889. Ashton's career was closely associated with Sullivan's, especially on the stage. He was in the cast of Sullivan's stage vehicle, *Honest Hearts and Willing Hands*, when he died aged 29 from a poisoned arm on January 6, 1893. The crowds in Brooklyn were "tremendous" until February 1, and so they were at Harry Miner's Eighth Ave. Theater in the Bowery from February 3 to 8. When they sparred at Cronheim's in Hoboken, "thousands were turned away daily and nightly," Naughton told the *Referee*. Cronheim's had 2,000 seats.

The party moved to Boston, where Jackson and Ashton exhibited on January 29. Peter had been getting $2,000 a week, doled out by Davies, but now he was big time. His one appearance in Boston netted $800. That night was important. An attempt was made to have the exhibition banned, even though neither the Union Athletic Association nor the Boston authorities made any objection. It was Sullivan's friends, according to Naughton, who wanted the exhibition prohibited. It is not clear why, unless it was that Sullivan's people thought that Ashton had contractual obligations.

That evening Sullivan came to the Boston Music Hall along with 2,500 others, and sat up on the stage. Unkind people suggested that Ashton was instructed to put Peter through his paces so that Sullivan could study the black contender. Peter had never set eyes on Sullivan, and although he was on the stage, Peter fought unaware of him. "I did not see him," he told the *San Francisco Chronicle*'s Boston correspondent. "They told me he was on the stage two or three yards from me, but I did not see him."

The *Chicago Tribune*, reproducing an article dated Boston, March 25, 1889, quoted Sullivan as saying, "Now that I have settled that Mississippi trouble I want to attend to Jackson's claim to the championship. I am anxious to have one more battle before I retire from the ring, and of course Jackson is the only man to be thought of just now." He wanted the 20 grand because such funds as he had accumulated had vanished in legal costs. He said he would fight with gloves because he was sick of illegalities.

The *Cincinnati Enquirer* published a notice from New York on March 31: "That Sullivan does not underrate Jackson's pugilistic prowess, I have the best reasons in the world of knowing," wrote the commentator. "The 'big fellow' saw Jackson spar with his old side-partner, Jack Ashton, in Boston and on that occasion I am satisfied Ashton did all in his power to put Peter to his trumps and expose his style of fighting for Sully's benefit. The result of that go satisfied Sullivan thoroughly that Peter was remarkably quick and clever, but that he could defeat him. In a conversation I had with him a week or two after this bout, Sullivan told me that Jackson had a wonderful reach. Said he, 'in this respect he has an advantage over any fighter I know of, but he don't know how to make the best use of it.' He then stood up and illustrated Peter's style of attack and hitting perfectly."

But Sullivan's confidence leaked away with the weeks. On January 17 the *Daily Alta California* reported Sullivan in a telegram to Fulda now demanding $25,000 for any contest. The *St. Louis Post-Dispatch* of May 19, 1890, published an article sent from San Francisco headed "Does He Fear Jackson?" which reported that Sullivan was having second thoughts about fighting Peter. "But lately," said the article, "the big fellow has seen Jackson spar, and while he has announced to newspaper reporters that he could whip Peter easily, John knows and has acknowledged to his intimates that Jackson is a hard nut for anyone to crack."

After that important night in Boston, they went to various places, playing Miner's Theater in the Bowery from February 10 until the 15th. In Washington, D.C., they played Kernan's New Washington Theater from February 17, 1890. The *Washington Bee,* the local black paper, advertised them as the All-American Star Specialty Company, and specified ladies' matinees on Tuesday, Thursday and Saturday, including Washington's birthday. An appeal to women to attend Davies' shows was rare, and Washington ladies must have hinted to the *Bee* that they wanted to inspect the Great Black Hope for themselves, with a view to their daughters' prospects.

On February 20, 1890, Peter fought "Soldier" James Walker, Georgetown blacksmith and heavyweight, though tall and thinnish in build. They appeared at Kernan's before 3,000 people, the gallery "jammed with the colored brothers of the big pugilist, who were wildly impatient for his appearance." Thousands more were turned away. Eight-ounce gloves were used. Jackson sent a hard left into Walker's stomach and followed it with a right-hander that brought Walker to his knees. He quit. The bout had lasted 40 seconds. To placate the riotous crowd, Jackson and Ashton sparred. Walker was whipped by Frank Childs in January 1893, five days before Peter exhibited with Childs.

Also in Washington, on February 21 he fought "Guy the Gypsy," who wanted the $100 offered for standing up for four rounds. Because he is otherwise unknown to history, Guy may have been like Connie McVey from Philadelphia, who was employed to travel around and challenge J.J. Corbett using a different alias in every part of the country.[1] Guy was said to hail from Maryland, and was called "Herculean," being 6 feet and 1½ inches tall and weighing 247 pounds. When time was called, Guy went for Jackson, rushing him all round the stage and making him so mad that in the second round Jackson winded him then used a swinging right-hander to knock him to the floor. The contest was all over in 4 minutes and 26 seconds, but its legacy endured. On August 4, 1890, the *Rocky Mountain News* of Denver reported Davies saying that Peter's left hand was in bad shape at the Lambert fight because of Guy the Gypsy.

While in Washington they did the tourist sights, including the White House of President Harrison and the Capitol with the Senate Chambers. Peter was made the guest of the local Acanthus Club, the nationwide black association.

From Washington they proceeded to Baltimore, where he sparred with Ashton. Here there was a riot on February 26: "the negro population has gone wild over him," reported the *Daily Alta California*, "and their demonstrations at his exhibitions have been so offensive that the white toughs became exasperated." While Peter was dressing the mixed crowd outside attacked each other and when he appeared rotten eggs were thrown at him. "His colored admirers formed a wall, however, and protected him." This may have been the worst scene in Peter's journeying.

Arriving by train in Jersey City, they went at once to Brooklyn for a benefit for Fallon on March 4, in the Palace Bicycle Rink on Grand. It had been announced that Peter was to fight four rounds with "Professor" Ed Donnelly, a Brooklyn heavyweight, but in the event he exhibited with Fallon. This became two rounds of extreme aggression from Fallon, with Peter retaliating by punching for real, the crowd hissing the local boy Fallon until the police threw him out of his own benefit. George Dixon, the black featherweight, fresh from his championship fight in Boston with Cal McCarthy, was introduced to the crowd. He became a friend of Peter's.

They set out the next morning towards San Francisco. On March 5 at Troy in upstate New York, Jackson met the 240-pound Canadian Gustave Esdras ("Gus") Lambert in a another encounter that became a debacle. Lambert, born in Montreal in 1850, was a wrestler and strongman rather than a boxer and should never have been allowed in the ring with Jackson. He had been the first athlete in Canada with a traveling troupe of boxers, wrestlers and acrobats. Every night during their 1886 tour Lambert had offered $25 to any man wrestling him for 15 minutes. According to the *Examiner* of December 24, 1888, he had knocked out Jack Davis, another of Mace's protégés, had licked Dominick McCaffrey in 1883, and had somehow won the Canadian heavyweight championship from Jim Fell.[2] It is astonishing that he would stand up with Jackson for $100 like any tyro. Davies said it was because he needed cash.

The fight was held in Troy's Bicycle Hall, which doubled as a skating rink. In the first round, Jackson was careful and wary, while Lambert had mischief in his eye. After landing a right and a left, he received a damaging blow from Jackson's left on the head, and another on the ear. Lambert's blood got up and he grabbed Jackson round the waist and held him amid great uproar until they were separated.

In the second round, after a brisk exchange of blows, Lambert again clinched with Jackson, hugging him and not to be pried off. His sinewy arms, according to the report Naughton sent the *Referee*, were twined around Jackson's loins and shoulders, octopus-fashion.

In the third round, when Jackson saw that Lambert persisted in hugging him, he tried to fight him away, but Lambert picked Jackson up and ran across the platform with him and would have thrown him over the ropes if Ashton had not grabbed at him. They punched in a corner, and one blow by Lambert staggered Jackson.

In the fourth round, Lambert kept running round the ring eluding Jackson, who, unable to knock Lambert down by the end of the fight, had to pay over the cash.

The referee for this match had been a Troy saloon-keeper, one Killoran, insisted on by Lambert, who also had insisted on 8-ounce gloves and a 28-foot ring. The referee proved to be Lambert's backer and personal friend, and would not grant that Lambert was fouling. He merely smiled at Ashton's and Fitzpatrick's remonstrances.

At the end, pandemonium broke out. Lambert, who had won the $100, was carried round on the shoulders of his fans. Jackson refused to shake hands, saying: "No, I won't shake hands with a cur. If you had stood off and fought for one minute there would have been some satisfaction in meeting you; but you're a coward at heart, and you know it." The crowd hissed Jackson. A page illustrating incidents in the match was published in the *National Police Gazette* on March 22. Davies vowed to be more vigilant in checking Peter's opponents out. Fighting Peter Maher at the Pelican Club in London in 1891, Lambert lasted not two minutes.

After Troy, it was to be westward. On Friday and Saturday, March 7 and 8, they played to big houses in Cleveland. On Monday, March 10, in Detroit the crowd numbered 3,000. Then it was Indianapolis on March 17, then through Ohio to Dayton, Springfield and Columbus, doing "roaring business everywhere," according to Naughton, and arriving in Chicago on Monday morning March 24. The formula was always the same: sparring exhibitions, and short bouts with local pugs or would-be pugs. People just wanted to see Peter in action, as modern spectators have enjoyed seeing Teofilo Stevenson moving, and what he did in detail on stage didn't matter. The galleries were always packed and excited.

It surfaced in encounters with Lambert and Lynch, but nobody can doubt that Peter was battling prejudice every day of his life. He was happy when he could escape from white America into the company of other intelligent blacks.

After his engagement in Boston, when Sullivan checked him out, the party returned to New York, and there on Thursday, January 30, Peter was feted at its 1788 Third Avenue clubhouse by the Harlem Unique Club, the Gotham equivalent of the black club he belonged to in San Francisco.

Only 20 of the Unique Club's 140 members, nevertheless "leading colored men of the Empire City," attended the dinner. Apparently many members had objected to feting a boxer, while others declined because the function started at 1:00 A.M., after the performance at Hyde and Behman's. There were 10 courses on Sèvres china and with silver service. Davies, Naughton and Fitzpatrick were there, together with three journalists, Wilkinson of the Chicago *Daily News*, Hackett of the *New York World*, and W.E. Harding of the *Police Gazette*. John B. Nail was present. When the meal ended and choice brands of cigars were handed around, the master of ceremonies, Aaron Thompson, called on the president of the club, Howard A. Jones, to make a welcoming speech and Vice-President Shiloh to present Peter with a basket of flowers. According to the *New York Age*, which covered the event, Peter replied with thanks, saying: "He had been banqueted most royally in Europe and elsewhere, but he derived more genuine pleasure from this entertainment than any which he had ever before attended." Then he said: "I have been successful in my profession beyond my fondest hopes, and I shall try to conduct myself as a gentleman. I do not desire any title which is not my right. I believe in a fair field and no favor — the California Athletic Club's motto. I have never said that I could best any pugilist. If I do meet Mr. Sullivan I will do my best to win. I thank you, gentlemen."

Davies and others made speeches, and then Charles A. Cruso closed the night, or rather hailed Friday's dawn, with one of his stump speeches "which was especially enjoyed by Messrs. Jackson and Naughton, who were well acquainted with the 'Judge' while he was in Australia," touring with the Georgia Minstrels in 1879. Maybe Cruso made some Sydney-versus-Melbourne quips!

Peter was happy to spend time with other blacks, even though his life required him to be in the company of whites so often, even though whites said repeatedly that he was a white man in all but his color. In January 1890 he remarked about George Dixon to the *London Sportsman*: "He is of the colored class like myself." Unfortunately the records of his black connections have largely vanished. We catch only glimpses in the extant black papers of Peter staying in blacks' houses, Peter being entertained and feted by blacks, Peter writing to blacks.

The loss of so much of the black newspapers makes it difficult to gauge exactly the stature of Peter among his peers, but it was extraordinarily high.[3] Even as early as 1889 hardly a black paper felt obliged to explain to its readers who Peter was. It is obvious that the blacks were not dependent on the black press for their information about him. The *Indianapolis Freeman*, however, thought it worthwhile in July 1892 to reproduce an article from England which provided a "Synopsis of the Life and Pugilistic Career of this Famous Afro-American."

In San Francisco he had a strong following. "When McAuliffe and Jackson fought, Ireland and Africa were largely represented and trouble was anticipated," said the *Chronicle* on December 29. "Whenever the lookout announced anything favorable to McAuliffe the Irish contingent cheered wildly. When an announcement favorable to Jackson was made the colored men struck up plantation melodies and danced jigs, the Hibernians patting time for the dusky shufflers. Jackson's victory was celebrated with much music and hilarity. If anybody comes here and defeats Jackson the colored population will meet with financial disaster." They were betting all their cash on Peter now. As for the primitive mosh pit, this must have been duplicated in many places.

Wherever he appeared, the cheaper seats were fully occupied by blacks. Some enterprising manufacturer put out yellow clip-on tin tags for Peter's fans to wear in their lapels, about the size of a quarter and bearing the words "Peter Jackson" framing a crude silhouette of him hitting an opponent. The man being punched could have been Godfrey, but the tag was for wearing over and over again.[4] In every town, troops of black boys ran behind his carriage cheering. In Portland, Oregon, it was remarked that numerous young black women were in the audience, too, and probably their sisters were in other places. They were bridling and ogling him because Peter was a great catch. Sometimes it was necessary to protect Peter from the crush of his admirers.

In every city blacks were told to go see Peter acting in *Uncle Tom's Cabin*. Along with Misto' George Godfrey and Misto' George Dixon, Misto' Peter Jackson was one of the greatest heroes of the plebs, said the *Chronicle*. The bands regularly played "See the Conquering Hero Comes," and after 1896 "All Coons Look Alike to Me." Said the *Freeman* on June 10, 1893: "The greatest fighter of them all, and the only gentleman, sailed across the blue last week. Before his departure, his Chicago admirers, whose names are legion, banqueted him." In the cities he visited, private parties and at-homes were given in his honor. In Washington, D.C., in February 1890, for example, as reported by the *Washington Bee*: "Mr. Peter Jackson, the Champion colored pugilist, was entertained by Mr. and Mrs. Griffin Reed last week, at their residence 1920 11 st. n.w. Among the invited guests were Messrs. Bennett, Harris, Johnson, of Philadelphia, Rodges, McKenley, and Fitzpatrick." And doubtless at many other such gatherings Sam Fitzpatrick was the token white.

Many of Peter's black friends were reported at the "Sailor" Brown fight in Chicago. "After he had taken his seat in his corner, a small colored man stepped upon the stage and presented him with a silver-headed umbrella and a large bouquet of flowers, a present from his colored admirers." In Washington, at the "Soldier" Walker fight, "the galleries were jammed with the colored brothers of the big pugilist, who were wildly impatient for his appearance," according to the *Evening Star*. At Denver in May 1890 he "was enthusiastically received by the large number of colored men who were present."

After his triumph in St. Louis, Peter and his team boarded the Ohio & Mississippi train for Louisville and Cincinnati. Their stand in Louisville, Kentucky, marks the only time that Peter ever fought in the South. Louisville in 1890 was the seventh largest black city in the United States. Its population was about 160,000 of whom about 20,000 were black. There were fans galore to fill the Buckingham Theater during their stay. The whites all put up at the Louisville Hotel, while Peter stayed at 1216 West Madison in the home of William Coats, a black saloon keeper.

"When Peter Jackson stepped onto the stage there was uproarious applause," said the *Louisville Courier Journal* on March 27, "especially from the gallery, where the colored men were packed like sardines." Peter wore red and white for Denmark and Shango. The *Courier Journal* said "his torso was muscled like a giant's and as richly brown as chocolate." He sparred with Ashton as usual, but they were hissed because, the paper suggested, "the modern public are more bloodthirsty than old Romans."

The next night, Thursday, March 27, Peter boxed to win or to pay $100 to the man who could stand up four rounds with him. In Louisville they had been much exercised to find Peter an opponent, and had settled on Dick Keating, an experienced fighter who traveled all the way from Lafayette, Indiana. Mike McCarty, a local saloon keeper who had beaten Keating, put his name down. Ed G. Green, a local black slugger, also wanted a go. The fight with Keating was brief. Peter knocked him out in 90 seconds.

About the time Peter and Keating were in the ring, Louisville was hit by a tornado that cut a swath through the city, killing more than 100 people. It demolished some blocks on Madison where he was staying, and it hit the Louisville Hotel, killing six women in the laundry.

When Peter reached Cincinnati, 100 miles away, he was two days late, arriving on Tuesday, April 1, by the O. & M. just after midnight, when he should have got there on Sunday morning. On Monday evening 2,000 spectators had turned up at the People's Theater for what was advertised as "Bennett Bros' Big Show and Peter Jackson," and had left disappointed. When asked why, Peter said nothing about the tornado. "There was a misunderstanding about Sunday," he told the *Cincinnati Times-Star*. "I was not aware that I was to appear on Sunday and consequently made no effort to start until Monday." It was almost as if he had been traumatized by the Louisville tornado, and as if this replay of the destruction of Frederiksted by the hurricane of 1867 had been pushed down into his unconscious. The pressmen concluded that he had been dead drunk for three days or shacked up with somebody, been "on a big hurrah," as the *Commercial Gazette* put it. He was asked point-blank if he hadn't been drinking in Louisville, because the Louisville papers had printed tales about his flying high, being "on a drunk" and the like. Peter, backed up by Naughton, unwisely called such tales typical newspaper misrepresentations. The reporters were offended by this and kept him under surveillance.

He went straight from being grilled by the pressman to the People's Theater at 13th and Vine for his first matinee in Cincinnati. The place was packed to the walls. The police would not allow him to box nor even to spar with Ashton, so the two punched the ball. The spectators were suitably impressed, but because it couldn't find anything to say the *Cincinnati Commercial Gazette* was obliged to report on his attire, especially his singlet. "When he appeared on stage last night he was dressed in white tights and a sleeveless undershirt, which showed to good advantage his muscular arms and shoulders." The *Cincinnati Enquirer* filled up by describing Peter's ball-punching: When he hit the ball a very savage punch, a boy in the gallery yelled: 'That ain't John L. before you, Peter.' He broke into a guffaw. 'No, I know it,' said Peter in a low tone of voice. 'John L. Sullivan would make a better fight than this ball.'"

Between the matinee and evening shows he was interviewed at Walnut House, the hotel where he was staying. The *Cincinnati Evening Post* noted that the black man was dressed in light trousers, flowered blue vest and dark cassimere coat, and that "on the bureau, by the side of his dressing case, lay a copy of the popular novel, *Thou Shalt Not.*" He was civil to the reporter.

At the People's Theater on Saturday, April 5, Peter dared Davies for $75 to don full boxing gear, to put on the gloves, and punch the ball on stage. The 1,900 spectators were highly amused by his hitting the ball less often than it hit him. Davies donated his winnings to the victims of the tornado, then headed off to Chicago.

Afterwards, Peter made a night of bar-crawling through resorts in downtown Cincinnati and in "Over The Rhine," that is, in the German part of town where beer flowed plentifully. It is unclear what precisely these "resorts" were, probably bars frequented by tight men and loose women, but "it was 2 A.M. before the colored champion got through, and then he went home on the invitation of a policeman, who was trying to settle a quarrel in the party growing out of the charge that one of the gang had robbed another of $151." The *Commercial Gazette* said on Monday that "his stay in this city was marked by one continual debauch, as there was hardly a night that he did not pass the time till the early morning hours in cracking bottles of champagne with his numerous admiring friends." It said that on Friday night between midnight and 7 A.M., in a saloon on Vine, Peter and an unstated number of friends worked their way through 42 bottles of champagne, and that Peter was so merry he entertained the crowd with songs. He knew Irish-American comic songs like "Down Went McGinty" and "I Owe Ten Dollars To O'Grady." In fact, in Brooklyn two months before, when he played on the same bill as Sheadon and Flynn who wrote the early "McGinty" songs, he had plausibly not only polished his stage-Irish accent with them but acquired some appropriate stage business. He was certainly letting off steam.[5] On April 6, the *Cincinnati Commercial Gazette*, which had a column headed "Our Colored Citizens," said Peter left on an O. & M. train for St. Louis.

On the same day, Davies in Chicago made an enigmatic statement to journalists who asked when Peter and Sullivan would be fighting. He said: "We are not particularly anxious for a match of that kind. You want a few plain truths. I am making bread and butter out of Peter Jackson, and, white or black, no athlete can ever come to me and say I have not been faithful to his interests." Davies said Sullivan was quite out of condition and said if Corbett and he were matched then Corbett would quite likely beat him. So that thereafter Davies and Peter would no longer be interested in Sullivan.

Davies then announced that Peter had hurt his right hand while sparring Guy the Gypsy, so they would be going to Mount Clemens for a fortnight's rest. There had been no mention of his right hand's being hurt when he fought Lambert, nor had a sore right hand hindered his ball-punching in Cincinnati. Davies may have been telling a white lie; indeed, the *Rocky Mountain News* reported it as his left hand.

When Peter reached St. Louis, he intended to give an exhibition with Ashton, Tom Kelly to be master of ceremonies, but the vigilant police banned it. Instead they punched a ball suspended from a stake at Brotherhood Park. As a sporting event, the visit to St. Louis was small beer, but the visit was the peak of his success in African American society.

For days beforehand, the *St. Louis Post-Dispatch* reported: "The colored population is worked up over the coming of Peter Jackson." Perhaps 500 blacks gathered at the train depot to give him a wild welcome. After an official welcome, Henry Bridgewater, billiardist, the "well-known colored sport," took Peter to his house on Glasgow Avenue, while the rest of the party, Ashton, Naughton and Fitzpatrick, checked into the Southern Hotel. Shakespiere, "the colored sport from Chicago," described as an old friend of Peter's, was in town and joined the group.

Peter was given a lunchtime reception in the Union Bethel Hall at Twelfth and Pine, with prominent blacks present, gentlemen variously reported as numbering 75 and 200. Ashton also attended. Bridgewater acted as MC. The address of welcome was given by the most famous black to come out of St. Louis, and one of the best-known black men in the United States.

This was James Milton Turner, a prominent educator whom President Grant appointed Minister Resident and Consul General to Liberia, and who served there from 1871 to 1878 under Grant and President Hayes. Later he turned to actively promoting black Freemasonry. It cannot be pretended that everywhere Peter was greeted by such eminent blacks, but it appears that wherever he went the locals rolled out their best red carpet. But still, apart from Frederick Douglass himself, scarcely a black in America had a higher profile than Turner. That he should have been asked to officiate at a banquet for a boxer, and that he should have agreed to do so, is a measure of how highly Peter was regarded. Peter "responded in his usual modest manner" to Turner's address.[6]

The *Referee* suggested the following year that he himself should emulate Douglass and lead his people. It even suggested that he should make his home in the South! But when Peter spoke of retiring, it was to Australia, or to England, never to Dixie. In any case, Peter was staying at good white hotels in the years when Frederick Douglass, if traveling by train, was obliged to sit in the caboose.

No American commentator ever made the same suggestion, though when interviewed on March 31, 1893, in the Knutsford Hotel in Salt Lake City, Peter was asked by the *Tribune* reporter: "Are you the idol of the colored people much as Sullivan was the idol of the Irish?" Peter replied at once, "Idol of the colored people? No! Why should I be the idol of the colored people? I never go with them, seldom meet them. They do nothing for me except go out on the street and hollow [*sic*] or yell — and I'm not after that." The reporter pressed on: "But don't the colored people rally round you, look upon you as a prominent representative, and back you as far as they can?" Rejecting any imputation of demagoguery, Peter said firmly: "No! Assuredly not!"

Turner may have inspired Peter to this limited extent, however, that some months later, back in Australia, Peter was initiated into Freemasonry.

The blacks were not certain of what attitude to assume in regard to Peter. This was before W.E.B. Du Bois had visited Germany, and two decades before the founding of the National Association for the Advancement of Colored People, of which John Nail became the first life member. Booker T. Washington had not yet delivered the "Atlanta Address." Pastors and ministers and teachers were taking black leadership positions. Douglass had encouraged his slave pupils to behave like intellectual, moral, and accountable beings rather than spending the sabbath in wrestling, boxing, and drinking whisky, back in the 1830s. This shows how soon boxing was pushed to the low end of black sport in the quest for respectability. In those dreadful Jim Crow years they were putting their emphasis on respectability, urging education and the creation of a middle class led by decent clergy, but they were forced to accept that the best advertisement around for black talent was a prize fighter. Moreover, Peter was a boxer who could expertly use his "shalls" and his "wills" and who had the habit of quoting Shakespeare.

The *Cleveland Gazette* paid attention to sports from 1889, noting the doings of George Dixon, of Peter, of the Cuban Giants baseball team and their manager S.K. Govern, etc. The *Freeman* started up a sporting column in April 1890, apparently just so it could say: "Peter Jackson does this generation a service by proving that a man can be both a prize-fighter and a gentleman." On May 5, 1890, in the *Freeman,* the journalist James M. Vena, who usually reported on social matters and who reported Peter's reception in St. Louis, wrote a few paragraphs on Peter, "Lion of the Hour," whom he interviewed the previous Sunday. Vena called him "the man pre-eminent in elevating a calling frequently debased by its other representatives." Ike Hines had in his famed Professional Club in New York a room covered with portraits of black achievers. As James Weldon Johnson described it in 1912: "There were pictures of Frederick Douglass and of Peter Jackson, of all the lesser lights of the prize-fighting ring, of all the famous jockeys and the stage celebrities...."[7]

But the black bourgeoisie had spent so much time trying to shuck off the darky image which included gambling and prizefighting, only to discover that the most famous black man, not just in the United States but across the world, was a boxer. They were bemused.

The young, however, were not necessarily transfixed by their parents' dilemma. In 1892 a black cycling club in New York city numbered over 100 wheelmen. In the 1890s, black colleges like Tougalou and Howard University began to foster track and field sports and to create baseball and football teams. Intervarsity competitions were set up. In October 1892, before any black YMCA had moved from spiritual exercises to athletic, and 40 years before any YMCA at all for Texas blacks, a set of young black men in Austin, Texas, led by Professor E.L. Blackshear, set up an athletic organization. They promoted all kinds of manly sports and called themselves "The Peter Jackson Club."[8]

"Old Sport," in the *New York Age* of August 8, 1891, took the positive line of saying about Jackson, Harris "Black Pearl" Martin of Minneapolis, and Dixon: "I don't care what it is, if one of the race is best at it, it helps." The *Washington Bee* occasionally noticed boxing, even in San Francisco. The *Cleveland Gazette* started to reprint in January 1893 a column called "The Talk of the Ring" which was edited by "Bantam" of the *New Orleans Picayune.* By January 1897 the *Freeman* itself felt so unconstrained by respectability as to list all the "pugilistic events by Negro professionals" during 1896, noting their opponents as "white" where appropriate.

Frederick Douglass himself viewed Peter differently. In his last years, James Weldon Johnson reported in *Along This Way* (1931) that, after his service in Haiti and while meditating on Toussaint L'Ouverture and the physical heroism of black males, "Frederick Douglass had a picture of Peter Jackson in his study, and he used to point to it and say, 'Peter is doing a great deal with his fists to solve the Negro question.'"[9]

After the triumph in St. Louis, the Jackson traveling players vacationed at Mount Clemens, north of Detroit near Lake Saint Clair, a spa resort with mineral springs and nothing to do but lie around and unwind and nurse that right hand. The rest did Peter good, but still he talked about going back to Australia for a visit, to see everybody there and to take two relaxed trips across the Pacific. At Mount Clemens, Peter gave away the bull terriers and the black-and-tans he had acquired in England, and released the English songbirds from their cages where they had been languishing all those months. It is to be hoped that Peter's dogs found good homes, and that his skylarks were happy among the clouds over Michigan for as long as they lasted.

Back in Chicago again, on May 19 he fought "Denver" Ed Smith, an Englishman who started fighting when he was an 18-year-old sailor. Tom Allen, the former champion, enticed Smith off his ship in Baltimore Harbor, and gave him his first ideas of the American ring. Smith joined the Jack Burke combination and ended up in Colorado, where he was promoted by Bat Masterson and fought a couple of bouts. But he and Masterson fell out and he went up Oregon way. In 1890 Smith threw in his lot with Kilrain and Muldoon and their boxing-wrestling combination. With them in Chicago he fought Peter under electric lights at Battery D.

Smith, who stripped to all blue, was seconded by Tom Cleary and Tom Allen. Jackson was seconded by Fitzpatrick and Ashton, and taking off his ulster and "a loose gauze undergarment" was all in white. The *National Police Gazette* said he looked like an ebony statue, but heavy and somewhat out of training. Davies and Muldoon kept time, and Pat Carroll was referee. Four-ounce gloves were used, but one ounce of hair was taken out of each of them before the start.

First Round

Jackson went at Smith, driving him onto the ropes, and the fighting was lively at close range. Smith swung his right and landed on Jackson's mouth, drawing first blood. This seemed to infuriate Jackson, and he rushed at Smith like a maddened bull. Pushing Smith into his corner and swinging his right, he landed on Smith's left eye, scoring a clean knockdown. Smith came up groggy and it seemed Jackson would finish him then and there. He was unable to do so, however, the dazed Smith clinching and going down several times to avoid punishment. The round closed with the men against the ropes in a clinch.

Second Round

Smith's left eye was closing rapidly. He landed several times with his left, but Jackson rushed him to the ropes and landed several times with both hands without receiving a return. Smith was knocked down against one of the posts. Then they worked to the center of the ring, and a right-hand swing by Jackson sent Smith to the floor. He was up in a moment, but was sent down again by a right-hand swing that caught the back of his neck. He was up in a second and at work again with a flurry of both fists. The fist work began to tell on Jackson, and his blows lacked force. Smith kept at his work gamely, and landed several times on chin and neck without a return. Once he rushed Jackson to the ropes. The round closed with the men sparring at long range. Smith had fallen six times thus far.

Third Round

Both men came up smiling and went right to work. But soon the clinching started. The *National Police Gazette* said that Smith was hugging Jackson as if he loved him. Jackson tried to finish his man with a punch on his neck, but didn't succeed. Smith in turn landed a straight shoulder blow on Jackson's neck. Smith would clinch and then go down, and Jackson was unable to land a knockout blow. At the close of the round neither was any too strong.

Fourth Round

Smith went onto the floor, a result of both getting hit and slipping. Smith came up surprisingly fresh, and when Jackson started at him with right- and left-handers that pushed him to his knees, fought back with great cleverness. Every rush was met, and Smith landed time and again at close range, one being a right to the jaw. Jackson seemed tired and his blows lacked force, but he still knocked Smith down again.

Fifth Round

The men shook hands, then Jackson led with his left. Smith again lost advantages by striking short, but one stinging left hand caught Jackson's jaw. Jackson attempted to finish his man, but could land no effectual blow. He had Smith on the ropes but let him escape. Smith was fighting him off with both hands when time was called. Smith's left eye was almost closed, and his forehead had been scratched by a rip in Jackson's glove. The referee should not have lightened the gloves.

The decision was given to Jackson. The *Denver Times* said Smith "has proven to the world that he has a heart and that it is in the proper place." In April 1893 Smith challenged Peter, saying that he had almost won in Chicago in five rounds and would win now if given more space, but was rebuffed. Smith did not resent this for long, however, and at the end of 1899 he played an important role in Peter's life.

The party left Chicago for California on May 24. At the train depot in Denver at 7:00 A.M.: "a delegation of sporting men and colored citizens assembled" to meet the Burlington train from Omaha. John Murphy acted as M.C. that night, when Peter boxed Ashton in the Grand Opera House in "a three-round set-to for scientific points," to the delight of the colored men who were present. The train left at 3:00 A.M. on May 25 for Salt Lake City and Ogden. James D. Barton was the sporting editor of the *Ogden Evening News*. He and John Russell, manager of the Novelty Theater, offered Peter $1,000 if he would stop off in Ogden for "a stop-off one-night show." He would! They met him at the railway depot with a carriage drawn by four pure white horses proudly carrying red plumes. He was paraded around the town, which turned out en masse to see him. He sparred with an unnamed lightweight dubbed "Siwash Wonder."

Ashton drops out of Peter's story at this point. He rejoined Sullivan's entourage. At the end of May, Peter re-entered San Francisco more than satisfied with the offensive he had conducted over two years. All his friends were there to greet him, with gossip about events he had missed.

According to the *Chronicle*, Herget intended to marry in late 1889, but didn't do so. With his savings from Australia, and with Professor Walter Watson as his partner, he invested in 1889 in a saloon on Market, at Golden Gate Avenue and Taylor. Watson, a Yorkshireman who emigrated to America in 1883, had fought Mike Donovan in 1884 for the right to become the boxing instructor of the New York Athletic Club. Donovan won, and Watson moved to California to teach, at first opening his own San Francisco Boxing Club and in time becoming boxing instructor at the Olympic Club, where he was succeeded by J.J. Corbett early in 1888. He had seconded Herget in his Pacific Coast title fight with Tom Cleary. According to Van Court, Watson "taught the English system which consisted entirely of straight blows with the exception of a left hand swing to the body. His system consisted of foot work, feinting, slipping the head and correct hitting."[10] Probably Watson, who had pupils to instruct at the Acme Athletic Club in Oakland, was largely a silent partner. In 1895 Herget's place had *Tamale Cafe* painted on it, and plain *Mitchell's*.[11]

In 1890, 1,400 licensed bars in San Francisco, plus unlicensed dives, served a population of around 300,000, but apparently the city's thirst had no limit. Herget's bar was in the Upper Tenderloin, a small White Way with theaters and restaurants and bars and swank hotels. The walls of his bar were covered with photographs of boxers. The following year, Peter would open a bar of his own, on Turk just round the corner from Watson and Herget's.

Around New Year 1890, when Peter was back in America from Europe but long before he reappeared in San Francisco, a news item was published by the *London Graphic* on December 28, 1889 and the *Referee* on February 12, 1890. It was to the effect that Peter was in love with a pretty white woman, a young widow with more than $100,000, and she in love with him. It was said that he had undertaken the trip to Britain in order to cool their relationship. Their black-and-white marriage would have to be performed in a foreign country or on a ship three miles off the California coast. The sports of San Francisco were shocked by the interracial marriage but far more alarmed at the prospect of Peter's retiring to easy street. Then it was leaked that the lady was an octoroon so there would be no miscegenation. In 1890 Will Corbett asked him directly what was the strength of this story. Peter replied that the lady in question was the sister of his best friend, a San Francisco businessman, and that their friendship was the screen which allowed him to be in the sister's company without scandal. San Francisco heard no more about this liaison, but Peter told Will that they were still in love when he returned to San Francisco in 1897.

Peter's contract with the California Athletic Club expired in June 1890, so that when he did go into the club he found not the banquet Fulda had promised but still a surprise: Sullivan was offering to fight him, now apparently not for a prize but for a fee of $30,000 — and in Texas.

Then, on June 9 Frank La Rue caused the death of Harry McBride in a San Francisco fight. These men were waiters and quarreling over a prostitute, but the Golden Gate Athletic Club had offered them its premises for settling their dispute and was therefore implicated in McBride's death. The death was treated so seriously that the police had forbidden all fights. This was reason enough to revive the idea mooted in May, about returning to Sydney before the Sullivan match.

The *Chronicle* had reported in late June 1890 that for this reason Billy Murphy was going back to Australia after beating Ike "Belfast Spider" Weir, and taking with him his featherweight champion belt. "Billy will be back soon," said the *Chronicle*, "as he has discovered that California is a very attractive land for a man who is disposed to place his spare shekels in the savings bank and invest them in suburban sandlots. Billy has declared his intention of becoming a citizen, solemnly foresworn his allegiance to her most gracious majesty Queen Victoria and taken to wearing the Stars and Stripes around his wasp-like waist when he goes into the ring. In this respect he is a noteworthy contrast to most of the foreign athletes, who are willing to earn American dollars but very loth to give this country credit for anything worth living for." The scope of this reproach included Peter.

However, the *San Francisco Wasp*, a satirical magazine, was able to report in 1890: "California adopted Peter Jackson with generous hospitality. He came here an Australian and a 'coon.' He slugged himself into our hearts, and when he left us he was a full-blooded Californian. His triumphs have been Californian triumphs."[12] Peter did not share the *Wasp*'s view.

After he got back to San Francisco, Peter bought from a stables in Seminary Park a brown pacer called Careless Boy for a price estimated by the *Chronicle* of June 15 as more than $1,000. As well he bought a single carriage and speed cart. Whether Peter ever raced Careless Boy is unknown, but in 1891 at Joe Dieves' place in San Leandro, Peter was "out in the yard tying a horse," perhaps Careless Boy, when the reporter Annie Laurie interviewed him on May 18. And it could have been Careless Boy that spilled him out of his dog-cart in Oakland shortly before the Corbett fight.

In the middle of June, Peter was involved in a brawl with some Germans at Joe Dieves' place. The press reports were contradictory. On the one hand he was said to have been set upon by half a dozen men led by one Herman Helmick, on the other to have beaten up two men of whom one was an Oakland grocer called Conrad Helmke. The *Examiner*, strangely, took the second view and said in its article on June 17, "Knocked Out by Petah," that his deplorable attack on "two good natured Germans out for a day's pleasure with their wives and children" destroyed forever the myth of the gentlemanly, peaceable Jackson. The other view, in the *Evening News* (London) and reproduced in the *Albury Border Post* of August 15, 1890, said Helmick "began to get insulting to the colored man whom he did not know," the usual inducement for Peter to get wild. Thirty-five years later, Van Court retold this story in his memoirs, saying that six German brewerymen lost a bet with Dieves and proved bad losers, attacking Peter with a bucket when he tried to smooth things over, so he punched three of them in the stomach. The little sensation quickly subsided.

On June 23 the *Chronicle* said: "Fistic Affairs at a Complete Standstill," and on June 30: "Prominent Pugilists Leaving San Francisco." Peter was in most things realistic. "Peter Jackson is talking about returning to the colonies by the next steamer, and taking a vacation under the Southern Cross," the *Examiner* said. "He will return when the present chilling gale of public opinion and official hostility shall have blown over." There was no point in hanging around San Francisco.

He left town, and at Marysville north of Sacramento on July 22 he fought Tom C. Johnson, a hard-hitting local heavyweight who had been spoiling to meet him. Peter was introduced by the manager of the Marysville Athletic Club as "Peter Jackson, of Australia." They boxed according to the Queensberry rules in the Marysville Theater, which had a capacity of 800. Ladies were cordially invited to attend. The *Marysville Daily Appeal* said: "The exhibition between Jackson and Johnson was highly interesting, for all one-sided," and said: "Johnson did credit to himself, as was creditably admitted by both Jackson and his trainer." Several San Franciscans had traveled up to Marysville to learn whether Peter had improved on his old form. They decided he had, but he could not demonstrate it in San Francisco.

The *Daily Alta California* noted on July 26, 1890: "A Colored Bruiser Off." Accompanied by Fitzpatrick, on July 28 Peter left on the *Mariposa*. At the dock waving his return ticket, he said, "I won't say good-bye, for I am coming back again."

CHAPTER 6

Diamonds and Schlenters, 1890–1892

After the *Mariposa* reached Honolulu on Saturday, August 2, Peter was busy fulfilling arrangements made with a local entrepreneur, James Welsh, to give an exhibition. "Peter the Great" at the Honolulu Music Hall or Hawaiian Opera House, "assisted by local talent," had been advertised.

The Oceanic dock was crowded with fans and sightseers. When he strode down the gangplank he was greeted by the crowd, many of whom then followed his carriage. Welsh took Sam and him all round Honolulu, which was small, numbering about 20,000. The Hawaiian Opera House was diagonally across the road from the brand-new Iolani Palace. Beyond the Kawaiahao Church and the Gothic-revival tomb of King David Lunalilo, there was as far as Diamond Head only a humble settlement called Waikiki.

The two-story Music Hall or Opera House, which seated almost seven hundred, was full, with many navy men. "The house was crowded, especially the gallery," the *Daily Bulletin* reported, "and the appreciation of the spectators was frequently manifested by shouts of applause."

Starting at eight in the evening, Welsh acted as master of ceremonies. Apparently navy men supplied most of the sporting talent in Honolulu. Tom Sharkey would start his career there. One of the preliminary bouts was between Sailor Kelly from the American *Nipsic* and Sailor Hudson from the English ship *Acorn*, "a plucky little fellow" according to the *Daily Bulletin*. This Kelly-Hudson fight stirred national antagonisms. A reluctant Fitzpatrick sparred with a man called Barron because the latter's antagonist vamoosed.

Peter boxed in his favorite outfit, white pants and red sox. His antagonist was "Sailor" Devine from the USFS *Charleston*, an armored cruiser built in San Francisco. The *Daily Bulletin* was disappointed that in fighting with an amateur, Peter could not show his quality.

The *Mariposa* sailed the following morning. The ship pulled away from the dock and the wharf rats dove in, scrambling for coins. Peter loved Honolulu, its people with their beautiful singing, and the rioting flowers which made the warm evening air balmy with their fragrance. It was almost Santa Cruz with its orange groves again.

On August 21, 1890, the *Mariposa* sailed through the Heads of Port Jackson to find an amazing spectacle. Dozens of boats had traveled down Sydney Harbor to greet him, two of them being chartered steamers, the *Birkenhead* and the *Pacific*, crowded with well-wishers. The *Birkenhead* had been rented by John Feneley, his old buddy, the other by the "Welcome Home" committee organized by Will Corbett. When Peter was within earshot, the musicians struck up "Home, Sweet Home" and everybody sang it. Then they played "Our Jack's Come

Prize Ring Photographs.

Cabinet Pictures, Satin Finished, of all the Pugilists in Fighting Costume as they Appear in the Ring.

PRICE, 10 CENTS EACH.

1. James J. Corbett, champion of the world
2. Peter Jackson, the Australian champion
3. John L. Sullivan, ex-champion of the world
4. Charles Mitchell, England's champion boxer
5. Ed Smith, Denver (Col.) heavyweight
6. Jack McAuliffe, lightweight champion
7. Jack Dempsey, the "Nonpareil"
8. Bob Fitzsimmons, middleweight champion
9. Jim Hall, Australian middleweight
10. Joe Goddard, Australian heavyweight
11. George Godfrey, the colored boxer
12. Jake Kilrain, heavyweight of Baltimore
13. Dick Burge, England's champion welterweight
14. Jimmy Carroll, famous lightweight
15. Ike Weir, the "Belfast Spider"
16. Billy Edwards, ex-champion lightweight
17. George Dixon, featherweight champion
18. Billy Plimmer, bantam champion
19. Solly Smith, California featherweight
20. George LaBlanche, the "Marine"
21. Billy Smith, the "Mysterious One"
22. Ted Pritchard, middleweight champion of England
23. Frank P. Slavin, the Australian heavyw'ght
24. Jack Skelly, Brooklyn (N. Y.), featherweight
25. Paddy Ryan, ex-champion of America
26. Jem Smith, English heavyweight
27. Johnny Murphy, Boston featherweight
28. Tommy Kelly, "The Harlem Spider"
29. Jim Daly, Corbett's ex-sparring partner
30. Alec Greggains, Australian middleweight
31. Jem Carney, the famous English lightweight
32. Andy Bowen, Southern lightweight
33. Billy Meyer, "The Streator Cyclone"

These are a few names taken from a collection of 30,000 cabinet photos—any three of which will be sent you, postage paid, on receipt of 25 cents, 6 for 50 cents, 12 for $1.00.

Large photos, suitable for framing, for Saloons, Cafes, e'c., size 11x14 inches are 50 cents each; 21x24 inches are $1.50 each.

For complete catalogue send 2c. stamp. Address

RICHARD K. FOX,
Franklin Square, **New York.**

This advertisement for Fox photographs, listing those boxers of the day who had the most fans, appeared in the *National Police Gazette* on March 31, 1894.

Home To-day," and "See the Conquering Hero Comes." This flotilla accompanied the *Mariposa* up the harbor and then Peter was taken off and brought to the Prince's stairs at Circular Quay, where thousands of people had gathered. Along thronged streets he was taken in an open carriage, standing up to acknowledge the cheering. He was banqueted at the Sydney Amateur Gymnastic Club's rooms, the attenders paying 5 shillings each unless they had received one of the 150 invitation cards bearing Peter's photograph. The rooms were decorated with greenery and bunting. Along the gallery in gold on azure ran the words: "WELCOME HOME PETER." In the center of the room was a photograph of Peter, patriotically surmounted by the Australian flag held by a large stuffed kangaroo.

Sid Broomfield chaired the banquet in the absence of Colonel McDonald, and concluded his speech by saying: "Peter Jackson has done more to advertize Australia as a great land of sport, and its inhabitants as good sports, than any other man ever did."[1]

Peter had been promising himself a rest after three years of intense activity. He needed to unwind by going to Bondi Beach, swimming at the baths, drinking with his friends and acquaintances, going to the race track, lying late in bed and reading a book or two. He really needed to restore himself physically and mentally. And he did these relaxing things, but if he did slow down it was almost imperceptible. His public was avid for him, and it seems that he was touched by the amazing goodwill toward him that the Australians were manifesting. All Australia wanted to hail, or at least inspect, Peter. He decided to tour.

With some associates he went to Newcastle, showing at the Victoria theater before enthusiastic crowds. Gillies of the *Maitland Mercury* had always treated Sam Fitch with levity, but in 1890 when he returned in Peter's entourage, though maintaining the quotation marks when he printed the Fitzpatrick name, Gillies was far more respectful. In response to his and others' requests Fitzpatrick promised a Jackson fight at Maitland, but it never occurred.

The *Sydney Bulletin* published a photo of Peter by O. Brand of 37 Park, copies of which were presumably for sale. In January 1894 Messrs. Brand and Co. were selling photographs of Harry Laing, the New Zealand champion, large at one shilling and sixpence and small at a shilling. Peter's doubtless cost more because his achievements were greater than Laing's.

He looked around to compose a touring company. He found three clubs in Sydney in 1890. Foley ran the Australian Club, assisted by Billy "Shadow" Maber and Jack Molloy. Then there was the California Athletic Club, run by Sam Mathews, back from San Francisco. The third was the Sydney Athletic Club, run by Mick Dooley and George Dawson, the lightweight champion of Australia, Dowridge's pupil who would be trained by Teddy Alexander and go to America. Peter picked his team.

The combination consisted of Peter, George Dawson, and the new featherweight Champion of the World by virtue of his defeat of "Torpedo" Billy Murphy the previous Tuesday. This was Albert Griffiths, "Griffo" in the advertisements (twice called "young" because he was 18) and ever after in Australia. In America, however, he was always called the composite "Young Griffo."[2] The rest of the party consisted of Fitzpatrick, Jack Bateman, who was Griffo's trainer, and Will Corbett, who had put the combination together and acted as M.C.

On Saturday, September 6, the combination visited Wagga Wagga. It was the weekend of the local fair and the show was held in the Victoria Skating Rink. Peter was advertised to box Jack Farrell, who had accepted Peter's standard offer of £20 for 4 rounds standing. Hundreds of people turned out to root for the local boy. No result was given on September 9 in the *Wagga Wagga Advertiser*'s report of the night, but in fact Peter allowed Farrell to win the £20 and his townsmen's respect.

They reached Melbourne the next day, welcomed at the Spencer Street railway depot by a crowd of about 10,000 including Mr. Power, chairman of the Melbourne Athletic Club, and Montague Sweet, its secretary.

"He blushed," said the *Sporting Standard*, "if colored men can be said to blush — and hung his head in maiden modesty. 'Welcome to Melbourne, Peter,' shouted a hundred voices. 'Three cheers for the biggest white man in Australia,' yelled out a dozen more. 'Tip us your flipper,' 'Chuck us your fin, old son,' and 'Room for Brother Peter,' were among the many welcoming epithets hurled at the head of the fighting man. Everybody tried to get him by the hand, and in default they seized him by the coat-tails."

Their progress in a four-horse drag, along Collins, Elizabeth, and Bourke to "Buffalo" Costello's Lounge Hotel in the city's tenderloin, was slowed by cheering crowds. It was almost enough to erase the Farnan debacle, but Peter was aware how hostile many of the Melbourne fancy were. He was careful to tell the crowd at his exhibition on the evening of September 9, "I'm an Australian, and you all know me. I do not belong to any one of these colonies, to Victoria or New South Wales."

Costello had arranged the reception at the Apollo Music Hall, which he now partly owned. Responding to the toast of "Long life and prosperity to Peter Jackson" from chairman Power, Peter gave a wide-ranging speech which showed that the inarticulate man of 1887 had indeed learned to talk. According to the *Sporting Standard*, he told them among other things,

He had never done a crooked thing to any man and it was that which pulled him through where he went.... He was not egotistical to say that had always acted fair and square and upright. When he landed first in America he was an utter stranger. There was a great prejudice against colored fighting men there, but he was pleased to say he had overcome that prejudice.... The prejudice against colored men could not abate until white men would fight them. Well, if he was a colored man, he was also a British born subject ... and what was more, he was an Australian. For he had been brought up here from childhood, and this was the land of his adoption. It was gratifying to himself to know that he had sustained the credit of his country, and that no Australian could be ashamed of anything he had done.

That evening Peter gave a four-round exhibition with Costello.

Leaving Melbourne on September 15, Peter pushed on towards South Australia with Sam, Costello, Griffo, Bateman, Jim Hall and Peter Boland. The troupe was supposed to visit Geelong on September 15, and a notice appeared in the *Geelong Advertiser* about the team of Peter Jackson (Champion Boxer of the World), Costello, Bateman and Fitzpatrick (the Australian Comet), and Griffo. The Geelong crowd who turned up at the Exhibition Theater on a stormy night were chagrined to find no Jackson troupe. No apology was tendered.

On the following night, September 16, "Australia's Boxing Wonders" showed in Ballarat at the Columbian Skating Rink. "A gold medal," said the advertisement in the *Ballarat Star*, "will be given for a local light-weight contest." The report the next day was hardly two sentences: the attendance was "very large" and Peter went four rounds with Costello.

Peter and his party arrived in Adelaide early on September 18 by the express train. Adelaide was not a strong city for boxing, but one enterprising promoter lived there. George McLaughlin, the licensee of the Marquis of Queensberry Hotel on Pirie together with Mac's Athletic Hall next door, was trying to make himself a star. He had even managed to get his portrait, with a caption saying "A Fearless Bettor" into the *National Police Gazette* of July 5, 1890.

A "very large and eager crowd," according to the *Observer*, were at the depot to welcome Peter and the others, all known in South Australia only by repute. They were advertised as "a combination that a man sees but once in a lifetime," and certainly McLaughlin was lucky to have procured it for Adelaide. As Peter emerged from the train depot a band struck up "See, the Conquering Hero Comes." A drag and four took them along North Terrace and round to Hindmarsh Square, where the hotel stood covered with bunting and bannerets inscribed "Welcome Peter." William Wicksteed from the Adelaide Brewing and Malting Company presided over a luncheon where, the *Observer* archly noted, several toasts were drunk — in champagne.

In the evening, in a packed hall, Fitzpatrick boxed three rounds with Billy Williams, the opponent he had defeated in those long-ago White Horse days. Peter wore his white and light-blue gear. Called on to "Give us a speech, Peter," before his exhibition with Costello, "he good naturedly responded by saying how pleased he was with his reception, and how he intended to uphold the colors under which he had fought and would always fight — those of Australia. He was an Australian, and although he might not always be victorious, as he was only one man among millions, he would do his best to win honestly whenever he entered the ring, and if he had to go down eventually it would not be for want of trying to beat his opponent." The little speech was noisily applauded. Peter had not found it necessary in Adelaide, as he had in Melbourne, to claim to have been British born and bred, though at the luncheon he did explain that he was brought to Sydney from the West Indies when he was five years old. The *Express and Telegraph* commented: "He is obviously proud of being an 'Australian,' a free country where a man's color is no bar to him if he has acquirements of which he can boast, whether his honors be gained in the arena or on the rostrum." The paper put quotes around the word "Australian" presumably because in 1890 there was no political entity called Australia but only the Australian continent divided among several colonies, though their federation was being mooted.

The next day the party caught the train back to Melbourne. At the Melbourne Athletic Club, Peter undertook a gentlemanly demonstration with Billy Power, the Victorian amateur heavyweight and middleweight champion. Mr. Power got carried away and began fighting in earnest, bloodying Peter's mouth. Peter at once unleashed all his professional expertise and laid Power on the canvas. Referee Miller jumped into the ring and pinioned Peter, who yelled at the staggering Power: "If you want to box I'll box; if you want to fight, I'll fight!" Peter's outburst, considered less than gentlemanly, was inevitably marked down against him in Melbourne.

Peter was convinced that as a professional he could not fight an amateur, let alone a non-boxer, but, moreover, as a black he could not punch out a white.[3] Interviewed by Annie Laurie for the *Examiner*, he complained on March 5, 1893: "It hurts me very much to be considered as a prize-fighter instead of as a man. I have been talking to a man, sometimes, and we have been drawn into an argument. Let me express my opinion, as any other man would, and what happens? The fellow who's arguing with me says, 'Oh, well, I can't contradict you; you are a professional fighter.' What can I do?" The celebrity felt constricted by the role he played and was made to play.

Hales reported to his *Referee* readers on October 1 that back in Sydney and staying at Botany: "Peter Othello Jackson has started training at the Sydney Athletic Club for his match with Joseph Goddard." Peter, writing aboard the *Mariposa* a letter captioned "My Visit to Australia" which appeared in the *Examiner* on December 21, said he trained only to please his friends who craved to see him in action again. He wrote that he expected the eight rounds to "only be such rounds as two men commonly box without especial preparation." But the end of September was leaving it late to prepare, even for what Peter referred to as "my exhibition with Goddard."

Peter wrote that in Sydney, "I continued my indulgence in social pleasures and really had as good time as a man could." As part of this indulgence he became a Freemason. Peter walked where Du Bois and Turner had pointed. He took to Freemasonry, not only to the ritual and arcana but to the brotherliness and drink. And he appreciated the fact that Australian lodges made no difficulties about admitting a black, whereas in the United States lodges were either for whites or for blacks.[4]

Twenty years later, Jack Johnson was initiated in 1911 into Lodge Forfar and Kincardine No. 225 in Scotland, an event oddly unnoticed in *Unforgivable Blackness*. The news was telegraphed to the *New York Times* on October 29 and caused such a scandal, with American lodges threatening to boycott the Grand Lodge of Scotland, that Johnson's membership was canceled and Lodge Forfar and Kincardine itself temporarily suspended. The ostensible reason was not Johnson's race but his being by profession "the champion brute of the world"; and technically, along with messy paperwork, this may have been the case. The Freemasons excluded unsuitable men, including the divorced and the crippled. Normally in America black Freemasonry was quite separated from white, and while Voorhis showed that there were a number of isolated cases of black freemasons in white lodges in the nineteenth century, presumably none were boxers.[5] After all, without causing outrage, a Scottish lodge had initiated Bert Williams and other black non-boxers from the *In Dahomey* company.

Jackson's pastor and teacher at St. Paul's, John DuBois, was chaplain to the Frederiksted lodge. Another man in Jackson's life, the boxer Larry Foley, joined a lodge in 1885 though a Catholic; but he soon lapsed, maybe after priestly pressure. How many other Masons Jackson met is unknown, but the upper class in England favored Masonry, and Prince Eddy, until his sudden death, was being groomed to head English Freemasonry. And then in St. Louis he met Turner. It was that year, 1890, that Turner became a Freemason, being initiated into the Widow's Son Lodge.

Turner's act may have inspired Peter. He was initiated in Balmain at Lodge General Gordon No. 166, United Grand Lodge of New South Wales. The event went unnoticed by the press, but among the Freemasons a brouhaha about his initiation arose. There were irregularities with his sponsorship, because he was on a visit from the United States and not strictly a resident of Balmain. The Master of Lodge General Gordon was called on "to explain the circumstances under which the initiation of a pugilist took place in the said lodge, and to produce nomination and other papers in respect of the occurrence." But it seems to have been mainly the question of his occupation, not technicalities and not his race. Peter, like Johnson, was a boxer. As the Masonic paper the *Australasian Keyhole* wrote on February 3, 1891, "Is a pugilist a man and a brother?" The Masons debated it, but according to official records he was initiated on October 1, becoming an Entered Apprentice; took the second degree (Fellowcraft) on the 14th before leaving for Melbourne to face Goddard; and the third (Master Mason) on the 23th.[6] This degree had as its password "Tubal Cain," the legendary inventor of metal-working, and thus evoked Shango. Taking the three degrees so quickly meant a tremendous amount of book-learning on Peter's part. He rose no higher in the Craft, but Bro. Jackson's membership was never revoked and he was a Mason till his death. *Sporting Life* of Philadelphia reported on December 27, 1890: "Peter Jackson is a member of the General Gordon Lodge of Free and Accepted Masons, Sydney," and commented that "the event is probably unique in the history of the pugilistic ring or of Masonry."

On October 17 Fitzpatrick, Will, and Peter left for Melbourne, so that Peter could box Joe Goddard for eight rounds on Monday, October 20. Peter had taught Goddard years before at the White Horse. Peter told the *Examiner* that he was "feeling comfortable and fat" when he arrived.

The Victorians declared the national championship to be vacant, and had Mick Dooley from Sydney fight the Victorian champion for it: this was Goddard. The new "Australian" champion had had a series of victories over nonentities in Melbourne over the past year, plus two in Broken Hill, which permitted him to style himself "The Barrier Champion."

As if Melbourne had not enough hotels already, Peter went out on a lodge-crawl, drinking with his fellow Masons. The *Maitland Mercury* said that he embarked on "one long round of gaiety, a mixture of Masonic entertainments and Buffalo reunions."[7] Moreover, the Caulfield Cup was run on the day itself, and he attended the races. Peter got drunk and, "as full as the proverbial tick" in Will's words, was taken back to his hotel by his companion, the publican Patrick Reynolds, who had been Paddy Slavin's great fan and still was. He had to be dried out quick-smart before the evening, Fitzpatrick using violent rubbing and a hot bath laced with ammonia.

Fred Diamond began his report of the fight, dated October 22 and appearing in the

6. *Diamonds and Schlenters, 1890–1892*

This photograph shows Joe "Barrier Champion" Goddard in late 1890 with his brother and second Herbert, and his trainer Jack Marshall, who had trained Farnan for his 1884 fights with Jackson. Photograph courtesy of National Library of Australia [nla.pic-3258820].

National Police Gazette on December 13 just before Peter's arrival back in San Francisco, by saying that "every one except Goddard's supporters were surprised at Jackson's failure to win."

It was held in the Crystal Palace at Richmond, and tickets were sold at 2 guineas, £1 and 10 shillings, and 5 shillings. Expensive, but the fight started at 9:00 P.M. before a crowd of 3,000.

Jackson was half an inch taller than Goddard and some 15 pounds heavier. Reporters exaggerated these differences in order to characterize the 28-year-old Goddard as underdog. Goddard's seconds were his brother Herbert Goddard, his trainer Jack Marshall, who had trained Farnan, and Foley's old opponent Abe Hicken. Jackson's seconds were Costello, Hall, and Fitzpatrick. Mr. Curran was the judge for Goddard and Will the judge for Jackson. William Miller refereed American-style, that is, inside the ring.

Round One

They sparred for an opening. Jackson led off on the ribs. Goddard steadied his opponent with hot ones on both sides of the face. A rally ensued, Jackson going for the body with a venom that showed he meant to get through his contract as soon as possible. Goddard got his left and right on the body, and Jackson replied with both hands on the head. After sparring for a moment or two, Goddard rushed with a right and a left aimed at the head, but Jackson, ducking, neatly escaped the threat. Goddard went in gamely at close quarters and punched Jackson all over the ring, getting him almost on the ropes in the defensive. Still forcing the fighting, Goddard got his antagonist on the ribs. Jackson replied vigorously with both hands. When they broke away from each other, Jackson feinted with his left at the body, and got his right heavily on to Goddard's head. After a clinch against the ropes, on separating Goddard tried his right at the mark, but was short. Jackson also failed with his left. Goddard battered Jackson's head. Jackson retaliated with one on the mouth. Goddard went in with one of his characteristic rushes and gave some warm punishment at close quarters. A rally finished the round.

Round Two

Goddard led off at the body, and Jackson responded with both hands, and they were at it again in give-and-take work. Jackson tried his left bunch of fives, but Goddard, stopping, pressed him back towards the ropes for another heavy rally. On breaking, Jackson ducked away with the lithe panther-like movement which had helped make him famous. Goddard kept at the champion and they gave it to each other with both hands until they clinched and the referee stepped between them. Goddard got both hands heavily on both sides of the ribs. Jackson appeared to be surprised at Goddard's tactics. Goddard landed a left-hander on the ribs and a right on the jaw, and Jackson gave ground to the onslaught before sailing in and steadying Goddard with one on the side of the head. Goddard, however, stood manfully up to his adversary. There were some more sharp exchanges, in which for the first time Jackson had the advantage, and the round closed in Jackson's favor.

Round Three

Goddard led off with his left and right on the jaw. Jackson hit Goddard smartly on the body, shifting him on his legs, but when he rushed in to follow up his advantage he found Goddard ready for him. A rally and a clinch led to Jackson's mouth being visited by the left, but when Goddard tried for the point of the jaw he received a heavy one in the same place. Jackson caught Goddard one on the ear which brought him to his knees, where he took his ten seconds. On facing each other again Jackson led off with his left. After sparring for wind, Goddard dashed in and, hitting Jackson's ribs with his right and forcing him near the ropes, delivered the left on the jaw. Jackson kept both hands going like piston rods, and out of the clinch brought Goddard down with a right on the ear. Goddard got a heavy right on Jackson's ribs. Jackson reached Goddard's mouth with the left, and his ear with the right, and Goddard responded with rib-benders. They were sparring when time was called.

Round Four

Jackson led off this time with his right at the ribs, Goddard responding with his right on Jackson's jaw. Then Goddard got smartly on Jackson's ribs, and Jackson's counter went round Goddard's neck, causing him to go down for some seconds. Jackson got one on Goddard's face lightly and Goddard repaid it with one on the ribs, Jackson doing the same. Goddard led off again with his left on the ribs, and on the jaw, then giving punishment on the ribs with his right and on the jaw with the left. A clinch, and Jackson again got it on the mouth with Goddard's active left. Jackson avoided a heavy swinging right, and time was called.

Round Five

Goddard led off again with his left, Jackson ducking, and after a clinch landed Goddard one on his ear. Some heavy countering ensued and both men went down. Goddard recovered his legs first, and chivalrously extended his hand and helped his opponent to a standing position. Some sparring was followed by a very heavy rally. Goddard with his left got a blow clear on Jackson's face, the latter only managing to get to the rear of Goddard's head. Goddard again led off with his left, Jackson closing. Goddard forced the fighting, and got his left heavily on the ribs, Jackson clinching. Goddard got his right in heavily on the body and his left across the ear, and then some very heavy rallying took place, Goddard forcing the fight all over the ring. Another clinch, then Jackson got in one on Goddard's ribs with his right, and the latter retaliated with his own right across the face and a ringing left on the ribs, forcing Jackson across the ropes. Both men had their mettle up, and met in heavy rallying order, until Miller broke them apart. Jackson showed signs of distress and was sweating fearfully, while Goddard looked a bit weary. When they faced each other again Jackson tried to lead off but was met by Goddard on the ribs very smartly. Goddard got his left in again on the ribs, and right under the ear as time was called.

Round Six

Respectful sparring ensued until Goddard punched with his left and right on the ribs. Jackson returned, and the two men clinched. Jackson tried his left on the ribs and his right on the ear, but was met with a right-hander on the ribs, and a clinch followed. Both went for the body. Goddard launched out with a tremendous left-hander for Jackson's ribs but missed him. He got in his left in the same place just afterwards, and received a counter from Jackson's left on his own jaw. Stung by the blow, he returned his right on Jackson's ear, receiving in return a heavy right-hander from Jackson on the ribs, which the latter improved on with a right-handed stinger on the ear. Goddard retaliated with his left on the ribs. Jackson tried to reply with his right, but was too close to be effective, and received a heavy left on his chin. Then they clinched, and when they separated Jackson stood off a bit, and directed his attack against Goddard's body. Goddard stopped the diversion with a right on the ear, then followed up with both hands, planting his left cleverly on Jackson's chest, and just missing his head with his right before the bell.

Round Seven

Jackson commenced operations with an ominous look on his face, shaking his head like an enraged bull. He hit savagely with his left, but Goddard, seeing the danger, ducked cleverly, and it swung harmlessly over his head. A clinch followed, and while the referee was parting them, Jackson received a blow. His seconds immediately claimed a foul, but it was disallowed. Goddard reopened hostilities with a left on the jaw and a right on the ribs, receiving in return a left on his own ribs. Jackson fought a bit more warily from this point, avoided a very heavy right round-armer, and cleverly managed to get in a stinger on Goddard's jaw, and managed to plant his right fist on his opponent's ribs. He was repaid by a right-handed one on the jaw, which he at once returned. A well-timed spring on his part enabled him to escape a crusher just above the belt. Jackson tried with his left, and then went for Goddard and put in his right heavily on his side. Goddard sent in his left, and Jackson followed suit across the ear, and then they clinched. Miller passed between them and divided the men, but before they were properly separated, Jackson hit Goddard with his right on the side of the head, but the foul claimed was disallowed. Goddard again forced with his right on the ribs, and received Jackson's left in the same place; and, as corners were called, the men were busily engaged in the midst of a rally.

Round Eight

Jackson appeared to time shaking his head, and led off right and left. Goddard followed him up and got both hands in heavily on each side of the head. Rally and clinch. Jackson tried a left on the body, Goddard returned his left twice in succession on Jackson's face and his right on the side. Jackson tried very hard to wind his man, but Goddard stood up to him and let go both hands strongly, and then got home on Jackson's face. Jackson led off lightly, and Goddard stopped him, rushing in and landing his left heavily on the ribs. Goddard tried his left on Jackson's body, but the latter was away too quickly and got in his left on Goddard's face. Goddard followed up, but Jackson stopped him with one in the ribs. Jackson again tried his left ineffectually, Goddard following up with left on the body and then with his right and left on Jackson's face. The latter let out at his opponent's body, and then time was called.

At the end of the agreed eight rounds, one judge was for Jackson and the other for Goddard. Miller declared it a draw.

Peter was shaken. He blamed Miller for not estimating his skills higher than Goddard's energy. But more importantly, he had failed to win! It would be so easy, then, for him to lose! But even more worse than his injured self-esteem was the news, spread all around the boxing world by the *National Police Gazette* and other papers, that Peter was not beaten yet but not invincible. The *St. Louis Post-Dispatch* actually headed its report on November 23: "Jackson Vanquished, Joe Goddard Beats the Colored Giant in a Glove Contest." Only careful reading showed that Jackson had not stopped Goddard within the stipulated eight rounds.

Peter's lithe style made it hard for him to deal with rock-like opponents like Goddard and Farnan. George Beans, an Australian sport who saw the bout, told American papers, for instance the *St. Louis Post-Dispatch* of December 1, 1890, that Goddard "knows nothing at all about the game, regarding it from a scientific point of view, but what he lacks in other ways he makes up by bulldog determination, indifference to punishment, brute strength, and ferocity." Peter did not handle such fighters easily. This was what Jim Jeffries would be, only with far more science, eight years later.

In his 1918 biography Will said he took Peter to their hotel, gave him another ammonia bath, and put him into bed with iced bottles of champagne and a glass. Then: "A mob of Melbourne sports, headed by Sam Fitzpatrick, Victor Becker and Buffalo Costello, raided the room between 3 and 4 in the morning. Each one of these unannounced visitors appeared to have two bottles of wine and a supply of Melbourne's famous flounders in his hands. What Peter called a barbecue followed, and continued till, singly and in couples and threes, the company gradually spread itself out on the floor." The word "barbecue," common in America and originally West Indian, was not yet naturalized in Australia.

Peter himself blamed not Goddard's style but his own carelessness. In May of the following year, straight after the Corbett fight, he told the *Examiner* that he was returning to Australia next month, "going home" as he expressed it, to fight Goddard, but this time fully alert. However, because of the way Dooley also was treated when he fought Goddard on November 1, he refused to fight again in Melbourne.

At the end of 1890 Richard Fox published one of his illustrated books on boxing. It was titled *Lives and Battles of Famous Black Pugilists*, alternatively *The Black Champions of the Prize-Ring from Molineaux to Jackson*. So Peter was acknowledged as crowning one tradition! But he was out for more than that. The "human fighting machine" was about to take on his biggest challenges.

"Before his departure,," said the *Maitland Mercury* on November 29, 1890, "Jackson was the recipient of a banquet and a purse of sovereigns from many of his Sydney admirers." But, also before he left, he made one of his very few overt political gestures. The year had been one of strikes across the world, the Australian Labor Party emerging out of the Australian unionists' struggles. On November 18 a "monster athletic and boxing tournament" was given at Foley's Gaiety Theater to raise cash for the *Sunday Times* Strike Relief Fund, "for the widows and children of the strikers." Many boxers appeared: Griffo, Foley himself,

Sam Matthews, Mick Dooley and others, even Joe Choynski. Peter headed the star cast. Thousands were turned away so another entertainment was given on Wednesday, November 26, but Peter had sailed for San Francisco that day.

The *Mariposa* reached Honolulu before dawn on Saturday, December 13, having been delayed by head winds. Peter had little time, but the *Evening Bulletin* said he "renewed his acquaintance with a number of friends while here." On December 20 Peter arrived in San Francisco but he announced he was "sick, worn out," and was going up to Byron Springs to recuperate. Like Mount Clemens, Byron Springs was another Calistoga, the Harrogate of California, with its own depot along the railroad to Sacramento. It had a grand hotel and separate cottages, as well as the springhouses. One drank the warm spring waters for various complaints, one submerged oneself in the mud baths, one also swam in a pool naturally always at 88 degrees Fahrenheit with bubbles coming up like a Jacuzzi. With tennis and billiards, horse-riding, walking, it was the perfect place for Peter to be pampered and unwind, hopefully to get rid of his rheumatism.[8]

The *San Francisco Evening Post* had found out more about Peter's health. "It is just possible that Peter Jackson will, after putting in a few weeks at the hot springs, make a trip to Honolulu and remain there for a month or six weeks. When Jackson was complaining of rheumatism in the colonies he was advised to try electric baths. He did so, and states that he derived more harm than benefit from the treatment." Earlier the *Evening Post* had said: "He has suffered a good deal from rheumatics since he returned to Australia, and taken altogether, has not enjoyed nearly such good health as he had in San Francisco." These were the first mentions of the rheumatism or sciatica which he would later say he felt first in 1900.

"The sports of Honolulu are very anxious to have Jackson amongst them for a while," the *Evening Post* said. The delightful climate of the Hawaiian Islands would suit Peter fine, also he could dash back to San Francisco if anything happened on the boxing front. Honolulu must have been desperate for sports, for in November, Corbett was invited there to fight Peter while the *Mariposa* was in port, but refused.

Immediately after his spell at Byron Springs, Peter left on the Southern Pacific for New Orleans, a two-day journey, in order to witness the match at the Olympic Club on January 14, 1891, between two men he knew well, his pupil Bob Fitzsimmons and Jack Dempsey. Corbett, who had fought Kilrain in New Orleans a year earlier, also attended. At stake were $12,000 and the title of middleweight champion of the world. It was Peter's first visit to the South, except for his wild time in Louisville the April before. It was also his last.

Fitzsimmons knocked Dempsey out in the 13th. Newspapers, the *St. Louis Post-Dispatch* for one, addressed the defeated Dempsey on January 27, saying: "Retire from the ring you have so well adorned, Jack, and follow Iago's advice, 'Put money in thy purse.'" Maybe this syndicated allusion caught the eye of Peter Othello Jackson. At the end of October 1891, Jack Dempsey went to Portland to settle his affairs before touring the country with a boxing combination that included Herget.

Peter returned from New Orleans on the Sunset Limited via El Paso and Los Angeles, in time to exhibit with Joe Bowers on the 21st. He noted the mild climate of El Paso, where in January 1889 the Bacchus Sporting House had offered $10,000 for a Sullivan-Kilrain fight. When El Paso was mentioned as a venue for his fight with Corbett, he looked forward to training there, according to a correspondent of the *Melbourne Sportsman* on April 17, 1894.

Those aches and pains sounded warning bells. Peter was almost thirty. He began thinking about his future, and George Godfrey's advice came to mind. The *St. Louis Post-Dispatch* had declared on November 5, upon what authority is unknown, that Peter "has made lots of money in his native land and is now better off financially than any other pugilist in the world." But if that was correct, it did not cheer Peter up.

In the letter, or mini-article, which he wrote for the *Examiner* and was published just before Christmas 1890, he wrote:

> I feel since getting acquainted with George Godfrey of Boston that I have made several great mistakes in my way of conducting my affairs. While Godfrey was here we talked several times about the pecuniary phases of a boxer's life, and he often urged the wisdom of banking or investing the proceeds of matches as soon as they were received. His argument was that, during the golden days of a boxer's life, he would have friends in plenty, and if taken sick would receive the best of care, but if permanent disability should come and the boxer be compelled to seek other employment, no one would hold out a helping hand.... I felt that the sun could not shine always and I made up my mind to do a little hay-making before the storms came, and that is what I am here for now.

Mindful of descriptions of California as an attractive land for investing spare shekels in suburban sandlots, when he got back he looked for an investment and found one in a saloon at 25 Turk, just off Market and close to Herget's place and the Baldwin Hotel. It was opposite the Turk Street Hotel at 22–24. This was a good position, among buildings of four and five floors in the uptown tenderloin. In this part of town, nonstop action was going on from which Peter could profit. On May 20, 1891, the *St. Louis Post-Dispatch* remarked that, when considering where to put his money, "as a rule a prize fighter invests in a saloon business, if any, as his reputation is a drawing card." Peter leased the place for seven or ten years.

His sporting saloon opened in February 1891. He knew about the trade from his unsuccessful years in Sydney hotels, but even an idiot could not fail in the liquor business in San Francisco. It had more saloons per head of population than any other American city, having 3,117 licensed premises in 1890, one to about every 100 inhabitants, while south of Market alone in 1899 were 440 saloons plus uncounted "blind tigers" and "blind pigs" in barbershops and even furniture stores.[9]

Peter kept the business until 1892, when he sold it though leasing the premises until 1899. It is uncertain how often he worked the bar himself. He had a business partner in 1891 and 1892, the barman Samuel Hess. Jack Miles, known as "Circus Jack," also tended the bar. These were the years when American mixed drinks became fashionable, even on the other side of the Atlantic among those who could afford them: Blue Blazers and Fisherman's Prayers, Corpse-Revivers and Bosom-Carezzas, Too-Toos, Locomotives and Alabazans, etc. As early as 1882 a Brandy Smash was described as "one of the 365 American drinks" by the *Sydney Slang Dictionary*. In what else Peter invested is unknown.[10]

In the middle of July 1891, Paddy, who had beaten Kilrain in nine on June 16, declined a $10,000 purse offered by the California Athletic Club for a contest between himself and Peter. He said he would fight Jackson or Corbett after it had been decided which of the pair was the better man. Peter's attitude was this: "Will I fight? Yes, I am ready to fight anybody who is in the business — Slavin, Sullivan or any other man, I don't care who he is. I don't say I can whip any man in the world, but I am willing to try. I will go wherever the most money is offered." In December he was offered and accepted a fight with Corbett with a purse of $8,500 for the winner and $1,500 for the loser.

With his bar established he settled into training for the Corbett fight. Peter's regimen was described over the years, and it varied little. In 1888 before the Godfrey fight, when he trained at Sausalito with Fitzpatrick, the San Francisco papers reported that he rose each morning at 6:30, and he did so now at Alameda.

He ate whatever was placed before him. Mrs. Dieves died in April 1894, when Peter was in Boston touring with *Uncle Tom's Cabin*. Hearing of her death, he said "she was an American mother to him, and he never forgot her kindness to him while he was training." He walked, he punched the bag, he was rubbed down with bay rum by Fitzpatrick. He retired for the night at 9 with a book.

One of his pillow-books is recorded: in Cincinnati in 1890 he was reading a new novel, *Thou Shalt Not*, written by "Albert Ross," author of *Her Husband's Friend* and other novels. The book is the only clue we have to Peter's reading when not scaling the heights of Shakespeare. *Thou Shalt Not* was a runaway bestseller. Set among the fast crowd in New York City, it was a melodrama about adultery, with echoes of *The Picture of Dorian Gray*, recounting the re-education of "Hector Greyburn, the libertine, the practiced seducer," who, led on by a series of sensational intrigues and disasters, dies for others and so redeems himself. *Thou Shalt Not* was as daring a fiction as anything one could legally buy in 1889 in Comstock's United States, but of course Peter was able to read much naughtier novels in French.

In Brighton in 1889 he followed much the same training routine, and in 1891 at Alameda, and in England in 1892 before the Slavin fight, and as late as 1898 when he was at Alameda again training for his fight with Jeffries. He scarcely needed a trainer because he was a self-starter and not lazy.

On Sunday, April 5, Peter had a road accident. He had gone from Alameda to Oakland by dogcart, then by ferry to San Francisco, where he farewelled friends going to Australia. Back in Oakland, according to Naughton, he was in his dogcart when the horse took fright at some flapping paper, overturned the cart on the streetcar rail, and ran away. Peter was left with a wrenched ankle. On April 17 the *St. Louis Post-Dispatch*'s correspondent reported tartly he had been so drunk that he fell out of the buggy. He was on crutches until April 21, and had physiotherapy, water cures and "electrical" treatments. Considerable doubt was expressed, by partisans like Davies and Bat Masterson, whether he would be fit to fight. In retrospect, he should have deferred the date. According to Naughton in *Kings of the Queensberry Realm* (1902), however, both Peter and Fitzpatrick considered that the fight could not last more than 5 or 6 rounds, 10 at the outside, so that his ankle was not a liability. This expectation was thwarted by Corbett's strategy of prolonging the fight indefinitely. Peter had never seen Corbett fight, whereas Corbett had many occasions to see Peter fight, though in his memoirs he denied it. Particularly at the Godfrey bout, when Corbett acted as Godfrey's timekeeper, he was able to note Peter's style. When they met, Corbett let Jackson do everything, himself dancing away from him. Jackson had counted upon a stand-up fight which he would win quickly and not trouble his leg too much, but in the event Corbett dragged the fight out to more than four hours, during which Peter was in agony.

On May 21, a Thursday, the preliminaries, beginning at 8:30 P.M., included 4 rounds between Bill and Jack Slavin, Paddy's brothers who had arrived from Australia on May 14. At 9:00 P.M. Jackson and Corbett entered the ring simultaneously, according to the *Examiner* and the *Chronicle*, whereas according to the *Morning Call* Corbett was seated and being cheered before Jackson appeared. The story, in Corbett's *Roar of the Crowd: The True Tale of the Rise and Fall of a Champion* (1925), about his tricking Jackson into entering first was untrue.

They both wore overcoats. Peter's went almost to his heels; it was the Calcutta veteran. Corbett's was also brown. When they doffed these, Peter was wearing his "Australian" outfit again, sporting the white and blue of Australia in white flannel knee breeches with two blue stripes running down to light blue stockings, and black shoes. He had on the small of his back a large porous plaster, the top of which appeared above his belt.

Corbett entered wearing pants, but stripped to almost nothing. "Jim was not hampered with costume," Naughton wrote to the *Referee*, "wearing merely socks, shoes, and a thin silken breech clout. His colors were red, white and blue, with a green rosette added in deference to the wishes of his father, who hails from the Emerald Isle." Corbett's wife had lovingly sewed his belt. "It is a dainty and elaborate thing, made of light but strong webbing, and covered with red, white and blue satin ribbons," said the *Examiner*. "In front, on either side of the fastening straps, are rosettes, one of ribbons to match the colors of the covering; the other, at Corbett's special request, is a large rosette of green satin."

Corbett fancied his butt and showed it off whenever he could, but not everybody else did. His outfit was so shocking in 1891 that the *Examiner's* artist discreetly drew him in little shorts, and the scandalized *Chronicle* made its artist portray him in full-length pants. Peter was asked by an excited reporter what he thought of Corbett's gear, and replied calmly that he had himself, like the American sprinter J.M. Johnson, worn a sporting slip (tight briefs) in 1884. "Eight years ago I used the same 'rig,'" he said. "In fact, I have used all sorts of dress for sparring and fighting, including the flannel trousers and the woolen knee pants which athletes usually wear." The athletes at San Francisco's Olympic Club, including their star Louis Brandt, were all wearing slips when they were photographed by Muybridge in 1879 for his book on animals in motion.[11] In the famous poster that the *National Police Gazette* printed in May 1894, in expectation of the Corbett-Jackson heavyweight title fight, "WITH THEM IN FIGHTING ATTITUDES," the artist portrayed both Corbett and Jackson in slips, but it does not appear Peter ever fought in one. Corbett was a model of fashion, and slips caught on. As to buttocks, the 1888 Taber photo had showed the world more of Peter's than Corbett ever showed of his, at least in public.

John Donaldson from the Cardiff fight, Billy Delaney, and Corbett's brother Harry acted as seconds for Corbett. Fitzpatrick, Herget and Billy Smith were Peter's seconds. George Harting was again timekeeper for Jackson, and Jimmy Wakeley for Corbett. Bob Roberts of the Frahman's Dramatic Company was Corbett's bottle-holder, while Peter's was Billy Field, the blacksmith at Alameda, who taught Peter smithing. Forge-work is under the protection of Shango. Peter made little iron souvenirs under Field's tutelage and presented them to his visitors.

Hiram Cook refereed, carrying a silver-headed cane and wearing a plug hat. Adhering more closely to the Queensberry rules than was usual in San Francisco, he stayed outside the ropes during the fight, entering the ring only twice, in the first round, to break clinches. There was no tossing for corners or for gloves, which were five-ouncers in tan-colored buckskin.

Naughton estimated 100 reporters in the club that night, and 12 telegraph operators at ringside tapped out the events as they happened, so that many versions were published. The following account is conflated from the *Examiner*, which often referred to "Peter" in its coverage and never to "Jim," usually to "the Californian," and from the *Chronicle*, which wrote of "Peter" and "Jim," and "the local man." Their stories were published on May 22. Naughton's report for the *Referee*, written on May 26 and published in Sydney on June 24, has also been used.

Round One

No more graceful big men ever lifted their hands, said the *Examiner*. Jackson leaned forward just a trifle out of plumb, and Corbett pointed gracefully in the opposite direction. Both carried a low guard, Corbett seeming to have scarcely any, carrying his hands at his side most of the time. Jackson assumed the aggressive after 20 seconds of long-range sparring. He shot his left into Corbett's ribs. The blow was pretty high, and Corbett was already going away from it. Corbett jumped to a clinch and dropped his left into Jackson's ribs as he did so. They separated, and Corbett drove his left into Jackson's stomach with the swing that the man's friends have been talking about so much, and which Jackson's friends claimed would never reach home. They were mistaken. Jackson's hula-hula contortion came too late and Corbett's glove reached his abdomen with a resounding whack that made the crowd cheer. As the blow fell, Corbett showed Jackson a new trick in clinching. His left continued on around Jackson's stomach to the small of his back and his right went up over his shoulder and then made a grip that left Jackson powerless. Corbett was evidently fond of this hug, or else he wanted to test it thoroughly, for he hung on for a full half-minute, squeezing Jackson lovingly and testing his ability to escape. Hiram Cook had to step into the ring before he would let go. Jackson drove out a straight left when they separated, but did not come within a foot of Corbett's face. Corbett baited him three times in succession, practicing a new dodge every time and never so much as feeling the wind of Jackson's glove. The fourth time Jackson got to his ribs lightly, and Corbett again put on his clinch. It lasted nearly as long as before, and Jackson could not get away until Cook climbed through the ropes. When the sparring commenced again Corbett landed his left swing into Jackson's stomach solidly and without a return. His next visit was on Jackson's mouth, and his next on the ribs, and in all three he escaped without a scratch. He danced in and out as lightly as a featherweight and eluded Jackson's lightning drives, the *Examiner* said, so surprised that it used a simile, "like a bit of thistledown"; according to the *Chronicle*, "as nimble as a fawn." So many happenings in three minutes (only two, if one minute for clinches is subtracted) meant the action in this first round was furious. It got progressively slower.

Round Two

Jackson squared off cautiously and Corbett drove his left into the short ribs. Corbett put his clinch on with it, but reversed holds this time, throwing his left over the shoulder and his right under. After the break Jackson reached for him and missed by reason of Corbett's duck. He shifted his front and guard from left to right, and Corbett punched him in the stomach while he was changing. Jackson's first good solid one came in just after the clinch, his left landing under Corbett's ear. Corbett clinched and swung his right on the break, but missed. He kept Jackson guessing very hard for a minute, feigning and dancing about and occasionally digging out with his left for Jackson's stomach. There was but one light exchange in the round. Corbett was on the back retreat most of the time, but stopped twice long enough to land his left on Jackson's stomach. The second time he followed the blow with a powerful uppercut, and the crowd cheered.

Round Three

Jackson opened by a right lead that did not come within a foot of Corbett's nose. Corbett was gracefully teetering on his toes when Jackson's glove started; he made a beautiful back jump and his feet seemed to scarcely touch the floor before they impelled him forward and let his left find its usual resting place on Jackson's soft spot. Jackson came back viciously and covered with perspiration. He reached for Corbett's pompadour, but the young fellow went under his arm and drove is right into Jackson's short ribs as he passed by. Corbett landed his left on the dark stomach three times in succession, following with an affectionate clinch each time. Jackson followed Corbett round the ring, Corbett laughing as Jackson tried to hit him and failed.

Round Four

The men walked around each other cautiously for a full minute, then Jackson missed Corbett twice. There was some beautiful boxing in this round, during which Corbett scored three clean hits without a return. One was a straight smash on the mouth and the other two were swing drives into Jackson's stomach and short ribs. His inevitable clinches came in every time and somewhat marred the performance, but it was beautiful work, cleaner and prettier than the California A.C. had ever seen before. Corbett's protection consisted of ducks and dodges, and Jackson did not seem able to reach him. When he led high, Corbett was under him, and when he led low Corbett was around behind him, hitting him in the small of the back. Corbett's stock went up 100 percent, and it became a question of whether he was punching hard enough to bring Jackson down to his weight before he tired himself out. As for Jackson, he did not seem to have deteriorated any, but Corbett was so awfully clever that he could not do anything with him.

Round Five

Jackson landed two light ones on Corbett's face as he was on the retreat, and then came the first close work. Corbett stopped Jackson's advance with a left drive, low, and then traded half-arm hits with him. He was quite as good as Jackson, and the crowd cheered while Jackson clinched. Corbett landed once on the mouth and once on the stomach in the subsequent sparring, and closed the round with another to the stomach. Both men kept smiling. Jackson started to limp.

Round Six

Corbett opened with a left swing into Jackson's short ribs and got away from his vicious cross-counter. The boxing for the remainder of the round was light, both hitting a trifle short until, just as the gong sounded, Corbett landed his low left swing again. Jackson was forcing, but Corbett's dodging was very clever.

Round Seven

Both men were extremely careful. There was a lot of preliminary sparring, Jackson threatening and Corbett beguiling him into leading, in the hope of an opening. Jackson landed heavily on Corbett's breast, and this was the only blow in the round.

Round Eight

Jackson kept on leading. Corbett missed his pet swing and left an opening for an awful right-hander, but Jackson was not quick enough to beat the lightning clinch. Jackson landed low with an uppercut intended for Corbett's jaw, and Corbett came back so fiercely as to push him to the ropes. He tried to hold him with one hand and punch with the other; but Jackson drove him away with a smart punch on the nose. Corbett wound up the round with a swinging right on Jackson's neck.

Round Nine

When Jackson came up for the ninth a little blood dripped from his lips and spotted his white tights. The crowd went wild! Corbett called his attention to it. Jackson laughed, and answered with a vicious swipe that would have knocked his head off if the nimble Corbett had not taken it out of the way. Corbett paid his effort with a drive into the stomach, which closed the round.

Round Ten

Corbett opened by landing his left on Jackson's ribs. Jackson tried to hold him off on the clinch and succeeded until he had planted three hot right-handers on Corbett's short ribs. Corbett landed two of his of his low left drives, and the round ended in a clinch.

Round Eleven

Corbett played his left into Jackson's ribs and then gave him one on the mouth when Jackson prepared for the supposed inevitable clinch. Jackson tried for Corbett's stomach, but Corbett avoided. Jackson landed twice on the side of the head in the long-range sparring and some rough wrestling followed. Jackson led again for Corbett's head, but the latter countered him heavily with his left and drove his right into the short ribs with a force that made Jackson grunt. They pummeled each other and fell against the ropes.

Round Twelve

Both men seemed contented to rest and nothing but light taps were exchanged.

Round Thirteen

Both men exhibited a coltish tendency to skip about and laugh but not go in for heavy punching. They clinched and Corbett punched Jackson's nose.

Round Fourteen

Corbett enlivened matters by landing his left solidly on Jackson' stomach and ducking under a cross-counter that made the air sizzle with its velocity. Corbett landed his left again, but this time he got a rib-roaster so low that his duck was unavailing. He slapped Jackson's mouth and nose smartly and Jackson returned the compliment. Quite a little pool of blood from his mouth had accumulated in Jackson's corner by this time, while Corbett's damage seemed limited to a swelled right eye and a very red back.

Round Fifteen

Little or nothing was done during the whole round, though Corbett punched Jackson once so hard on the face that it drove his head back.

Round Sixteen

Corbett led for wind, but Jackson escaped. The men exchanged a few light blows and near the end Corbett caught Jackson heavily on the jaw twice, which brought out great applause.

Round Seventeen

Jackson opened by a wild and ineffective rush. Corbett was either under him or clinching, and it was not until the breakaway that Jackson landed a good solid left on the corner of Corbett's jaw. Jackson rushed in and landed on Corbett's ribs. Then Corbett hit him twice on the side of the face with left and right. Some short-arm work followed and Jackson landed two to Corbett's one on the rib roasting. Jackson got his stomach out of the way three times in succession and his stock took an upward turn until Corbett finally got there just as the gong sounded, despite Jackson's cleverest bit of subtraction of that suffering organ. Both men went to their seats blowing from the warm work.

Round Eighteen

Jackson came up vigorous, but missed two leads and got Corbett's gloves on his kidneys in both the clinches that followed. In the remaining sparring Corbett landed three swings on Jackson's head, and his friends began to fear for his tender hands. But Corbett delivered a left-hander, which the *Chronicle* called "one of the best blows of the fight," right on Jackson's chin and made him stagger.

Round Nineteen

Nothing but smart boxing, bearing no resemblance to fighting.

Round Twenty

Corbett gave Jackson the back of his head for a landing for a right drive, and then made a standoff of the infighting that followed. Corbett rushed Jackson into a corner and pounded him on the head with right and left until Jackson clinched. Corbett's lip split and blood ran down his chin.

Round Twenty-One

It began like the others: they fiddled around for a minute, and then Corbett landed as usual. Then he landed again. Jackson slapped him on the shoulders, and just as they seemed about to get into a rally the gong sounded.

Round Twenty-Two

This was the twenty-first over again until Corbett made his usual lead. He missed it, and before he had got his arm back he found Jackson's left on his cheek. It was one of the nastiest blows delivered up to that time, and Corbett swung no more during that round. His upper lip swelled and showed red.

Round Twenty-Three

Jackson led for Corbett's wind for a change. He did not reach it. There was one pretty piece of boxing: they were within half-arm range and both went to work. The ducking matched the striking, and not a blow went home.

Round Twenty-Four

This was merely a repetition of what had gone before. Corbett punched Jackson's nose once, but his blows seemed a little wild, and not a bit of damage was done.

Round Twenty-Five

Not a single blow was struck. Two easily avoided leads by Corbett made up the whole of the fighting.

Round Twenty-Six

Corbett had not struck a blow with his right for half a dozen rounds, and the rumor spread around that he had broken it. Jackson was beginning to get over his respect for the idle member and left both hands up. Broken or not, Corbett drove his right into Jackson's stomach with a whole lot of vim.

Round Twenty-Seven

Jackson countered Corbett heavily and Corbett staggered a bit. Jackson got in a middleweight right-hander before he had wholly recovered, but just as the gong sounded Corbett got back with a stinging left-hander.

Round Twenty-Eight

This was livelier. Punch followed punch and clinch followed clinch, but the blows were muffled in the maze of swinging. They quit their pretty boxing tricks and got down to first principles. Jackson had the best of it at first. He got in a left-hand straight blow and a fierce uppercut. It looked rocky for Corbett but he did some lively ducking and got out all right.

Round Twenty-Nine

This was another fierce one. Corbett landed first on Jackson's face, but Jackson gave as good as he got. Jackson hit him again in the face, but Corbett drove his right into Jackson's stomach with double force. Then Jackson looked weak. He was beaten back to the ropes, and got the worst of a red-hot rally. Corbett showed that he did know something about ring tricks. He was very tired, and he leaned on Jackson and rested, and Jackson could not prevent it.

Round Thirty

It was a bit slow at the start, but Jackson livened it up a bit with two good passes on Corbett's face. Corbett got even when he got Jackson against a post and gave him right and left in quick succession. They were both too tired to do any decisive work, but Corbett's blows were the harder, and he punched Jackson's stomach so that it seemed a miracle that he could stand up.

Round Thirty-One

It began with a clinch. They were still tired and both were willing to go slow for a minute. There were a couple of pretty rallies in which Corbett's superior skill counted. He dodged two of Jackson's drives that would have brought the end near had they struck, and the crowd cheered him for his cleverness. Before the round was over Corbett had reached Jackson's stomach again, and apparently as hard as ever.

Rounds Thirty-Two to Forty

Both men were tired, and there was little action over this nine round stretch. By the 39th round the crowd began to lose patience with the boxers.

Rounds Forty-One to Fifty-Five

At this point the *Examiner* gave up its round-by-round reporting, and presented a general account of the rounds, saying that from round 42 on it was extremely tiresome. Scarcely a blow was struck in a dozen rounds. The *Chronicle* persisted but found little to report: in round 46 Jackson suddenly landed a left on Corbett's jaw and staggered him, Corbett punched Jackson in the throat and in the heart; and in round 48 the two were chatting and laughing while sparring when Jackson hit Corbett about the head and drove him onto the ropes. Corbett's hands were sore and Jackson's stomach so tender, the *Examiner* explained, that neither cared to risk conclusions. Jackson was the stronger on his legs, but he did not dare to take his hands away from his stomach, and Corbett was afraid to hit him on the hard head on account of his hands. They simply faced each other and walked around and sparred at the air. Jackson's game seemed to be to tire Corbett's legs out. Every round or so he answered the demands of the crowd by making a lead or two, and usually for Corbett's head. Sometimes he got there, but Corbett always came back with a rap in the stomach, and Jackson again became respectful. There never was the appearance of a finish until the fifty-fifth round, when Jackson became vicious, but only for a moment.

Rounds Fifty-Six and Fifty-Seven

The time was now 1 A.M. The round started just as tamely as the forties and fifties had been, and both men walked through it without making a lead. The next round was no better, and the crowd commenced to hiss and make loud demands that the two men wind it up or quit.

Rounds Fifty-Eight to Sixty

Jackson squared off as though he intended to comply, but Corbett anticipated him with a spirited punch in the stomach, and the fight settled into the same old dreary affair. It dragged along for two more rounds without even the pretense of a punch, and the crowd commenced to sleep, go home, and make sarcastic remarks. It was now 1:30 in the morning of the 22nd, and the pair had been fighting for four hours.

The directors consulted in their box about what best to do. Cook called both men over to him at the call of time, and advised them to put a little life into the contest. "This is not a walking match," he concluded. "Ain't it?" queried Corbett, grinning, "I thought it was." Jackson told Cook, in Naughton's hearing: "I am doing the best I can, and I'm not going to take any chances if I have to stay here all night." Then Cook asked, "What is the matter with you, Corbett? Are your hands injured?" Corbett replied, "I am not going to give my business away in front of Jackson," but he said *sotto voce* to Major McLaughlin, Peter's patron, "My left hand is in pretty bad shape, but my right has nothing the matter with it," or, according to his own letter to the *Examiner* on May 24: "My left hand is a little off, but my right hand is good."

Round Sixty-One and Last

Both men sought the center of the ring, and walked through another round. By now it was obvious that nothing more was going to happen in this fight. There were loud cries of "Draw!" and "No draw!" at the edge of the crowd. Indeed, according to the *Chronicle*, Jackson himself proposed a draw, but Corbett objected, so Jackson said: "Well, go on, and I'll stay with you," as they resumed walking.

The directors and Cook went into busy consultation. Both men were questioned as to their condition. Corbett's second answered for him that his hands were gone. He crippled them both when he forgot his legitimate target, Jackson's stomach, and delivered those swings on either side of Jackson's hard head. Jackson frankly confessed that he was sore about the abdomen and that his leg was swelling and giving him much trouble.

"I don't think he can lick me in a year and I am not going to whip myself trying to whip him. I am too tired," said Peter.

This settled it. Cook entered the ring, put up his hand, and said: "Gentlemen, this contest is becoming very unsatisfactory to you and the directors of the club. Both men have admitted that they cannot go on to a satisfactory conclusion. You have had ample evidence that they cannot go on except as walkers, and I therefore declare the entertainment ended and that it is no contest." The fight ended at 1:33 A.M., more than four hours after it began.

Calling it a "No Contest" was not the same thing as declaring it a draw. It meant in effect that the fight had not taken place, that the last four hours had never happened. The announcement was extremely controversial. It will be understood that large sums of money had been laid on Corbett to win or Jackson to win. The *Chronicle* estimated on May 21 that $100,000 had been wagered on the fight. Jim Wakely had wagered $3,000 on Corbett, Owen Hogo $10,000, Lee Little $3,000, Harry Heims $3,000 and Asa Hamilton $1,000. Mose Gunst had bet $5,000 on Jackson, Davies $1,000, Bat Masterson $1,000, Charles Archer $10,000, Charles Dexter $1,500 and Charles Kingsley $3,000. These wagers, not to speak of the California A.C. officials, plus the innumerable lesser bettors, all could now put their money back in their hip pockets. Henry Ash had been specific: he had bet $3,000 that the fight would not last 20 rounds, but he too was saved from paying out anything because of the decision. Not lasted 20 rounds! Notionally, it had not lasted one second. Since nobody had lost any money, hopes were still high. "Frank Phillips wanted to be Corbett's backer right away," the *Examiner* reported. "'There is $10,000 to be had in a minute,' he said, 'that Corbett can whip Jackson on the turf, London rules, with or without gloves, in three or four months from date.'"

The fight had stirred up the blacks, who bet thousands on Peter. The *Chronicle* said: "For weeks it was the main topic of conversation, and as the critical time approached interest rose to fever pitch. Around the Lotus and Stevenson-street clubs and other colored resorts in that neighborhood the heat was tempered only by the fact that hardly anyone could be found to talk Corbett, and so disputes were few."

Generally, the bettors were happy with Cook's decision. The boxers were not. "Both contestants looked blank," said the *Examiner*. They were now dependent on the California directors for any payment they might get for their exertions. Corbett was mobbed by his fans, while Peter, whose ankle was the size of his thigh and whose left shoulder-blade was hurting him, sank back against the ropes limp and, according to the *Chronicle*, actually pale.

At the end of the fight, Herget went round to shake Corbett's hand and said, "Jim, we are both Californians, and I think we are good for the world." Corbett was saying, "I'm champion of America tonight, that's sure." He added, "Well, I'm up pretty well, anyhow, and with Sullivan out I can have a shy for the championship. Australia can't have two champions; let Slavin and Jackson settle that, and I'll be on hand to represent America when the turn-up for the championship of the world comes off." It is not quite clear what he meant by saying Sullivan was out, his own title fight with Sullivan being 16 months in the future. By January 23, 1893, in a letter written to the *Chicago Tribune*, he said he would not meet Goddard until he became champion of Australia, presumably by defeating Peter. "I am the champion of America and of the world," Corbett wrote, "and I claim the right to say whom I shall meet."

After confabulations, the California Athletic Club's management offered them each $2,500, that is a quarter of the prize which either might have won, and not the half of it, which might have been given had the decision been a draw. Corbett at first refused to take the $2,500, demanding $4,000, but he finally accepted it. On May 25, Peter said he was unwilling to take what he was offered. "I am a poor man," he said, "and I may have to accept it but I do not think it would be just or fair. The purse ought to be divided between us." But he was in a contractual situation. "I am in the hands of the club, however, and I suppose they will do about as they want with me." He ended up taking the $2,500 as better than nothing.

There was a good deal of rumbling about the no-contest decision, and many thought the club lost credibility because of it. Corbett said he was boycotting the club thereafter. He wrote a long letter to the *Examiner* called "My Fight With Jackson," published on May 24, justifying his inaction or, rather, defending his tactics. He said, "I cannot recollect a single time when I took the lead." On August 10 the *Examiner* published a second letter from Corbett, this one called "How I Fought Jackson," in which he claimed to have been taken ill in New Orleans and not recovered by the time of the fight, nor indeed by August. He blamed Hiram Cook for prejudiced refereeing. He said he had been denied, by a few rounds, the victory that he was planning to win. But these were Parthian shots, for by August he was galloping toward his date with Sullivan.

So loud was the murmuring that President Fulda felt obliged to issue a long statement, ostensibly a justification of the decision, which was published on June 15. It was, however, more a rationale for Cook's having called a halt to the proceedings than a justification of the no-contest verdict. In regard to that, Fulda said: "Suffice it to say, for our own part, that we only knew at the time, from their own utterances and our own observation, their true condition, and judged them accordingly." Fulda's language veiled his meaning, but what the directors had concluded was that neither Peter nor Corbett was intending to fight with the risk of losing, so the fight had been at heart a sham and could be justifiably canceled.

One of the most perceptive things Fulda wrote was: "The club's purposes and objects are not confined to the giving of such exhibitions of professional boxing as have given it its present renown in the sporting world nor to the maintenance of a pugilistic aristocracy in opulence and idleness rendering no equivalent to their patrons and supporters, the public or the art itself, nor to the imposition upon the sporting world of so-called champions, made so, not by deeds of daring, but by courtesy of friends and friendly journals, for truly can it be said that in the creation of latter-day champions the pen is mightier than the sword." Fulda could understand, already in 1891, that the sporting press was throwing off its restraints and creating the modern sports world with its celebrities.[12]

But the fight was one great bore, and only in retrospect, after Corbett defeated Sullivan, did it become of importance. Billy Woods, the Denver heavyweight, commented in a letter to Tom Kelly in St. Louis: "Corbett was worn out from running round the ring, and the big colored Australian from endeavoring to catch him. Corbett never led once during the contest." He ducked and weaved and danced away. And, like a faun or like a bit of thistledown, for years afterward James J. Corbett continued to dance away from Peter Jackson.

Not a week after the fight, on May 27, a Wednesday evening, Peter set eyes and one finger on John L. Sullivan, who was performing in San Francisco in the play that he was soon to carry to Australia for a season. After his performance at the Bush Street Theater, Sullivan went on a bar crawl and ended up, intentionally by chance, on Turk Street and in Peter's saloon. He had been shadowed by an *Examiner* reporter. Sullivan yelled at Sam Hess, who was tending bar, "Where's de mug that runs this place and thinks he's a fighter!" Peter was momentarily out of the bar. Sullivan then said, "Oh, say, he's no good. Black men ain't no good, anyhow. He's a duffer. I'd like to tell him so, see? There's kids in New York can lick carloads of Jacksons." At this point Peter returned to the bar, tapped Sullivan on the shoulder, and said, "You're talking through your hat." Sullivan said, "Say, come off! You're a chump." Peter repeated he was talking through his hat. Sullivan took off his coat and struck out at Peter, but Peter eluded his fist. Sullivan's companions bundled him home to the Baldwin Hotel.

The *Examiner* in particular followed this incident up. At the theater on Saturday evening, May 30, 1891, a few minutes into the performance, Sullivan stopped the show and addressed his audience, which included an *Examiner* reporter:

> Lades and genelmen, I've been lied about. Lades and genelmen, I wonner say a nigger's no good. If God wonned a nigger ter fight why did'ne make him white? Nigger's no good. I'kn lick'im — lick any nigger. I wish ter say somethin' an' I'm gon ter say it. Lades an' genelmen, th' newspapers — yes, the newspapers, the newspapers — say I say "mudder." It's not so. I can say mudder. See! Mudder! I can fight any nigger an' lick him in a minit. A nigger can't fight. He ain't no good. Ain't as good as a white man, anyhow. No nigger is; if he was he'd be white. Now the Exam'ner says — yes, the Exam'ner newspaper, the Exam'ner — I was drunk an' had fight with Jackson. I knows newspapers an' I know newspaper reporters. I knows 'em pretty well.... I'm John L. Sullivan an' they're reporters. But I tell you, lades an' genelmen, I pay fer what I drink. Th' ed'tor of the Exam'ner don' pay fer my drinks. I was born in Boston an' I can lick any nigger. If no lades was here I'd give my opinion of de Exam'ner.

The *Examiner*'s reporter noted that "many ladies retired, presumably to give Mr. Sullivan an opportunity of giving his views without restraint," though all he said was: "Well, never min' boys. I was goin' to sing but I won't. P'raps I've been drinkin' a bit. I dunno. I can lick any nigger, though, that ever lived. 'Sides I pay fer everything I drink myself." When the play resumed, a boy in the gallery yelled out, "Say Mudder! John, say Mudder!"

Sullivan left for his tour of Australia on June 26, 1891, intending to return in September. Fulda went to the dock and up to stateroom E on the *Mariposa* to pay his respects.

It was then that Peter and Sullivan were formally introduced. We have two firsthand accounts of their famous meeting, published in the *Examiner* and the *Chronicle* on June 27 and unadulterated by the activities of memory. A third account, in the *Morning Call*, was short because the paper (with a pioneering woman editor) was averse to reporting anything much about Peter and detested the celebrity whom it called "John Lush Sullivan."

The *Chronicle* reporter wrote:

> Just then W.W. Naughton, a well-known sporting man, made his appearance and shook hands with Sullivan. "I want to introduce Peter Jackson to you," said he. "What for?" asked the champion. "Because I have known him since he was a boy, and I think you two champions should meet." "Bring him along," replied the great John L. as he gave his hand a royal wave.
>
> The crowd on the dock was not aware of the expected meeting, and when Jackson arrived in a hack considerable excitement was created. Sullivan and party left the cabin and went round to the port side of the steamer, where the introduction took place. Jackson, all smiles, approached the gathering with Naughton. Jack Barnett, turning to John L. Sullivan, said: "This is Mr. Jackson, Mr. Sullivan."
>
> The two champions, one white, the other black, looked at each other on the sizing up principle, when Sullivan spoke: "How are you, Jackson?" "How do you do, Sullivan?" responded the black champion as he extended his hand in a manly way. Both shook hands in a friendly manner. "You are a big fellow. Do you think you could fight me?" asked John L. Sullivan a moment later. "I bar no one!" responded Jackson quickly. Here friends called out to Sullivan that the occasion was only a friendly introduction. "Well," said Jackson, "Mr. Sullivan, I sincerely wish you success on your trip to Australia." "Thank you," responded the world's champion, and the two shook hands again and parted.
>
> "What do you think of Peter Jackson?" asked a reporter of Sullivan. "I am better pleased with him than I expected to be. This is the first time I ever spoke to him in my life. But he is a nigger, and that settles it with me. God did not intend him to be as good as a white man or he would have changed his color, see?" And the pugilist retired to test the quality of the ship's goods.

So the *Chronicle*. It is interesting that Sullivan denied that the two of them had spoken before. Either he had simply forgotten the episode in Peter's saloon, or else he hadn't realized that the black man who tapped him on the shoulder a month before was Peter.

On Wednesday, September 23, 1891, Peter refereed the Young Mitchell versus Reddy Gallagher bout at the Occidental Athletic Club. Fitzpatrick had trained Herget, and the *Examiner*, that is to say Naughton, said, "A word of praise is due to Sam Fitzpatrick for the splendid condition in which he sent Mitchell into the ring." For what it was worth, Naughton also said that Herget had "better shoulders and sturdier and more shapely legs" than Gallagher. Sam also seconded Herget, along with "Nonpareil" Dempsey. For seconds, Gallagher had Jimmy Carroll and his backer Bat Masterson. Peter did not have much to do beside reciting the Queensberry rules at the start and unclinching the two in the second round. The fight ended with Masterson throwing a towel into the air, a variation from the usual sponge, and stomping off to his hotel — so that Peter did not even have to decide the winner. His unique appearance in America as a referee was because Herget was fighting.

Sullivan returned to San Francisco aboard the *Alameda* on October 29, 1891, disgruntled after a tour that was panned and lost money. He told the reporters at the Spreckles wharf, "There ain't a dozen decent sports in the bloomin' place, but more hoodlums to the square inch can be found there than at any place in the world." Choynski, sporting a mustache, was on the same boat after a few profitable months fighting in Australia and he said of Australia, that he liked the people and "It's a great sporting country, too."

On November 10, 1891, Peter issued a challenge, something he rarely did, to Paddy, inviting him to fight him. "Mr. Slavin, I see, claims to be heavy weight champion of Australia," wrote Peter, "a title which I won, still hold, and am open to defend against all comers. If he can defeat me he will honestly be entitled to what he now claims and be in a better position to meet Mr. Sullivan for the world's championship when the time comes. I trust Mr. Slavin will see the force of what I say and favor me with an early acceptance of my offer." Peter suggested the California Club as the venue, for $10,000.

No direct reply to this challenge came, but on November 16 the first news of a fight with Paddy in London was published. The National Sporting Club's agent in America, Captain James Cook of the *Boston Police News*, wired Peter that the club was putting up $10,000 in prize money, plus it would pay Peter $500 for his expenses. The proviso, a concession to Paddy, was that the fight must take place during Derby Week in June 1892. "It will decide who is really the champion of Australia and which of the two is the proper man to pit against," Paddy was reported as saying. And the chance of $10,000 was something Paddy could not afford to pass by. Gillies of the *Maitland Mercury* wrote on May 21, 1892: "Slavin and Jackson will be able to settle the moot and vexed question as to who is the champion boxer of Australia."

The arrangements suggested by Cook suited Peter well enough, and he prepared for the trip. The *St. Louis Post-Dispatch* of December 6, 1891, said: "Jackson has cabled to Lord Lonsdale that he will sign the articles for his proposed contest with Slavin before the National Club as soon as they reach him. The Earl took a great fancy to Peter when the latter was in England two years ago. The black trained for his bout with Jem Smith on Lord Lonsdale's grounds, and it is probable that he will be invited to train there for this affair. Jackson has not improved since he met Smith. He has lived too well, and champagne has had its effect on him. This was painfully evident in his contest with Corbett." The injured foot, which many accepted as sufficient explanation for his performance, was by some people treated as the wages of sin because when his horse bolted Peter was drunk on the Sabbath.

The main thing to be organized was the Turk Street bar. He sold the business, though not to Sam Hess, who had apparently left town. Instead, he said it to W.B. Holloway, but he retained his lease of the property.

Peter left San Francisco for the east, taking with him Riordan as his trainer and sparring partner, on January 2, 1892. On the same day, in London, the Pelican Club, not merely the organization but its premises, was officially pronounced dead. It resurrected immediately as the National Sporting Club. A splendid new building was being constructed. The plaster on the ceilings was still damp the night Peter and Paddy fought. The stuffed pelican and the stuffed flamingo and the mounted mustachios were conveyed to the new premises, and the cast of characters stayed the same, minus only Queensberry.

Going east, Peter and Riordan stopped on January 6 in Denver on the invitation of

Bat Masterson and Johnny Murphy, leaving the next day, according to the *Colorado Sun*. They were in Kansas City on January 7. The local black paper, the *American Citizen*, said on January 8 that Peter had arrived and was staying with Dan Lucas. He would be exhibiting with Riordan on Saturday night at the Turner Hall. Peter was accorded a reception by his fans, and the *American Citizen* offered Peter a tour of Kansas City. It then said: "Welcome King Jackson to the city. If you don't see what you want ask for it." Peter declined the invitation to cruise Kansas City in the company of a reporter, and the paper accused him of having grown too big for his boots. "Besides," it said, "Lucas' champagne and dollar-a-piece cigars got the better of him." It was rarely that Peter offended a reporter.

Peter with Riordan reached Chicago on January 11, 1892. On Tuesday, January 12, in Battery D he first fought Jack King, a local heavyweight, who had once fought Mervine Thompson. King, who "seemed frightened to death almost," according to the *Chicago Tribune*, quit in the third and was hissed. As a wind-up to the night, Peter fought John Dalton, who once whipped Gus Lambert. During the first, in a clinch, the two of them fell down on the stage. For the rest Dalton fought gamely until he was knocked out in the third. Coming to, he wanted to fight Jackson with bare fists but his friends drew him away. Dalton turned a handspring to show he was strong yet, said the reporter.

The most interesting aspect of the evening was that Paddy attended, with Charley Mitchell and Fred Gallagher. These three were in town on their theatrical tour with Paulding's *Struggle of Life*. On Wednesday night Peter, Davies and Hall reciprocated by going to the Windsor Theater to watch Paddy and Mitchell spar on stage. Paddy and Peter met and talked "for the first time in years," according to the *Chicago Tribune*, but it had been a little less than two years.

They continued to New York City. Between January 18 and 23, 1892, at Hyde & Behman's in Brooklyn, Peter showed as part of "Parson Davies' Athletic and Speciality Company." This consisted of Peter and Riordan, with acts by William Jerome, Gus Bruno, Sam Dearin, the Three Judges (acrobats) and the Braatz Sisters. The Davies company would be followed there in February by Muldoon and his athletes, then by Corbett.

At the start of February, Peter was given a benefit at Hyde & Behman's theater in Brooklyn. After the turns Peter gave a little speech of thanks, and some joker yelled out, "Don't go to Bruges!" The *Referee* said Peter responded, according to the New York correspondent of the *London Hawk* on February 6: "No fear, boys, about me getting fair play if I hold a good hand. I've never been treated so well in all the places I've been to as I was in England (loud cheers and hurrahs). Having a 'square deal' gives me no worry or anxiety, I got it with the English champion, Jem Smith, and I shall get it again. I am not going to meet a dunce, as we have met as boxers before in Australia. I don't say I shall win, but I do say I will try to do so, and if I am whipped it will be because I have found a better man than myself." This was almost the only occasion on which Peter referred to his punch-up with Paddy in the White Horse, or else those early encounters before their Kiama reunion.

On March 25 Peter and Riordan sailed for England on the White Star steamer *Britannic*, arriving on Friday, April 4, 1892, in Liverpool. He was interviewed on the wharf and at the North Western Hotel. The next day they traveled to London. He was interviewed by a *Sportsman* reporter at Euston depot. *Reporter*: "You met Slavin in America?" *Jackson*: "Yes, I met Frank twice, once in Chicago and once in St. Louis. He was looking, I thought, very

6. Diamonds and Schlenters, 1890–1892

well indeed." *Reporter*: "It was a friendly meeting, I suppose?" *Jackson*: "Certainly, in every way." Peter did not encourage press beat-ups.

The *St. Louis Post-Dispatch* of April 23 quoted an unnamed English source that said Peter and Paddy were readying themselves. "Over in the land of the kangaroos," it reported, "the standing of the two is in dispute. Slavin is regarded as the champion at Melbourne, his home, and the Sydney sports swear by Jackson, who resides at that point when in Australia. While the pair have never met in the ring yet they did have a rough-and-tumble encounter in a barroom at home." It is strange that Goddard was not Melbourne's choice by then.

At Euston an engine with a carriage was waiting "so that the ordinary passengers should escape the crowd which it was anticipated would be at the terminus," and it took him and Riordan on to Holborn Viaduct depot. He was met by "Peggy" Bettinson, E. Dewhurst and H. King from the Belsize Boxing Club, T. Jones of the Middlesex Polo Club, his old pupil Billy McCarthy, and J.T. Hulls from *Sporting Life* with other pressmen. Also present was W. Smith, who was described as Peter's *fidus Achates*, which suggests a long-term relationship, and must have been "Australian" Billy Smith, Peter's favorite pupil. From there a four-horse coach driven by Ambrose Preece conveyed him to his hotel, and in the evening to the Empire Theatre of Varieties and Sam Adams's Trocadero Music Hall.

In between entertainments he called in at the National Sporting Club to inspect the new premises. Bettinson, John Fleming, and George Piesse the perfumer, Paddy's Svengali, showed him around. He was impressed, for the building was state-of-the-art sports architecture. Peter managed to say a couple of nice things about Jem Smith.

Next day he visited the *Sporting Life* office to renew acquaintances, and then to Ware in Hertfordshire to stay with friends. He and Riordan quarreled, and Riordan was heading back to America. Riordan was drinking too much. But he stayed beyond April 2, and he was still in England in June, about to fight Jack Slavin and being advertised variously as "of California" and "of Melbourne." Davies would be leaving New York on April 30, and probably Davies had told Riordan to cool it until he arrived. Paddy and Charley Mitchell reached London on March 31.

Peter was going back to Brighton after three weeks but was advised that it was too crowded with holidaymakers. So on April 5 he went temporarily into Buckinghamshire to train, to a quiet suburb near Stoke Poges not far from Slough, from where it was easy to travel to downtown London.

When he did transfer to Brighton he was lucky in being able to take up residence above the oyster shop where he had stayed before his fight with Smith. He took morning and afternoon swims at Brill's Baths. In the afternoons he would stroll round to Ike Da Costa's club, where he met a large circle of friends who made time pass pleasantly. From there he would call in at Brighton Athletic Club's quarters under the Dome Assembly Hall. The unseasonably hot weather made him languid. He kept well, but on May 28 the *Sportsman* said: "The rumors about his having had several hemorrhages have not been officially denied." He had to bestir himself to train Jem Young, the East London boxer with whom he had sparred in 1889. Davies reached England on the *Germanic*, with Choynski and Davies's new boxer, the 24-year-old Australian Jim Hall, arrived in London on May 13, proceeded to Brighton the next day.

The fight was written about in the sports section of every cheaper newspaper. The *Sporting Life* carried advertisements that read: "Jackson and Slavin. Portraits from life in boxing costume of the above celebrities can be obtained from J. Robinson and Sons, Photographers, 172 Regent-street. Cabinets 2s.; large size for framing, 7s. 6d." Who got what out of these charges is unknown, but Peter must have taken a percentage.

Sporting Life made an interesting nationalistic comment on the matching of Peter and Paddy. "With their home at the other end of this terrestrial hall," it said, "they are nevertheless British subjects. Their flag is the Union Jack, their emblem the rose, with (just to show that they belong to Greater Britain) the wattle intertwined." *Sporting Life* was dreaming an imperial fantasy. On their colors no roses or wattle were to be seen. The Union Jack was displayed only as a component of Australian flags and coats-of-arms, and, as before, the Stars-and-Stripes logo on Peter's colors was as big as the one for Australia. Only the former reference to the California Athletic Club had been omitted.

Jackson's train arrived at the Victoria depot from Brighton at 3:32 P.M. He was met by Choynski, Billy Smith and Fallon. He spent some hours at the Colosseum Hotel on Great Portland, and from there about 8:30 left for the fight venue, where milling outside the National Sporting Club he found lots and lots of blacks. Making a joking allusion to Mrs. Jellyby in Dickens's *Bleak House*, the *Sportsman* said: "It might have been a May Meeting for the promotion of the mission to Borioboola Gha, or a movement to supply Africa with respirators, so numerous were the members of the race of Africa on view in the neighbourhood of Exeter Hall." Only about 500 blacks lived in London, and even including seamen and other transients it sounds as if most black men had turned out to encourage their hero.[13] Paddy arrived from the Cliff Hotel in Dovercourt at 3:15, went to the barber's for haircut and shave, then straight to the National Sporting Club.

Several authoritative accounts of this fight appeared in the newspapers at the time, together with more than a few versions over the years corrupted by the vagaries of memory. But among the eccentric 12 volumes of his *Famous Fights, Past and Present,* published across 1901–1903, Harold Furniss gave a nice account of the match, at which he had been present.[14] And as late as 1925 reliable details were given in his published memoirs by Bernard Angle. One of the authoritative accounts was written by Hales, who was sent to London from Sydney to cover the match, probably the only instance of a *Referee* reporter's being dispatched overseas.

Angle refereed. The seconds for Slavin were Tom Williams, the Australian club-swinger, and Tom Burrows, the champion lightweight of Australia, with Jack Slavin as bottle holder. The seconds for Jackson were Davies and Choynski. The Club's timekeeper was Tom Anderson. It was the boxers' timekeepers that showed which powers were in play that night, because Jackson's timekeeper was Lord Lonsdale and Slavin's was "Rats" Piesse.

At 10:50 P.M. Slavin entered the ring in a loose gray coat. He wore dark-blue knee breeches, light-blue stockings, and russet leather shoes. He had shaved off his trademark bushy mustache. He sat there chewing a lump of ice, crunching the rosin under his feet and waving at friends. Jackson came a few minutes later in his old brown ulster, with under it white drawers, white socks, and black leather shoes. Each of them wore a strengthening plaster. Slavin was said to be notably shorter than Jackson, but because they were in fact equally tall and Jackson was wearing his heel-less, cloth-soled boots, the reported difference in height must be put down to the impressiveness of Jackson's body or else to enhance the threat he posed. The fight, or rather contest as the National Sporting Club preferred to call it, started at 11:20 P.M.

Round One

Jackson landed on the chest lightly with the left. Tried again, and Slavin countered in stomach hard. Short-armed exchanges at the head and face in favor of Slavin. Slavin landed a hard one on the side of the head, but Jackson countered hard in the face. Slavin landed a hard one on Jackson's ribs, and got one in the stomach, which made Slavin wince. Both were very cautious, and clinched several times.

Round Two

Slavin rushed at Jackson, but was slipped. He then tried at the stomach, but Jackson gave him a hard punch in the left eye, and amidst cries of "Don't hold!" Slavin hugged his opponent. Jackson planted a hard one in the stomach. Slavin then crossed on the jaw. Slavin landed several facers, but Jackson's left-handers were always in the face.

Round Three

Slavin tried to swing for his antagonist's jaw, but Jackson slipped his man, and landed a couple of little facers, straight-countering his man on the nose. Several swings on the part of Slavin were woefully short, but Jackson's left-handers on the nose were straight and heavy. He feinted for the stomach, and as Slavin's head came forward he caught Slavin on the left eye, raising a big bump. When he went to his corner he looked tired, and Jackson was fresh.

Round Four

Slavin now adopted different tactics. He tried at the face, and then hooked his man. Jackson timed him, and landed two or three heavy stomach and rib blows. "Then Jackson reached the nose and mouth," reported the *Sporting Life*, "drawing copious streams of carmine." Furniss said Slavin's blood "spurted in ruddy jets half-way across the ring." The *Sportsman* did not see any blood flow.

Round Five

Slavin again tried to rush his man, but was met with a straight left in the face. His next attempt at the stomach was a hard rap. Twice Slavin swung for the jaw, but was too far round. Then Jackson nailed his man on the nose, and getting him going he landed very hard on the jaw with the right. Slavin "reached the nose," said the *Sporting Life*, "and the distillery at once began to work, but the white man got a severe rap in the stomach." Furniss saw blood "pouring down Jackson's dusky body, and showing plainly when it reached the white drawers." The *Sportsman* missed this bloodshed, too.

Round Six

Slavin showed a big lump under his left eye, but he was first at the face, Jackson relying on his straight left-handed counters on the nose. Slavin tried a swinger at the head but miscalculated and was met with a stiff punch in the chest. Slavin backed slowly away, guarding his head with the right and his body with his left arm. Cautiously Jackson stepped in, stepping nine inches forward and six back, weaving artfully, when suddenly bang went his fist full and flush on Slavin's sore nose, and instantly the red stream was again trickling down Slavin's upper lip and dropping on to his brawny chest. Both men were very tired, but Jackson rallied first, and punished his man severely in the face, reaching the stomach once.

Round Seven

Jackson was the first to make play this time but gave only light blows, while Slavin landed three good body blows, and then reached the face very heavily. Jackson was evidently resting. Comparatively light exchanges filled up the round until the end, when just as time was called, Jackson caught Slavin a tremendous smack on the jaw with the right, which sent him reeling and dizzy to his corner.

Round Eight

Slavin gave Jackson a couple of left-handers on the nose and got punched hard in return. A succession of light punches then ended with shooting home his right onto Jackson's jaw and sending him tottering across the ring. Choynski yelled to Jackson, "Steady yourself, Peter. It'll soon be over. Don't waste your chance. You've got him licked. Watch your man." When Slavin moved in to finish him off with body punches, a revived Jackson gave him smash after smash in the face, driving his head backward jerkily with every blow.

Round Nine

A quiet spar opened the round, and both missed with the left, when a another spar followed. Slavin was the first to try, and he soon drove Jackson back, the latter getting out of danger easily. Slavin tried a rush with left and right cross, but Jackson popped the dexter on the side of the head. Then Slavin made an attempt with the left and right on the body, but after reaching lightly Jackson closed with him. Meeting Slavin's next attack with the shoulder, Jackson received a tap on the face, but gave a very sharp one in reply, and as Slavin went back, Jackson smashed in a one, two, sending Slavin up against the ropes. Slavin tried a hurricane attack with a torrent of hits. Then, again, just before the call of time Jackson got blows home, two on each side of the jaw and two straight smashes on the nose and mouth. In 1937 Lonsdale recalled that at the end of this round, Slavin being urged to surrender, he said, "Give in? Not I! Never to a black man!" The reporting at the time says nothing about any such urging or any such speech.

Round Ten and Last

After a quiet spar Slavin let go with the left, but only touched the face lightly. He was again short at the face, and then rushed in with left and right, but Jackson jumped out of danger. Another spar and Slavin came the left and right dodge, but once more did little. As he tried a third time Jackson went at him and with terrific force landed right and left on the jaw, Slavin fairly reeling under the blows. He tried to avoid, but rolled about, and made a big effort to turn the tables but he was powerless to harm. Jackson went after him and rained blows upon him as he worked round the ring, trying with the greatest pluck to keep going. Several times Slavin faced round, but could hardly defend himself, and Jackson at last sent him down with a right-hander. Several little face hits were indulged in, then he began in earnest. First he landed one in the stomach, which brought Slavin's head forward, and before he could get out of danger Jackson found his jaw with an awful punch, which made him reel and in a moment Jackson's left hand struck the side of the head. "Poor Slavin," said Furniss, "looked in pitiful plight — one eye, the left, was completely closed, and his lips and cheeks were swollen to a frightful extent. He was dazed from the last three punches. He wandered about aimlessly." Jackson knocked him onto the ropes, where he half stood and half hung in a very helpless manner. The rain of blows recommenced, but Slavin instinctively turned round and sank down.

The *Sportsman* said: "Towards the close he was almost oblivious to all around him, clutched Jackson round the legs, and the latter appealed in dumb fashion to the referee, hardly knowing what to do." Jackson stepped back with his arms by his side and looked toward the referee. Eugene Corri heard him ask, "Have I won?" but nobody else did. Angle said "Box on!" Peter said: "I must finish him then?" It was the Lees fight and the Cardiff fight over again. As quickly as he could he gave Slavin a number of savage punches on the head and a final right to the jaw, so that Slavin collapsed in a senseless heap on the floor.

It is hard to know what passed before Hales's eyes, but he wrote: "To the everlasting honor of Peter Jackson be it recorded, that instead of striking the beaten man he opened his brawny arms and caught him and held him from falling to the floor; and even then Slavin tried to struggle away and lifted his arms for a blow. Jackson turned and made a mute but eloquent appeal to the referee, which went unheeded." According to the end of Chapter 20 in Hales's 1910 novel: "Peter, standing a yard or two away, looked round at the referee and threw out his hands with an appealing gesture, mutely asking if it were absolutely necessary for him to strike this already-beaten man. The referee nodded to him to go on and finish; there was no alternative." Following in Hales's track, accounts of the 10th round grew ever more romantic.

The 10 seconds allowed rapidly ran out, and thus, 1 minute and 25 seconds into the 10th round, amid deafening applause, Peter Jackson was declared the winner of what was hailed as one of the most scientific glove contests yet seen. He remained, as he had been since 1886, the champion of Australia. Bettinson went round to see Paddy the following morning, in his room where he had been sleeping it off, and Paddy said: "They won't believe it in Melbourne."[15]

They had to believe it, however. The *Melbourne Argus* wrote, grudgingly, on July 13 that "no one in this country gave him credit for the ability to stand up to, much less defeat, the redoubtable Frank Slavin, the champion boxer of the world." Paddy's Melbourne reputation had clearly exceeded reality. Peter was photographed with Naughton, both in top hats and Prince Albert coats and holding canes, standing on either side of an floral display spelling out:

P. JACKSON THE CHAMPION.

On a small table lay a belt, evidently Peter's belt displayed to show everybody that he had always had the right to it. This was the photograph of which Peter sent a copy to John Dunlop at Bondi and no doubt sent copies to other figures from his past, even to some obdurate Melbournites.[16]

But within a few days of Peter's victory the popular trouper Harry Allnutt performed on a Melbourne stage a song that appeared later that year in the *Australian Melodist Number 20*:

> *I am crazy! And I'm cranky!*
> *And I'm mad with wild delight,*
> *For a cable tells me lanky*
> *Peter Jackson's won the fight*
> *From the lanky Paddy Slavin,*
> *Our picked pet pugilist—*
> *Who's been knocked out by great Peter*
> *With his beautiful black fist.*

And so it went on. The "wild delight" Melburnians supposedly took was because the finally *national* Jackson might "sully 'Sully's' name" in a world championship bout, a hope soon dashed by events in New Orleans.

Peter never did well again. He never was able to fight his greatest fight, that is the fight with Corbett the champion. He cannot be deemed to have lost his knack immediately. But he had only four fights (as distinct from exhibitions) after the Paddy Slavin fight. In one (against Jeffries, a 26-year-old) he was defeated when he was 37; and when he was 38 he was effectively defeated in three fights by Jeffords, a 24-year-old.

The day after his victory, June 1, Peter went to Epsom to see the running of the Derby. A whole party of National Sporting Club members and others were driven down by Ambrose Preece, who was the National Sporting Club's chauffeur. Godfrey was in the party and an unnamed friend of Peter's "whose figure is well known at the Hoffman House, New York," possibly Billy Edwards, who was the bouncer at 1111 Broadway. Peter was in the best of spirits, as well he might be, being champion of the Pacific Slope, colored champion of the world, and finally the undisputed champion of Australia. Moreover, he was in luck that Derby Day, for he drew Lord Bradford's "Sir Hugo" in a sweep and the horse won.

Paddy had wanted the victor to take the whole purse. Peter had said: "We can't both win, Paddy," and insisted that the purse be split between winner and loser. When they called at the National Sporting Club the day after the Derby, June 2, to get their shares, Fleming handed Peter a check for £1,750 and Paddy one for £250. "Ah, Paddy," Peter was reported as saying, "you wouldn't have got that but for me." Paddy tore up the check and threw it into the fireplace. It was a grand gesture. The following day Paddy got himself a replacement. This anecdote, which appeared in 1929 in Fleischer's valedictory article about Paddy, and which seems to embody a recollection of Choynski's, is not what the *Sportsman* wrote at the time.[17]

While they were in the National Sporting Club office, a dialog took place which the *Sportsman* did report:

6. Diamonds and Schlenters, 1890–1892

SLAVIN: Well, Peter, I own you surprised me. You boxed tons better than I thought you would, and I have no excuse for my defeat. I hope we are just as good friends as ever.

JACKSON: Yes, certainly. If I thought I could not be friends with a man after a contest, I tell you I would not enter the ring with him.

SLAVIN: We have known each other for over 10 years, and I thought I would prove too good for you. There's no doubt I was over confident. I felt well, and when there is nothing wrong with a man he naturally fancies himself. Maybe, if we meet again, I'll come off best, and perhaps you will win again.

Peter tried to close off this topic:

JACKSON: Just so. As far as Monday is concerned I did my best, and I am quite sure you did the same.

SLAVIN: You bet I did. Halfway through I thought I had you set. I told my second, Tom Williams, you were tired, but you came again, which I did not expect, and you won, that's all about it.

Peter was obviously bored with Paddy's self-pitying stoicism so he changed the subject entirely, to Jack Slavin's match with Con Riordan in the Ormonde Club that night:

JACKSON: Do you second your brother to fight against Riordan?

SLAVIN: I do, and I'll bet you a tenner he wins.

JACKSON: That's a wager.

They shook hands on the deal, said the *Sportsman*, and then they talked about old times and their doings in the colonies. Their closeness would become even more apparent at Peter's farewell dinner in October. The inveterate antagonism between them had been another newspaper fabrication.

On Monday, June 6, Peter and Paddy boxed at the Central Hall, High Holborn, five rounds starting at 10 P.M. before a crowd of 4,000. "Perhaps the only occasion Jackson and Slavin will box in public," said the advertising, and it was. The referee was Joe Steers, the heavyweight and middleweight amateur champion. George Godfrey was brought onto the stage and was cheered. He said he was over in England not for business but for the pleasure of seeing Jackson and Slavin fight. "Jem Mace was next presented, and loyally received. He said: 'I wish it was my day now, and I'd have a go.'" Mace was still fighting five years after this. The match proved to be only an exhibition, in fact. Both Paddy and Peter were extremely tired, but after all the years of being tantalized the customers were satisfied just to have seen them in a ring together.

Davies crossed over to Ireland again for a visit. Peter went sparring on stage as before, but he was having trouble with his right hand and discovered that "in my fight with I broke one of the small bones in my right hand, just back of the little finger." The fracture may have been a legacy of his trouble in 1890 when he fought Guy the Gypsy in Washington. His wrist was put into a sling and he ceased all boxing activities.

In July, Peter went to the Continent with Davies and Choynski. Davies had been asked before to exhibit his little troupe across the Channel, but the money offered had been too slight. Now Peter was out of action anyway, so they paid their own way. They started a tour of Germany on July 9 at Aachen (Aix-la-Chapelle), and made their way across to Berlin. Peter enjoyed being idle for once. He was planning to get back to San Francisco by Christmas. On July 11 they were already in Berlin. Peter was said to be slowly improving but unfit to fight for some time. On July 27 a letter from Choynski in Germany told that Peter's hand was still bad and that he would stay in Europe for another six weeks. Davies and Choynski, with a New York sport called Warren Lewis, at one time "Nonpareil" Dempsey's manager, left England on August 26, 1892, sailing on the *City of Rome* to witness the Sullivan-Corbett fight in New Orleans. Peter stayed on because he wanted to be a tourist for a little longer. He was back in England and at Doncaster when the news of Corbett's victory came though.

Davies, Lewis and Choynski, after being placed in quarantine at Sandy Hook over a cholera scare, went down to New Orleans for the great tournament there, but also apparently to arrange another fight for Peter with Corbett. They traveled from Washington in Corbett's special train, and Davies used his hours on board to reconcile Corbett and Choynski, who had been enemies for years. Davies also managed to organize a match between Choynski and Godfrey at Coney Island in December.

In June, Peter had been asked by reporters if he would now challenge Sullivan, and replied: "No. Sullivan has announced his intention of retiring from the ring, and I will not force him to break his resolution. But I want to settle matters with Corbett, and 'Parson' Davies will be in New Orleans when Sullivan and Corbett meet to arrange a match with the Californian, whether he wins or loses with Sullivan."

Four fights were originally in the New Orleans tourney. The first was Jack McAuliffe versus Billy Myer for the lightweight title, a reprise of the fight they had had on February 23, 1889. The championship fight between two featherweights involved Dixon, a black, and Jack Skelly, a white. "Negroes," said the *Chicago Tribune* on September 1, 1892, reporting from New Orleans, "will be admitted to the Dixon-Skelly fight, but will be kept in a gallery by themselves and will be passed into the arena by a separate entrance. They will be admitted to the Myer-McAuliffe fight, but are not wanted much, while the doors will be barred to them when Sullivan and Corbett do battle."

So the heavyweight contest between Sullivan and Corbett could be viewed only by white men who were rich enough to pay $15 for a seat. However, one shining exception would be made: Peter Jackson was allowed to see it. Perhaps that was the reason Peter chose to avoid New Orleans. But he told nobody and he was expected as late as September 1, with quarters still reserved for him at the Senate Club.

As it was, when Dixon beat Skelly for the featherweight championship, in the process turning his face into hash, the most tremendous wave of fear and indignation swept the South. Blacks were roughed up all over, and the New Orleans authorities declared that no interracial bouts would ever be permitted thereafter in the Crescent City. Peter took careful note of the Southern climate.

The projected middleweight match, between the Britisher Ted Pritchard and the titleholder Fitzsimmons, was canceled. It was the heavyweight match that was sensational. After ten years Sullivan had lost his title. Davies had bet on Corbett and he was happy.

Clinging to a ring-post, Sullivan said, "I am glad that an American defeated me and none of those blarsted foreigners." Corbett became, in American terms, the champion of the world. Peter's opinion was, rather: "There is no champion of the world now, and I am desirous of having a chance for the honor with anyone else that is after it. Corbett, of course, is champion of America by virtue of his defeat of Sullivan." Taking the same line, on September 14 the *Referee* published a picture of the man it styled, pointedly, "James Corbett Champion Heavy-Weight Pugilist of America."

When asked had he ever fought Sullivan, Peter replied, choosing his words with extreme care: "No, he barred me, he said, on account of color." One coherent explanation of Sullivan's actions was given by him on May 28, 1905, to the *San Francisco Sunday Call*, in a page-length article titled "Jolts from John L.," which may have meant the *Call* had softened in its attitude toward him. "A white man has nothing to gain by swapping punches with a negro," Sullivan wrote or dictated. "I have twice been almost goaded into meeting the colored brother, but I took a second think in time. A club in San Francisco hung up a fortune for me to meet Peter Jackson — there was $20,000 in it, and nobody ever questioned my ability to win it — but I ducked. I was insulted from one end of the country to the other in the attempt to stampede me into that fight, and I was angry enough at one time to throw principle to the winds and give Jackson his. Another time I almost came to a set-to with George Godfrey, but I'm glad to say I didn't."

Before the date of the fight Peter was asked his intentions, and said as he almost always did, "No, I shall not challenge the winner, but I am hopeful that I will be able to get on a match with Corbett. When I say I will not challenge the winner, I mean that I do not intend to make a bid, but I stand ready to make a match with anyone." Paddy, who was now so prosperous that he owned two bars, said that he would challenge the winner for $10,000. After Corbett's victory Peter went to the States but he took his time, staying in London until October 26.

Peter was given a big send-off in London, to which he invited Paddy. The *Sportsman* reckoned that 150 members of the National Sporting Club feted him on Saturday, October 22. He was eulogized, and spoke about his hopes of meeting Corbett and then returning to England. Paddy was seated on the other hand of the chairman, F.W. Hobson, who was standing in for Sir John Astley. "Concerning my old friend Slavin here," said Peter, "we have been brought up together — we were boys together, and played together, and the hatchet is buried between us. We met in the ring as men, and we meet out of it in the same way. I have no animosity against any man, and I know Slavin is no enemy of mine. From the bottom of my heart I thank you all, and in conclusion I would like to propose the health of Frank Slavin."

In response to this suave though sincere speech, Paddy said gallantly: "As regards Jackson's remarks about the hatchet, I did not know that there was one to bury. We met in the ring and Peter proved successful. I had no ill-feeling towards him before we fought, and nor had I any when it was all over. I have business to attend to, and must retire for a while. I hope that Jackson will get on a match with Corbett, and if he wins I trust to have one more trial with him and then spend the rest of my days here in England."

These things did not come to pass.

Peter left Liverpool the following Wednesday, October 24, on the *Teutonic*, with a costly diamond ring "from a number of friends," and with several valuable canes, the gifts of employees of various hotels. He told reporters that he was ready to quit the fight game and probably return to Sydney, "which is my first love," because he was now 31 years of age. Actually he was 32. The champion of Australia reached New York by the *Teutonic* on October 27, 1892.

On November 1 he was in Philadelphia already, at the Academy of Music at Broad and Locust, in his "first appearance in America since defeating FRANK P. SLAVIN, Champion of England," implying if not stating that Peter now held the title. He was said to be going to box four rounds with an unknown, which meant that out of a number of local contenders, including Joe Lannon, one would be selected. The advertisement called him "The Invincible Fistic Marvel." In the event, he boxed John McVey, described as big and fat, puffing and panting, and Peter scarcely bothered with him.

He was in Philadelphia again at the end of November with his own "Big Specialty Co. 12 — Strong Acts —12" at the Lyceum. The performances were simply vaudeville acts hastily strung together by Davies. The performances concluded with a little play, called *The Judge*, in which all the troupers appeared. It was the first strictly theatrical piece in which Peter had ever appeared, even though in it he seems to have done little more than spar with Fallon.

On December 1 he fought three rounds with Billy Leedom of Philadelphia at the Lyceum. In the first round he sent Leedom into the scenery, and toyed with him in the other two rounds. On December 2 he sparred four rounds with local boy Joe Butler, for the last fortnight the colored middleweight champion, one of the few black boxers Jackson ever met in the ring. The Lyceum Theater was crowded from pit to dome. Two of Butler's punches reached Jackson's face. According to the *Philadelphia Inquirer*, Jackson "seemed pleased that he had met a man who was not afraid to spar with him." At the end, Jackson's fans and Butler's supporters cheered them both. Butler eventually fought Paddy twice and Johnson once.

In New York, Tom O'Rourke, who made his specialty the managing of black boxers, had booked him into the Occidental Hotel in the Bowery. From New York, Peter went to San Francisco directly. At the California Athletic Club he found gifts waiting for him: several boxes of cigars and more canes, four of them gold-headed and one in ivory. Such canes, by manufacturers like Thomas Briggs and James Smith, cost at the time something like $400 each. He did not guess that his seven good years were ending and that seven bad years were on their way. Since 1885 it had been all successes, rolling along a macadamized highway, but soon he would be on a corduroy road which would get him over uncertain ground, though his ride would be a jolting one. His lucky star deserted him and he became dreadfully unhappy and ended up wrecked.

In 1892, however, there remained only the matter of bringing the new heavyweight champion, Corbett, into the ring. The *Chicago Tribune* published an interview on December 6, 1892, in which Peter said: "Still I am the champion of Australia and the champion of the Pacific Coast by virtue of my victory over Joe McAuliffe, and I should think Corbett would be after the championship of the World." He laid no claim to be the champion of England. Peter realized that he couldn't go on forever. He told the *Chicago Tribune*: "When my powers are declining, then I don't know what I will do, probably go back to Australia. I shall go back there some day to stay." He was getting older, and if he was to have one last fight then he wanted it to be, win or lose, his fight for the championship of the world.

CHAPTER 7

Waiting in the Wings, 1893–1894

Peter never got another match with Corbett, not during the years when he was champion nor after his defeat by Fitzsimmons. But because Peter didn't fight against anyone from 1892 to 1898, against nobody between Slavin and Jeffries, he earned no income from prize money and side bets. Nor was he again taken on as instructor at the California club. He had sold his bar business though keeping the lease on the Turk Street property, so that he had a steady but small income from subleasing it. The fight game was always uncertain; indeed, life itself was risky. Following Godfrey's advice, Peter had done some hay-making by the end of 1892 in San Francisco and Chicago, though it is uncertain how much.

Meanwhile the boxing scene in California and throughout the United States was dismal. City after city was prohibiting fights, and boxers were either retiring or going abroad to fight. Peter fought some exhibition matches but gained no steady income. Everybody was scared of him, the mice not daring to approach the lion. Nobody was left to fight except the champion, who refused. The offensive tour had failed of its full effect. It was at this point, it seems, that he and Fitzpatrick broke up. Early in June, after hanging about in San Francisco, Fitzpatrick headed east "in search of dollars and renown," and for the next 30 years was contactable in New York City and environs. By June 12 the *Chicago Tribune* called him "Jackson's old second." The question was what Peter could do to earn his living, while waiting for his chance at the Pompadour.

Peter arrived in New York on October 28. He attended the Choynski-Godfrey fight on October 31 at the Coney Island Athletic Club, and according to the *National Police Gazette* "received a tremendous ovation" from the 5,000 spectators.

On November 18, Peter and Choynski were in Philadelphia, and Corbett was staying at the same hotel. In the lobby, Peter put out his hand, saying, "Mr. Corbett, I congratulate you on your splendid victory," upon which Corbett muttered some words. On November 28, Peter dished Denis Kelliher in four rounds in Philadelphia. The following evening he gave a three-round exhibition with Professor Billy McLean, the veteran. McLean, who had fought Joe Coburn in the 1860s, was 60 years old though remarkably active and retaining some of the cunning tactics of his youth. Peter courteously let McLean set the pace, and the exhibition, while tame, moved along briskly and pleased the spectators. It might seem that this match could only have been put together by an archaeologist, but in fact in those years McLean showed in Philadelphia with Corbett, Andy Watson, and Fitzsimmons, as well as with Peter. He thus made himself into a bridge between the bare-fisted and the gloved generations.

Peter exhibited again in Philadelphia, including a *déjà-vu* experience with Butler and another with Leedom, then he and Choynski went to Chicago. Here on December 5 he sparred with Tom Chandler and Jim Douglass at Battery D, but the *Chicago Tribune* said that "both were not even useful enough to give the audience an idea of the big Australian's power." He and Davies left Chicago for the West on December 10, doing some shows en route to San Francisco.

Peter arrived back in San Francisco in January 1893. He wired Naughton from Ogden, and Naughton went up to Reno to join him and Davies on the Southern Pacific train. Naughton noted the absence of bulldogs and skylarks. Naughton told the *Referee*'s readers that Peter was "just the same even-tempered, level-headed old stick-in-the-mud that he has always been." But he was about to change.

The *St. Louis Post-Dispatch* of November 28, 1892, had reported: "Joe Choynski, the boxer, believes that he is built for an actor. He intends, it is said, to have a play written around himself, and to star under Davies' management." Choynski knew he was handsome, with his blond chrysanthemum-cut hair, and why not show the world so, especially the ladies? This was the germ of the *Uncle Tom's Cabin* project. In the train coming down from Reno, Peter said: "I might take to the stage if nothing else was left for me to do, but I doubt if there would be any money in playing 'Othello.' Colored actors are not popular in America, so I will stick to my old profession. Pugilism can not give way entirely to the stage. The sport is too popular to be downed simply because some of the bright lights in it are seeking fame in a histrionic sense." Then he confessed: "Several playwrights have spoken about writing a play for me. I can't say, however, that I am in love with the idea of acting." Referring to Sullivan and Corbett, he said with a slight curl of the lip, "There are too many of my kind acting now." When he did become an actor, Peter said: "I have always thought that I would like to play Othello, if the part wasn't such a hard one. I believe I could look the character all right, and I wouldn't have to use walnut juice or any kind of complexion wafers at that. I have made a study of Ethiopian and Moorish history, and if ever I get myself up as the jealous Moor, people, I am sure, would admit that I looked the character, even if I didn't fill the bill any other way. I would have a genuine Moorish warrior's costume, no matter what it cost, and I would have bangles on my arms." This confession suggests that Peter secretly felt more than a literary connection with Othello.[1] On the other hand, C.B. Lowe, the Australian racehorse breeder, met Peter again in San Francisco early in 1893 and, according to his letter in the *Maitland Mercury* of September 16, not only was Peter well informed about African question but "it was quite apparent that he considers himself an offshoot of the Zulus, nor was it difficult, when looking at his stalwart frame and honest face, to imagine him another Umslopogaas evolved out of a few generations of contact with civilization." Lowe had been reading *Allan Quatermain* (1887).

But there was no alternative, and he played Tom in *Uncle Tom's Cabin*.

Many Tom shows toured the United States in the 1890s, but none of them starred a black. Indeed, it appears that only one black, Sam Lucas, had ever played Uncle Tom before, and his performance had been praised in 1879 by Harriet Beecher Stowe herself. Naughton called this one "Uncle Pete's Cabin." The *National Police Gazette* disapproved, saying Peter should have had a play written for him called *The Colored Gladiator* which would be "far more suitable than his playing the character of 'Uncle Tom.'" Also, it said, people would want to see him box, which was precisely why the Sullivan and Corbett stage vehicles had fight scenes built into them.[2]

In Los Angeles, in the Turnverein Hall on January 19, 1893, Peter gave a four-round exhibition of "scientific sparring" with Frank Childs, "the Los Angeles Favorite," as the *Los Angeles Times* called him, a local black aged 25. Childs, who had just trounced James "Soldier" Walker at the Palo Alto Club in San Francisco, was "honored" to fight Peter. He had a brighter future than Peter might have guessed.

Peter then turned to his acting. The general idea was to take *Uncle Tom's Cabin* from San Francisco to Chicago for the spring, so that it could play during the World's Fair. The organizers of the World's Fair had a policy of excluding blacks, so that *Uncle Pete's Cabin* would have to play outside the White City. Then they would break for the summer and Peter would go to England. In January 1893 J.J. Corbett told the *Chicago Tribune* that he predicted that in the coming year his earnings from theatrical performances would amount to $150,000. The Tom show was expected to turn a good profit.

Lincoln R. Stockwell owned and managed the Alcazar Theatre Stock Company. The company alternately worked in San Francisco at the Alcazar Theatre and toured the Pacific Slope towns from 1886 to the end of 1893, when it disbanded. The Alcazar Theater was at 629 O'Farrell. It seated 1,434 plus the eight boxes. It had an impressive facade but was made all of wood like so many San Francisco buildings, and it burned to the ground in 1906.[3]

Ironically, Davies played the auctioneer. "Little Eva will be portrayed by Georgie Woodthorpe, a pretty little damsel with the proverbial golden locks. She and Peter are on good terms already," said the *Chronicle*. Peter had to wear a white wig, white mustache and even white eyebrows, and people kept telling him he was too limber for the part. According to notices published in Sydney by the *Bird O' Freedom* on March 11, probably sent by Naughton, Peter responded by asserting: "It is all wrong to make Uncle Tom out an old stiff. Tom was only about 45 years of age, even if he was grey, and I know lots of fellows myself who are that age and a bit more, too, and still consider themselves young." The image of Harry Sallars might have recurred to him. Peter weighed so much that Stockwell hired two strong fellows to play Sambo and Quimbo, Legree's slaves, and after the whipping carry him away to his deathbed.

They talked of out-of-town runs in Santa Rosa, San Jose and Sacramento, but in the event the only tryouts were in Santa Rosa on February 19 and at the Macdonough Theater in Oakland, with its 1,337 seats, two nights and a matinee starting on February 21. The issues of the *Oakland Tribune* for February have gone missing with its review of the performance, but the *San Francisco Call* of February 22 applauded his "frostbitten eyebrows and snowy Pierpont whiskers" and said "Nick Long has so carefully coached him that the hardened critic finds it very difficult to pick any flaws in Peter Jackson's make-up, stage action, gesture, voice, reading or interpretation of the character created by Mrs. Harriet Beecher Stowe.... The simple truth is that Peter is an ideal Uncle Tom."

The San Francisco season began on Monday, February 27, 1893, at the Alcazar. On the first night it attracted a number of blacks and particularly Peter's buddies from the Lotus Club, "who," said the *Chronicle*, "occupied one of the proscenium boxes, and more conspicuously emphasized the desire of the colored population to claim the actor for their own." The theater was quite full. Peter's acting was judged adequate, with one reservation: "He has a sing-song tone that almost forces a smile from the listener at times." It was extremely difficult for a Cruzan educated by DuBois and long exposed to Australian and Californian talkers to catch Uncle Tom's accent, especially as Peter had only ever spent about four days in the South.

After three successful weeks the company set out for Chicago, starting in Cheyenne, Wyoming, on April 4 followed by Kansas City from April 10 to 15. All this was timely. By the end of February, the athletic clubs of San Francisco were being closed down, according to the *Examiner* of February 28, because of a boxer's death in the ring.

The reception of his production by the San Francisco audiences was so gratifying to Stockwell that his fancy took flight. He conceived the grandiose idea of starring Peter in a steamy Kanaka melodrama to be written for him, all palm trees, grass skirts and pyrotechnic volcanoes; and, astoundingly, of co-starring with him 55-year-old Liliuokalani, the Queen of Hawaii, who had been deposed several weeks earlier by a posse of Americans and had been put under house arrest by a provisional government. Stockwell wrote a letter to ex–Queen Liliuokalani offering her the chance of playing in his production not only the female lead, but opposite Peter Jackson the boxer. And forget San Francisco, the play would premiere in New York! It is most unlikely that Stockwell ever received any reply from Honolulu. Nor is it mysterious why he went bankrupt within the year.[4]

Stockwell had limitless ambitions but limited resources. For the tour of the eastern states after the summer break, Davies had to organize the bookings because Stockwell didn't know the scene beyond Chicago. Finally, just when *Uncle Tom's Cabin* was playing New York City for the second time, Stockwell's company went broke. The *New York Sun* reported on December 17, 1893: "A determined and worthy effort to establish a stock company in San Francisco, L.R. Stockwell being the manager, has resulted in bankruptcy, with rent and salaries unpaid."

So Peter and Davies together bought up the production and carried it over into 1894 with a largely new cast. Little Georgie Cooper was replaced by Little Anna Laughlin, Minnie Elseworth as Topsy gave way to Louise Miller, and George R. Caine replaced H.R. Jewett as Simon Legree, while Davies now doubled as George Harris. An arresting wall poster was designed in Chicago: announcing "Chas. E. Davies' Spectacular Production," with a large red "Uncle Tom's Cabin" at the top and an even larger red "Peter Jackson" at the bottom. In between the lines was the curious device of Peter's bust, in natural colors with folded arms, atop a pedestal decked with laurel leaves and a placard with lines from Pope's *Essay on Man*: "Honour and Shame from No Condition Rise — Act Well Your Part — There All the Honour Lies." It is hard to say whether the quotation was Davies's choice or Peter's. The poster was pasted up across America.

This portrait dates from the first week in May 1893, when *Uncle Tom's Cabin* was playing in Chicago at the Haymarket Theatre. William Morrison's studio was in the building from 1889 to 1899. Jackson's turned-in left eye can be seen. Photograph courtesy of Harvard Art Museum, Fine Arts Library [119.1976.3373].

In the middle of January 1894 the *Freeman* reported from Springfield, Ohio: "The abundant new scenery used in Charles E. Davis' 'Uncle Tom's Cabin' is pronounced simply gorgeous. The company is certainly one of the most expensive on the road." The *Freeman* said the scenery cost $20,000, but the ability of Davies and Peter to raise such a sum is doubtful.

Their tour was a matter of week-long showings and one-night stands for 12 months all told. In 1893 they progressed town by town to Chicago. Here they played during the second week of the Exposition, which had started raggedly on May 1, in the Haymarket at West Madison and Halstead with its 2,196 seats. After the summer break they did Washington, D.C., and Toronto, and all the towns between. They were twice in New York. The first time, October 16–22, they showed at Hyde & Behman's New Park Theater at Broadway and 35th, renamed the Herald Square Theater.[5]

Their itinerary can be followed in the *New York Dramatic Mirror*. The troupe were always getting on trains and getting off trains. Most of the whistle-stops they visited were not places where a purely pugilistic evening could be mounted. Thus audiences quite unfamiliar with the ring saw a boxer in the flesh performing, and it was the great Peter Jackson. Especially was it a novelty for women. The *Washington Post* said on March 6, 1894, that "it is quite possible that a great many ladies understood for the first time last night what there is about a gloved contest that possesses so much fascination for the masculine mind." Women had never been admitted to fights, but Davies guaranteed "three scientific rounds with none of the disgusting details of the prize ring." Many women would later attend boxing films— without thumps, without blood.

Reckless of the old saying that the worst two weeks in show business are the week before Christmas and any week at all in Toledo, Ohio, they played New York again in Christmas week, at Jacobs' 3rd Avenue Theatre (hard to fill, with its 2,100 seats). They were touring Massachusetts by New Year's Day, 1894. They hardly ceased. They played Cleveland. They played Boston. They did play Toledo, Ohio. They played every spot that would yield dollars, and carried Peter's fame to Main Streets far and wide. The only place they did not go was the South, not even to Louisville.

During the tour the big draw card was the boxing. As early as February 7, 1893, Naughton reported talk about having boxing in *Uncle Tom's Cabin*. But he said: "If there is to be any it will be during a plantation scene, and before Peter has made up in white Limericks and cotton-batting eyebrows for the pious old slave character he represents." Someone suggested casting Goddard as Little Eva.

On January 10 there had been a reception for Peter and Choynski in the Orpheum Theater, where the two had sparred three rounds. Now, two weeks into the San Francisco season of *Uncle Tom's Cabin*, a segment of sparring with Choynski was introduced, though not into the plantation scene. The audience was thinning in the huge Alcazar (especially in the orchestra) and was restless until the third act, when "Uncle Tom" first appeared. Something had to be done, so Choynski was induced to spar three rounds with Peter between Acts I and II. He stayed on for the tour, saying it was steady money, sparring and playing at first Haley the slave driver, then George Shelby. Moreover, he married the second Topsy, Louise Anderson Miller. With "three friendly and scientific rounds" included early in the performance, the audiences improved at once. Peter's three weeks at the Alcazar in 1893 were described as "a very respectable run for butterfly San Francisco." Over the next 15 months Peter sparred with Choynski on the *Uncle Tom's Cabin* stage nightly and at matinees.

The boxing was the attraction, but to everyone's surprise Peter proved a good actor. The *St. Louis Post-Dispatch* said, when the tour was drawing to an end: "It must be said that the Australian-African actor-pugilist is surprisingly good in his stage work, all things considered." He was big and had great physical presence on the stage, like Paul Robeson. His beautiful baritone voice, rich and mellow, delighted audiences, and he could project it. Peter said that *Gentleman Jack*, Corbett's stage piece, "was especially written to suit him and he fits into it, while I am compelled to assume a character that makes me to a certain extent appear ridiculous. It appears inconsistent that a pugilist should take the part of that very religiously inclined 'old darky,' but my friends credit me with giving a good representation, and I suppose I will have to continue on the stage for a season or two at least." What most surprised audiences was an Uncle Tom who was not a white in blackface but a black, and moreover one who came on stage and boxed a white man as fair as Little Eva.

Some blacks at least must have read a political message into these goings-on. At one of the early performances in San Francisco, when Peter was offering his splendid torso to the lash, one excited young fellow in the gallery yelled out, "Paste him, Peter," urging Uncle Tom to stand up and punch Simon Legree out!

A couple of the reviews may be quoted. A favorable one is from the *Kansas City Star* in April 1893: "His big shambling form and loose walk are peculiarly fitted to the requirements of the part of Uncle Tom and his voice has the deep resonance that one would expect to find in that old plantation darky. The chief fault in Jackson's acting is his elocution. He has yet to learn the importance of distinct enunciation. In the emotional scenes the black actor is hardly equal to the demands of the occasion, but nevertheless he is as good as most of the Uncle Toms that the stage has seen in recent years." The shambling walk had been perfected at Foley's hotel when he played stumblebum for his customers; Peter's off-stage walk was habitually a stately one. And the *Star* could not resist saying: "The Australian negro is not only infinitely the superior of the lamented [Sullivan] in dramatic ability, but he is a better actor than Corbett."

Peter was sweetly natural in his scenes with Little Eva, and could deliver Tom's last lines (in the George Aiken version) with convincing pathos: "Don't call me poor fellow. I *have* been poor fellow but that's all past and gone now. I'm right in the door, going into glory! Oh, Massa George! *Heaven has come!* I've got the victory, the Lord has given it to me! Glory be to his name! (*Dies*)."[6] The programs said "N.B.— Keep your seats-wait for the transformation," meaning perhaps a stained-glass tableau.

Peter seems to have felt his humiliation more sharply than spectators did, because no oreo-type slurs were heard. The *Washington Bee* of December 9, 1893, said that Philadelphia audiences "pronounce him the equal of the best 'Uncle Toms' of our day." Unfortunately, the copy of the *Bee* containing its own review of Peter's performance is missing. The *Indianapolis Freeman* said on January 20, 1894: "Mr. Jackson plays Uncle Tom to perfection, and has the finest show of the kind on the road."[7]

Even the jaded *New York Dramatic Mirror* reported in October: "Jackson is much better as Uncle Tom than could have been expected, although there is no surety that he will legitimately win half as much attention as an actor as he has as a fighter." At Christmas it said that "this novel company has before been seen in the city but will be very popular, evidently, on the East-Side this week," while the *New York Herald* said on December 19, 1893, that the Christmas week production was "greeted with enthusiasm last night." New York has never been easy.

By March 1894, however, the reviews of the play in the Grand Opera House at Decatur suggest the performers had lost interest, even the sparring sequence being lackluster. In spite of the buck and wing dancing, the Jubilee singing, and the host of pleasing specialties, the *Decatur Morning Herald* called the show "worse than rotten," but said: "The people who bought tickets were satisfied when they had seen the celebrated colored pugilist." It reported "a small crowd down stairs, a packed balcony and gallery," that is, while richer people at 75 cents were sparse, working men and blacks at 25 or 50 cents were there in force. The *Decatur Daily Review* confirmed that Peter was the attraction, saying: "The gallery howled for him and the balcony stamped for him. The more sedate below clapped their hands for him." And it noted: "After the boxing was over there were plenty of empty seats all over the house," which had 1,500 places.

The prospect of a Corbett fight in May 1894 marked the end of *Uncle Tom's Cabin*. Peter swore off liquor from February. His friends in St. Louis, by which the *St. Louis Post-Dispatch* of March 4 seems to have meant his black friends, gave him a reception at the Central Turner Hall under the aegis of the Gentleman's Athletic Club. Their last performance in St. Louis was on March 13, whereupon they made their way to Boston, where *Uncle Tom's Cabin* wound up. The scenery ended up in Chicago with Davies and was left to rot. The fate of the bloodhounds is unknown. Peter resented Davies for not making arrangements to dissolve their theatrical partnership. In March 1894 he went back directly to San Francisco to get in shape.

Only two events connected with their touring require notice.

In May 1894 when he was playing Boston again, according to the *Indianapolis Freeman* of June 2: "Peter Jackson has found a long lost brother in Boston in the person of James Jackson." They had not seen each other since 1888 when Peter left Sydney. James was described as a porter, like his father. It is not clear whether James had failed to contact Peter when he was in Boston six months before, or whether James had not been living in Boston at that time.

The second noteworthy event was that Peter went to a New York doctor about his nosebleeds. Dr. John Wilson Gibbs had often treated Sullivan. Peter was forced there by Davies.[8] The bleeding had been going on for three years! and three times a day! and for half an hour at a time! but he had not seen about it, probably because of the old Santa Cruz suspicion of white medicine.

At first Gibbs claimed to find no evidence of injury to Peter's nose. "I examined Jackson thoroughly," the *Chronicle* of January 3 reported Gibbs as saying, "but could find no apparent

Joe Choynski together with Charles "Parson" Davies at the Massachusetts resort of Lake Quinsigamond in May 1894 after their *Uncle Tom's Cabin* tour. Photograph courtesy of C.J. LaForce, with W. Schutte.

cause for the trouble. I attribute it to some organic trouble of the liver. I examined Peter thoroughly. He is sound in every other respect." It was leaked to the press that the cause was Paddy's having punched Peter over the liver. When he fully realized that he was dealing with a professional boxer, Gibbs looked harder for a lesion inside the nostril and dealt with the bleeding by scarring the offending vein with one of the miniscule hot irons that were the new electric cauteries. He prescribed medicine which Peter took for some time. The remedies must have worked, for no more reports of distressing nosebleeds came — nor of liver troubles.

In March, Peter wrote to San Francisco about having seen Gibbs. "I agreed to this principally to offset the ridiculous reports that were going round about me as a physical wreck. The doctor, as you noticed probably, reported that I was all right, and I hope the news will be satisfactory to my friends in San Francisco." The *Police Gazette* of March 31, 1894, gave the matter national publicity, saying: 'Jackson has suffered ever since his fight with Slavin from a blow delivered by the latter just over his liver. This brought about hemorrhages from the nose at the slightest tap. About ten weeks ago the black fellow began to treat himself for this affection and he announces with a sense of pleasure now that a fair blow on the nasal organ with a baseball bat might flatten it — the bat — but wouldn't make his nose bleed." Peter was being jocular, but the nose was always his weak point from then on.

While he was there, Peter got Gibbs to measure him carefully. He was 6 feet ¼ inch tall. His neck measured 15½ inches, his chest 39 inches with an expansion of 2½ inches, abdomen 33, waist 32. The length of his right arm was 34 inches, left arm 32¾, with the shoulder 18. (In 1898 when he was measured for the Jeffries fight, his reach, from fingertip to fingertip, was 73 inches.) His right bicep was 12½ inches round, his left bicep 13, right forearm 11, left forearm 11½, right wrist and left wrists 7 inches. His right thigh measured 31½ inches round, left thigh 32, right calf 14½, and left calf 15 inches. Peter was in most respects a little bigger on his left side.

Far more important than those two events, however, was Peter's return to England in the summer of 1893, between the two seasons of *Uncle Tom's Cabin*. It was his third visit to Britain and the first without professional commitments. Fitzpatrick had left him by now, and he engaged as his trainer Dan Murphy, dubbed "Handsome Dan," Sullivan's bottle holder in 1890 and an opponent of Johnson's in 1902. Peter needed few of Murphy's services, being intent upon pleasure.

The arrangements were hastily made. He had wanted to travel via Jamaica, but finding no boat sailing for a week he decided to do England first. "Peter will stop in England for about four weeks, and from there he will go directly to his home in the West Indies," the *Cleveland Gazette* on June 10 told its readers, after the event. Here "his home" meant Jamaica. The *Syracuse Daily Courier* said on May 23, 1893, that Peter would be traveling to Jamaica with Bat Masterson, friend since the Gallagher-Herget match in September 1891, at least; but he sailed alone for England on the *Teutonic* on May 31, intending to return via Kingston in August.

Peter was always happiest in England. The *Freeman*, back in July 1892 when Peter and his buddies were still in England after the fight, published an article about London called "The World's Metropolis: One Spot Where The Negro Is A Man." It was signed "Athos," and it can be guessed that, vis-à-vis Peter's D'Artagnan, the others called themselves the Three Musketeers. The article by "Athos" can be attributed on internal evidence to

Naughton. It was announced as being the first of several articles to deal with "The Negro in London," but as no others appeared in the *Freeman* we have to take this as representing the opinions of Peter's party. They found no discrimination in restaurants, in theaters, in hotels and so on; none in political activities; none in the relations between men and women; and none in the sporting world; indeed, "Athos" pointed out that "during the contest with Slavin, an English Peer of the Realm, Lord Lonsdale, conferred upon Jackson the exceptional honor of acting as his time keeper."

The article concluded with the rosy statement: "With sufficient energy and capacity any foreigner, Negro included, may get on well in England, and if he can only manage to excite a friendly interest with some prominent individual of influence, his ultimate success is assured." That the *Freeman* would print a white's account of a black's happy experiences in England probably shows that its American readership craved some light in those darkening years. "Athos" even quoted approvingly the line from *Othello*: "Bound slaves and pagans shall our statesmen be," a theme that the *Referee* had sounded three years before when linking Peter with Douglass.

Since it was a private visit, Peter's movements were not much covered by the press. He attended the races and socialized with his buddies. Peter was said by Davies in January 1893 to have made plenty of money since his fight with Slavin, and to be planning to invest it in real estate, in either San Francisco or in Chicago where, with the World's Fair about to start, property would appreciate. They expected the Fair's slogan to be "Progress and Plunder." The annual estimate by the *Chicago Tribune* on New Year's Day 1892 of boxers' earnings for 1891 allowed Peter $2,500. This was respectable but nothing like Fitzsimmons' $11,000 and much less than Herget's $7,250. These estimates refer only to money earned through boxing. Peter was probably taking in about $250 a week and probably spending most of it, in London rather more.

On July 6 he witnessed the wedding of Prince George and Princess May of Teck, who would have married Prince Eddy had he lived. Accounts of the wedding suggest that, along with Queen Victoria's Diamond Jubilee procession in 1897, it was the most splendid spectacle that the British Empire produced. Everybody was happy and even the weather was brilliant. At the end of his stay, Peter told a *Sportsman* reporter on July 27: "The Royal Marriage was a sight in itself, and a sight that's seldom seen. I have traveled round the world and have never seen anything like it for brilliancy and grandeur, and perhaps never will again."

In May 1893, George Harting, being "a strong supporter of Peter Jackson" according to the *San Francisco Call*, tackled Corbett about his reluctance to fight Peter. In the presence of a small crowd Corbett said he was willing, and Harting made him put it in writing. Harting handed Corbett's letter to the *Call*, which published it on June 13. Corbett then sent Peter a cable promising him a fight. On July 12 Peter cabled New York to say he was delighted and was coming back. But he left London only on July 19, with Ambrose Preece.

Maybe as a result of Harting's intervention, Corbett sent Peter another telegram on July 18 saying that he was prepared to fight him at Coney Island on November 1. At once Peter wired the *Sportsman*: "I leave Euston by the special at 8:55 on Wednesday morning. Mr. Preece accompanies me to America." The *Sportsman* commented that, "Jackson's stay in England has been all too short. Business matters, however, call for his return to the States. Mr. Preece, who accompanies him, is the well known whip and the gentleman who handles the ribbons when the National Sports Clubbists go for their coaching trips down the green lanes of old England." He rushed across the Atlantic with Preece, whose role is unclear. But the Coney Island project went into smoke. Peter said a year later: "Now I don't know what transpired while I was on my way back here, but on my arrival I was informed that sundry conferences had been held and that the fight was to take place in June. When June came Corbett was in England." Somebody was confused, because the fight was proposed in July, to take place in November.

In Jamaica, the *Daily Gleaner* reported that he was expected in Kingston on July 22, by the *Floridian* from Liverpool. And then he was to come on August 3 by the *Medway* from Southampton. His friends were disappointed when he was not on that, either, disappointed that he didn't wire, and very disappointed when they read, in the next *National Police Gazette* to arrive in Kingston, that he had returned from London directly to New York.

In August he went back to San Francisco for a short visit. On Friday, August 11, there was "a road party." In a carriage pulled by four grays, a dozen of Peter's buddies went on an excursion along El Camino Real out Millbrae and San Mateo Way. They consumed boiled chickens, oysters, big yellow peaches and lots of alcohol; they sang as they went along, they sang themselves hoarse. Peter and Herget "supplied the clown comedy portion of the outing." It was a happy day. Later, summoned by telegrams from Chicago, he quit San Francisco on August 14.

He went to Mount Clemens, where Davies was sojourning before the next season of the Tom show. At Mount Clemens he began a drying-out process, and in New York he was said to have ceased drinking several pints of beer hourly, to be content with an occasional glass of champagne, and soon to be going on the wagon. He was happy enough to hang out in Steve Brodie's saloon at 114 the Bowery with the many pugs who frequented the place. He swallowed his disappointment over Corbett's first summoning him and then avoiding him.

In order to understand these events, it must be understood that Corbett was unwilling to meet Peter. On September 8, 1892, Delaney said: "Corbett will never meet Jackson again. We are against fighting negroes any more. Besides, Corbett has bested Jackson already, and there is nothing to be gained by fighting again." Corbett must have realized that this would not cut any ice, since (unlike Sullivan, who got as far as signing articles to fight Godfrey but pulled out, and also as far as saying he would fight Peter) the two had already fought. Moreover, in their no-contest he had not bested him.

And so Corbett began the process of wearing Peter out. "I will not fight anybody or talk fight for a year," he said three days later in Atlanta. "I am engaged until then, and I don't know what I will do after that. However, Jackson has the first and best claim to my attention. He has shown that he is a representative heavyweight man, and I consider he is alone entitled to my attention." In their fight in San Francisco, Corbett had danced away. He continued to dance away.[9]

The events of the next three years, 1892–1894, fall into a pattern of avoidance. Corbett wanted money and he knew, as did everyone else in the fight game, that the champion of the world made more money by performing in theaters and endorsing products than by entering the ring. Moreover, by not fighting anybody he guaranteed that he would continue as champion of the world. Corbett made jokes, but he was not at all sure that Peter was no threat, for he might take away not only Corbett's title but also his meal ticket. Corbett did everything he could to keep up public interest in a contest with Peter (who charged that it was in order to increase Corbett's box-office takings), and simultaneously to defer the match until Peter would be too old.

That was why at first he had Delaney announce that he would not fight Peter because of the color line, but then must have realized that, if this decision was acted upon, it meant that he could not use Peter to keep the pot boiling for his publicity. So the color-line story was forgotten and there began a never-ending and heavily publicized quest for just the right time and just the right venue.

In May 1893, Naughton revisited Sydney, and at that early date in the negotiations for a Corbett-Jackson fight he told the *Referee*: "But the truth of the whole business is that Corbett is avoiding Jackson until such time as he feels thoroughly sure that Peter is a back number." Naughton said that he had been told by Delaney that the whole idea was to keep Peter on the shelf until he was altogether too old to fight Corbett. "Jackson is not so young as he used to be by long chalks," Naughton said when Peter was 33, "and, moreover, he is at that period in his life — from an athletic point of view — when there are exceedingly few brilliant performances left in him."

Early in 1896, Naughton wrote the *Referee* that Corbett said to him: "I will be in the ring again at the right time. I put Jackson on the shelf, and Sullivan and Mitchell out of the game, and what I did once I can do again." Naughton said these were "Jim's own words." He went on to say:

> He kept Jackson on the anxious seat for something like 4 or 5 years after they fought at the California Club, just kidding him along with the idea that they were to meet again, and having not the slightest idea of giving poor old Peter a return match. When Corbett was training for his fight with Mitchell

This page-length engraving appeared in the Boston *Illustrated Police News* on May 18, 1893.

at Florida he was under contract to fight Peter Jackson a few months later. The exact location of the battle had not been decided upon, but everyone believed that both men were in earnest. Yet Billy Delaney, Corbett's trainer and confidential man, told me that the whole party were going to England after the Mitchell fight. I looked at Delaney in surprise and remarked, "How about the fight with Jackson?" It was then Delaney's turn to look puzzled, and he smiled and said to me, "I guess you had better say nothing about the English trip until you hear from Jim himself or somebody else." I heard about it with the rest of the world in due time. It was part of the process of putting Peter Jackson "on the shelf," and if Peter was good for the next twenty years to come Jim would still be putting him on the shelf, or, in other words, avoiding him.

We should believe this testimony of Naughton's, especially as he showed no animosity to Corbett in his *Kings of the Queensberry Realm* (1902) and *Heavy-Weight Champions* (1910), which appeared after Peter died.

As the months passed, and the years, Peter's unhappiness increased. At various times Corbett suggested fights in Jacksonville, in El Paso, at Coney Island, in Sioux City, at Wagoner in Indian Territory, even over the border on an island near Orilla in Ontario. And though the dates were always set well in advance to accommodate Corbett's theatrical engagements, they never suited him when the time approached. As well, he wanted an unlimited number of rounds, whereas Peter said grimly that 10 should be sufficient. It was announced in London on April 21, 1894, that "the chief financial backer of the National Club says he will never consent to a fight to the finish, and Corbett declares he will not fight a limited number of rounds." Corbett said the California A.C. and the National Sporting Club were prejudiced against him and biased in favor of Peter, so that he would not fight in either place. Meanwhile the list of which American cities would permit boxing, or tolerate boxing, or turn a blind eye to boxing, was continually altering. Nothing could be settled. Peter did not trust Corbett, but he hoped to nail him finally, somewhere. The *Chicago Tribune* said on June 29, 1894: "The match has been talked of so much and the principals have been so verbose over it that the public has lost nearly all interest in the episode."

After his last performance in *Uncle Tom's Cabin* in March 1894, Peter made his way back to San Francisco and started to train for the fight with Corbett, which everybody believed would happen. He took up residence in the Baldwin Hotel, among the two or three best hotels in San Francisco. The Baldwin's theater and hotel complex had five stories and 250 rooms, plus attics all *oeil-de-boeuf*, with its roof culminating in a fantasy hexagonal dome 168 feet high. It had steam-powered elevators, carpets that had cost $30 a yard, and a Tiffany clock in the lobby worth $25,000. In short, it was a Gilded-Age extravaganza and all in wood. It was in the middle of town at 932–936 Market, occupying the whole block between Powell and Ellis. Peter was cashed up from his Tom tour, and he could certainly afford a room there, since they started at $2 a night. He was slated to fight the champion. He was bankable. Though he was a black he was made welcome by the owner, Elias J. "Lucky" Baldwin, a well-known sport who lived on the premises. Baldwin doubtless saw Peter as attracting people to his establishment. Peter lived there during the spring and summer of 1894.[10]

While Peter was at the Baldwin he was featured in the *Examiner*, in articles on two Sundays, May 20 and 27, which discussed the perfect man. The strongman and bodybuilder, Eugen Sandow, whose contests with Samson in 1889 had interested Peter, was in San Francisco for the Midwinter Exposition. He was hailed by some as having the ideal male body. But, according to the *Sportsman* of April 17, 1894, "a well-known contributor" to the *New York Herald* said while *Uncle Tom's Cabin* was playing New York City: "If I were a sculptor, and wanted a model of a perfect figure to illustrate the happiest possible combination of strength and agility — a between of Hercules and Mercury — I would choose Peter Jackson." Sandow's physique and Jackson's were seriously compared in San Francisco.

The *Examiner* quizzed San Francisco painters and sculptors on whether Sandow's body or Peter's represented the ideal male physique. Peter and Sandow themselves both contributed to the coverage. Peter said, apropos of using classical sculptures as the standard of beauty: "The inclination nowadays, of course, is to compare alleged perfect men with the old Grecian athletes and Roman gladiators. I think these ancients must have looked better in statues than they did in the flesh." Asked by the reporter which he considered the perfect man, he discreetly replied: "I consider Highland Scotchmen to come as near to my idea of perfection as any. I have also seen splendidly put-up Sikhs and Hindoos of an athletic turn, while if photographs and pictures are to count for anything the Zulus have some splendid specimens of manhood among them." He had evidently not forgotten the Zulu War diorama. He was discreet not to name an individual, but brave to exalt dark bodies.

The articles held other surprises. They were illustrated by an engraving by Langford of three male figures posed like the Three Graces: the Apollo Belvedere at center, with on his left Sandow in his trademark sandals and a fig leaf, and on his right Peter in the nude

THE THREE TYPES OF MANLY FORM.
[Jackson and Sandow, from photographs by Taber.]

This wood engraving of Jackson and Sandow flanking the Apollo Belvedere was published in the *San Francisco Examiner* on May 20, 1894.

pose that had caused such a sensation in 1889 in the *Dead Bird*. It was surprising that a black should be brought into such a debate. Even more surprising, the consensus of the connoisseurs, voiced by John Stanton from the School of Design, was in effect: "Peter Jackson to my mind approaches the nearer the elegant proportions of the old Greek statues than Sandow. The lines of his contour of figure are more finely drawn, more delicate than those of Sandow." A black more Greek than a white! Most surprising of all, the *Examiner* articles made no mention of Peter's race except for one word in one subtitle, and the whole debate was conducted in terms of body types: Herculean versus Apollonian.[11]

The following year his lithographed portrait — bare torso, arms folded, full face clearly showing his turning left eye, from the Taber photograph originally reproduced in 1888–89 on the tiny "Creole" card — appeared as Plate Number 6 in *The College of Life*, a success manual for blacks. It was captioned, "Fine Specimen of Physical Development, PETER JACKSON, Athlete."[12] The Sandow incident was remembered, though it became slightly blurred. His obituary in the *Freeman* stated: "Jackson in his prime was said to have been the finest specimen of physical manhood in the United States and he posed before a number of artists and sculptors."

As well as chatting about Greek sculpture, however, Peter was training for his bout with Corbett in May 1894. This bout was so certain that on May 10, in conjunction with its Issue 872, the *National Police Gazette* published a 23-inch-by-16-inch chromolithograph wall poster with an artist's impression of Peter and Corbett facing off in the ring; "in fighting attitudes," as the *Gazette* said. It was on heavy paper "printed in 12 Rich Colors," and cost 10c mailed in a tube. Both men were shown in slips with no socks wearing skin gloves. Peter's legs looked more massive than they were. Corbett's waist was girded by Old Glory, whereas Peter's sash was in the red and white of Shango and Denmark. In the top corners were oval vignettes of Delaney with a blue towel and Davies looking judicious with a red towel.[13] But the event never transpired. Corbett slipped away to Paris.

In 1894 two illustrated publications came out, with a picture of Peter and letterpress, along with similar coverage of other boxers. One was the *Pugilistic Magazine*, published by the American News Company of New York, 11 issues of which came out across the year. Peter was in Issue 1, along with Corbett, Choynski, and Jack Burke. Sullivan was in Issue 2 with Kilrain and others. All in all the *Pugilistic Magazine* carried photographs of about 100 boxers, plus, in Issue 7, Griffo and Jack McAuliffe illustrating boxing technique in 24 pictures. The other publication was a book compiled by Billy Edwards, the former lightweight champion, and was titled *Gladiators of the Prize Ring; or, Pugilists of America and their Contemporaries*. This folio volume also consisted of letterpress and pictures, but these were steel engravings. Along with Fox's postcards, these publications raised the boxers included into a pugilistic pantheon.

The process had begun in 1887 with ten boxers in Allen & Ginter's beautifully crafted cigarette-card set: "World's Champions," and was furthered when other cigarette-card sets, less beautiful, were put out.[14]

In 1889 or early 1890 Peter, like other sportsmen before him and theater folk such as Lillian Russell, appeared in the famous series of cabinet cards for Newsboy Plug Tobacco. Sullivan was said to be the most widely recognized person in the world after Queen Victoria, because of cigarette cards and his posters in every barbershop. It was by these means that sportsmen were turned into stars by visual representation, even before the movies.

On February 14, 1894, the London photographers Cadbury Jones advertised a picture of Peter in fighting gear. "It is a photogravure from a painting of the famous and favorite black boxer, whose manly figure, pleasant face, and graceful bearing have been carefully caught by the artist A.D. Bastin." This was perhaps the painting presented to Peter in January 1890. Known for his figure painting, Alfred Dickman Bastin (1849–1913) lived in West Worthing and perhaps met Peter in 1889 at nearby Brighton.[15]

An instance of star-making featured in the *Examiner* on June 2, 1894, when half a page was given to Peter's learning to ride a bike, illustrated by three pictures of him at the cyclery enclosure on Stanyan, pedaling in a suit and a bowler hat while waiting, according to the article, to acquire a bicycle suit. He said he was going to take up professional cycling if nothing happened in the fight game. When he was losing control of the bike, he said to it: "Be a gentleman," but it crashed. He informed his onlookers: "It's the grandest sport I've tackled, though; it beats boxing, rowing and swimming all to pieces." The article was sheer gossip designed to keep him before the public while Corbett shilly-shallied and San Francisco boxing was moribund. On June 30 the *National Police Gazette* told its readers: "Peter Jackson has got the bicycle fever, and he rides about the streets of San Francisco."

On May 6, 1894, the *Boston Sunday Globe* told its readers that Peter was crazy about checkers. It said: "Peter is also a fine Shakespearean reader, and many times has corrected persons who were rated high in that line while they were giving quotations from the bard's immortal works. He carries a large volume of the plays with him, and during his leisure moments, when not playing checkers, he reads them." Publicity gossip. But the greatest instrument for publicizing sportsmen had just been invented: this was the movie camera.

Peter arranged a rendezvous in Santa

This notice of a poster, published in the *National Police Gazette* on June 9, 1894, advertised a Jackson-Corbett championship fight that never happened.

Cruz with his brother James and left San Francisco on August 6, 1894, for New York and the Danish West Indies.

The night before, there was an incident at the Baldwin Hotel. He was in the fabulous bar, being farewelled by his buddies, among them Lucky Baldwin himself. Joe McAuliffe began to aggress Herget, complaining that he had taken down McAuliffe's photo from his wall.

Herget had cleaned up the walls of his bar, which were covered in about 300 boxing photographs, many fading and tatty. He did not put up a new photo of every boxer and McAuliffe's was one of those omitted. McAuliffe had been proud that his photo appeared on that wall, and was offended that it did so no longer. In 1901 Furniss, in *His Famous Fights Past and Present* magazine, told another story, namely that Herget deliberately banished it after McAuliffe's defeat by Paddy on September 27, 1890. In 1894 McAuliffe's career was ending. He had been beaten by Goddard in June 1892 and had only drawn with Maher in October 1893. He fought twice later and was beaten both times. He was sensitive to his declining powers.

In Lucky Baldwin's bar, McAuliffe raised the matter of the photograph with Peter, saying: "He's got no use for me, the young — — —, and he threw me out of his house. He's a —." Peter rushed to Herget's defense, saying: "Here, here, you are talking about my friend, and I won't stand it. Now, Joe, you know that Mitchell is the best friend I've got in the world, and don't you talk like that to me." McAuliffe retorted: "Why, you —, who the — are you?" Peter said that McAuliffe "called me a name which in my country would have meant death to him." Coats came off. A policeman was called, wanted to arrest everybody in sight, and then had to be got rid of by Baldwin. This performance of Peter's did not amuse him. The *Chronicle* recalled the incident on September 22, 1897, and in the *Bulletin* on the following day "a prominent sporting man" mentioned it: "The big fellow thinks the world of Young Mitchell. It will be remembered that a few years ago he came within an ace of whipping Joe McAuliffe because he offered some uncomplimentary remarks about his friend. And Young Mitchell has a warm spot in his heart for Jackson."

The next day Peter left. In Chicago on August 7 he and Davies had a quarrel, apparently because Davies told Peter to cease with the Corbett farce, advising him to forget Corbett and get on with his life. This quarrel got mixed up with the one about "Uncle Tom" scenery and other concerns. Peter got so angry with Davies that he wired O'Rourke in New York, who managed Dixon, Joe Walcott and some other blacks, asking him if he would take over as his *pro tem* manager.

On August 11 the *Chicago Tribune* mentioned that the managers of Edison's new invention, a machine that produced moving images, were making an offer for a Corbett-Jackson fight. The Kinetoscope Exhibition Company asked to film Peter and Corbett boxing in a 10-foot ring. Peter was agreeable, but Corbett said he would not do it. When Davies discussed the offer, he clearly did not know what he was talking about because he said: "If the people behind this machine can find a battleground I shall be satisfied — still more so if they can bring off a match. Neither Peter nor I cares what sort of an instrument the fight takes place before if there only is a fight, but I see little chance of the men ever meeting, even with machines for assistance." And yet Edison's invention had been demonstrated as far back as May in the Masonic Temple in Chicago, the second place in the world. It was advertised as "More wonderful than anything you saw at the World's Fair." Peter, who was not in Chicago when Davies made bitter fun of the proposal, may himself have seen the kinetoscope in San Francisco, because its first showings there, the third place in the world, had been on June 1 in Peter Bacigalupi's "Edison Phonograph Arcade" at 946 Market, in the Baldwin Hotel building. He may have been especially interested because one of the films on show was *Sandow*.[16]

The machine, the kinetoscope, was indeed new. It was a kind of peepshow. One looked into a box to see a view with little figures — only these figures were moving. With the help of celluloid, Edison had invented the motion picture. The first motion pictures were made only in March 1894 at Edison's establishment, one of them being of Sandow before he left for California. The first boxing film, shot on June 14, 1894, captured a match between Mike Leonard and Jack Cushing. Kinetoscopes had no future; that belonged to the projected films pioneered in Berlin by the Skladanowsky brothers and in Paris by the Lumiére brothers in late 1895. Edison joined their league later, calling his projected films "Vitascope" productions and recycling many of his kinetoscope films for the screen.

On September 7 in a 10-foot ring Corbett boxed half a dozen 1-minute rounds with Peter Courtney, an "old-time prize fighter" and a fourth-rate pug. This was for the Lathams and in front of Edison's immobile camera inside the "Black Maria" at Orange, New Jersey. When released the film was promoted by flyers saying: "The Great Corbett-Courtney Fight, Six Rounds with Knock-Out and Other Scenes, etc." which were the first ever movie advertisements. "And even now," it was said two years later by the *Referee*, "the result is on exhibition all over the civilised world, care being taken to exploit the affair as one of the most desperate encounters on record." The encounter may have been more desperate than its promoters imagined, for a month after the filming, on October 7, 1894, Courtney was fighting Maher at the Nonpareil Club in Philadelphia when he collapsed, could not get up, and was carried off the stage; in May 1896, he died of tuberculosis. The film played for years, in kinetoscope and Vitascope forms. Corbett ended up getting $5,000 from Edison and $15,000 from royalties.[17] Still, now, Corbett may be seen moving, boxing, on the Library of Congress "American Memory" Web site. But thanks to him we have no film of Peter[18]; and it is no consolation that Professor Welton's boxing cats, filmed at Edison's studio in July 1894 and still on view, were called (the pale one) Corbett and (the parti-colored black one) Jackson.[19]

When the *Chicago Tribune* announced on September 1 that O'Rourke claimed to be representing Jackson, Peter, referred to as "the Australian," said: "I also hear that O'Rourke, Dixon's manager, is to manage me in future, but I have made no such arrangements." What he meant was that O'Rourke had handled him in New York City, but that Davies was still his manager. He intended taking the Tom show on the road again with the Davies company. However, shortly there would be nothing of Peter's business for Davies to manage.

Peter left Chicago on August 12. The final scene in the tragic Corbett farce was played out in the Grand Central Hotel in New York City on Monday, August 13, 1894. The *London Sportsman* gave a detailed account of the event. Except for that salutation in the Philadelphia hotel lobby in November 1892, Peter and Corbett had not talked to one another since the night of their fight. Now in the hotel room Peter, Corbett, Delaney and O'Rourke discussed where and when the fight would occur. Corbett would not fight in England or America, except in the South, preferably Jacksonville, where he had beaten Charley Mitchell; and Peter would not fight in Florida. The debate became acrimonious. The South, London, and the North were canvassed to exhaustion, but at no point did anybody suggest that a suitable venue might be found in Australia.

This scene in the Grand Central Hotel effectively marked the end of the Corbett business. Peter gave up all hope in Corbett's promises, all faith in his good will. He left for Santa Cruz and for England, where he stayed for the next three years.

On August 17 the *New York World* published a long statement written and signed by Peter, exposing his view of Corbett's dodging and weaving. He claimed that Corbett had forced him back and back to the only place they might meet, the South (and that was if Corbett did not renege about Jacksonville, too, in the end). He therefore provided a careful and dignified explanation of why he would not fight in America below the Mason-Dixon line. He wrote: "I will not fight in the South. I have too much respect for myself. And no self-respecting colored man would go down there." He said that battling Corbett was the least of his fears: that the "mob of whites, who despise my people and would jeer and insult me," could mob him if he won, insult him and mistreat him and his friends. Moreover, he insisted upon his respectability, his dignity. If he went South, "I could not live at good hotels, in the surroundings I have been used to. I would have to go into low and dirty surroundings, into company I don't care for. A respectable white man doesn't want to travel with low whites. In the same way I don't want to associate with the low of my own race and color. I couldn't even ride in the first-class cars."

Peter's riding in first-class cars and living in good hotels, "in the surroundings I have been used to," at Gilman Houses and International Hotels, became impossible not long after, even outside the South. Peter had pursued his American career at the dawning of Jim Crow's day.[20]

Peter also wrote an open letter to the papers which concluded with: "I do not propose to stay awake nights thinking of replies to fit Corbett's unfair assertions." And he added: "My present plans, which I will alter only in the event that Corbett agrees to an early meeting, are to sail from New York for the West Indies, September 15, where I will visit my mother, whom I have not seen for years. Then I will go to England and, if things are agreeable, will take on Frank Slavin. Corbett has not treated me in a sportsmanlike manner and I will bother him no more."

It was the end of a dream, almost.

CHAPTER 8

Corduroy Road, 1894–1900

When Peter and James met up in May 1894 in Boston, they arranged to visit Santa Cruz for a grand family reunion and to fix up various loose ends, emotional and other.

In 1893, before the *Uncle Tom* rehearsals, the news had come to San Francisco cabled from Brisbane, from Jack Dowridge, that Peter's parents were dead. The news went from the West Indies to London to Brisbane, then was sent on by Dowridge to the *Examiner* office, the only place in the world where messages for vagabond Peter could confidently be sent. The unsigned cable made Peter most upset. He said he was pained that someone could play such a cruel joke, his mother and father having died years before. The cable was doubly mysterious, because what hoaxer in Santa Cruz knew Dowridge's address?

Naughton said of the cablegram that all the world knew Julia and Joseph had been dead for a long time but that was untrue. When Peter left San Francisco for Santa Cruz he said he was going there to visit his mother and was believed. Davies said in a press release from Chicago on August 14, "Jackson will, after a short visit here, leave for his boyhood home in the West Indies and visit his mother, whom he has not seen since he was seven years old." Here was the deserted-in-Australia story again. In New York, Peter said he was going to Santa Cruz to visit his mother but also his brother. Probably because he declined to explain again where Santa Cruz was, New York wired London that Peter was heading for Cuba.

O'Rourke with the Nail brothers and several other sports gave him a farewell dinner. The *World* reported: "Jackson does not know when he will return to this country." At noon on September 15, 1894, he took the British ship H.M.S. *Caribbee* from New York for the six-day

A photograph of Peter, James and Felix Jackson, with James's wife, at Estate Orange Grove on St. Croix, was taken in September 1894 and published in *The Referee* (Sydney) on February 20, 1918, on a page since destroyed. The picture was preserved by A. Thomas.

183

voyage to the Danish West Indies. He would not see New York again for three years. The *Caribbee* unloaded 290 packages and Peter in Frederiksted on September 22, then proceeded to Barbados.[1]

Peter was met at the dock by two of his sisters and his brother Felix, now aged 30 and a policeman. He scarcely knew them. He scarcely knew Frederiksted, which had been burned to the ground and rebuilt since he saw it last. But the garrison soldiers in Fort Frederik were there, still waiting for their rum issue and now polishing Krag-Jörgensen rifles. And the wharf laborers were there, still shoveling coal at 10 cents a ton. That could have been his fate, but Peter was doing better than that. The governor of the Danish West Indies was on a salary of $4,000 a year. Peter was doing considerably better than that. In the 1890s the bishop of Antigua was on a stipend of £2,000, roughly is $10,000 a year. Peter was doing better than his Lordship!

Writing in late September to Fred Nail, and to San Francisco, to Herget probably, he was uncertain whether James would come down to Frederiksted, but he came with his wife. One day in early October they went out to the estate where their father had been a slave. "Next Wednesday's Instalment," said the *Referee* on February 20, 1918, repeating what Peter had told Corbett, "will refer to Peter Jackson's boyhood days and some experiences of his early childhood. A picture of the house where he was born, showing himself and several relatives seated on the front steps, will be published." The three brothers and James's wife were photographed on the dilapidated steps of the great house together with a crowd of twenty-odd people, servants and old plantation figures, barefoot boys and even one toddler. The visit to Estate Orange Grove apparently effected a closure for Peter. The sorrows of his youth were now almost done with.

Peter was in Frederiksted from September 22 to October 15, effectively for three weeks. He left aboard the new sloop *Bessie* via Christiansted for St. Thomas, where on the verandah of the seafront Commercial Hotel he could drink a nostalgic Cherry Heering. At Charlotte Amalie he caught the *Caribbee* again and sailed to Barbados. He was there for four or five days, and was feted by the innumerable Dowridges and Walcotts in Bridgetown. He said that "he was made the hero of sundry flying-fish dinners," thus fulfilling another of his youthful aspirations. Altogether he had such a good time in the West Indies that he was reluctant to leave.

But he quit Barbados on October 22 aboard the R.M.S. *Orinoco* heading for Southampton. The *Barbados Globe* reported seven passengers, 6 of them named, a list on which Peter did not figure. He was the 7th passenger, concealed behind the letters "D.B.S.," meaning a "Distressed British Seaman" entitled to a free passage. Peter must have asked that for reasons of anonymity his presence be so disguised. He reached London on Monday night, October 31, with no reporters alerted. He went to Joe Fallows' Bull and Gate tavern in Kentish Town.

The next day he and Fallows went to see people. He was interviewed at the National Sporting Club by the *Sportsman*. He denounced Corbett, saying: "Corbett is no man. He is a liar, and my words can be put in print. He caused me to waste my time and my money running after him and never once did he intend acting up to what he said through the papers. Corbett had no idea of fighting me, a fact I found out when he turned tail after I had given way and agreed to all his propositions."[2] This was a fair summary of what Corbett did. It had also been a rerun of Paddy's story in Australia seven years before.

Then he spoke wildly about going to India. "I am here on business. I want a job, and am prepared to box any man in the world for any reasonable sum." And asked how long he intended staying, Peter replied: "As long as I possibly can. I can perhaps accept engagements and spar. I cannot be idle, and after my stay in England I shall probably go on to Calcutta. I would like to remain in England altogether, but this cannot happen just now."[3]

Why he could not stay in England, and just which opportunity beckoned in Calcutta, are obscure matters. The *Melbourne Sportsman* described the efforts of one boxing teacher, George Smith, to introduce fisticuffs into Calcutta, but for that he had to collect sailors from Lal Bazaar. Calcutta papers, the *Englishman* and the *Indian Planters' Gazette and Sporting News,* which both reported on the explosion of sports in the city during 1894, especially football, soccer as well as Rugby, ignored Peter that year. The huge urban park Maidan could not accommodate all the scheduled Saturday matches.

Peter's contacts there might have asked him to establish a boxing school. In addition to the older Bengal Club (1827) and the Bengal United Service Club (1845), and clubs for cricket, rowing, football and golf, several new social clubs had opened, the Saturday Club on Wood in 1878 and the New Club on Park that very year.[4] M.H. Hayes described the sporting world in Calcutta at the time, called Peter "the best prize-fighter of the present day," and claimed to know Sir John Astley's third son, Jack (1874–1896), who had recently been sent east for his health. Sir John thought highly of Peter, saying in 1893 in his memoirs that "a very civil, well-spoken man is Peter Jackson" and that he "perhaps ought this day to be champion of the world."[5] Through his son, "The Mate" may have been Peter's Calcutta connection. But if Peter did provisionally agree to teach boxing in one of these clubs, his obituary in Calcutta's weekly *Indian Planters' Gazette and Sporting News* said nothing about the scheme.

Back in London, Peter set about enjoying himself. The *National Police Gazette* had the previous February said: "Jackson is a great favorite in London, owing to his gentlemanly manners, and from the way he keeps his money circulating." He circulated it. On November 8 he chaired the Bohemian Concert of the Highgate Wheelers' Cycling Club. Soon afterwards he saw the Lord Mayor's Show and was reported as "the great centre of attraction; his reception, whenever he cared to make himself visible, was very hearty and spontaneous." Phil May was one of the Pelicans and a friend of Peter's. They went to a masked ball in costumes punningly designed by May: Peter the pug as "a *Punch* artist," presumably with smock and palette, and May, the notorious spendthrift, as "a brass-finisher." Almost certainly Peter had known him back in Australia from 1886 to 1888 when May was a cartoonist for the *Sydney Bulletin*.[6] There were always people to meet and have a drink with.

Peter would have to earn his living as he had done earlier, by sparring in music-halls. He looked around for a partner. An enormous young Welshman called David St. John was boxing in London. He was a coalminer from Wales. Familiarly called Dai, he came from a mining townlet and his first language was Welsh. He was 6 feet and 3 inches tall, and broad, bull-necked and with beetling brows. Though only twenty years old, he looked a tough customer and a plausible opponent for Peter. When he appeared with Peter in 3 rounds at the National Sporting Club on December 3, 1894, Peter's first appearance in England since the fight, it was said: "Big as is Jackson, he actually looked small by the side of the gigantic Welshman." Peter jokingly urged St. John to put his hand up and unhook one of the electric chandeliers.

It was the lumbering St. John's physique, and not so much his talent, that led to his becoming a boxer. He had beaten Tom James at the People's Park in Pontypridd and at

Merthyr, then was brought to London by Bob Habbijam to box at his West End School of Arms. In early October, St. John had cross words with Paddy Slavin, and they scuffled. He challenged Paddy to a fight, but Paddy disdained the invitation. However, St. John's pluck may have endeared him to Peter. It was arranged that he would become Peter's sparring partner and that they would have a season in Paris at the Folies Bergére.

The Folies had a habit of putting Anglo-American sportsmen on display. Cannon wrestled there in 1889. The billiards champion Frank C. Ives performed there in 1892, and in April 1893 the *Chicago Tribune* declared: "Gay French Capital the Mecca of All Cue Experts." Ives returned in 1894. Corbett went to Paris in May 1894, giving sparring exhibitions at the Folies and at the Nouveau Cirque. The city was pasted over with his portrait, "Champion du Monde" below it. "At the Folies Bergère where Corbett is the attraction, the crowds are large with 'standing room only' signs out," said the *Sportsman*. Peter and St. John were the latest in this parade.

For some years Fred Boon, the boxing impresario, had been putting on fights at his gymnasium in the Nouveau Cirque and lately in the Rue Colisée. He had imported Wag Ward of Hoxton who, it was said in 1894, "is almost a Frenchman by now," and to fight Ward a succession of other British boxers. Boon had patiently built up a Parisian public for English boxing. How much Peter and St. John were paid is unknown. Peter was earning the equivalent of 400 francs a night in London, but he may have taken a little less because it was, after all, Paris.[7]

The duo were well received by the Parisian public, Peter being the first of many black boxers to be feted in France over the next 40 years. At the Folies, Peter and St. John followed a troupe of acrobats and an illusionist. On the bill with them was "Mlle. Polaire," long-time Folies favorite, and an act (probably salacious) called "Tableaux Vivants from the Palace Theater in London." Across town, the Olympia on the Boulevard des Capucines was featuring an act by "The Australian Firemen," whatever they did. Around the music-hall circuit was also a boxing kangaroo, with Professor Dick Landermann as its wrangler and opponent. Australia was briefly fashionable in Paris.

Peter and St. John appeared for eight nights, with matinees on Sundays and public holidays, in the huge hall at 32 Rue Richter, with its horseshoe-shaped gallery lit by enormous chandeliers, its orchestra directed by maestro Métra, its chorus girls and trapeze artists, its overdressed and underdressed women immortalized by Maupassant, its barmaids immortalized by Manet. Peter was able to drink all the champagne he desired: 12 francs for a bottle of Moët, 15 francs for Veuve Cliquot and for Roederer.

The most advanced section of the Parisian cultural scene ignored Peter, *Le Soir* disdaining even to accept classified advertisements for the music halls. But in his column "Courrier des Théâtres," Georges Boyer, the entertainment reporter for *Le Figaro*, made up for the neglect of the others. "The Australian champion is a magnificent negro," Boyer wrote, "with muscles beyond compare (*musclé comme pas vu*) who has already defeated more than 150 opponents. He is so far the only boxer whom Jim Corbett hasn't beaten." Boyer enthused about Peter's boxing so marvelously, and about his not resting content being the foremost boxer but being also an actor. Peter must have been embroidering a little, or else his French had gotten shakier, for Boyer reported him playing in *La Case de l'Oncle Tom* across America and round Australia too. He said the champion Australian negro and the champion of Wales had to be back in London by December 20 because Peter would be fighting there for a purse of 50,000 francs.[8]

8. Corduroy Road, 1894–1900

On Saturday, December 15, Boyer predicted that all the American and English colony in Paris would turn up to applaud Peter on the last night, and thus crown his uninterrupted successes at the Folies Bergère. He was hailed as "First Among Boxers." The act was so popular that their engagement seems to have been extended for a couple of days, but then Peter, called by Boyer "le champion boxeur nègre," yielded to Captain Martin, an American sharpshooter, with Polaire and the Palace Theatre troupe again, and a "four-handed horseman," perhaps a trained ape. They had done well, though it is doubtful that they made more money than Corbett had done.

Encouraged by their success, Peter and St. John talked of going to America in April 1895. Peter wrote Naughton: "My sparring partner is David St. John, the Welshman. He is a big strapping fellow and fairly clever. I don't know whether I shall meet someone in England in a real contest before I come to the United States. My plans are not made up as yet." The *St. Louis Post-Dispatch* reported in January 1895 that Peter intended to bring "the leekeater" to America and was inviting challenges to St. John. They never went.

On the evening of December 17, back in London at the annual benefit for Fleming in the National Sporting Club, Peter put on a friendly exhibition with the amateur champion of England, George Sykes of the Mincing-Lane Boxing and Athletic Club. This was not for a purse of 50,000 francs and not for even £5, Sykes the amateur being severely policed. "Sykes was a resolute boxer with a straight left and a good style," said Bernard Angle, a famous amateur boxer and more famous referee. Mr. George Sykes did not get carried away like Mr. Billy Power in Melbourne. Angle said Peter never gave better exhibitions than those he did with Sykes. The *Sportsman* reported on the 18th that "the two retired amid a torrent of cheers."⁹

Three days later the *Sportsman* put out *The Sportsman Almanac for 1895*, a large single sheet for pinning up, with oval pictures of famous athletes and sports. The first portrait was Peter. Dr. W.G. Grace came after him, and along the line was Champion J.J. Corbett.

In 1894, Frank "Coffee Cooler" Craig was performing at Gatti's Palace of Variety in London. Born in New York in 1870 of a black Cuban father and a Canadian Indian mother, he was noticed on October 1, 1892, in the *National Police Gazette* as the "Harlem Coffee Cooler, Frank Kreig." He had now come to England and, according to the *Referee,* commanded more money than any other boxer appearing before the British public. He was the first boxer to appear in Britain in a robe or dressing gown, as distinct from a Peter-type greatcoat. Lonsdale said Craig also introduced chew-

Jackson as a race icon, from H.D. Northrop et al., *The College of Life* (1895). His turned-in left eye is obvious.

ing gum for boxers. In his act he sparred, but he also played a harmonica and performed plantation dances. He lasted just over 4 minutes with Maher in July 1894. He lasted 2 rounds with O'Brien, the middleweight who had bested St. John.

On November 9 Craig challenged Peter, telling the *Sportsman*: "I can hit as hard as Jackson, am equally as clever, and have youth on my side." Peter did not respond. Just before Christmas Craig challenged him again, through his manager Ed Holske, who said: "If Jackson has retired from pugilism let him say so, and I will seek elsewhere for a customer, but until such times as Peter declares himself out of the business I shall certainly insist on the meeting." Peter did not respond. Early in January 1895 Craig expressed his frustration in the *Sportsman*. Peter was questioned in Glasgow and his reply was published on January 9. "The answer, straight and candid, was that neither Jackson nor his friends considered Craig sufficient class to seriously regard the challenge, nor will Jackson take notice so as to allow Craig to trade upon his name. He considered it *infra dig.* to reply to Craig's offer of a match for such a sum as £250." The Coffee Cooler obtained a match with Paddy. He wrote to the *National Police Gazette*, saying: "If I defeat Slavin I am going to make Peter Jackson fight or jump out of England." On March 11, 1895, Paddy, described by the *Penny Illustrated Paper* as "a Victorian, born at Maitland, Melbourne, in 1863," downed Craig in 70 seconds.

With the start of 1895, Peter and St. John began performing around Britain, in London in the summer, often at the Aquarium, and during the winters in the provinces. Peter's three years in England coincided with an explosion of entertainments. In central London alone, between 1890 and 1897 some sixteen new theaters, legitimate and music-hall, were built. Entertainers like Dan Leno and Little Tich, Vesta Tilley and Marie Lloyd, became household names. The depression was over and people had more disposable income.[10] The *Illustrated Buffalo Express* reported on March 24, 1895, that "Peter Jackson will shortly open in the London variety theaters in a sensational sketch by Fred Bower, and one of the scenes will represent a celebrated London sporting club during a glove contest." This syndicated news had no sequel.

So widely were Peter's doings reported that the *Cleveland Gazette* of December 1 quoted from the *London Sporting Life* an item about Peter's attitude to performing in music-halls: "In the matter of hippodroming he naturally considers that a very difficult business, but where his reputation — for which he has always worked hard and often had the worst end of the deal as regards pecuniary considerations — is at stake he stipulates for everything fair and no favors." Will Corbett said Peter's pay for sparring displays in America and England never dropped lower than $1,500 (£300) weekly, and that "for months he showed at three music-halls in London in one night," apparently meaning he thus earned much more than $1,500 a week. He managed himself or more probably had a good agent, essential for booking an act in the provinces. There were any number of theatrical agents whom Peter could have got to handle him. Tom Holmes, who had been a comedian, and William Oliver, a former comic singer, had offices on York Road in 1895, and Peter may have dealt with them because Holmes was a black.

For the next year and a half Peter and St. John sparred their way around England, Scotland and Wales, at the Variety Theatre in Hoxton, at the Corn Exchange in Northampton, at the Miners' Hall in Durham, at the Hammersmith Theater of Varieties, at Brighton's Empire Theater of Varieties, and so on. At the Scotia Variety Theater in Glasgow, with Peter billed as THE CHAMPION PUGILIST OF THE WORLD and St. John as THE CHAM-

PION OF WALES, the theater was "packed in its every corner." They appeared with a marvelous farmyard mimic; Joe Edmonds, a black comedian, dancer and banjo-player; the Sisters Slater, and other acts. In Glasgow and elsewhere the story was always the same: one or two shows a night at the local venue and wildly enthusiastic crowds. Their warmest reception came at Pontypridd in Wales, where they exhibited at the Empire before a large crowd of Dai's compatriots. In 1896 he and Bob Fitzsimmons were both touring, and coincided in Cardiff for their first meeting since the days at the White Horse. They may have sparred for old times' sake.[11]

This routine was rarely broken by significant events. After his defeat by Corbett the year before, at Jacksonville, Florida, Charley Mitchell asked to fight Peter, who said he would, but only at the National Sporting Club. The club, when asked about such a fight, replied on January 30, 1895: "The National Sporting Club cannot see its way clear to entertain the proposed match between Peter Jackson and Charles Mitchell." And that was the end of that. In 1896 Mitchell fought his last fight, against Steve O'Donnell. Eventually, his autobiography was ghosted by "Smiler" Hales.

Towards the end of January 1895, Peter had written a private letter to Fred Nail in New York, portions of which were published in February as far afield as the *St. Louis Post-Dispatch*. Peter said: "When I was in America Peter Maher wanted to meet me. When I was in Scotland Jem Stewart, the Scotch giant, challenged me. Then Frank Craig, the Harlem Coffee-cooler, asked for a trial, and since then Charley Mitchell wants to fight me. It seems to me that these men only want to gain cheap notoriety. There is only one man I want to fight, and he is James J. Corbett, and had I known he would have refused to fight me I would have retired long ago from the ring." Stewart must have wanted to fight their canceled 1887 fight.

Rub the lamp and the genie rears up! In January and again in the middle of 1895 Corbett reopened the question of a contest with Peter. He still craved the publicity that their infinitely postponed match gave him. He first said he would fight at the end of 1895 at the National Sporting Club, adhering to their rules, though once he had said that he wouldn't do so even "if he were given Windsor Castle for the job." Peter rejected a date so vague and so remote, saying: "It is now January, I have waited three years, and why should I be asked to wait 10 months more, perhaps a year?" He asked for a match within 4 months. In his letter to Fred Nail he said that he would return to America in May.

Nothing more came from Corbett. Then in May, Brady cabled Fleming at the National Sporting Club announcing that Corbett was ready to fight Peter there in August or September. Fleming referred the announcement to the members, and amid comments like "Let Corbett apologize," and "Corbett has insulted the club, we don't want the match," Brady's patronizing offer was unanimously rejected on May 13.

Peter was not working that night. "There were loud calls for Peter Jackson, who was in the club at the time," the *Sportsman* reported, "and promptly the coloured champion took the ring. In a few well-chosen words Peter said he was sorry the affair had fallen through. Corbett was the one man left he wished to meet. He could not go against the ruling of the club, anxious as he was to settle the old dispute. No one was left to fight, therefore he must retire from active participation in a profession he had, he trusted, followed in an honourable manner. Jackson was lustily cheered, and an end came to the business." He stuck by his words for a while, in January 1897 refusing to fight Bob Armstrong, Davies' new black discovery, who had just beaten Charles Strong in New York and so claimed to be the colored champion of the world. Peter's right to that title was passing to others.

Corbett's reaction to being rejected, according to the *National Police Gazette* of June 1, was rage and invective: "What, apologize to that crowd? Never; for they owe me more of an apology than I do them. The London club is made up of first-class snobs whose only claim to distinction is the possession of a lot of titles. They are the flimsiest excuses for men and sportsmen that ever disgraced a community." The man who would devise the Lonsdale Belt scheme could not have appreciated the Pompadour's insult, but almost certainly he and his colleagues lost no sleep over it. The *Arrow* of March 14, 1896, described Corbett as: "Cute, aye, cute as a pet fox!"

In December 1895 the National Sporting Club put on its annual benefit for manager Fleming. Mace didn't come, but Craig was there. Wag Ward, the toast of Paris, got floored. Dick Burge fought three rounds with Jem Smith, whom the National Sporting Club had almost forgiven for Bruges. Peter was stylish, being "in morning dress, as distinguished from the other professionals, who wore tight pantaloons, showing off every muscle in their legs." That evening he remained strictly decorative because his opponent didn't show.

In March 1896, Steve O'Donnell came to England to box Dick "Queensland Giant" Barker at the National Sporting Club. He came over with Fitzpatrick and with George "Kid" Lavigne, Fitzpatrick's latest discovery. O'Donnell fought Owen Sullivan, who was back from Africa, and then Peter gave a few exhibitions with Sullivan. At this time South African boxing was busy, fed by the gold and diamond mining. Jake Hildebrandt from Johannesburg offered O'Donnell a fight in South Africa with Goddard, who had gone there. O'Donnell preferred to return to America looking for a fight with "Denver" Ed Smith. But Smith himself went to South Africa and on November 7, 1896, fought Goddard for the South African title and lost. Just before he dashed off to New York, Hildebrandt offered Peter $20,000 to fight Corbett in South Africa. He gently declined to scratch at his scars. In June 1896 the visiting Abe Hicken was given a benefit in London, and both Peter and Mace performed. Fitzpatrick saw Peter. "I was very much surprised," he told Naughton, who told the *Referee*, "to see him looking so well after all I had heard about him. There is another good fight left in Jackson without a doubt. He looked much better than he did three days before he went in training for his go with Joe McAuliffe. He was dressed in the height of fashion, and appeared to have plenty of the long green." Naughton felt it necessary to explain to his Australian readers that "long green" meant dollars. But in truth he had less long green to circulate.

It was about this time, when he was 23, that St. John parted company with Peter and enlisted, donning the uniform of the Grenadier Guards. By mid–1896 St. John had either sickened of his vagabond existence, realizing that he would never go beyond sparring with Peter, or else he fancied himself grasping the Lee-Metford rifle with its bayonet, looking smart in the scarlet tunic with the bearskin cap and the white drill jacket with the blue pill-box. The pay of 13 pence a day was hardly attractive. Private St. John became the Grenadier Guard's champion boxer. In the late summer of 1898 he served in the Sudan, winning a medal at the Battle of Omdurman when the English recaptured Khartoum.

Or else St. John simply sickened of Peter's perpetual drinking. Hotels were everywhere and, after everything else closed, the Market House Tavern in Covent Garden opened at 2:00 A.M. Peter was fond of Gurnia's pub on Church, whose host was the champion bird mimic of England. He had many, all too many other favorite pubs, and Peter was not always fit to perform. On July 28, 1896, the *Oswego Daily Times* reported from London that "Peter Jackson, the colored heavyweight pugilist, was arrested last night outside the Tivoli music hall for being drunk and disorderly. He was arraigned in the Bow street police court this morning, found guilty, and fined five shillings." The tough St. John got going.

On October 6, 1896, the *Sportsman* had to tell its readers: "The colored champion is still in the trade. Peter the Great has been fulfilling lucrative engagements in the provinces, and next month he commences a sparring engagement at Oldham." Oldham was a cotton-spinning town near Manchester. The boxer who once took San Francisco and Paris by storm let papers know he was working Oldham. About this time Angle saw him sparring with William "Coddy" Meddings, and there will have been other partners, briefly. Two months later the *Sportsman* said he had successfully toured the south coast and that he and Bill Slavin would soon be appearing at Hackney.

In the 1890s the *London Sportsman* was discreet about Peter's private life, but Australian and American papers portrayed him as a womanizer and a lush, always reporting on his physical decline and dissipated lifestyle. It is hard to make out the reality behind the innuendoes and the prudery. Boxing gossip spread all around the world. The word was, in America and Australia, that Peter lived an extravagant life. The word used by the gossipers was "gay." He was said to be "leading a gay life." Fitzpatrick in 1894 used the phrase "broken down by disease or gay living." So that when we find the *Referee* reporting him among "the gayest of the gay" we have nowadays to inquire what was understood then by "gay."

It did not mean indulging in man-to-man sexual activity. In the 1890s the word "gay" had a spread of connotations, the most important of which was that of female prostitution. The drab prostitution of Whitechapel and African Broadway was less strongly implied than the bejeweled prostitution of the Everleigh Club in Chicago, of the Folies Bergère and other grand theaters. According to the 1882 *Sydney Slang Dictionary*, gay meant "loose, dissipated," and a "gay woman" meant a kept mistress or a prostitute. A "gay house" was a brothel. To be told that Peter was "leading a gay life" would be to understand, at that time, that he was visiting expensive brothels, trifling with "actresses" and skirt-dancers, and patronizing the fancy women who received gentlemen in fashionable hotel rooms. Along with this activity went gambling on horseraces, roulette and chemin-de-fer, wheeling and dealing with a criminal element and, almost proverbially, Havanas and hashish. Most importantly, Peter was becoming an alcoholic. He was making merry with Widow Cliquot and Widow Monnier, they said. He was making a fortune but drinking what he didn't gamble. He made money hand over fist, it was said, but it passed through his fingers like sand. Thus Peter was supposed to live his gay life in the chiaroscuro world of gaiety.

In its obituary, the *Melbourne Sportsman* was only repeating the usual tale of wine, women, and song when it wrote:

> "Wein, weib, und gesang" will in time knock out the doughtiest and stoutest boxer or athlete of any other kind that ever lived. Strong as the Biblical Samson was, his "weib" was too much for him. He could pull down the gates of Gaza and with the jawbone of an ass, put up a world's record in the slaughtering of Philistines. But the cooing of Delilah finally brought him to grief—coupled with the chronological equivalent of Perrier Jouet, Moet and Chandon, or whatever Samson's favorite brand may have been. The "wine that sparkles in the cup," and the Delilahs of London, New York, San Francisco, and other large cities, helped materially to bring about the downfall of Peter Jackson.

The *Sportsman* seemed unable to trace any ill effects back to song. Nor did it mention gambling. Billy Brady wrote that in his experience most boxers died poor. "The trouble is," he said, "most of them come of poor parents and, uneducated in the use of money, when prosperity comes it knocks them off their pins."[12]

With St. John now a Grenadier, Peter replaced him with Bill Slavin, Paddy's elder brother who resembled him. The *St. Louis Post-Dispatch* for November 2, 1891 said: "They possess the same shaped limbs, the same straight backs, thick chests, wide shoulders and sturdy necks. Bill has the stern, resolute look of Paddy, his mustache is quite as bristling, and his eyebrows are as heavy. His nose has the same rainbow shape," whatever that meant. Bill had showed with Peter in Brisbane, in Newcastle, and at Foley's, he had fought with Jack a preliminary before the Corbett fight, and he had met Craig the year before. Unlike St. John, Bill was not bigger than Peter; in fact, he was a middleweight and about the same height, but he was white.

In September 1892 Paddy bought the Swan and Sugar-Loaf Hotel in Fetter Lane, which, with his wife Edith as barmaid, he ran like his Rose Hotel on Jermyn. Now, in December 1894, Paddy gave up both hotels and quit London for South Africa. He was given a "grand send off" at the huge Central Hall in Holborn. At the start of 1897, Jack Slavin, the third brother, went to Johannesburg. "Denver" Ed Smith was already there, and so was Goddard; so were a number of lesser lights. Paddy hadn't stayed long, having gone to Canada to box and dabble in mining.

With his brothers abroad, Bill found it convenient to be employed by Peter. It was reported in Australia that the two were giving successful boxing exhibitions in London and provincial music-halls, Bill wearing a high silk hat like Peter's and acquiring the London polish. At New Year 1897 the *Sydney Arrow* reported: "Peter Jackson and Bill Slavin have been drawing good business in England lately by their sporting show, which is held to be nearly as good as anything of the kind could be." Two weeks later it reported: "Bill has for some time past been acting as Peter Jackson's sparring partner in the provincial and London music-halls. They've been very successful, too." Bill was acting as the "sparring partner with Peter Jackson (when Peter feels fit)," the *Arrow* said.

Peter was drinking heavily, but he had not lost it entirely. Before a packed house at Fleming's annual benefit at the NSC on December 14, 1896, he boxed Josh "Brum" Cosnett, who had seconded Paddy at Bruges. "The appearance of Peter Jackson and Josh Cosnett," said the *Sportsman*, "was the signal for a round of cheering. The sable warrior was attired in green jersey and white pants. He acknowledged the plaudits with all the grace for which he is noted. The hero of the finest fight ever seen between two big men, viz. his battle with Slavin, and the white man had an interesting if not a particularly heavy spar." But his bread-and-butter employment was disappearing. He wrote Will on March 6, 1897, that "exhibition boxing in the provinces is at a complete standstill," and in London it was little better. In the *Referee* of April 21 Will commented on the letter, gently suggesting that Peter should return to America, knock second-raters over, take the prize money, and run. But he was too proud.

Actually, in December of 1896, through Naughton, President Rivers of the California Athletic Club had offered him a fight with an unknown. Peter took the attitude that Naughton would not steer him in the wrong direction. The unknown was Paddy Slavin — but nothing came of the offer, then. The *Police Gazette* wrote on January 9, 1897: "Tom O'Rourke will give Peter Jackson the chance to show he isn't a has-been. O'Rourke will match him against Peter Maher in NYC at Broadway Athletic Club." This offer did not make Peter's heart pound. Something bigger was bound to turn up and put some money into his coffers again.

8. Corduroy Road, 1894–1900

In Reno, Nevada, on March 17, 1897, Corbett lost his title to Fitzsimmons, who used the solar plexus punch to put the Pompadour down. After the fight, Corbett, crying with rage, and "jabbering insanely" according to the *Chronicle*, went over to Fitzsimmons in his corner and attacked him. He had to be dragged off him. As reported by Naughton, the new champion of the world said smugly: "I have promised never to fight again. I met the enemy and he is mine."

Peter had become a member of the Harmony Club, which had its rooms in Fitzroy Square, nearby to Marylebone. At the end of 1896 he planned a boxing academy in conjunction with the Harmony Club. He wrote Will that he was starting "a class in London for a little while prior to my going back to the States." On March 20, three days after Fitzsimmons became champion, the academy opened inside the Harmony Club's premises at 38 and 39 Fitzroy Square. Peter intended teaching two nights a week. The sons of "dukes, earls, lords, and commoners" were reported enrolling for lessons. The launch saw four exhibitions between boxers from London clubs, interspersed with vaudeville turns, singers and dancers and a trick-cycling juvenile. To close, Peter and Bill sparred. But the academy may not have been successful, for the *Sportsman* never mentioned it again. Comments in newspaper interviews suggest Peter's interest in his academy ended by September 1897, after not six months.

On May 7, 1897, a smoke-concert was arranged for Bill Slavin, who had been invited to South Africa by his brother Jack to prospect for gold on his mining claim near Johannesburg. Jack had been boxing in South Africa, but now he wanted to emulate Paddy's Canadian mining success. Peter chaired the evening. Bill left for South Africa the next day. Good reports of the two brothers' prosperity in Johannesburg filtered back to England and Australia. Then in July 1898 came the news that Bill was dead of typhoid in Pietermaritzburg.

The earlier plan to have Peter fight an unknown who was Paddy had a sequel. In the middle of May, after Bill left, cables from America announced that Peter and Paddy would fight in San Francisco in July. On May 31, 1897, in San Francisco, Paddy fought Butler, with whom Peter had exhibited in Philadelphia five years earlier when he was a middleweight. Then cables announced that Peter and Paddy would fight in the new California Athletic Club. But Peter was warned in June that Paddy was in Alaska and he should ignore any cables about a fight. In early August, however, San Francisco complained that Peter ignored telegrams.

Peter didn't reply to those telegrams because he seems to have sunk into apathy after Bill left. E.S. Tremayne Rodd, the Sydney amateur middleweight, wrote to Will from the National Sporting Club in May saying he had met Peter there. Peter looked well, was a grand toff with his top hat, claimed to be Australian to the backbone, said he had always worn the Australian colors with honor, said Sydney was his home. Rodd did not notice the melancholy that normally afflicted Peter, and Peter probably was cheered by seeing Rodd and his companion Captain Scott from the old White Horse days. Dan Creedon, however, who also met him about this time, wrote to the *Referee*: "He sits looking sleepy and tired, the nerves in his neck twitching his head unconsciously; he plainly takes interest in few things."

Reporting the Derby for 1896, the *Times* ignored commoners, so Peter's presence at Epsom that day is hypothetical. But when *Punch* came out on June 19, it brought a delightful surprise for Peter. In the middle of the magazine, on heavy art paper, appeared the most elaborate of all Phil May's drawings. It was a double spread titled: "A Diamond Jubilee Dream of Victorian Derby Days." It contained more than 100 figures, most of them portraits of great and famous people from the 60 years of Victoria's reign. *Punch* supplied no key, and it is difficult now to identify more than a few, but May drew the Duke of Wellington and Lord Brougham, Disraeli and Gladstone, Queen Alexandra and Florence Nightingale, Tennyson, Darwin, Dickens and many more notables. In the lower left corner, Carlyle (whose proto-fascist politics must have been anathema to May) was shown as a cardsharp, trying a card trick on a couple of dudes, probably J.A. Froude and Anthony Trollope, who published racist books about the West Indies. In the lower right corner, Mr. Punch astride a toy horse saluted the Prince of Wales, whose own horse "Persimmon" had won the Derby two weeks before. At the top of the picture, higher than other figures, as if standing on a wagon, were a white and a black sparring, and another white with a fierce mustache gesturing "Behold." The hawker is another of May's portraits of Paddy, and the white sparring partner was probably meant as Bill Slavin, being too thin for Jem Smith. The black must be Peter, for he is even shown in the Wood-Mayo pose. Thus May set Peter Jackson firmly in the context of England's great age.

In 1897 Peter roused himself and made a move. He had needed motivating, and the spur to action was news that Mace at 66 and Mike Donovan at 48 had engaged in two contests. The first was an exhibition in New York, at the Broadway Athletic Club in December 1896. The second, on September 3, 1897, was in the Olympic Club at Birmingham. This was billed as being for the "veteran championship of the world." The rounds were only of two minutes but the action ceased after the third with both veterans blowing like grampuses, the result tactfully declared a draw. But if at 66 Mace could keep going, why should not Peter try again at 36?

Soon afterward Peter returned to the United States. He told the *Sportsman* that he was going to San Francisco on private business but also to have a fight if anything offered. On the Cunard liner *Servia* crossing the Atlantic, in first class with him was Donovan, relaxed after his encounter with Mace, while in second class was Maher. The two Peters chatted before they disembarked.

It was September 15 when Peter arrived in New York, stopping in a hotel "where a big crowd made him welcome." He was interviewed by a *New York World* reporter. "'Yes,' said he, 'I've come here to fight. It's my business and that's what I'm here for. I'll take one, or I'll take them all one by one. I've got money to back me, and I'm looking for a battle.' 'You won't dodge Fitz?' someone asked him. 'I'll fight anyone,' he responded. 'Fitzsimmons included?' Jackson threw out his chest, breathed hard, and replied: 'Mr. Fitzsimmons will be more than welcome.'" He then left for Chicago and San Francisco.

Peter gave only vague reasons for his return. He told the *Chronicle* reporter on September 21, 1897, "I intend to remain here indefinitely, and although I am here solely to look after some business matters which require my attention, you may say that I am open to any engagements which will give me a chance to prove myself all that my friends have claimed for me".

The *New York World* said of Peter's return to America: "Jackson, to be sure, has money behind him. Curiously enough it lies in Wall Street, and if he can pull off a fight he can raise all the money he needs. Much of his old-time popularity sticks to him, and the Wall Street men — men by the way not often seen at the ringside — have guaranteed to stand by him. So Peter's talk of fight is, as he says, pure business." And the *Chicago Tribune* reported that Peter was in America for a few months attending to business matters, saying, "Jackson is a man of means and has varied financial interests, stocks, and mortgages." Both newspapers were reporting only what Peter told them. It is not certain that any such financial resources existed by then, nor any such backers, though the Nail brothers were sometimes still called his backers. And perhaps he did own some government bonds.

On September 19 the *Chicago Tribune* called him the Umslopogaas of the prize ring, a complimentary reference to the great Zulu warrior who was a character in several wildly popular novels by H. Rider Haggard. He met Armstrong in Chicago where he stopped for one day, and was favorably impressed.

Immediately after Fitzsimmons's victory over Corbett, a *Chronicle* reporter recorded a dialog between Mrs. Fitzsimmons and Bob, she saying: "He is too good a man and too healthy ever to be defeated. I shall ask him never to fight again," and Fitzsimmons replying: "Rose, my dear, I never will fight again. I think I have fought enough and when you ask me not to fight again I don't think I could refuse unless it is for your own protection." On September 25, 1897, the *Chronicle* reported Fitzsimmons in Rye, New York, repeating his announcement of March. "This is positive," he said. "I have retired permanently from the ring and will never fight Corbett or any one else again." Choynski told the *Chronicle* in early November 1897: "The general impression in the East is that Corbett and Fitzsimmons will not meet again as Fitzsimmons' announcement of his retirement from the ring is deemed genuine. It is believed that Corbett will retire also. This leaves the championship question badly mixed, but the coming contests between leading heavy-weights ought to get it into a condition so that the real champion can be ascertained."

In fact, on March 20, after his victory, Fitzsimmons had sent off what the *Chronicle* described as "notifications to Corbett, Goddard, Choynski, Sullivan, Sharkey and Maher, declaring his intentions and requesting them to battle among themselves for the honors he had laid aside." Peter had not been sent a telegram, but evidently he returned to America for the knockout competition. As it turned out, Fitzsimmons announced in December of 1897 that he or Mrs. Fitzsimmons had changed his mind, and he would certainly defend his title. But then he went off on a theatrical tour, leaving the championship undefended until 1899.

Traveling on the Southern Pacific's Overland route, Peter wired ahead to Naughton, and Naughton went to Sacramento to meet him. He wore a tall silk hat, a sky-blue shirt and a stylish Prince Albert coat of the latest London cut. He carried a gold-headed umbrella. While in the depot at Oakland he jumped on the scales and showed reporters he weighed 215 pounds.

On Tuesday, September 21, he reached San Francisco. The sidewheeler ferry from Oakland was met by friends. "Young Mitchell was the first to shout 'Hello, Peter' at the champion of Australia and England, and then J.D. Gibb, of the National Club, voiced a welcome." Herget had branched out from his bar business, and had now taken over the management of the Occidental Club. His brother August ("Gus") had likewise taken over the Alpine Club, founded in 1889 "to foster all kinds of out door sports." The *Bulletin* reported that Peter showed no ravages from whisky. "As far as looks cut any figure," it said, "the great, dusky fellow disproves these statements in toto. Instead of being decrepit, he is a model of health. He walks erect, and with a step firm as an army captain."

Peter checked into the Baldwin, having forgotten the McAuliffe incident three years before. The party then headed for the bar, where more buddies joined them for drinks. Lucky Baldwin came across the jolly group and was not pleased, not at all. Peter was a foreigner, he was long past being the contender, and he was black — moreover, he was no longer well cashed up. Before another ruckus could occur, Baldwin ordered Peter's baggage moved to the hotel's annex, a separate building through a walkway, and had his signature in the register erased. A year later the world champion, Fitzsimmons, was denied service in the restaurant of the Gilsey House in New York City. J.H. Breslin, the manager of the hotel, expelled him, saying "I don't want you or any of your profession in my house." Fitzsimmons, who was a white and now an American citizen, set about suing the Gilsey House. Peter was in good company.

Peter said with justice: "In Australia, throughout the United States and in England I have stopped at the leading hotels, and this is the first time such a thing has happened to me. Even when I was here before I stopped at the Baldwin and no objection was ever raised." The *San Francisco Call* reported this as: "No," he said, "It was because of my color. For the first time in my life I had the color line drawn on me." The *Call* said nothing about the McAuliffe incident, and printed the opinion of a black bootblack: "It's a shame to refuse to give a room to such a gentleman as Peter Jackson. Didn't he walk arm in arm with the Marquis of Queensberry in Piccadilly? Didn't he shake the hand of the Prince of Wales? Ain't he the best fighter in the world?" The details were legendary but the tenor of the remarks was plain.

The Baldwin's management was not talking, but the clerk at another big hotel said suavely: "It is a law in all first-class hotels throughout the country never to give accommodation to negroes." If such a rule existed it was an extremely new rule, part of the Jim Crow regulations that were gripping the country. The incident is probably an index of how quickly the freedom of blacks was being curtailed in the 1890s. In the *Bulletin* on September 23, "a prominent sporting man" reminisced, saying that "the big fellow thinks the world of Young Mitchell. It will be remembered that a few years ago he came within an ace of whipping Joe McAuliffe because he offered some uncomplimentary remarks about his friend. And Young Mitchell has a warm spot in his heart for Jackson." The *Chronicle* did refer to the 1894 incident, but it too viewed Lucky Baldwin's actions as racially motivated. The Palace Hotel had sacked the last of over 200 black employees the year before.

He stayed perforce in the Baldwin's annex overnight, then checked out. The *Bulletin* reported him sauntering along Market the next day, accompanied by a coterie of admirers. He attended the theater drunk, it said, but acting sober. He made his headquarters at "Young Mitchell's sporting resort," by which presumably the *Bulletin* meant he was bunking in the back of Herget's bar on Taylor. Soon he took lodgings along the street at 1130 Market in the Vienna Bazaar, a four-story building. It had the advantage of being a couple of minutes' walk along Market to the Tamale Cafe, Herget's place.[13]

The *Bulletin* of September 27 reported that Peter was seen on Powell yesterday. He had been hitting the bottle. "His massive shoulders, once admired by thousands, were stooped and bent. His legs, once straight and firm, wobbled. Indeed, he was a sad sight. He looked but the tottering wreck of his former self. He was followed by a mob of hoodlums, who cheered in his steps. Tales from London were here verified: tales which sporting men had hoped were groundless." But the *Bulletin* was relieved to report: "Even in his state of intoxication the whilom idol of the world acted only the part of a gentleman. His language was as polite as that of a parson." From this sad spectacle the *Examiner* averted its eyes.

In the evening Peter staggered into a saloon and was introduced to Tom Sharkey, who was in San Francisco for his November 18 fight with Goddard and had sworn the day before he would never fight Peter because he was black. They sat down together, watched by a crowd that included at least one reporter. Peter took a Scotch, Sharkey drank chartreuse. They said little, not even reminiscing about Honolulu. In the following November, Sharkey offered to meet anyone in the world, thus erasing the color line, and was immediately challenged through O'Rourke to meet Walcott.

On November 3, 1897, an alcoholic incident occurred. Harry Corbett, proprietor of a poolroom at 30 Ellis and Gentleman Jim's elder brother, punched Peter in a saloon at 12 Ellis, called by the *National Police Gazette* "one of San Francisco's most famous gilded sporting resorts." Harry and his buddy Andy McDowell had been drinking and found Peter propped up on the bar about 1:30 A.M. The three had a drink or two. Harry made provocative remarks to Peter about his brother, and Peter said uncomplimentary things about the Pompadour. Harry knocked the drunken Peter to the floor and McDowell pulled a knife on him. He suffered no physical damage, but a dramatic picture and high-colored letterpress on November 3 carried the news of Peter's enfeebled condition into every barbershop in America that took the *National Police Gazette*. Other men probably picked a fight with a drunken Peter Jackson in order to say, like Jim McMahon back in Lane Cove, that they had licked him once. The Baldwin was not Peter's luckiest place, even its environs. A year later he had the satisfaction of hearing that in the early hours of November 23, 1898, the wooden Baldwin burned, or had been burned, to the ground.

On October 4 George Dixon, who had been in the city since at least July, fought Solly Smith for the featherweight championship in Woodward's Pavilion. Peter had met Dixon in Brooklyn at the Jack Fallon debacle on March 4, 1890. He attended to see his little friend win, and proved that the crowds had not forgotten him. "When Peter Jackson, beaming all over and tipping his hat gayly to his friends, entered the pavilion they cheered themselves hoarse," the *Examiner* reported. Dixon was still managed by Tom O'Rourke. They spent time together while Dixon was in town, went hunting bears together. Peter had always been a good shot.

By this time Peter badly needed money. The *Bulletin* reported on October 13 that he was going to revive *Uncle Tom's Cabin* and tour the West Coast. Things were desperate!

He had officially engaged Naughton as his manager. The *Bulletin* had a jaundiced view of the *Examiner*'s Naughton, saying that "the sporting scribe has hooked his talons on Jackson and will arrange his dates in California." Already, by the end of September, Naughton was talking to Eddie Graney about getting a fight on with Choynski. Fitzpatrick in New York was looking after Peter's interests by talking to Brady. But nothing came of these talks beyond a report on November 19 that Peter would fight Choynski if he beat Jeffries on November 30. Choynski didn't. Naughton suggested to the *Referee* in November: "Two or three propositions confront Jackson. He can have the winner of the Choynski-Jeffries contest, or the winner of the Goddard-Sharkey affair provided Goddard happens to be the man. He can also have a go with Peter Maher."

The *San Francisco Call* reported on December 12 that Peter and Jim Jeffries were matched for February, and that "the Colored Champion will tour through the Northwest before he starts to train." Peter supposedly signed for a month's tour up the coast as far as Eureka, Portland and Astoria, to Puget Sound with Tacoma and Seattle, ending in Victoria, British Columbia; in short, said the *Call*, touring "all of the cities of the Northwest showing any signs of sporting life." It was not the Royal Westminster Aquarium and the Folies Bergère, but it promised money — because it was to be, according to the *Bulletin* of October 13 and the *San Francisco Call* of October 29, a revival of *Uncle Tom's Cabin* managed by a no-longer-bankrupt Lincoln R. Stockwell! Billy Elmer, "the thespian pugilist," who boxed Dick Case in San Francisco in September 1897 and Frank McConnell in Oakland in November 1897, would replace Choynski. If this was not already a pipe dream it ended when Peter was offered a February fight with Peter Maher — as well, that is, as the February fight with Jeffries. Elmer went to Portland alone for a second fight with Case on January 17, 1898, and eventually to make numerous movies, his last being Orson Welles's *The Magnificent Ambersons*.

The idea of a tour up north, however, stayed with Peter.

In early December he signed the contract for 20 rounds in February 1898 with Maher at the Occidental Club. Herget was now managing Peter, and the Occidental Club had exclusive control over any of his matches. Maher would get 65 percent of the gross receipts. Maher's American backer scented a winner in matching the two Peters again, 10 years after their sad little encounter in Dublin. One thing could be said about Maher, he was an "Anytime Annie" and would fight anyone. All the boys had him at least once over the years.

On January 13, 1898, it was reported that Peter would fight Maher at Herget's Occidental Club between March 1 and 15. The *St. Louis Post-Dispatch* commented that since Peter fought "the then formidable Frank Slavin" he had only played in *Uncle Tom's Cabin* and drunk a lot of "Uncle Tom" gin. Then it was announced that the Police Committee of the Board of Supervisors would not grant the license for the Occidental Club to stage the Jackson-Maher fight. On January 21, Peter was training at Alameda, getting ready to fight Maher "in the near future." He wrote Fitzpatrick in New York that he was in strict training at Alameda "for anything that may turn up in the way of a match." He wrote he had seen Jeffries in training at Alameda, and described him to Sam as "a corking heavyweight." On January 29 it was announced that under license from the Health and Police Committee of the Board of Supervisors, Jackson and Maher would fight at Woodward's Pavilion on Wednesday, March 16, at the Occidental Club.

"The contest between Peter Jackson and Peter Maher will create a great deal of talk and guessing," said the *Chronicle*. "Jackson may fool those who consider that his retirement from the ring since he knocked out Frank Slavin has so far affected him that he is no longer his former self. The little training he has done has wrought a wonderful change in him. Just what his vitality and power of endurance are will never be known until he gets into the ring. Jackson will have the advantage in reach, height, weight and cleverness, Maher in youth and punching powers."

But this arrangement somehow fell through, and maybe the permission had been an invention of Herget's to force the issue. Peter was now urged to meet Maher in Philadelphia, but Peter refused to budge.

At this time, the licensing of boxing clubs involved political favor and graft. From 1891 to 1901 the Democratic Party under Gavin McNab ruled San Francisco. Everybody had to do deals with City Hall. Even the coroner took bribes! The city worked so mysteriously that by 1897 the police commissioner was Mose Gunst. On January 22, 1898, the *Chronicle* reported: "The policy seems to be to grant the applications of the Empire and the National Club, but not those of the Occidental Club, as Manager John L. Mitchell has had a falling out with the powers that be." It is plausible that Herget got no permits for his Occidental

Club because he would not offer sweeteners to the Democratic Party. The *Bulletin* of December 22 said that all matches were banned purely "in order to prevent Young Mitchell from holding his contest."[14]

While announcements were being made about Maher, Peter signed on December 4, 1897, to fight Jeffries at the Occidental Club early in February 1898 for 75 percent of the take. Herget and Delaney agreed to this. Herget could obtain no permit for the Jackson-Jeffries fight, either. "The managers of the clubs which have been left out in the cold are somewhat at a loss to understand why the applications should have been rejected and the Empire Club favored." The Empire Club, out at Vallejo, was managed by Frank Burns, who must have paid his dues. On February 5, the *Chronicle* announced: "The Peter Jackson-Jim Jeffries match, scheduled for the Olympic Club sometime between March 20 and April 4, probably on Friday, March 25." On February 12 the date was settled as Tuesday, March 22, at Woodward's Pavilion. Peter was at Croll's in Alameda, as ever, and Jeffries was training at the Reliance Club in Oakland. Then the grand jury suggested that the Board of Supervisors had no right to license fighting!

The situation was confused and confusing. By 1898 the situation of boxing in America was so dismal that the *Chronicle* was obliged to state on January 22 in large type that NO MATCHES OF ANY IMPORTANCE CAN BE BROUGHT OFF ANYWHERE ELSE OUTSIDE OF NEVADA AND POSSIBLY NEW YORK CITY. The confusion dissipated in San Francisco: all fights were put on hold except two. The Jackson-Jeffries and the Choynski-Sharkey matches could proceed.

Peter, who had not fought for 6 years, not since the Slavin fight in London, had never wanted to fight Maher and was not keen on Jeffries. But he was compelled to fight Jeffries because he had no money and nobody else was offering. The *San Francisco Call* of December 3 said that "Peter Jackson, the colored heavyweight champion of England and Australia has at last secured a match." In Herget's saloon, Herget signed for Jackson and Billy Delaney for Jeffries.

Peter went into serious training at J.G. Croll's "Neptune Gardens" at Alameda. The papers pictured him greeting his fans and on a training run in long pants, a polo-neck jaeger and a peaked cap, with a retriever running alongside. He used to run over to Dieves's old place. Afternoons he boxed with Vincent White, John Miller (who had fought Sharkey in 1895), and his official trainer Patsy Corrigan, the Australian who had been in San Francisco for a couple of years and was an undistinguished lightweight. As ever, Peter really trained himself.

Many people told Peter to his face that he should not have gone six years without a proper fight. He said: "The argument that I have been a long time away from the ring is one that can be used two ways. Possibly had I fought right along during the past five years I would have been stale now from overtraining. Who can tell?" On March 17 the *San Francisco Call* reported him saying, "I will allow that since my contest with Slavin I have enjoyed myself"; and he said that "until I am whipped my wish is that the sporting people of this city will refrain from cauterizing me because I may not have lived an abstemious life since then." On the 22nd the *Call* described him as "the sensitive and proud champion of England and the Australians."

For the Olympic Club he was twice checked by Dr. Charles E. Parent of 926 Sutter, who also checked Jeffries. Parent stated: "I consider the men to be in the best of condition." On the eve of the fight, the last time his measurements were officially taken, he had a 40-

inch chest and a 33-inch waist. His reach was 77½ inches between fingertips, and he weighed 195 pounds. Perhaps his last photographs by a professional were taken by Fred H. Bushnell's Photo Company and published on the front page of the *Call*.

An assiduous watcher at Alameda was Prince André Poniatowski. If not the pretender to the Polish throne, Poniatowski was a scion of the former royal house of Poland and was born in Paris. In 1894, in San Francisco's wedding of the year, he had married Beth Sperry, the flour-milling heiress from Stockton, and thus married into the Crockers, the banking family of San Francisco. Poniatowski was living in Burlingame near the other Crockers, and so could drop in on Peter daily. Was Peter attracting eminent patronage again?[15] Maybe like Herbert "Hype" Igoe the prince witnessed a strange incident at Alameda. In 1935 Igoe recounted his visit as a cub reporter to Peter's training camp in 1898. He said he saw Peter punched out by Corrigan but Naughton making light of it. Igoe reported some impossible things in his time, but this may have happened.[16] Will Corbett wrote from Sydney urging him not to fight with the young Hercules from the orange belt. He understood that, at 37, Peter was not up to fighting 26-year-old boilermakers. But advice from Down Under sounded faintly at Alameda.

Peter fought Jeffries at Woodward's Pavilion on March 22, 1898, and was defeated for the first time since Farnan. This was a public event, unlike Peter's other fights in San Francisco, which had been in the California Club. The gallery was filled with blacks, and while they waited one played a banjo.

Jeffries's seconds were his brother Jack, the San Franciscan boxer "Spider" Kelly, and Delaney. Peter had said, just a few days earlier: "I do not care to have too many men around me when I am boxing. As a rule, I do not take cues from my seconds. I size my man up to the best of my ability and make my fight accordingly. Too many handlers bother a man in my opinion." But he used Corrigan, White, and Herget. The referee was Jim McDonald, better known as a baseball umpire. The master of ceremonies was William Kennedy from the Olympic Club.

Peter arrived first, and in 1910 in *My Life and Battles* Jeffries said: "Jackson, standing in his corner, bowed to me very politely and smiled as if we were about to play a game of handball instead of trying to knock each other's head off. This surprised me a little, as most of the men I had fought tried to look ugly and throw a scare into me. I managed to grin a little and bow to him in return."[17]

Jackson wore his brown ulster, out of its mothballs. He wore white fighting drawers reaching halfway to the knees, and white sox leaving most of his legs bare. Jeffries wore dark blue trunks with a red and white belt, and black stockings rolled down to the ankles leaving his legs bare. The gloves were tan colored.

They had a consultation with the referee and agreed not to hit in the clinches. Peter strangely broke this agreement, showing how unnerved he was beneath the calm. The fight started at 9:11 P.M.

Round One

Both men went cautiously to the center. Jackson stood in the middle of the ring, feinting, and Jeffries walked in a circle around him. Finally Jeffries tried a left swing for the head. Jackson raised his left guard and the blow touched the tip of his glove. Jeffries landed his left on Jackson's chest. Jackson feinted a couple of times and Jeffries backed away. Then Jeffries rushed, lashing out with the left, and Jackson ducked the blow. They clinched. Both broke away immediately. Jackson was clearly trying to draw on his man, and purposely leaving an opening. Jeffries held his left guard high and pressed in, making a right drive for the heart. He barely touched Jackson's ribs, and Jackson struck him a right-hander in the body before he could draw out. Jeffries threw his head low and made a left dig at the stomach. Jackson drew back from it. Jeffries landed a right swing on the neck. Then he rushed Jackson to the ropes, landing two on the ribs and a left on the neck again. Jackson got out of range. Jeffries stepped after him and swung at his head. Jackson ducked neatly and both rushed to a clinch. Jeffries tried with his left for the face. Jackson ducked from the blow and shot in a stiff left on the stomach. Jeffries rushed and Jackson threw aside a left and put in a hard right under the heart. Jackson stepped in close and drove the right in at the heart again. They clinched. After the break Jeffries swung his left on the ear, and Jackson his right on the body. Another clinch, Jackson put in a straight left between the eyes. Jeffries grinned and kept away for a moment. Then Jeffries sent in a straight left on the stomach. Jeffries rushed two or three times in succession and was met with solid right punches under the heart. They were clinching at the call of time. Jackson's body blows were the cleanest ones landed, but, taken all in all, honors were even during the round.

Round Two

Jackson took the center of the ring again, and Jeffries worked around. Jeffries met Jackson with a light tap, then swung with a vicious left but was short. Again Jeffries swung with the left and was short. Jackson put in a straight left on the face, and was countered with the left. Now they mixed it, Jeffries landing his left on the side of Jackson's face and Jackson pumping in hot ones with the right under the heart. There were a good many clinches, but the men broke at a word from the referee. Jackson directed his attention mostly to the heart. He ducked some swift left-handers from Jeffries, who held his right high, and tried a vicious swing at the head. He missed Jackson's chin by about an inch. They clinched, and Jackson punched Jeffries in the body, contrary to what they agreed with referee McDonald. Jeffries tried for the body with the left and was short. Jackson sent in a straight left stab on the mouth, and backed away to the ropes to get out of the way of Jeffries' rush. Jackson ducked cleverly under some left-handers from Jeffries. The crowd cheered wildly at every duck. Jackson put in another jarring left on the face, and Jeffries dropped his hands and backed away. Jackson accepted a left on the jaw in order to get in another of his heart blows. Jackson stepped too close to put in a heart blow, and Jeffries struck him with a left on the jaw. Jackson dropped onto his haunches and rolled over on his side, then he scrambled slowly to his feet. He was dizzy and hurt. He got up in about seven seconds, and Jeffries waited quietly for him. Jeffries swung his left again, catching Jackson on the chin, and again Jackson went down on his back. He rolled to the ropes, and was himself to his feet when the gong sounded for the end of the round. Jeffries's friends were cheering wildly, and Jackson was very dizzy as his seconds dragged him to his corner and threw water over him. He recuperated, however, after a minute's rest.

Round Three

Jeffries was now full of confidence. He did not try to guard Jackson's heart blows, but swung with his left for the face. Jackson got in one heart punch, and took a hard left on the jaw. Again Jackson tried with his right for the body, and Jeffries landed several hard left-handers on the face. Jackson was all but gone. He staggered, but kept his feet. Jeffries kept hammering him on the face with lefts, and Jackson tottered back to the ropes. An extra hard left-hander from Jeffries placed Jackson in a sitting posture on the lower rope, with his arms hanging outside.

The referee stepped between the fighters. Cries arose on all sides of "Stop the fight." Jeffries drew back for McDonald to count; but McDonald said, "I can't do any counting, because he isn't down." His head was drooping; he was powerless and helpless. Jeffries said to McDonald, "He's done, Jim," and, as he related in 1927, "walked over, pulled his arms inside the ropes, and then his body, without support, slipped to the floor, and the great old Peter was counted out." While McDonald was still counting, Captain Gillen of the police stepped into the ring, and had Jackson lifted to his corner. As soon as McDonald could make himself heard, he said: "The police have stopped the fight, and I proclaim Jeffries the victor." The whole thing had lasted a quarter of an hour, and the spectators, who had paid from $1 up to $10, were indignant.

"There was no scene of wild enthusiasm when the decision was announced," Naughton told the *Referee*. "There were cheers for Jeffries, of course, and there were just as vociferous cheers for Peter as he pulled himself together and made his way out of the ring. No more popular pugilist ever had a decision recorded against him." Peter issued a press release, which concluded: "I have had done to me to-night what I have done to many others in my day, but it is hard to see the reputation which it has taken me 15 years to earn swept away in a few minutes." His reputation would suffer worse damage the next year.

Much anger was directed toward Dr. Parent, whose pronouncement that Peter was in the best of conditions had been represented by the *Examiner* as saying he was in perfect condition, and by many interpreted as saying that he was in winning shape. Many bettors had lost money on account of Dr. Parent, and so, according to the *Chronicle*, he was "very harshly criticized by Jackson's friends and backers."

In *Two-Fisted Jeff*, published in 1929, Jeffries appeared not even to remember the fight, expressing solely the regret that Peter hadn't lasted longer and provided him with a more educative experience. "I was disappointed," he or his ghost-writer said in 1929, "because it was said he was the master of all heavy weight boxers, and I expected to learn something of ring tactics from him, but it proved to be one of the few fights from which I got nothing but the big end of the purse."[18] But in two earlier accounts of the fight, one in J.W. McConaughy's *Big Jim Jeffries: His 12 Greatest Battles,* published in 1910, and one in *James J. Jeffries' Life and Fights*, published in parts in the Sydney *Referee* in 1927, Jeffries was more explicit. In 1910 he said: "I realized that the hard fight I had expected was never to come off. Jackson looked like a champion, but London had robbed him of his stamina." In 1927 he said: "I did not have the heart to tear into him savagely. I just kept hitting him with jolting punches, hoping that he would give up. But Peter was too game for that."

The *Los Angeles Daily Times* headed its article on the fight: "Peter Peters Out." He got the loser's 30 percent of the fighters' 60 percent of the take (originally quoted as 75 percent), which amounted to $1,878. He would have got more had the promoters used the Mechanics'

Pavilion instead of the smaller Woodward's Pavilion. As it was, hundreds of people were turned away.

In his dressing room Peter told the *Los Angeles Daily Times* reporter: "It's the fortune of war. The youngest and strongest man won, and, as I said before the fight, I will not murmur as I was fairly whipped. I counted on skill and long experience to carry me through, but it was no use against the great strength of Jeffries." To the *Chronicle* reporter he said: "I am sorry that my friends have been disappointed and that they have lost their money, but I feel that this beating, though it may have thrown me out of the race for good, has not disgraced me or hurt my record. Jeffries is wonderfully strong and active, and I was up against it hard. That is all there is about it. I am not a youngster any more, and we must all find our finish sooner or later, I guess." He said: "It'll all be the same in a thousand years. What's the diff?" He concluded his *Chronicle* interview by saying: "I can't talk about my plans at this time, and I don't care to say yet whether I intend to abandon the business or not. I think I will, but I won't say for sure."

He went to Herget's bar and brooded. A *Bulletin* reporter found him there alone, with his arms stretched out along the brass rail of the bar. "He stared hard at nothing," said the *Bulletin*, "and his name had to repeated before he was aware of the presence of another. Then he showed the gold in his teeth while he smiled in recognition." Peter denied he was retiring, but not sure what he would be doing. The paper headed its article: "'Hail, Jeffries, Adios, Peter,' Say Sports." The *Chronicle* said: "The black hero of the prize-ring, the idol of the galleries, and one of the cleanest and cleverest fighters that ever stood in a ring is a 'has been,' finally and for always."

The next day Peter raced down to the *Alameda* before it sailed and gave a verbal message to one of the officers, for him to pass on to Will in Sydney, to the effect that he was "not a has been." Will reported it to his readers. But Will had been severe when the news first came through, blaming "a palpably wrecked constitution brought about by too free indulgence in the temptations of a life of absolute inertia, extending over five years, spent among the gayest of the gay in one of the fastest cities of the world — London." Will's charge of absolute inertia was unwarranted, since the man had been sparring most nights during those five years. Peter thought that the Jeffries fight was not a fair test of his ability. Everyone else, however, thought that indeed, in 1898, it was. Peter himself predicted that Jeffries would become the champion, which he did the next year when Jeffries stepped into the ring with Peter's pupil Fitzsimmons at Coney Island on June 9, 1899 and stepped out of it heavyweight champion of the world. Peter's next opponent and his last, Jim Jeffords, would have nothing of Jeffries' stature.

The *St. Louis Post-Dispatch* was told: "Peter Jackson celebrated his defeat by Jim Jeffries at San Francisco by getting gloriously drunk," and for months after the Jeffries fight Peter did little except drink. The *Call* wrote on March 26, 1898: "Jackson is about town drinking heavily again. Before he was matched eastern papers called on the negro race to provide a testimonial fund for Jackson, who had done so much for them, instead of letting him go down to defeat in his older days."

On April 26 Peter was drinking in a Mission Street saloon with a woman known as Lottie Douglas, who was no lady. She stole his $150 diamond pin and pawned it. She was arrested and charged with grand larceny and vagrancy. This is the only time Peter was reported in a woman's company; and his naivety is shown by his flashing the diamonds. Soon there would be none to flash.

On June 11, 1898, Peter told Fitzpatrick, who at once told the *St. Louis Post-Dispatch*, that he might return to England and become a boxing instructor. The Harmony Club venture had disintegrated when he left, but he was hoping for a job somewhere. It was time for thinking about Calcutta again. What else could he do? Take up some of the challenges that people now dared to issue? In Aesop's fable the dead lion is kicked by jackals, and Peter now got many offers to fight from men who previously were afraid to meet him, offers he proudly rejected. Too proudly, given his financial situation.

What could he do? He could have taken up refereeing, something he had done on a few occasions. He could have gone on the vaudeville circuit. This had been canvassed in 1894, when the *Examiner* said: "It is positively painful to hear Peter affect a negro dialect, and while he has a natural bent for Irish funnyisms and costermonger songs, he feels he cannot make up for the parts, and everyone knows that in stage business the make up is half of the battle." He could not, or would not, play Mr. Bones, but if only he had persevered Peter might have carried the term "Black Irish" into a new dimension. He could have taken $25 a week as a bouncer. "The bouncer for a big saloon," said the *Examiner* in 1891, "is usually a retired prize-fighter. An ex-champion is most desirable. His record is more use than he is himself." Then came the bouncers at the concert halls along Grant Avenue. Below them were bouncers at dance halls on the Barbary Coast, paid a few bits a week plus liquor. The *Examiner* considered: "When a man becomes a bouncer for a dance hall he is about as low down on the social scale as he can get. It's about time for him to die." Peter was not ready to die yet.

In June he injured a leg climbing into a buggy. He had to be operated on in St. Luke's Hospital, which was an Episcopalian hospital on Valencia between 27th and 28th, and where "no distinction is made between the various nationalities, creeds, or opinions, its doors being open to all," according to its entry in the *Crocker-Langley San Francisco Directory*.

Peter was laid up for three weeks, and though he wrote Will that "I will be going East among the big guns shortly," he stayed in San Francisco and gave himself over to socializing. His assets were disposed of one after another, the diamond pin, the goldheaded canes, the fly and dumb-bell stickpin, and he drank the proceeds. The man who once quaffed Veuve Cliquot champagne now drank steam beer at five cents. As for food, if ever he felt like food, he probably acted like the hero of Frank Norris's *Vandover and the Brute,* who worked a dozen saloons on the Barbary Coast offering free lunch. "He paid five cents for a glass of beer and ate his morning's meal at the lunch counter: stew, bread, and cheese. At noon he made his dinner at the second saloon on his route. Here he had another glass of beer, a great plate of soup, potato salad, and pretzels." Vandover hoped that no bartender would get wise. Peter could do that too.[19]

A furnished room in San Francisco rented for about $8 a month, bed and breakfast cost around $15, and a room with board cost $20-plus a month. The prices at Alameda were probably somewhat less. In 1899 he was living at 24 Turk, renting a room in the building he had once leased. All he had left was the trust account that he had set up for his old age. But then, he became aware that he was not altogether well, what with those night sweats and that persistent cough, and he began to pester his trustees to let him break into the fund now.

The *St. Louis Post-Dispatch* of August 18, 1898, said, quoting "an old sporting man" who remembered how beautiful Peter was, that Peter was a total wreck, utterly broke, spending his days and nights in saloons, going to bed drunk on whisky. He said Peter toddled, and lived in a saloon near Turk and Market. This must have been the property at No. 25. The saloon, or presumably its second floor, was not Godfrey's "nice little home," but it was free. He would sell the lease within the year, however, as his cash dwindled. On March 18, 1899, Edward Tweedie, champion featherweight of New South Wales, ran into Peter on his way to Oregon. He wrote the *Referee*: "Poor Peter looks broke up, and I don't think he will fight any more. He doesn't look that way."

His degeneration had become so evident to others that the colored championship of the world, the title which Peter had won from Godfrey in 1888 but had not defended and now never would, was fought for officially. In Chicago on January 29, 1898, Childs, with whom Peter sparred in 1893 and who had left Los Angeles for Chicago, met Armstrong, whom Peter had refused to fight two years earlier. Childs won. In March 1899 they fought again at the Stag Athletic club in Cincinnati. "This will be in every respect a championship match," said the *National Police Gazette*, "for Peter Jackson is conceded to be out of the game now.' But he wasn't, not completely.

The *Chronicle* reported on June 11, 1898: "Peter Jackson has been living quietly in Alameda since his go with Jeffries, but says he is desirous of entering the ring again. He says he is willing to take on any of the heavyweights, and that he has money for a side bet." He was occasionally reported in the papers beastly drunk.

In March 1899 he was at Croll's hotel in Alameda. His drunkenness was scandalous. He went through his money. He fell into arrears with his rent, paying none for months and by the middle of the year owing $78 to his landlady, who wanted to evict him and impounded his few possessions pending payment. In July 1899, a few days after he officially turned 38, his friends bundled him out of San Francisco.

The *Chronicle* headlined its story "Peter Jackson's Pitiful Condition," but what was unknown to the *Chronicle*, and even to Peter himself, was that in the previous year he had contracted tuberculosis. It was hard to diagnose tuberculosis, and in any case Peter would never run to doctors with little things. He was checked by Dr. Parent before the Jeffries fight. He was well when he fought, the reporting suggesting merely that at 36 he was outboxed by a 23-year-old. The diagnosis made by Dr. L'Estrange in the middle of 1901, arrived at from a physical examination and from asking him about his symptoms, was that the tuberculosis dated back two years, that is to the middle of 1899. Peter dated obvious symptoms to then, but these were the eruption of subterranean activity. He contracted tuberculosis after the Jeffries fight, and obscurely realized it. His lifestyle predisposed him to catching the disease: smoky barrooms, spittoons, chewing tobacco, raised wooden sidewalks, and alcohol that destroyed vitamins, not to speak of the meat from tubercular cattle which the city's poorest bought, not being able to catch healthy cane rats.

A scheme was devised to send him up to the chocolate-box wilderness of British Columbia, to take the Canadian-Pacific Railway across Canada, exhibiting at whistle stops as far as Toronto and thence New York City. Peter wired Fitzpatrick, who was managing the Westchester Athletic Club, and made the proposal. After consulting with O'Rourke, who was managing the new Lenox Athletic Club in New York City, Fitzpatrick thought that once in New York Peter might be matched, ten years on, against a 40-year-old Kilrain. Behind this desperate Canadian scheme was the realization that people would pay to see celebrities "in person," even though the celebrities were past their prime. If people queued in New York to see films of Corbett, surely Peter Jackson in the flesh could still attract a paying crowd in Medicine Hat, Beavermouth and Moose Jaw.[20]

The *Chronicle* said on June 25 that there would be a benefit for Peter before Thursday, July 6. Herget put it together. They hoped for Jeffries but he would be too late arriving back in San Francisco. Eventually, it was held on Friday, June 30, 1889, in Woodward's Pavilion. Though only about 1,000 spectators came, most of them gallery regulars and most of these blacks, it was "a very good crowd, considering that San Franciscans do not turn out well at exhibitions." Billy Madden refereed. Gus Ruhlin, Charlie Goff, Jack Stelzner, Billy Otts and Al Neill appeared. These were not luminaries of the ring. It had been reported that "Sharkey says he will put off his departure for the east and do some sparring with Peter," but he couldn't wait the few days, so that "the announcement that Tom Sharkey telegraphed his regrets was received with mingled cheers and hisses." To close, Alex Greggains, the founder of the San Francisco Athletic Club in 1882 and a respectable heavyweight who had fought Sharkey and LaBlanche, went three rounds with Peter.

Accompanied or rather chaperoned by an Australian, Charley Long, who was noted in the *Daily Colonist* as "his manager, Mr. C.H. Long," Peter went on the *City of Puebla* up to Victoria, the capital city of British Columbia. On Saturday, July 22, signing himself "Peter Jackson Australia," he checked into the refurbished Hotel Victoria. Rooms were $1 and $1.25 a night. He could afford that. Thereupon he challenged anybody who might care to put on gloves with him and reached for a whisky.

That evening he ran into Paddy, who was awaiting the arrival from England of Edith and their three children. He and "Denver" Ed Smith had done well in the Yukon. Mining towns were always good for boxing, gold-rush towns the best. Dawson City was paying favorite entertainers with gold ingots! Besides that, he had interests in gold prospecting and in the lumber industry. He was said to be worth $15,000. Peter and Frank had much to talk about over drinks that night, but of course they had especially to talk about poor dead Bill.

Long excused himself and returned to San Francisco where he reported: "I left the big fellow up north enjoying himself. He seems to have a lot of friends there. He started to drink up all the liquor in sight as soon as he arrived in Victoria." In 1899 about 300 blacks lived in Victoria and on Vancouver Island, a number also being West Indian, among whom would have been admirers of Peter. He found drinking buddies but nobody to accept his challenge. As his money trickled away he started buying gins.[21]

At Portland on his way back to San Francisco, Charley Long met up with Jim Jeffords, the pride of Sonora, and suggested that he should arrange a fight with Peter. Jeffords didn't do so, but unnamed friends of Peter's organized a 20-round fight with Jeffords which somehow turned into three shorter fights at Victoria, Vancouver, and Nanaimo. The articles were signed in Portland by proxies about July 25.

Peter started training at the Colonist Hotel, on Simcoe at Beacon Hill Park in Victoria, which was run by "Denver" Ed Smith, Peter's old opponent and buddy. It was almost like family! Peter enlisted as his local manager John B. Simpson, licensee of the nearby Brown Jug Saloon at 174½ Yates.[22]

Peter's match, Jeffords, had been born in Cornwall, England, in 1875 and in California had started out at Sonora as a Cornish-style wrestler, turning to boxing only the year before. He was managed by Biddy Bishop, a small-time boxer. The *San Francisco Chronicle* described him as "a big, strong, whirlwind fighter." He claimed to the *Vancouver Daily World* to have drawn twice with Jeffries the champion of the world. Just the month before, however, Jeffries had ostentatiously refused to fight Jeffords. Pressed, Jeffords admitted to the reporter that he had only sparred with Jeffries at a mining camp in California.

As soon as word of his Portland deal with Peter reached San Francisco, all sorts of remonstrances went up to Victoria saying that Jeffords was an inferior fighter. Naughton thought Peter stupid to fight "lusty young know-nothings at this stage of the game." The *Bulletin* said on July 27: "Jeffords and Jackson! What a match! Can anyone think of a worse one: Jeffords a rank incompetent and Jackson an 18-karat has-been. Let us be grateful that the farce is to take place far away." But Peter could not afford to be concerned with his image when he needed money. The contract said the winner took all and the loser got nothing. Peter must have been confident, and his proxy signed it.

The three matches were held across one week. Nanaimo, along Vancouver Island some 50 miles by train from Victoria, was a mining town of 10,000 inhabitants. The fight took place on Thursday, August 17, in the Nanaimo Opera House. It was advertised as a "Grand Ten Round Boxing Contest under the Marquis of Queensberry Rules. Peter Jackson of Australia and Jim Jefford [sic] of San Francisco." Jeffords was little known. The *Nanaimo Free Press* of August 18 improperly called them "Peter Jackson the Champion of Australia and England" and "Jim Jeffords the Champion of the Pacific Coast." The preliminaries were to involve "local aspirants to the noble art." Said the advertisement: "A Good Evening's Sport Assured. Popular Prices." The *Nanaimo Free Press* presented Jeffords as a Hercules. "Standing 6 feet 1½ inches in height, he presented a perfect picture seldom seen in this section of the country." Bishop said "Peter will certainly know that he has been to a fight." Simpson accompanied Peter and, it was said, "will attend to his business affairs while here," meaning that he was his manager. A party of friends and hangers-on came along with Peter.

The Opera House was almost full and the 10 rounds began. The audience was sadly disappointed that no local men were taking part in the exhibition. No arrangements had been made with Nanaimo boxers, nor had they even been contacted until the night! The star turn, which was the only turn, was nothing more than the two pugilists taking a little exercise at the expense of the spectators, said one disgruntled reporter. "It was certainly one of the tamest affairs seen in Nanaimo for some time, the two principals trading on past reputations to obtain an easy living." The *Nanaimo Free Press* disdained to mention the next two fights.

The second fight took place in the Savoy Theater at Victoria on August 21. It was a 5-round contest for points. The venue, holding about 1000, was crowded. Police were on hand to ensure no slugging. The fight was taps and feintings, and the result another draw. "Jackson has not lost any of his cleverness," said the *Daily Colonist* in its one-paragraph coverage, "and to those who have seen him dragging himself along the street, his cat-like movements were a revelation." Jeffords was bothered by his breathing, and "he has a lot to learn before he will be a match for such an old general of the ring as Peter Jackson." The *Daily Colonist* printed his name as "Jeffers."

The fight in Vancouver, by far the most important of the three, took place on Wednesday, August 23, at the Savoy Theater at 133 Cordova, near the harbor. The *Vancouver Daily News-Advertiser's* advertisement simply said "Boxing Contest between Peter Jackson and Jim Jeffords." Jeffords was described as "a fast fighter of the hurricane order." The *Vancouver Daily World* published a list of Jeffords's fights: the two B.C. ones against Peter were labeled "Draw." Peter arrived on Wednesday with his manager Simpson and "a large delegation of Jackson's admirers." He said he was in great shape, and "I will convince Mr. Jeffords of this before we have boxed many rounds tonight." Bishop said: "We have had two draws with Jackson and I am anxious for Jeff to win this bout."

The fight was witnessed by a full house. Most spectators were disappointed by the match. It seemed that Jackson went on drunk, and spectators shouted down at the stage that it was a poor proposition to bring a drunken man into the ring. Friends and acquaintances were said have been treating him drinks and he had suffered overmuch at their hands. Jeffords outclassed his opponent and could apparently have finished the fight by a knockout blow with 10 seconds' notice at any stage of the fight.

The first round was nothing but a display of pussyfooting that drew cries of "Fake!" from the house. But by the end of the second round Jackson's nose was streaming, and Jeffords knocked him back against the ropes in a vicious way that could have put him entirely out of the ring, into the footlights or down the five-foot drop beyond. Jeffords followed this by easy fighting in the 3rd round.

In the 4th, Jackson came up with a leery grin on a bloodstained face and he was simply pummeled to the knockout. He was so befuddled that he ceased defending himself, and the crowd started yelling out, "Don't hit a drunken man." But Jeffords struck him repeatedly on the jaw and body until Jackson did go over backwards into the footlights area. At the count of 5, Jackson staggered back through the ropes. He started to wander out of the ring until someone pointed him back. Jeffords punched him furiously and he would have fallen except that he had backed up against what the *Province* called "a wall," the fire wall or a backdrop. Jeffords let him out a foot or two from the wall and then punched him back again. At this point Chief of Police J.M. Stewart climbed into the ring and stopped the massacre, just as the "Time" to end the 4th was sounded. The decision was given to Jeffords.

Then Jeffords addressed the spectators from the stage, and Jackson did too, apparently now lucid. Both expressed their willingness to meet each other again at any time or any place. The Savoy's managers maintained that the engagement was an entirely bona fide and sporting one. Every effort had been made, they said, to keep Jackson from the "pottle pot," and they supposed he was fine until a winder or two from Jeffords's 7-ounce punches jolted and dazed him.

Jeffords's victory lifted him up from what Bishop had called "the Deacon Jones-Mexican Pete-Mike Morrissey class." A Seattle club offered him $1000 to fight Peter in a return match but Bishop said he might allow Jeffords only to fight "Young Peter Jackson" (Seth Thompson). Jeffords left for Portland, where on Tuesday, August 29, he fought local boy Nick Burley in the Olympic Club gymnasium, defeating him with a KO in two minutes.

Peter wrote a letter from Portland to a Denver paper, published on September 11 by the *San Francisco Chronicle*, along with Jeffords's comments to a reporter. A frantic dash to Portland and back is not impossible, but implausible given Peter's condition: the Denver letter may have been posted in Vancouver. Peter wrote: "As you doubtless know I recently boxed a man by the name of Jeffords at Vancouver, B.C. Our agreement was to box a series of exhibition bouts, one at Nanaimo, one at Victoria, and one at Vancouver. We boxed the first two and in the third bout Jeffords saw that I was intoxicated and took advantage of me. He was given the decision in 4 rounds though I was far from being out. I came to this city yesterday to offer to beat him in 6 rounds, but he heard of my coming and left for your city."

Peter wrote this letter probably on August 30. Jeffords commented that everyone knew he left Portland because of the Denver offer. And he said that Peter's intoxication was an *ex post facto* explanation of his defeat. He said: "There were a lot of Englishmen there who had seen Jackson box in England several years ago and who were betting wildly on him, and as soon as he lost they set up this cry about his being drunk. He knew it was to be a fight and it is not likely an old fighter like Jackson would go into the ring drunk." Certainly the referee had not noticed Peter's intoxicated state when he was instructing the combatants. Peter's letter was disingenuous, moreover, the reporting never suggesting the three Jeffords bouts were exhibitions. Peter was echoing his excuse after the Goddard fight, that he thought it not a serious event. He had not trained, he was slack from good living, he almost lost to a slugger. But now after Jeffords he was penniless and desperate. And the *Vancouver Province* had called him "the old colored man."

After the victory in Portland, O'Rourke wired Jeffords from the prestigious Lenox Club offering him a fight with Gus Ruhlin in New York, and Jeffords dumped Bishop. He had a short career. Twice he fought Peter Maher, as everybody did, and was twice knocked out. He was also knocked out by Joe Jeannette, knocked out by Bob Armstrong, and knocked out by Jack Johnson. In 1909 he terminated his inglorious career, but it must be said of Jeffords that he never drew the color line.

In *Jack Read's Boxing Annual* for 1939, Biddy Bishop wrote an article about Australian fighters in the days of his youth. It was excerpted in the *Western Star* of Roma on July 12, 1940. Bishop praised Peter, against whom he recalled setting his "mitt-slinger," a Cornishman named Jim Jeffords. "This last contest of Jackson's marked the passing, in my opinion," wrote Bishop, "of the greatest heavyweight ever to rub a shoe in resin."

On the morning of September 1, Peter and Paddy took the ferry to Victoria, to take passage to Alaska. Peter said that Dawson would be his future home.

Paddy must have told Edith that he was going back to northern Canada after scarcely a month's reunion. He and Peter left Victoria for the Yukon on the SS *City of Seattle*, sailing north to spar in the Arctic. Peter told skeptical reporters that he would spend the coming winter in Dawson City, playing the vaudeville houses. The voyage ended in disaster. Peter went 1000 miles up the coast as far as Skagway in Alaska, from where it was by land to Dawson. When he reached Skagway, he fell ill. He had to be taken back south.[23]

In July 1918 the *Referee* reproduced a letter from London, from a man who had drinks with Paddy. Paddy told him he arranged a benefit in Skagway and handed the proceeds to Peter, but it appears Paddy simply tucked a roll of bills into the delirious Peter's pocket and left for Dawson City. It was the last service he could do for the friend of his youth. Peter was shipped back to Victoria and admitted on September 14 to the Royal Jubilee Hospital, where he was treated for three months. Those spectators in British Columbia were the last who ever saw Peter Jackson box.

The Royal Jubilee Hospital on Fort was a small hospital staffed by a matron, a steward, and 4 nurses. It usually held around 40 patients who were discharged after a day and a half stay on average. The temperature was a controlled 60 degrees. An X-ray machine had been installed in July. In December the management noted a great need for one or two air or water beds for the use of helpless patients. Peter's treatment may have proven this need, for he was kept immobilized in his bed for three months.

For the 82 days he was in the Royal Jubilee Hospital, from September 14 until December 5, Peter was in the care of Dr. Frank W. Hall, who had graduated from the Detroit College of Medicine in 1885. Hall could do little but stabilize his condition, employing a regimen of immobility. A decade later, in 1910, he was on a train from Winnipeg to Calgary when Will Corbett was traveling across Canada. They chatted as strangers do until they had a big recognition scene. The surprised Hall told the amazed Will that "he had charge of Peter Jackson's case in the hospital, and said he never, in a very long experience, met a man possessing such fortitude and patience, and who gave so little trouble to anybody."

On September 21 a headline, "Peter Jackson Dying," was sent out from Victoria with an article saying he was in the hospital "and it is feared cannot recover." The diagnoses were announced as pleurisy-sciatica and pneumonia-typhoid, screens for the truth. *Referee* readers were told by Will that "for months, perhaps a year or more, pneumonia has been slowly working its way into his system." Here "pneumonia" is so obviously a euphemism for "tuberculosis" that it is hard to credit Corbett's protestations that before 1901 he never suspected that Peter was consumptive.

While Peter was in the hospital, one of his exhibition partners died. Probably Peter learned only much later that Dai St. John was killed in the Boer War fighting with the Grenadier Guards at the Battle of Belmont on November 23, 1899. Thirty-six Grenadier Guards died that day. St. John was 26. He bayoneted a Boer and, while tugging at his Lee-Metford to pull out the bayonet, was shot by another Boer. The *Sportsman*, the *Sporting Life* and the *South Wales Daily News* published obituaries, and the *London Graphic* of February 3 published his photograph — but Peter never saw them.

By this time Peter was again broke. Nothing was left of Paddy's money. In early December he sent off distress messages in all directions, to Philadelphia friends, and to others including Elijah Smith, the superintendent of the Polk Street Bridge in Chicago. Smith contacted Davies in New Orleans. Smith wrote O'Rourke and the Considine brothers in New York City, even J.J. Corbett, asking for contributions. Smith's messages must have been badly composed because Corbett, for one, so little understood how sick Peter was that he offered not money but to spar with him at any benefit that might be organized. Peter's credit ran out and Dr. Hall told him to leave the Royal Jubilee Hospital, recommending Arizona or southern California, anywhere with a warm dry climate.

Peter was taken in at "Denver" Ed's hotel. On December 12, the *Daily Colonist* reported that Peter, after "his recent battle with pneumonia and typhoid in conjunction," was "resting and quietly recuperating" in the Colonist Hotel at Beacon Hill Park, and noted that "it is big Peter's intention to leave shortly, either for Southern California or his old home, Australia." No mention was made of Santa Cruz, where he had a brother and sisters and nephews.

One day in January somebody from Seattle called in at the Colonist Hotel to visit Peter. The caller went home and published a devastating account of his visit in the *Seattle Daily Times* of January 26, 1900. The article was republished by the *Bulletin* on January 30, 1900, then reprised in the *Police Gazette* on February 10 and doubtless by other papers. It washed up across the Pacific in the *Referee* on March 14.

"Well, I won't complain," said Jackson to his visitor:

> I have made lots of money and I've spent it. No man can say I owe him a cent; no man can say I ever asked for charity. If it were not for the fact that I would like to repay in kind some of those who were my presumed friends when I was prosperous I would give up the fight now. But the treatment they have accorded me is the one thing I wish to repay. They never wanted for anything while I had it — it was theirs for the asking. But I will not cry about it. If I had the whole thing to go again I don't know but what I'd be in the running. Experience is a great teacher, but I believe I've done some good in my life and the

good I've done I'm thankful for. All I want is my health back. Give me that and Jackson wants no odds from any person. And I'll get it back, my boy, if willpower and determination to reciprocate will pull me through. Who's treating me unjustly? Well now, don't worry about them. They know. It's not my way to "squeal." What I am I am. What I've done for others is my affair. What they've done for me — well, as Kipling says, "That's another story."

Peter was presented as broke, friendless and in a dying condition, in the home of charitable acquaintances, sitting in a chair by the fire, scarcely speaking above a whisper and ending in a fit of coughing. Peter was upset by the article and wrote an unconvincing refutation of it, but the details were in accord with tuberculosis.

Peter did not readily blame others. His thriftlessness, his spectacular spending, were part of the culture of poverty when you ate today and fasted tomorrow, exhibiting the fatalism of the Caribbean where a hurricane could wreck your luxurious home at any time. Peter was not sorry for himself. He had had meaty years and now was having pickled-herring years — that was all. The most lasting impression left by the *Seattle Times* article is that of Peter's serenity in the midst of afflictions.

Nevertheless, he could not continue serenely in the Colonist Hotel. "Denver" Ed was not a bank. Something had to be done, and quickly. Peter wrote to Lige (Elijah) Smith on February 1, 1900: "I have a severe cough and suffer with pains in my left side, and also shortness of breath, and I cannot walk faster than a child, but I hope with good care to be a well man again." The rest of his letter was as cheerful as could be, talking about the Dixon versus Terry McGovern fight and so on; but propped up beside the fireplace in the Colonist Hotel he agonized and obsessed. He longed to be rescued by another Captain Heering on another *Svanen*.

His longings were answered. Naughton ended the agonies, taking Peter's decision out of his hands by collecting money for a one-way fare across the Pacific. For his part, Paddy told a *Weekly Despatch* reporter in London in May 1916: "Well, I bucked around and collected 500 dollars for the old fellow and gave it to him, together with all sorts of good advice as to its disposal"— but he may have been misremembering his Skagway gesture. It was Naughton who sent Peter enough cash for some decent clothes. On December 21, 1890, Peter had told the *Examiner* that Australia "has been my home for many years and my oldest and warmest friends are in that far-off land." And now, ten years later, he was returning to sunny Sydney.

From Victoria he took the *Walla Walla*, 67 hours via Puget Sound ports down to San Francisco, and stepped off the boat at Broadway Wharf on Saturday, March 18, most conspicuous in a fashionable "golf suit," which was a Norfolk jacket worn with knickerbockers in the same tweed. The fellow had style! But the *San Francisco Call* noted his old man's walk and the ulster he wore though it was 70 degrees in the shade. On March 20, 1900, the *Examiner* published two photographs of Peter juxtaposed, one of the sable Apollo of 1889 and one of his ravaged face taken the day before. Naughton's article was headed: "Invalid Pugilist Seeks Health in Former Home." He said Peter had typhoid-pneumonia, but few were deceived. The *Vancouver Daily Province*, which had seen Peter only at the Jeffords fight 6 months before, wrote on March 24, "From photographs received he seems in the last stages of consumption."

On Saturday, March 24, 1900, the *Chronicle* reported: "Peter Jackson left this city for Australia last Wednesday evening on the steamer bound for his old home, where he expects to regain his strength. Some of his old friends brought him back from Victoria, B.C., and sent him where there may be a possible chance to lengthen his life, and where he can at least end his days in peace." The *Examiner* said stoutly that he would open a boxing school in Sydney.

On March 6, Wing Chung Ging, dead of an unknown disease, was found in the Globe Hotel in Chinatown. On March 11 it was identified as bubonic plague. The pestilence that had since 1894 been making its way around the world from China had finally reached the United States. This outbreak claimed 22 victims in San Francisco.[24] On the evening of March 21, 1900, Peter boarded the *Mariposa*. Defying the plague, a crowd of friends were at the Spreckles dock. The one who counted most was holding a streamer: Herget. The *Chronicle* interviewed him 17 months later, calling him the sporting man in America who had known Peter Jackson the most intimately.

This time Peter did say his goodbyes. The ship pulled away from the dock at 9:30 P.M. The last streamers broke. The stewards detached their remnants from the railings and let them drift down into the black waters below. The lights of San Francisco dwindled and were blotted out. The fogwhistle on the Farallones sounded to starboard. The pilot's boat cast off. The dark Pacific lay ahead. If he had a home anywhere, Peter Jackson was going home.

CHAPTER 9

Home from Home, 1900–1901

The *Mariposa* was making one of its last voyages. It carried 68 European and 7 Chinese passengers, as well as Peter Jackson, "the colored ex-pugilist, who is en route to Sydney for the benefit of his health." Peter was in the care of the ship's surgeon, Dr. A.J. Younger.

The *Mariposa* reached Honolulu on March 28 at 6 A.M. and sailed that night. "Peter Jackson," the *Evening Bulletin* reported, "for many years thought to be the cleverest man in the pugilistic profession, is a passenger in the *Mariposa* on his way to his old home in Australia."

The Iolani palace stood empty, now that the United States had annexed Hawaii. The old Music Hall had burned down in 1895 and been replaced by another. Plague was in Honolulu, too. Peter met up with friends in town. These included his 1890 entrepreneur Jim Welsh and the "Unbleached American," Ernest Hogan, the black entertainer. Dancer and singer, comedian with an elastic face, extremely talented man, in 1898 Hogan had had a great success with the first all-black musical revue on Broadway, *Clorindy or the Origin of the Cakewalk*. He was fresh from playing Australia with the Afro-American Minstrel Company of M.B. Curtis, which had also starred Peter's New York friend Billy McLain. Unfortunately Curtis went bankrupt and the tour was canceled.[1] Now Hogan was spending an enforced three months in Hawaii. Here was a shameful business: the troupe reached Honolulu and paid their passage to San Francisco, the shipping company taking their money and then refusing to carry them because they were blacks. Eventually they did recover their money, but meanwhile they had to put on an improvised series of minstrel shows at the Orpheum Theater to live and to raise enough money to get home—with another shipping company. Hogan starred in a hasty production of *Uncle Tom's Cabin*, maybe the first with an all-black cast. Between shows, the "Hoganites," a scratch team, played baseball for a share of the gate. The weekend Peter was in town they were playing the Stars of Honolulu on the Makiki diamond.

Hogan personally was a rich man by virtue of his coon songs which were wildly popular. In 1896 he composed the most famous of them, "All Coons Look Alike to Me: a Darkey Misunderstanding," which was estimated to have netted him over $40,000 through copyright and sales of over a million copies of the sheet music. Hogan's brisk and jaunty song developed the remark of an Irish rookie cop about arresting the correct black. It was, however, essentially a comic love song. It was popularized in Britain by Eugene Stratton, who had watched Peter fight in 1889. The song became the triumphal anthem at any victory by a black. In February 1898 a black jockey, "Long Shot" Conley, won two races at the Oakland track. Each win was followed by the band playing "All Coons Look Alike to Me." It was played in Sydney after Johnson defeated Burns in 1908 to show that blacks were not clones.

At some point before his death in 1909 Hogan told Herbert "Hype" Igoe, the sports journalist, that he had been cradling Peter's head when he died at Roma. "He talked of his early days in the West Indies," Hogan said. "He mentioned Paris and London, scenes of great triumphs in his life. Then came the name of a fellow warrior, his supreme antagonist — Jim Corbett! He kept repeating, 'Corbett... Corbett...' and the last two words he uttered on this earth were, 'Terrible Corbett.'" Igoe said in 1935 that Hogan wept as he recalled the scene.[2]

That must have been one of Hogan's finest performances, because when Peter died in Queensland in July 1901 the Unbleached American was wowing them on Broadway at the Cherry Blossom Grove, the revamped roof garden of the New York Theater. On an otherwise all-white bill topped by Little Tich over from London, Hogan "sang a bunch of coon songs with his accustomed art," according to the *New York Dramatic Mirror*. But maybe, to please the credulous Igoe, Hogan simply embroidered upon a scene in Honolulu when he became aware of how sick the great Peter Jackson had become. It may be added, that Igoe claimed in the same article to have been in Corbett's room when he died and to have heard him expire with Peter Jackson's name on his lips, but no recent biography of Corbett puts Igoe at the deathbed.

Peter wanted nobody else to know he was tubercular, not even Will, so he concocted a story about experiencing, soon after leaving Honolulu, his first twinges of sciatica. This he hoped would explain his difficulties in walking, and his frequent rests. The *Mariposa* reached Apia on April 4, and Auckland on April 11. The weather was perfect until the last stage, across the Tasman Sea, where storms delayed the *Mariposa*'s arrival in Sydney by 15 hours. Instead of being on schedule on Saturday, April 14, it arrived on Easter Day.

Peter was hoping for a resurrection. "I went up to Canada," he told Bill Doherty that year. "It was too cold for me up there. I got pneumonia. I've come back to sunny Australia now to get right again."[3] But he never did get right again. Neville Forder wrote in 1914 that "it was pitiful to look at his wasted frame and hear him express his bitter regrets," but generally he kept stoutly optimistic.

The headlines in Sydney that Easter read bravely: "Peter Jackson Home Again," and "Peter Jackson the Famous Colored Boxer Returns Home," but in contrast with his triumph in 1890, with chartered boats and "Home, Sweet Home" sung at the Heads and a parade through town, this time only Will with one or two others met him. As the next issue of the *Sydney Bulletin* put it: "Peter was met by a few friends, and wine was opened. The cheering thousands that greeted him 10 years ago when he returned loaded with scalps and still on top had something else to do this time." But there could have been another reason. The bubonic plague afflicting San Francisco and Honolulu was raging in Sydney and had been evident since January. The first of some 150 deaths had occurred on January 19. In downtown Sydney, especially along the wharves and in the Rocks area, rats were being exterminated in millions and streets of slum houses being ripped down. People were reluctant to go down to the *Mariposa*'s dock. It was a subdued return.[4]

Peter was extremely weak. He tottered down the gangplank and, said the *Referee*, he "couldn't hold his hands up if it made a difference of a thousand pounds to him." That night, rain and winds assailed the city. Sunny Sydney! The next day, Easter Monday, was the coldest April day in over 40 years. This did not stop him from going downtown and calling on Foley and some of his buddies for a drink or two. Then on Wednesday, April 18,

Peter attended the Charlie Weiner versus Ike Stewart fight at the Golden Gate Athletic Club. Stewart was an African American and Weiner was half-Aboriginal. "Peter Jackson was present, at the invitation of the proprietary," said the *Referee*, "and met with a reception the heartiness and thoroughness of which must have made him feel that he was still the world's champion, still the great boxer who opened the eyes of America and the old world to what it was possible for a big man to acquire in the way of cleverness." Peter entered the hall to applause, then the 600 people rose and cheered him repeatedly.

The weather was bad, and what with the adulation and the exertion and all the drinks, he had overdone it and he collapsed. He was carried off to Tom Saywell's Brighton Hotel at Lady Robinson's Beach on Botany Bay where he had trained for his fight with Lees in 1886, and lodged in a sickroom.

By the good offices of his friends, notably Will, his treatment was confided to Dr. Angel Money, who was best known as a pediatrician. A graduate of London University, he had once occupied rooms on Harley Street. He came to Australia for his health. After arriving in Sydney in 1892 he was appointed to the Sydney Hospital for Sick Children. But he had worked for some years at the City of London Hospital for Diseases of the Chest. He was therefore as good a lung man as any Peter could find in Sydney.[5]

Under Money's care Peter made what looked like good progress. He measured his progress in terms of weight and was delighted when he briefly attained 250 pounds. But weight was merely a phenomenon. Inexorably, his body degenerated.

The symptoms of advanced tuberculosis are disgusting and Peter suffered them every one, including bloody phlegm and fetid breath. The faces of consumptive blacks developed a chalky pallor. Death occurred in one of two ways: either by a seizure of violent coughing and choking, in which the rotted lungs were coughed up, or by blacking out and a slide into death. Peter's death, when it came, was of the latter kind. He now submitted to doctors without a murmur. Gone was the Peter whose nose bled daily for three years before he would consult a doctor.

By early June he had put on weight and was feeling sprightly. His remarks to the Sydney *Bulletin* about boxing in the USA caused a furor there and elicited a sneering rebuke from Davies. Peter's verdict on the American boxing scene was: "Most matches are 'arranged,' and unless a man will let himself be 'used,' 'Murkan managers don't want him. The 'ould dart' element finds most favor with followers of bruising struggles, and the more 'Irish' a pug has in his blood the more chances he gets — as instance Peter Maher, who has been licked a dozen times, perhaps, and is still allowed to hang on to the front rank. A colored man has a hard row to hoe, no matter how circumspect or inclined to knuckle under he may be." Davies snapped that Peter was an ingrate, which was a little harsh from the man who had taken 50 percent of his earnings.

That winter of 1900 a return match in Sydney between Bill Doherty and Peter Felix was arranged. The money was put up by Billy McLain, who was still touring Australia and was backing Felix. Felix was a Cruzan, born in 1866 on Estate Good Hope near Frederiksted, who had come to Australia about 1890 and begun fighting. He claimed Peter as "family," and maybe they were related, among the Jackson "cousins" on Santa Cruz, but certainly not closely. Peter agreed to train Felix, the *Arrow* saying "he did this at the request of Billy McLain, who is a friend of the famous colored boxer." Said the *Arrow*, "Peter Felix and Bill Doherty are getting on with their preparation in great style. Felix has had the benefit of advice from 'Peter the Great' during the past few days."[6]

They trained at Auburn at the well-equipped Royal Hotel. He was able to spar for 5 minutes with Felix, but 6 minutes would have been too many. He was happy. He talked about opening a lavishly appointed boxing hall and about private lessons for aspiring boxers, a revival of the Harmony Hall idea.

On Monday night, July 16, the Felix-Doherty bout took place at the Metropolitan Athletic Club Hall in Ultimo. Peter's advice had been to fight proactively but Felix was too pigheaded to obey, and Doherty won on points. "Peter Jackson looked on and commended the decision, which he said was beyond cavil." The next day, calling in at the office to collect Felix's earnings, Peter encountered Doherty and they had a short conversation. Doherty recalled: "He was not yet 40 years of age, but he was wasted to a shadow of his former self, and he looked both old and weak." His clothes were getting threadbare. Doherty well-meaningly passed him a £5 bill. Peter handed it back, saying that he didn't need charity because he had friends. Doherty was not one of them, presumably; and Peter may not have recognized in the husky champion that Melbourne stripling of 1884.[7] After the fight, cold and rainy weather put him back into bed complaining to Will of his sciatica, supposedly of "the excruciating pain down his leg" and "in the left hip."

In September he was offered work, which he accepted. Fitzgerald's' Circus was owned by Dan and Tom Fitzgerald. It was the premier circus in Australia.[8] There was a stock of Australian acts, and Tom had just returned from Europe where he had engaged a number of acts: Rosie Acquinaldo the great contortionist, Guillaume and Auguste the French clowns, equestrian acts, and so forth.[9]

After Sydney, the circus was leaving on its southern circuit, catching the crowds in town for Melbourne Cup week, and Dan Fitzgerald suggested that Peter came along in a sinecure position. He got paid and had nothing to do but circulate. The advertising for him said:

> Special Engagement by Mr. Dan Fitzgerald
> of the Renowned
> PETER JACKSON.
> WATCH FOR HIM.

The official name for his job was *attaché*. Apparently Dr. Money okayed Peter's tackling "the necessary rough life inseparable from a traveling show."

Peter left on the circus train in the middle of October, exhilarated by his change of fortune. Boarding the train he said: "Well, this is my old game — traveling; something that I had years of in America and England. And the fact that I am going away under engagement makes me, to a very great extent, feel that I am once more myself." Peter, his mother's favorite son, was as usual looking on the bright side. The truth was that his position was scarcely better than appearing in a dime museum, though not in a booth to be peered at like a freak. He could move around and manifest himself whenever he wished.

They talked of a ball-punching act, and of his playing ringmaster in the bronco act by putting eight white horses through their paces. His experience with Joe Dieves's trotters might still pay off. Neither performance would have required much walking around, but if he did them the newspapers did not notice. In its obituary on July 16, 1901, the *Melbourne Sportsman* said only: "For months past the ex-champion had been looked after by the Messrs. Fitzgerald Brothers, the well-known circus proprietors. During their last Victorian tour the tall figure and good-humored ebony colored face of the world-renowned boxer were noticeable in and around the tent afternoon and night."

While in Melbourne he was going to referee the match between "Cocker" Tweedie and Nicky Duggan on November 10, and that between Jack McGowan and Tim Hegarty on November 13, but in the event he refereed neither of them. He was not strong enough, probably. But he attended; and upon his strolling into the Victoria Hall where Farnan had beaten him, "the people cheered themselves hoarse with delight as the old champion bowed in acknowledgement of the kindly welcome extended to him."

After its Melbourne season the circus started for Adelaide by way of the railroad towns. They reached Geelong, some 50 miles west of Melbourne, on Tuesday, December 4. They gave two evening performances, with a matinee on Wednesday. There was some talk of Peter's giving boxing exhibitions as part of the program. On Thursday, December 6, at 5:00 A.M. the circus entrained for Ballarat — everybody, that is, but Peter, who was so ill, ostensibly with sciatica and lumbago, that he had to be left behind. On his return to Sydney he told Will that it had been cold in Geelong — but the temperature had in fact been 72 degrees Fahrenheit and the weather fine. The tuberculosis was galloping along.

The *Geelong Times*, published by James Bell, reported that he was a patient in the hospital. The publisher of the *Geelong Advertiser*, Frederic Montagu Douglass, undertook to look after Peter. Dan Fitzgerald paid the bill. Just as Peter had arranged to ship from Barbados as a D.B.S., so now he arranged to have his name and situation kept out of the *Geelong Advertiser* and the other Geelong papers too. Following a request from Peter through Douglass to Bell, after that first notice the *Geelong Times* also kept silent.

Peter dictated to Davidson a letter for Will. "At the best of times I am not a good correspondent," he said. "Now I am compelled to get a friend to write to you. I am in the Geelong Hospital. I have a room on my own, and am as comfortable as one placed in the position I occupy could well be. My trouble — sciatica — put in an appearance at Gippsland and it got me down in Geelong. I am round fairly, and live in hopes of seeing you on the Friday or Saturday before Christmas, when I shall have some lively anecdotes to relate about my traveling experiences."

By December 22 he was able take the train from Geelong to Melbourne and then the express to Sydney, reaching there on Christmas Eve. "It is good indeed," he said to Will about Dan Fitzgerald, "to know that one has such friends in one's adversity." Will, who so far had blindly accepted that Peter's tuberculosis was sciatica, explained that "he was fretting for action, consequently, when Mr. Dan Fitzgerald's kindly-meant offer of a trip with his circus and nothing to do came along, Peter jumped at it, and then his undoing began, for he met too many people anxious for his company, with the result that he broke up again, and catching a cold in Gippsland, was laid up in the Geelong Hospital, where he developed symptoms of consumption, and never got over it."

Peter went under the care of Dr. Money again, in Thornley's Grand Hotel near Botany Bay. He spent five weeks there. After Peter died the following year, Will wrote: "When he returned after those few weeks in Geelong Hospital I felt convinced the noble-natured fellow's days were limited. He didn't confess as much to me, nor did I let drop the slightest hint regarding my suspicions.... I am satisfied he never admitted to himself that the end was within measurable distance. All Peter would say was that he caught a cold in Gippsland and hadn't felt well once since." Will refused to recognize the tuberculosis.

At New Year, Jack Dowridge visited Sydney on one of his sweep-connected commutings between Brisbane and Tasmania. He was anxious for Peter to visit Brisbane, and he called apropos on Peter at Rockdale.

On January 1, 1901, the various colonies were joined into the Commonwealth of Australia. In Sydney, where the official inauguration was held, military units from all over the British Empire paraded. In conjunction with this, on Monday, January 7, and Wednesday 9, 1901, the Gaiety mounted an "assault-at-arms."[10] Peter refereed several boxing matches at the tourney. He had done refereeing before, for example in Newcastle in 1888 and 1890, and in September 1891 when he refereed the Young Mitchell versus Reddy Gallagher match in San Francisco. He would not have had the strength to referee an American fight, where the referee was in the ring with the boxers and moving about with them, but at this time in Australia, as in England, the referee watched from outside the ring during the rounds and entered the ring only when boxing was not going on. Will was master of ceremonies. "Peter Jackson (who met with a great reception) filled the office of referee for the boxing," said the *Daily Telegraph*. But appearances were deceptive. He was not getting better.

He refereed lightweights and middleweights the first night. "Poor old Peter hadn't moved about so spry since he came back to Australia," said the *Referee*, "and the glint which shone in his eyes plainly indicated that the old warhorse had got a whiff of the powder of the ring again, and was for the time being the man of a dozen years ago. He stepped down from the ring as lively as a two-year-old, and went home as cheery as a cricket." In one match on Wednesday night, "The referee, Peter Jackson (the famous colored pugilist) called for another round, explaining that the points scored so far were equal." This assault-at-arms was almost the last event involving the colonial defense forces, soon to be superseded by the Australian national defense force—and it was Peter's last appearance in any ring.

He kept on rallying but overall he was getting worse. Dr. Money came to the end of his science and advised him to go north, in effect pronouncing him incurable. The *Evening News* said, "Although the sciatica for which he was a sufferer for a long time has left him, he has not quite recovered from the cold which he contracted in Victoria a few weeks ago, and it is thought that a visit to the northern capital for a month or so will effect the necessary improvement in his health." He was going to Brisbane for "a few weeks in the warmth of the Bananaland capital," staying with Jack Dowridge.

Sam Fitzpatrick in New York was told that Peter was "stone broke and has to depend on charity." Fitzpatrick had no money to spare, as he was planning to move to Havana and open its first boxing academy. But instead he went to England with his latest discovery and lost a place in Cuban history to John Budenich. Somebody paid Peter's boat fare, and he left for Brisbane. Almost all his stuff stayed with Corbett for safekeeping: his belt, his account books, and his photographs, but not the old brown coat.

He chose to sail up as he had done in 1887. The *Peregrine* left on Saturday, January 26, 1901. Unfortunately, it ran onto a sandbar in the Brisbane River and the passengers spent a further night on board. When Peter arrived at Brisbane on Monday, January 28, the city was in mourning for Queen Victoria.[11]

Dowridge installed him in his Theater Royal Hotel. The next issue of the *Sports Observer* told its readers in the "Bits about Boxers" column by "Counter": "The great coloured pugilist, Peter Jackson, perhaps the most popular exponent of the art fistic—and deservedly so—that ever stepped into a ring in Australia, arrived in Brisbane in the early part of the week, and during his stay will be the guest of Mr. J. Dowridge. It is more than probable that a monster benefit will be tendered the gentlemanly black, who has many friends in Brisbane."

By Saturday he was no longer staying with Dowridge. Alas, he had many friends in

Brisbane and they all wanted to drink with him. He had to be removed to St. Helen's private hospital across the river in South Brisbane. It had been a hotel in the early 1890s. In front were two terraces which descended from the arcaded verandah to the steamy brown Brisbane River, where a fence of stakes formed a swimming pool.[12]

The matron was Annie Marshall. The hospital was advertised by Mrs. Marshall in the *Brisbane Courier* on New Year's Day 1901 as the "Largest and Best Equipped Private Hospital in Australia. Qualified Nurses. Excellent Cuisine. Patronised by Leading Physicians and Surgeons. One Wing of Building Reserved for Accouchement Cases." Each patient had a room. The appointments were lavish, with a dinner service of Royal Dalton china. At the end of 1901 the hospital was bought by Dr. E. Sandford Jackson, who already liaised with Matron Marshall and thus was one of the physicians serving St. Helen's while Peter was there. It is probable that Peter had carried a letter from Angel Money to Sandford Jackson.[13]

On February 9, after only a week, Peter was reported to be making good progress and was allowed to leave St. Helen's. Discharged, it was easy for him to visit the Theatre Royal adjoining the hotel, where Dowridge had procured the movie of the Jeffries-Corbett fight on May 11, 1900, in New York. But he didn't see it, unwilling to see his former rivals glorified and because it was only a reproduction of the fight, one of Siegmund Lubin's productions, with stand-ins enacting the bout after newspaper descriptions. This caused some scandal in Brisbane and cries of "Schlenter!"[14]

He went drinking in Billy Flynn's nearby Carlton Court Hotel, although he was reduced to ordering "stark nakeds," that is, straight gins. It was not only alcohol and idleness. Will wrote in 1918: "Often Peter said, 'I want to be a man among men,' and he tried hard to reach that standard. It was his religion." Will was exaggerating, but Peter did need the emotional support of men, of his fans, of anyone who would listen as he told endless stories about his fights. At times, now, he lost the thread of his memories and had to say he could use a drink. Knowing he was broke, his auditors would buy scotches for the most famous man they were ever likely to meet.

He went into the hospital. His left lung was completely gone. He had a high temperature and suffered lengthy night sweats, especially in the early morning hours. The deeper he slept the more copiously he sweated. He had a frequent harassing cough, especially when lying down or exerting himself. At times the coughing became violent and paroxysmal, and led to vomiting and to his spitting out blood in streaks, increasingly bright red and frothy, mixed with small clots. His breathing was distinctly audible, with groans from his lungs, crackling ones and coarse bubbling ones. His right lung breathed exaggeratedly to compensate for the destruction of the left. His hospital bills were piling up.

On March 27 he came out of the hospital once more. Ten days Peter wrote to Will for the first time, saying: "The doctor said he could patch me up, but one lung was going.... I think I had rather a rough trip up, with the wet weather and being stuck in the river and having to spend the night on board the steamer. It is very hot up here today."

Subtropical Brisbane was not good for a tuberculosis patient in the hospital right on the muggy river. He could have imagined himself back in Calcutta, moored on the Hooghly with corpses tangling round the anchor chains. He was suffocating in the thick air. It was a most unsuitable place for him.

In these years the Queensland government embarked upon a tuberculosis campaign, and organized several wards and even hospitals. However, advanced patients like Peter were not admitted to general tuberculosis hospitals. The suitability for a hospital at Roma, out on the plains of western Queensland, in the district named Maranoa, had been canvassed but decided against. Roma was 978 feet above sea level, with a mean temperature from May to September of 56 degrees and 69 percent humidity. Dr. David Hardie said in 1897 that Roma was not suitable for consumptives in winter, having variable temperatures and high rainfall.[15] In March 1914 "Boxer-Major" of the Sydney *Truth* received a letter from W. Moran in Bunbury, Western Australia, who remembered Peter in Brisbane, at Dowridge's hotel. "It was there that I saw Peter for the last time — an old, bowed man, leaning on his stick, and admired by young and old. Three days after I saw him he went to Roma, a place from which he never returned. He was always cheerful, with hopes of recovering from a bad cough he had — but his friends knew better."

Because the Brisbane Hospital had a link with the Roma Convalescent Home, Peter was sent there on the recommendation of Dr. Sandford Jackson and with the sanction of the state's Chief Secretary's Department. Peter had letters of introduction to Dr. Guy L'Estrange; to Eugene O'Connor, an accountant; and to the town's barber, Charles Conroy, who was the Roma agent for the *Referee*. Dowridge will have written the latter two.

Dr. Guy George Champagne L'Estrange, the Government Medical Officer in Roma, came from an Anglo-Irish military family with Indian connections, and had graduated from Trinity College in 1886. He was experienced with consumptives. When he met him at the end of 1901, Corbett described L'Estrange as a "well-built, handsome and athletic-looking man of, perhaps, 36, with finely-formed features, large dark eyes and bearing and manner that one takes to and feels at home with straight away. He is a fine type of an Irishman." He spoke charmingly with a slight brogue. He had played for Dublin's crack Rugby XV and had been a prominent member of the Dublin Boxing Club. In his early twenties at Christmas 1889, he probably watched the Jackson-Maher fight in Leinster Hall. Almost miraculously, Peter had found at Roma a doctor who understood his world. L'Estrange treated Peter without charge.[16]

Eugene O'Connor was an auctioneer and commission agent, the local representative of a couple of insurance firms, secretary to the Roma Cemetery Trustees, and the town poundkeeper. He had a wife, Mary Jane, who after 9 years of marriage had given him a son, Gerald, now aged 10, and then a daughter, Elizabeth, who was now 7.[17]

Roma and district had a population of just under 2,000. Peter went to what was dignified as the Roma Sanatorium, actually "Argyle Cottage," a quiet farmstead just over a mile to the northwest of Roma. L'Estrange told Will, "I have made him as cosy as I can on a farm here, which is used as a small sanatorium." To the Chief Secretary's Department he reported on May 21: "I have made satisfactory arrangements for Peter Jackson who expresses himself comfortable and satisfied. His condition I regret is markedly bad." Strictly, incurable consumptives could not be admitted to any of Roma's hospitals, and a special dispensation, in a letter dated May 31 from the Chief Secretary's Department, was granted for Peter.[18]

Argyle Cottage belonged to Donald McCullum. In the grounds was the room where Peter stayed, a roofed shed with roll-up canvas blinds for walls, in accordance with the Nordrach treatment. Peter, the special patient, was looked after by Mary "Minnie" McAnally. Minnie was in her early twenties, and seems to have specialized in nursing chronic cases. She brought Peter his meals and ensured that his person, and all his utensils and bed-linen, etc., were kept perfectly clean. As well as an enamel bottle for coughed-up sputum, Japanese handkerchiefs at 7 shillings the 1,000-tissue packet were used. At first Peter could not sleep for coughing, but L'Estrange ameliorated his cough, or did so until the rain. He could not take more than twenty steps. He was weighed with his famous overcoat on, and with thick underclothes, which all together weighed some 14 pounds. He told Will that he weighed 162 pounds, "thus making me (stripped) about 10st 11 lb. [151 lbs.]. You can imagine what a skeleton I am."

While Peter was laid up Will got an idea for earning cash. Peter should write his autobiography for his fans on three continents. Will lived at Botany, near the Brighton Hotel, and evenings he sat with Peter while the sick man could endure it, plying him with endless questions about his life and his boxing career. Will had access to the files of the *Referee* and those of other sporting papers; he had himself known Peter for 20 years and had collected documents about him. But Will had seen nothing of the life Peter had lived outside of Sydney. Moreover, he was interested to get Peter's version of those events that had been reported. What appeared in the *Referee* in 1901 was a mixture of Peter's memoirs in the third person and factual documentation.

Will's effort was trustworthy in most respects. By the time the first installment came out in March 1901, Peter had departed for Brisbane, but he only read the first four installments before he died at Roma on July 13, 1901. No protests or corrigenda were sent from Queensland, so that Peter in effect authorized what Will wrote. The 1901 series would falter and cease after Peter's death, only seven installments ever appearing.

Life at Argyle Cottage was extremely monotonous. L'Estrange observed that men long confined became argumentative and complainant. He said, "Mr. McCullum is very patient and longsuffering with his boarders and prefers any course to disturbance." But there is no record of other patients fighting with Peter. One patient was expelled because of what L'Estrange called "bad habits." These amounted to drinking. Every week Charlie Conroy would bring along the latest issue of the *Referee* with its page devoted to Peter's biography. Such irony! Peter's life had now come to wondering which cookies would come with tea today.

Conroy and L'Estrange and O'Connor did their best to amuse him. L'Estrange was a vice-president of the new Roma Amateur Race Club and Charles Conroy was its secretary. Eugene O'Connor was secretary of the older Western Queensland Racing Club. L'Estrange and O'Connor both took Peter out for drives, out through the rolling countryside to visit sheep and cattle stations where other racing club members welcomed Peter to their homes.

He used his blackthorn walking stick, the one he had bought in Queenstown on January 16, 1890. L'Estrange wrote on June 18 to Billy Mooney in Brisbane: "He is a general favorite here. All classes and ranks visit him, and all are impressed by with his frank, cheerful, sunny, nature."[19] During the last weeks O'Connor broke L'Estrange's rules, quietly supplying Peter with an occasional scotch-and-milk and asking himself what did bad habits matter any longer?

The Episcopalian clergyman called round to offer spiritual comfort, but Peter sent him away. He was confronted by a clergyman who wished to snatch his soul from the jaws of hell. Because the Presbyterian church in Roma had become an organizational mess, for 1900–1901 it was declared a Home Mission, and was served by a visiting minister, the Rev. James Stewart from Brisbane. When Stewart returned in late June for his monthly visit he called on Peter. He told him that the pleasures of Heaven would be our childhood happiness infinitely multiplied.[20]

With religious persons Peter was scrupulously polite but uncooperative.[21] Confronted by a sky pilot, in what Stewart described as "the soft, pleasant voice, so peculiar to the negro race, the pure speech with every sentence like a well-cut jewel," Peter said, "Well, now, that is very interesting. But I cannot help contrasting your life with my own. You have delightful memories of your home, your godly parents, and your general environment. Now mine were so different. I have very few memories of my parents, and I was out upon the world when I was only a youth, and I have never known much of the comforts of a real home. Ay, we live in a very funny world." Stewart could not draw Peter on his vision of heaven.

He told Stewart: "I want to be honest, sir, and I don't wish to say that I have been a church-going man, because I have not. But when I tell you that I don't wish you to think that I am devoid of a creed, or indifferent about religion." Later in their half-hour conversation he said: "I quite understand you. You refer to Bible truth, and, though I do not pose as a Bible student, I have read the Bible; and I have pondered over its truth more than many would think, and I have found great comfort in it." When Stewart said that after death he would be judged fairly, he commented: "Ah, that is a comforting thought, for human judgment is often harsh and unjust." And when Stewart said that God's judgment could not be guessed, he remarked: "Thanks for that crumb of comfort." He also said: "I usually take a philosophic view of things, and if there is a bright side in the circumstances of life I take that view." These remarks of Peter's were sincere, because he was not speaking to a reporter and he could not guess that Stewart would publish their conversation.[22]

L'Estrange wrote to Will on June 18: "I find that he is barely holding his own. Weight has decreased since his arrival, but not during the last fortnight. Taken all round, his troubles and symptoms point to an alleviation of suffering. His digestion is better; his cough relieved; he now can sleep at night, not kept awake by the persistent cough. If I can keep him in statu quo during the colder months, I may be able to assist him to some benefit during the Spring and Summer, but as I said before, I cannot, I am sorry to say, hold out any hope of his ultimate recovery. The disease is too well established."

The weather turned bad. After many dry months, at the end of June it began to rain steadily on Roma. It rained for a fortnight. Hope ended and the illness ended.

In his final days Peter was not at peace. He read in the June 26 *Referee* a report of Tom Meadows's death from tuberculosis. How long ago their voyage to San Francisco! Then Peter started going over the Farnan fights! Every week the *Referee* arrived at Argyle Cottage containing an installment of his own history. The last one he could possibly have read was episode 5, dealing with his meeting with Paddy, published in Sydney on the Wednesday before he died. The two installments dealing with the Farnan fights would follow it, though in the event they appeared months later.

"On his death-bed he kept fretting as to whether the public thought he was in on the swindle," that is to say, whether he had thrown the fight. Will wrote: "Just before going into the ring, Peter found himself dazed and half-paralysed. He had been doped." Peter had thought so at the time. Will had now been told by Jim "Soldier" Davis that he was "hocussed" by one of his attendants, possibly with potassium bromide, but Will could not tell Peter. All that last rainy fortnight Peter kept going over the first Farnan bout in his mind, denying again and again to L'Estrange and O'Connor, but more to himself, that his performance had been a schlenter. He had always been straight. He had not been shamming, he had not thrown the fight, there must have been something in his drink. He went over and over that night. He could not forget how they cried "Schlenter" and jeered him when he had always been straight. O'Connor and L'Estrange found Peter's obsession very sad.

He was dying. He was not fit to see his visitors, for example Jim Gredden, the high-jump champion. On Friday, July 12, L'Estrange wired Will and Dowridge summoning them to Roma if they wanted to say goodbye. On Saturday the 13th L'Estrange wired: "Peter very weak, would like very much to see you before the end." Will wired both L'Estrange and Peter that he would come. He booked on Monday's train up from Sydney but never took it. Monday was too late because L'Estrange wired on Sunday 14th: "Poor Peter died last night at 10 o'clock very quietly. Am writing."

O'Connor visited him with 10-year-old Gerald after dinner on Saturday, July 13, his last evening, and remained with him to the end. "The only persons present were the nurse, my son, and myself," O'Connor wrote. Minnie told O'Connor that Peter was on the point of death. "I asked him if he wished to leave any message. He could then only speak with great difficulty." He said: "Corbett understands me — if I should ever see him again." Those were his last words. Then, O'Connor said: "He wiped his big hand across his eyes and wept." O'Connor was holding his hand when at 9:47 Peter died without a struggle, like a tired man falling asleep. He had been a poor fellow but that was all past and gone now. L'Estrange said he died of exhaustion: "Tired out, poor Peter, and just slipped away."

Among the Jackson clan in St. Croix the story circulated that Peter was poisoned in an Australian hospital.

O'Connor went to inform L'Estrange, who wired Will and Dowridge. O'Connor made arrangements for a funeral at 2 P.M. on Monday, July 15. But a return telegram came from Dowridge saying that a funeral in Brisbane would allow more people to show their respect, so the body was embalmed by swabbing it over with formaldehyde and pouring some into the mouth, in order to transport it by train to Brisbane.[23]

The mail train left at 9:30 P.M. on Monday. The coffin was conveyed to the railroad depot with ceremony. The Roma Town Band and the Hibernian Band played the "Dead March" from *Saul*. Bearing torches, all the members of sporting clubs who were able to participate followed the hearse drawn by two black horses. The whole procession, at night, lit by flaring, flickering torches, was watched by almost everyone else in Roma. It proceeded to the train depot, where the coffin was put on board the mail train. Roma had done almost all that it could for its famous visitor.[24]

The train reached Brisbane at 12:40 the next day, July 16. Events were managed by John Smith of K.M. Smith's, the undertaker's on George, near Dowridge's hotel. Smith was a friend of Peter's from the St. Helen's Hospital weeks and also a friend of Charlie Conroy's at Roma. The coffin was unloaded at City Station and taken unobtrusively to the Theater Royal Hotel. Here several of Peter's friends inspected the corpse lying in what was described as "no mean-looking casket." Said the Brisbane correspondent of the *Sydney Sportsman*: "Looking at Peter in his last earthly shroud, his face bore a peaceful aspect of repose." It was at this point that a silver plate was affixed to the coffin. It bore the inscription: "Peter Jackson died at Roma, Saturday, July 13, aged 40 years."

The funeral left the Theater Royal Hotel at 2:00 P.M. Dowridge had ordered Smith's best hearse and two coaches for mourners. There were four pall bearers: the former New Zealand boxer Harry C. Perry, who wrote as "Bimana" for the weekly *Sports Observer*; his colleague Harry Macintosh, "Mac" of the *Evening Observer*, who counted himself a friend of Peter's for 20 years past; Jack Dowridge Junior, who at 21 was called "Queensland's cleverest boxer" and became for three years running the Australian amateur featherweight champion; and Dowridge. They walked beside the hearse for the four miles to the Brisbane General Cemetery at Toowong.

Wirth's Circus, with its hippodrome, circus, and menagerie, had set up in Brisbane the previous Friday, and the funeral procession was headed by Wirth's band assisted by some local bands. They played the "Dead March" and other anthems. All the men in Wirth's circus attended: the bear tamer, the three American triple-horizontal-bar acrobats, the clowns and the rest. These people were a token of that part of Peter's life which had been spent showing for audiences. The hearse was followed by the members of the Brisbane Gymnasium Club, the token of the other aspect of his career: the boxer of world-champion class. About 30 private vehicles followed containing most of the prominent sportsmen of Brisbane and many others. The whole cortege, three-quarters of a mile long, was claimed to be the largest funeral yet seen in Brisbane. About 500 people were at the graveside for the interment.

Dowridge owned three adjoining burial plots in the Episcopalian section at Toowong, one hallowed over the last 20 years by the remains of his infant daughter Mary Ann. The third plot he now proceeded to give over to Peter's body, ensuring that when he and his wife Julia eventually joined their little girl they would be adjacent to Peter. The grave was dug on Monday. He wrote to Will saying merely: "I selected a nice spot at Toowong for the grave, overlooking the town. I don't think the poor fellow could have had a better funeral in Sydney."

The funeral was conducted by the Reverend Samuel C. Harris from St. John's Cathedral. Peter, who had hardly ever set foot in an Episcopalian church since his youth in Frederiksted, was buried with his church's beautiful burial service, which culminates with these words: "Forasmuch as it hath pleased Almighty God of his great mercy to take unto himself the soul of our dear brother here departed, we therefore commit his body to the ground; earth to earth, ashes to ashes, dust to dust; in sure and certain hope of the Resurrection to eternal life, through our Lord Jesus Christ; who shall change our vile body, that it may be like unto his glorious body, according to the mighty working, whereby he is able to subdue all things to himself." There was no Masonic element at the graveside, no acacia, because nobody in Brisbane knew that Peter had become a Freemason 10 years before.

John Smith entered all the details of the funeral in his Day Book, including the 8 shillings for two notices in the *Courier* and 7 shillings for two in the *Telegraph,* the £2 and 5 shillings for the grave-digger, the 7 shillings and 6 pence for the clergyman. He concluded his entry with the words, "He was known (familiarly) as the Champion Boxer of the World." An addendum said : "Paid 6/8/1901."[25]

But, for all his scrupulous accounting, Smith must have been moved by this funeral, because he wrote a poem titled *IN MEMORIAM PETER JACKSON* for the *Brisbane Sportsman* two days later, the final stanza of which was carved on Peter's tomb.

Obituaries for Peter appeared in most newspapers and sporting papers around the world. Even the *Indian Planters' Gazette and Sporting News* recounted his career, competently except for identifying Peter as "the well-known Coffee Cooler."[26] For three weeks nobody outside of Australia knew he was dead. The news broke first in Victoria, British Columbia, on August 8, and spread from there. The *National Police Gazette*'s obituary appeared as late as August 31.

Three eulogies can stand for the rest. From Newcastle in Australia came these remarks: "The news of the death of big-hearted Peter Jackson was received here with general regret.

The great colored fighter was a universal favorite here, and on his many visits to Newcastle he was invariably received with open arms. Local 'sports' feel that they have lost a dear and sincere friend in Peter, a man of whom nothing but kindly words are uttered, and it is generally felt that we will never look upon his like again."[27] On August 24, 1901, the *Cleveland Gazette* gave his life and death more than a column on its front page, and stated what no white paper could bring itself to say plainly: "He was the only colored fighter who had the temerity to challenge John L. Sullivan for the championship when the latter held the title. John L. Sullivan refused to make a match, it is said, because he knew what the result would be — defeat for him." The *London Sportsman* in its obituary took the theme of Peter's uniqueness to a higher level, saying: "Whenever anyone wants to hold up to the world's observation a PARAGON OF THE ETHIOPIAN RACE they inevitably turn to Toussaint L'Ouverture, who is dubbed the 'Prince of the Blacks.' What he was in his country's politics, Peter Jackson was in the world of sport." No greater compliment was possible.

Will sent gifts up to Roma. To O'Connor, who had already appropriated Peter's blackthorn walking stick, he sent a sovereign-holder. To L'Estrange, who in late 1901 called at the *Referee* office, he gave a sovereign-holder cum matchbox. Both gifts were in gold with the initials of the recipient engraved. Minnie received a very neat lady's watch.

Will decided to set up a Jackson Memorial Fund. The committee in Sydney consisted of Will; Charley Campbell and Harry Beckett, two old pugs; and Foley. That in Brisbane was Dowridge; J.J. Knight, the editor of the *Evening Observer*; and the sports journalist Harry Perry. Will managed the fund, and delayed acting, much to the disgruntlement of the Brisbane people, especially Dowridge, who held the deeds of the grave. In September 1902 the *Sydney Sportsman* reprinted a polemical item from the Brisbane *Observer* which said with considerable justice: "It is well known that, notwithstanding the professed friendship of certain Sydney people, towards the late champion, his last days were made comfortable almost entirely at the expense of Brisbane sportsmen, to whom the man was practically unknown, save by his great reputation. When he died a fitting funeral and interment was given him, also at the expense of Brisbane friends, who were then and are still prepared to finish the work they commenced by putting a modest stone over the grave. A memorial subscription list was opened at Sydney, however, without consulting Brisbane." And they had additional grievances. Will for some deep reason had cast himself as the sole keeper of the flame.

The *Referee* did not specify the form the memorial would take. In October 1901 Will advocated a suitable memorial raised in some public place — probably the Centennial Park, Sydney. Plans like this were received coldly in Brisbane, where Peter's grave remained uncurbed with only a numbered cast-iron marker. In September, almost certainly as a result of the *Observer* letter's being reproduced in the *Sydney Sportsman*, Will said that a proper tomb had always been envisaged. The *Sydney Sportsman* itself had spoken pointedly of "the reprehensible dilatoriousness of Peter Jackson's 'friend' who has the handling of the fund." The quotes around the word friend must have stung Will.

Will now rushed to act, but the form of the memorial was not finally settled until February 1903. The money came in slowly. The fund was closed on June 1, 1902. The first contribution to the fund was the *Referee*'s own, of 5 guineas. Most contributions seem to have been from individuals. Some were old friends, like Captain Dick Taplin and Professor William Miller. Billy McLain, touring Australia with the Afro-American Minstrel Company, gave a pound. In Roma, Gredden the high-jumper raised £7 in 140 one-shilling donations from "the Mayor, many aldermen, commercial travellers, railway officials, hotelkeepers, storekeepers, drovers, shearers, station overseers and managers, jockeys, bookmakers, ladies, children, and people in all walks of life." Roma had not forgotten its exotic visitor. When Gredden moved to Brisbane he took upon himself the tending of Peter's grave.

Will collected only £130. Most people who knew Peter's story estimated that he had frittered away maybe a quarter-million dollars, and were disinclined to pay for him now. In deciding on a monument over Jackson's grave, Will stressed that to build Jackson a tomb would be English, and unlike the American practice of ignoring dead boxers. "Let us have something," he wrote, "as near as possible after the manner of those enduring memorials erected by Englishmen over the grave of Peter's great prototype, 'Gentleman' Jackson, and that of Tom Sayers. What has been done in the Old Country can, to a considerable extent, be done here." Finally, an advertisement was placed in Sydney and Brisbane papers in September 1902 which specified that the cost of the tender should not exceed £130. The winning design was by Lewis Pages, a monumental mason from Rookwood Cemetery. After a more detailed tender was extracted from him, Pages was told to execute it.

The work was done in two sections. The sandstone parts of the monument were cut in one of the Pyrmont quarries, in Hell-Hole or Paradise or Purgatory, and then cut to specification on the big machine at Saunders's sawing sheds, corner of Glebe Road and Wattle in Pyrmont. A bust of Peter and a sleeping lion in Carrara marble were carved by Pages himself in his workshops at Rookwood. The cast-iron railings were specially designed. On April 8, 1903, the monument was assembled and inspected by crowds of sightseers. It was then taken apart and its 10 tons shipped to Brisbane. On Thursday, April 23, Pages arrived in Brisbane with the components and began erecting the memorial. The unveiling was announced for Sunday, May 10, with a general invitation to all racing and sporting organizations.

On the day, a fine Sunday after a rainy Saturday, these sporting bodies made up a crowd calculated at some thousands. Edward Forrest, one of the two honorable Members for North Brisbane in the Legislative Assembly and "one of our sterling sports," spoke at 4:00 P.M., then unveiled the monument for all to inspect.

It was rectangular, 5 feet by 4½ feet, and just over 6 feet high; with a small lion on top and on the sides of the pediment mourning sprays of lilies and tendrils of ivy (signifying remembrance) carved, and a sprig of oak leaves together with acorns to signify athleticism. At the back of the monument was carved a monogram, in black and gilt: a P entwined with a J. On the right side (facing it) was an inscription which read:

> To the Memory of
> Peter Jackson
> ***
> Dead at Roma Q
> 13th July 1901
> +
> Aged 40 years.

Under the name was carved a sprig of acacia. Somebody, probably Will, had recalled that Peter died a Freemason. The cross under the date was not a true cross but four triangles that did not touch. On the left side (again facing the tomb) were carved into the sandstone some lines of verse, the third stanza of the poem written by John Smith.

Sleep, Peter, Sleep! Brave Champion
All hushed, we gather round the Ring
While snow-white flowers, moist-eyed we fling
Within a grave... The fight is done.
Sleep, Peter, Sleep! the hero's rest
Be thine in Mother Earth's broad breast.

At the front of the monument was a cartouche with a bust of Peter carved in high relief in unpolished white marble, the face in three-quarter profile.

At the top, said the *Courier*, was "a sleeping lion in Carrara marble, an appropriate design which is borrowed to some extent from a monument erected to the memory of the great English champion, Tom Sayers." This reference to Sayers's grave in Highgate Cemetery was somebody's lapsus, occasioned by the finely sculpted mastiff's being a representation of his dog called "Lion." Almost certainly the notion came rather from Timothy Butler's monument to "Gentleman" John Jackson, Lord Byron's boxing instructor, in Brompton Cemetery. Pages's lion was 37 inches long and 15 inches high at the crest of its mane. In position (surmounting) and in pose (couchant) it resembled Butler's mourning lion, but somewhere between Brompton and Toowong it had turned into a small feline with a stylized mane and fast asleep,

This picture appeared in the *Queenslander* on July 20, 1901. It was probably taken in London in 1895; Jackson used it for his cartes de visite. One of them was shown to the monumental mason to copy for the grave sculpture.

unfortunately resembling less a Trafalgar Square lion than a Staffordshire pottery cat.

As to the bust, the choice of dazzlingly white Carrara marble in which to portray the black boxer was probably not unmotivated. The portrait can be described charitably as that of a black in a suit. Pages must have worked from a photograph given him by Will, the photograph figuring on Peter's visiting cards through 1897 at least, which showed a prosperous bourgeois Peter with collar and tie, and a coat out of the pocket of which sprayed a fancy pleated handkerchief. Clearly Will's aim was to code his man as civilized and even dandified.[28] The carved handkerchief was far more fancifully pleated than in the photograph, the hair was a cap of tight ringlets, and—finally—the face was not Jackson's at all, not copied from the photograph, but was rather a generic negroid face. It was simply not a portrait of Peter Jackson! After all the delay, neither Will's choice of monument nor Pages's execution pleased the Brisbane committee, and their resentment simmered for years.

Will made Pages inscribe upon Peter's tomb effectively what Napoleon had said of Goethe, and Walt Whitman of Lincoln. In the sandstone below the bust in Olde Englishe lettering were cut Antony's words over the corpse of Brutus, with a reference: "'*This Was a Man*'—Shakespeare." The text reads like an echo of that on the diamond medal in 1888, which Will remembered; but he could not have known how close it came also to the words from *Hamlet* quoted by Bishop Branch for Peter's mentor, John DuBois.[29]

Left: "This was a man." The portrait sculpture by Lewis Pages in the Brisbane General Cemetery at Toowong. Photograph taken by Arnold Thomas and used with his permission. *Right:* This photograph of the Jackson tomb dates from circa 1920, when the subsiding grave was refurbished. Photograph courtesy of National Library of Australia [nla.pic-3768217].

Countless thousands have, like Jack Johnson, made their way to Toowong Cemetery to look at the memorial. In his 1924 book of reminiscences, "Peggy" Bettinson recalled the Australian light-heavyweight champion Albert Lloyd's saying to him in January 1922: "You know, Mr. Bettinson, the name of Jackson is worshiped in my country. Go to Queensland where he is buried, and if you be an average man you will visit his grave in the same way as the stranger to London would look at Westminster Abbey. The grave of Peter Jackson is and ever will be one of *the* sights of Queensland, and though I am a very young man, and Jackson lived long before my time, I feel that fighting Australia has its source and inspiration from him."[30]

On September 13, 1982 the sports journalist Cherra Heyliger, who had been reading Langley's biography, wrote regretfully in the *Virgin Islands Daily News*: "Even the monument which is lifted in his honor stands proudly in the sun in Australia. Yet the navel string of Peter Jackson is buried here and nothing can change that."

As the years passed, Peter's story was remembered ever more faintly by fewer and fewer people.

Peter's brother James was called "Kangaroo Jackson" after his Australian sojourn, and the sobriquet followed him into the U.S. army when, as reported in the *Referee* on September 25, 1898, during the Spanish-American War he enlisted as "Samuel Copeland" for some reason. He was stationed at the Presidio in San Francisco and remained cook to the garrison until at least 1917, when he was 62 years old. His pork chops and his biscuit were reckoned his best productions. He referred to himself extremely discreetly as "an employee and friend of Peter Jackson when the latter conducted a hotel in Sydney before he came to America." James said he had done some fighting himself, in California and the East. He used to drop George Dixon's name, and it is possible that in Boston he had put on the gloves with the lightweight champion who died in 1909, his younger brother's friend. The lives and deaths of Peter's other siblings have not been tracked.

In 1909 Mecca cigarettes included in their "Champion Athlete and Prize Fighter" series of cards one with Peter's portrait. It was perhaps the image of him which circulated most widely, in its millions. The cigarette card showed Peter stripped to the waist with white pants and red belt, standing in a fantastic tropical landscape with his dukes up. The Mecca artist, who usually drew his athletes in characteristic settings, was following the blurb written for the back of the card, where it says Peter was born "near Porto Rico."

In 1910 "Smiler" Hales produced his own fantasy, the *Romantic Career of Peter Jackson, His Fights Re-told*. It is a novel, which preserves some second-hand impressions of Peter when he was young and newly arrived in Sydney. Its extravagances have bedeviled the Jackson story ever since. From the 1889 hint of Peter's involvement with a rich widow with a drop of black blood, for instance, Hales elaborated the sentimental drama of Peter's love for an octoroon opera singer named Josephine Leon who is living in Roma when Peter arrives there. "Pete, Pete! God bless you for coming!" she sobs. They spend an hour together and he dies. The book has some value, but not in its narrative parts.

By 1917 Hales was claiming to be communicating directly with Peter at spiritualistic séances. In the *Referee* on June 3, 1918, Corbett quoted a letter from Hales. "I went to an occult meeting a good while back," he wrote Will on November 11, 1917, "and good old Peter Jackson came and gave me a lot of sane advice. He was always a straight man and a damned long way cleaner in principle than most white men we've met, eh? Say, is poor old Griffo dead? If not, I can't understand a message that was given to me recently. Peter said he was going to look after Griffo. So I opine that the most wonderful little fighter earth ever saw has gone West." Griffo died in 1927, but if Peter's message to Hales has any credit at all, it can be supposed that a decade of earthly years means little to dwellers in the Summerland.

Bill Naughton died in 1914. Paddy Gorman, the last of the 1888 *Alameda* trio, died in New York in 1916. Larry Foley died in July 1917 followed by Bob Fitzsimmons in October. John L. Sullivan died the following year.

Will realized that Peter was fading from memory. By 1915 any 15-year-olds who saw Peter fight Goddard in 1890 were now 40-year-old men. Will decided that the Toowong tomb was not enough, so he unearthed his unfinished 1901 biography and wrote the documents up in seventy-one weekly installments during 1918 and 1919. He explained in the *Referee* of January 2, 1918: "This was written up to 17 years ago while Jackson sat at my elbow supplying the matter for a book which would have been published in his interests a few months later had he lived." This large biography is the main source for Peter's own view of his life and career.

Charles "Parson" Davies died in 1920. Jack Dowridge died in April 1922, aged seventy-five, and was buried beside his beloved Julia and his little Mary Ann in his plot with its view of the Brisbane skyline. They lie next to Peter.

Sam Fitzpatrick died in September 1922. Writing after Johnson's defeat of Burns, Robert Edgren of the *New York Sporting World* wrote: "Since the Peter Jackson days Sam hasn't been picking gold up in the street. Everybody who knows Fitzpatrick is glad to see him win out. It'll be wine for Sam now instead of beer and cheese in a back room." But it was not. Johnson sacked him and Fitzpatrick went back to beer and cheese. Early in 1909, while he was still in Johnson's employ, Fitzpatrick talked with Frederick Hornibrook, English boxing aficionado and New Zealand promoter of Sandow. In his *Lure of the Ring*, written much later in 1946, Hornibrook recorded their conversation:

> I was fortunate enough to have a long chat one day with Sam Fitzpatrick who was Johnson's trainer and incidentally knew more about the psychology of negro pugilists than any man living as he had trained Peter Jackson, Joe Walcott and Johnson. I asked him, explaining that it was not for publication, which he thought was the better man — Peter Jackson or Johnson. He replied, "Peter Jackson was the best man in the world and would have beaten Johnson." I asked him why, and I shall always remember his answer — Peter was a heavyweight but he was like a featherweight on his feet. Johnson, on the other hand, is a flat-footed boxer who makes men come to him and then possesses this wonderful defence. Peter's left hand would have been too quick for that defence and he would have made Johnson come to him."

This was the opinion of the man who knew both Peter and Jack better than anybody else. Fitzpatrick didn't return to Australia after 1909 and so, because he hadn't seen Peter's grave at Toowong then, he never did see it. The *Maitland Mercury* noted his death below the forgiving headline: "Old Maitlander Dead."

William Francis Corbett died in 1923. Paddy Slavin died in 1929. Paddy had made his money in the Klondike, and had settled down in British Columbia. His son Jack was killed in the Great War, and Paddy enrolled in the Canadian army. In 1938 the first volume of Nat Fleischer's *Black Dynamite* sequence was published, with its chapter on Peter's life. Fleischer used the memories of living people to flesh out his story, for example the imaginative "Hype" Igoe, but it was difficult to find anyone.

In 1942, after Joe Louis became champion of the world, Warner Brothers released *Gentleman Jim* starring the Australian actor Errol Flynn as J.J. Corbett, and Ward Bond playing Sullivan with a thick Irish accent. It was the first of several films on white champions. No Peter character was shown in that movie, but his name appeared in a montage of newspaper headlines and he was discussed by the Sullivan and Corbett characters. Joe Choynski acted informally as one of the historical advisers for the film. Choynski himself died in 1943.

Lord Lonsdale died aged 87 in 1944. John Herget died at 77 on September 2, 1945. He lost a fight in September 1906, when Ad "Michigan Wildcat" Wolgast beat him. After failed ventures in the entertainment field he became San Francisco's chief storekeeper in the city's Bureau of Supply, a position from which he retired in 1938. The *New York Herald* described him in 1921 as "now a San Francisco alderman and political boss," and as having been the best middleweight of his time except for the Nonpareil. His death notice in the *Chronicle* proudly called him "a native of San Francisco." Among the last of Peter's acquaintances to go were Jim Jeffries and Tom Sharkey, who both died in 1953. Prince André Poniatowski died at ninety in March 1954. Jim Jeffords lived on until 1969.

Things like belts are more durable than people. The two pairs of gloves worn by Peter and Lees in their championship fight, with the red and white flashes, were auctioned in Melbourne by Christie's in 2002. Dr. L'Estrange brought Peter's lucky greatcoat back to

Sydney, and Will preserved it until one day Mrs. Corbett destroyed the rotted fabric. Until he died Will kept the sash Peter wore at the Slavin fight. Will had all Peter's papers; they have disappeared. As for the championship belt, after Will's death it found its way to England and stayed there until 1977 when the silver portion was auctioned at Christie's in Melbourne and sold to an Australian devotee of vintage silverware, in whose collection it remains.[31]

Eugene O'Connor did not need Peter's blackthorn stick to remember him. When he was in his seventies and had not long to live, he wrote under the name "Maranoa" an article about Peter's time in Roma and sent it to Will's son, Claude Corbett, at the *Sydney Sun*. The article was published on July 28, 1935. It was full of Peter's gentle humor. These were, thirty-four years after his death, the last of Peter's living words to come down to us.

In the course of that dreary fall, "You never married, Peter?" O'Connor had asked him directly. "No," he replied. "Any woman I wanted did not want me; and any woman who would have me I did not want." And O'Connor asked how come his opponents had not disfigured his nose. Silent about the Godfrey and the Slavin fights and the rest, Peter answered with a straight face that "none of them knew enough to hit me on the nose." O'Connor believed him.

Another time he asked Peter, "Did you ever take on any business in the States?" and Peter replied: "Yes, sir. I opened a saloon in 'Frisco once and struck both fun and trouble from it. My bartenders went on strike and had me posted by the union as a 'black' saloon. They warned their friends and then the skunks went a bit further and put up all and sundry to come in when I was doing my own bar-work and to ask for all sorts of awful drinks that I had never heard of—'Corpse Reviver,' 'Morning Glory,' 'Samson with His Hair On,' 'Last Kick,' and such like."

"How on earth did you manage?"

"Oh, easily enough. Just grabbed a few of the nearest bottles, mixed a little of each of them, set it up, and then jumped across the counter and asked them how they liked it. I never had a complaint all day."

An' den de wheel bend an' den de story end.

Notes

Chapter 1

1. G.C. Ward, *Unforgivable Blackness: The Rise and Fall of Jack Johnson* (New York: Knopf, 2004); J. Wells, *Boxing Day: The Fight that Changed the World* (Sydney: HarperSports, 1998); R. Broome, "The Australian reaction to Jack Johnson, black pugilist, 1907–9," in R. Cashman and M. McKernan, eds., *Sport in History: The Making of Modern Sporting History* (Brisbane: Queensland University Press, 1979), 343–363; D. Headon, "'World's fistanic history,' Sydney 1908: 'Flash Jack Johnson vs. Sinking Tommy Burns,'" *Sporting Traditions* 26, 2 (2009): 1–14.

2. J. Johnson, *My Life and Battles*, translated from *Ma Vie et mes combats* [1914] by C. Rivers (Westport [CT]: Praeger, 2007).

3. J. Johnson, *Jack Johnson Is a Dandy: An Autobiography* (New York: Signet, 1969) [originally titled *Jack Johnson In the Ring and Out*, 1927].

4. W. Corbett, "The Life and Reminiscences of Peter Jackson, I," *Referee*, 3/27/1901,1

5. N.T. Hall, *Slave Society in the Danish West Indies: St. Thomas, St. John, and St. Croix* (Baltimore: Johns Hopkins UP, 1992); I. Dookhan, *A History of the Virgin Islands of the United States* (Epping: Caribbean University Press, 1974).

6. B.M. Kuyk, *African Voices in the African American Heritage* (Bloomington: Indiana University Press, 2003). On naming in the United States, J.L. Dillard, *Black Names* (The Hague: Mouton, 1974) is useful.

7. W. Chapman, "Irreconcilable differences: urban residences in the Danish West Indies, 1700–1900," *Winterthur Portfolio* 30, 2/3 (1995): 129–172, and the same author's "Slave villages in the Danish West Indies," in T. Carter and B.L. Herman, eds., *Perspectives in Vernacular Architecture*, vol. 4 (Columbia, MO: University of Missouri Press, 1991), 108–120, 223–226; S. Brown, *Victorian Frederiksted: Details of 19th Century Caribbean Architecture of Frederiksted, St. Croix* (Christiansted: St. Croix Landmarks Society, 1981).

8. R.A. Watlington and S.H. Lincoln, eds., *Disaster and Disruption in 1867: Hurricane, Earthquake and Tsunami in the Danish West Indies, A Collection of Accounts and Reports* (St. Thomas: University of the Virgin Islands, 1997).

9. M.E. Lomax, *Black Baseball Entrepreneurs 1860–1901: Operating by Any Means Necessary* (Syracuse: Syracuse University Press, 2003), 50–51.

10. T. De Booy and J.T. Faris, *The Virgin Islands: Our New Possessions and the British Islands* (Philadelphia: Lippincott, 1918); L.K. Zabriskie, *The Virgin Islands of the United States of America: Historical and Descriptive Commercial and Industrial Facts, Figures, and Resources* (New York: Putnam, 1918); J.A. Jarvis, *The Virgin Islands and Their People* (Philadelphia: Dorrance, 1944).

11. A.G. Hales, *Romantic Career of Peter Jackson, His Fights Re-told* (running title: *Peter the Black Prince, A Tale of Love and Sport*) (Manchester: Umpire Publishing Company, n.d. [1910]), 16.

12. N.T. Jensen, "Safeguarding slaves: smallpox, vaccination, and governmental health policies among the enslaved population in the Danish West Indies," *Bulletin of the History of Medicine* 83, 1 (Spring 2009): 95–125; R.N. Buckley, "The Destruction of the British army in the West Indies 1793–1815: a medical history," *Journal of the Society for Army Historical Research* 56, 226 (Summer 1978): 79–92.

13. H.S. Whitehead, "Negro dialect of the Virgin Islands," *American Speech* 7, 3 (February 1932): 175–179. A website carries a vocabulary of contemporary Cruzan/ Crucian: this is www.cruciandictionary.com, with a printed version by Antilles Press (Christiansted) in 2008.

14. E.C. Parsons, *Folk-Lore of the Antilles, French and English* (New York: American Folklore Society, 3 vols., 1933, 1936, 1943). Michael Richards's stories are in vol. 2, 414–450.

15. *St. Croix Avis*, December 12, 1884, page 2; G. Weaver, *The History of Trinity College, Volume 1* (Hartford, CT: Trinity College Press, 1967); *St. Croix Avis*, April 27, 1878, 2.

16. C. Birchenough, *History of Elementary Education in England and Wales from 1800 to the Present Day* (London: University Tutorial Press, 1914); D. Salmon, ed., *The Practical Parts of Lancaster's Improvements and Bell's Experiment* (Cambridge: Cambridge University Press, 1932).

17. C.C. Tansill, *The Purchase of the Danish West Indies* (New York: Greenwood, 1968 [1932]).

18. C.E. Taylor, *Leaflets from the Danish West Indies: Descriptive of the Social, Political, and Commercial Condition of These Islands* (London: Dawson, 1888), 36 and 146.

19 Bard Tablet: notes taken in St. Paul's church on 10/29/2003.

20. H. Degenkolv, ed., *Oplysninger Vedrørende den Danske Flaades Skibe i Sidste Aarhundrede* (Copenhagen: Lehmann & Stage, 1906), 79–80 gives details of the *Dagmar* and its tours of duty.

21. E.H. Petersen, ed., *Peter F. Heering: The History of a Danish Firm During 125 Years* (Copenhagen: n.p., 1943); *Slægten Heering: personalhistoriske optegnelser* (Copenhagen: 1900); P.N. Heering, *Familiebogen: optegnelser om min slægt af Peter N. Heering, Christianshavn 19 Februar 1912* (Copenhagen: H.H. Thiels Bogtrykkeri, 1912). I thank Mr. Philip Sampson of Copenhagen for translating for me relevant passages from the latter two books.

22. P.H. Jensen, *From Serfdom to Fireburn and Strike: The History of Black Labor in the Danish West Indies 1848–1916* (Christiansted: Antilles Press, 1998); L.A. Pendleton, "Our new possessions — the Danish West Indies," *Journal of Negro History* 2, 3 (July 1917): 267–324; *American Churchman*, 11/30/1878, 640.

23. H. Asbury, *The Gangs of New York: An Informal History of the Underworld* (London: Arrow, 2003 [1927]); L. Sante, *Low Life: Lures and Snares of Old New York* (New York: Vintage, 1992); T.J. Gilfoyle, *City of Eros: New York City, Prostitution, and the Commercialization of Sex, 1790–1920* (New York: Norton, 1992), Chapter 10.

24. W.J. Bolster, *Black Jacks: African American Seamen in the Age of Sail* (Cambridge: Harvard University Press, 1997).

25. B. Lubbock, *The Blackwall Frigates* (Glasgow: Brown Son Ferguson, 1924); *The Down Easters: American Deep-Water Sailing Ships 1869–1929* (Glasgow: Brown Son Ferguson, 1929); *The Last of the Windjammers* (Glasgow: Brown Son Ferguson, 2 vols., 1929).

26. F.T. Bullen, *The Men of the Merchant Service: Being the Polity of the Mercantile Marine for 'Longshore Readers* (London: Smith Elder, 1900).

27. G. Weightman, *The Frozen Water Trade: How Ice from New England Kept the World Cool* (London: HarperCollins, 2001); "The ice trade between America and India," *The Mechanic's Magazine*, 4/9/1836; *New York Times*, 2/25/1878 and 8/16/1878.

28. H.E.A. Cotton, *Calcutta Old and New: A Historical and Descriptive Handbook to the City* (Calcutta: Newman, 1907); M. Massey, *Recollections of Calcutta for Over Half a Century* (Calcutta: Bibhash Gupta, 1986 [1916]).

29. I. Thornton, *Krakatau: The Destruction and Reassembly of an Island Ecosystem* (Cambridge: Harvard University Press, 1996); S. Winchester, *Krakatoa: The Day the World Exploded, 27 August 1883* (Bath: Chivers Press, 2003).

30. S.A. Buddingh, *Neêrlands-Oost-Indië: Reizen 1852–1857* (Rotterdam: Wijt & Zonen, 1859), 161–176 on Samarang, 402–415 on Banjoewangie; J. Tenison-Woods, "A Journey Through Java," *Sydney Morning Herald*, Part I, February 27, 1884.

Chapter 2

1. T. Watson, "Peeps into the past: stories by Tom Watson," *The Suburban Herald (The North Shore Champion)*, 1927; L.A. Clark, *North of the Harbour: A Brief History of Transport To and On the North Shore* (Newcastle: Newey & Beath, 1976). For a photograph of the bus, C. Warne's *Pictorial History: Lower North Shore* (Sydney: Kingsclear, 1995), 51. I owe this reference to Mr. B.G. McKelleher. K. Roberts, author of *Captain of the Push* (Melbourne: Lansdowne, 1963), 108–111, writes fiction and endows Peter with dialect.

2. K.D. Nichols, "Memoirs of W.H. Baker," *The Historian* 7, 1 (March 1978): 5–11; 9, 2 (June 1980): 11–14.

3. J. Ellicott, *Waterhouse and Smith: The Rise to Power of Two Racing Dynasties* (Melbourne: Hardie Grant, 2008), Chapter 1; B. Petersen, "Peter Jackson at Lane Cove," *Lane Cove Historical Society Newsletter*, No. 163, March 2001, 1–5.

4. R. Waterhouse, *From Minstrel Show to Vaudeville: The Australian Popular Stage 1788-1914* (Sydney: University of New South Wales Press, 1990), Cruso as "Bones" pictured figure 10 (66–67); M. Bellanta, "Leary kin: Australian larrikins and the blackface minstrel dandy," *Journal of Social History*, March 2009, 677–95.

5. There are few mentions of Feneley in the Jackson records.

6. N. Donnelly, *Self-Defence; or, The Art of Boxing* (London: Weldon, n.d. [1879]).

7. G.B. Shaw, *Cashel Byron's Profession* (London: Constable, 1932 [1881]), 16–22.

8. "L. Foley's reminiscences: IX," *Referee* 11/17/1897, 8.

9. P. McInnes, ed., *Fifty Years a Fighter: The Life story of Jem Mace (Retired Champion of the World) Told by Himself* (London: Caestus, 1998 [1908]; G. Gordon, *Master of the Ring: The Extraordinary Life of Jem Mace* (Wrea Green, UK: Milo, 2007). The entry by Tony Gee in the *Oxford Dictionary of National Biography* (2004) corrects earlier accounts.

10. "L. Foley's reminiscences: IX," *Referee* 11/17/1897, 8.

11. Details of the births in the baptismal register of St. John the Baptist Church at Maitland.

12. R. Bogdan, *Freak Show: Presenting Human Oddities for Amusement and Profit* (Chicago: University of Chicago Press, 1988), 182–184; R. Adams, *Sideshow U.S.A.: Freaks and the American Cultural Imagination* (Chicago: University of Chicago Press, 2001); R. Poignant, *Professional Savages: Captive Lives and Western Spectacle* (Sydney: University of New South Wales Press, 2004).

13. *Referee*, "Special Jubilee Issue," November 11, 1935; D.B. Welky, "Culture, media and sport: the *National Police Gazette* and the creation of an American

working-class world," *Culture Sport Society*, 1, 1 (1998): 78–100; C. Cunneen, "Elevating and recording the people's pastimes: Sydney sporting journalism 1886–1939," in R. Cashman and M. McKernan, eds., *Sport: Money, Morality and the Media* (Sydney: University of New South Wales, n.d. [1980]), 162–176; G. Reel, *The "National Police Gazette" and the Making of the Modern American Man 1879–1906*, (New York: Palgrave Macmillan, 2006).

14. *Sydney Australian Sportsman*, May 30, 1883, 1.

15. W.J. Doherty, *In the Days of the Giants: Memories of a Champion of the Prize-Ring* (London: Harrap, 1931), 47–50.

16. A. Sinclair and W. Henry, *Swimming* (London: Longmans Green, "Badminton Library of Sports," 3rd ed., 1903), 88–89; L.B. Rout, *The African Experience in Spanish America, 1502 to the present day* (Cambridge: Cambridge University Press, 1976),185–197; K. Dawson, "Swimming, surfing and underwater diving in early modern Atlantic Africa and the African Diaspora," in C.E. Ray and J. Rich, *Navigating African Maritime History* (St. John's Newfoundland: International Maritime Economic History Association, Research in Maritime History No. 41, 2009), 81–116. T.J.D. Obi, "Black terror: Bill Richmond's revolutionary boxing," *Journal of Sport History*, 36, 1 (Spring 2009): 99–114, evokes Peter's traditional African boxing skills.

17. *Referee*, 9/8/1916, 16.

18. P. McInnes, ed., *Bob Fitzsimmons: A Pugilistic Biography* (London: Caestus, 1998); D. Webb, *Prize Fighter: The Life and Times of Bob Fitzsimmons* (Edinburgh: Mainstream, 2000); A.J. Pollack, *In the Ring with Bob Fitzsimmons* (New York: WinByKO Publications, 2007).

19. *Referee*, November 13, 1912, 8. Corbett gave several episodes of his 1918–19 biography to Peter's teaching.

20. *Referee*, September 3, 1890, 8.

21. G. Deghy, *Noble and Manly: The History of the National Sporting Club* (London: Hutchinson, 1956), 108 and 121.

22. D. Deitcher, *Dear Friends: American Photographs of Men Together 1840–1918* (New York: Abrams, 2001); J.N. Katz, *Love Stories: Sex Between Men Before Homosexuality* (Chicago: University of Chicago Press, 2001); M. Chapman and G. Hendler, eds., *Sentimental Men: Masculinity and the Politics of Affect in American Culture* (Berkeley: University of California Press, 1999).

23. C. Wright, "Of public houses and private lives: female hotelkeepers as domestic entrepreneurs," *Australian Historical Studies*, 116 (April 2001): 57–75.

24. These facts are from the City of Sydney archives, as well as the annual *Sands' Sydney Directories* for the 1880s.

25. S. D'Amico, ed., *Enciclopedia dello Spettacolo* (Rome: Le Maschere, 1956), s.v. "Chiarini."

26. J.M. Houstone, "A Pugilistic antique: researching a rare piece of Australian silver," *Australasian Antique Collector* 19 (1979): 86–89.

27. T. Gee, *John L. Sullivan: Cradle to Grave* (Romford, Essex: Sporting Profiles, 1998), 44, reproducing the *New York Herald* of 2/3/1918.

28. *New Zealand Truth*, 12/20/1913.

29. A. Bayley, *Blue Haven: History of Kiama Municipality, New South Wales* (Kiama: Kiama Municipal Council, 2nd ed., 1976).

30. See the *Referee*, 1/16/1918 and 2/13/1918, for Dowridge reminiscences gathered by "Straight Left"; obituaries *Brisbane Courier*, 4/26/1922 and *Referee*, 5/3/1922.

31. G. Growden, *The Snowy Baker Story* (Sydney: Random House Australia, 2003), 25–26.

32. *Maitland Mercury*, 4/21/1888.

Chapter 3

1. D. Harris, *Eadweard Muybridge and the Photographic Panorama of San Francisco 1850–1880*, (Montreal: Centre Canadien d'Architecture, 1993).

2. D. Van Court, *The Making of Champions in California* (Los Angeles: Premier Printing, 1926); F.D. Somrack, *Boxing in San Francisco* (Charleston: Arcadia, "Images of Sports," 2005).

3. The best book on the blacks of San Francisco is D.H. Daniels, *Pioneer Urbanites: A Social and Cultural History of Black San Francisco* (Philadelphia: Temple University Press, 1980); useful is D.L. Beasley, *The Negro Trail Blazers of California* (Los Angeles: self-published, 1919).

4. *Referee*, 7/31/1918.

5. W.A. Brady, *The Fighting Man* (Indianapolis: Bobbs-Merrill, 1916), 61.

6. D. Van Court, *The Making of Champions in California*, 51.

7. This photo — a glass negative, mutilated — was offered on eBay by an Australian vendor in June 2000 as item #353880877.

8. Peter's swimming contretemps figures in one of the few copies extant of the *San Francisco Vindicator*, 11/17/1888, 2. A decade later, John Harris sued Adoph Sutro because he was not allowed to swim in the Cliff House baths, even when he was with white friends (*San Francisco Call*, 8/1/1897). The *Chronicle* did an article on the baths of San Francisco on 5/18/1890, describing the Palace and the Crystal as well as the Hammam at 11–13 Grant Avenue (Dupont). Peter was allowed into these Turkish or Chinese baths, but they were not for swimming in.

9. *Referee*, 1/27/1915.

10. *Daily Alta California*, 1/22/1889.

11. H.V. Carby, *Race Men* (Cambridge: Harvard University Press, 1998), 55–58; B.L. Michaels, "New light on F. Holland Day's photographs of African Americans," *History of Photography* 18, 4 (Winter 1994): 334–347.

12. J. Smalls, *The Homoerotic Photography of Carl Van Vechten: Public Face, Private Thoughts* (Philadelphia: Temple University Press, 2006).

Chapter 4

1. L. Dawson, *Lonsdale: The Authorised Life of Hugh Lowther, Fifth Earl of Lonsdale* (London: Odhams, 1946); D. Sutherland, *The Yellow Earl: The Life of Hugh Lowther 5th Earl of Lonsdale* (New York: Coward-McCann, 1966).
2. J. Cahn, *Julius Cahn's Official Theatrical Guide, Containing Information of the Leading Theatres and Attractions in America* (New York: Empire Theater Publications, 1896).
3. R. Cashman, *Sport in the National Imagination: Australian Sport in the Federation Decades* (Sydney: Walla Walla, 2002), 211.
4. M.T. Isenberg, *John L. Sullivan and His America* (Urbana: University of Illinois Press, 1988), 66–79.
5. G. Osofsky, *Harlem, the Making of a Ghetto: Negro New York 1890–1930* (New York: Harper & Row, Harper Torchbooks, 1971), 117–118.
6. Deghy's *Noble and Manly* is the fullest account of the NSC, its predecessor the Pelican Club, and their members.
7. Useful for the Aquarium are the two editions of R. Mander and J. Mitchenson, *The Lost Theatres of London* (London: Hart-Davis, 1968), 205–217, and (London: New English Library, 2nd ed., 1976), 89–95.
8. M. Pickering, "Eugene Stratton and early ragtime in Britain," *Black Music Research Journal* 20, 2 (Fall 2000): 151–180; and more generally J.A. Dormon, "Shaping the popular image of post-reconstruction American Blacks: the 'coon song' phenomenon of the gilded age," *American Quarterly* 40, 4 (1988): 450–471.
9. E.W. Gilbert, *Brighton: Old Ocean's Bauble* (London: Methuen, 1954).
10. A. Cook, *Prince Eddy: The King Britain Never Had* (Stroud, UK: Tempus, 2006).
11. J.E. Vincent, *His Royal Highness Duke of Clarence and Avondale: a memoir* (London: John Murray, 1893) leaps over the months of Peter's sojourn in London. I used the daily "Court Circular" in *The Times* to trace the prince's movements.
12. *Sportsman* (London), 3/7/1892.
13. *Ibid.*
14. S. Craddock, *City of Plagues: Disease, Poverty, and Deviance in San Francisco* (Minneapolis: Minnesota University Press, 2000), *passim* but especially Chapter 1.
15. J. Dignam, *The Dublin Guide* (Dublin: Eason, 1891), 62–63.
16. P. Myler, *The Fighting Irish* (Kerry: Brandon, 1987); M. Donnellon, *The Irish Champion Peter Maher* (Vancouver: Trafford, 2008).
17. *Boston Daily Globe*, 1/30/1890.
18. C.L. Ponce de Leon, *Self-Exposure: Human-Interest Journalism and the Emergence of Celebrity in America, 1890–1940* (Chapel Hill: University of North Carolina Press, 2002), 92–95.
19. P. Dresser, song lyrics, "Mother Told Me So," (Chicago: Lyon & Healy, 1887).

Chapter 5

1. Brady, *The Fighting Man*, 78–81.
2. M. Grieg, *Goin' the Distance: Canada's Boxing Heritage* (Toronto: MacMillan Canada, 1996); *National Police Gazette*, 5/12/1883, 4.
3. G.M. Campbell, *Extant Collections of Early Black Newspapers: A Research Guide to the Black Press 1880–1915* (Troy, NY: Whitston, 1981); J.W. Snorgrass, "The Black press in the San Francisco Bay area 1856–1900," *California History* 60, 4 (Winter 1981/82): 306–317.
4. One of these tags was auctioned on eBay in December 2000 as item #1105618942, being described as "rare as hen's teeth."
5. W.H.A. Williams, *'Twas Only an Irishman's Dream: The Image of Ireland and the Irish in American Popular Song Lyrics 1800–1920* (Urbana: Illinois University Press, 1996).
6. G.R. Kremer, "The World of make-believe: James Milton Turner and black masonry," *Missouri Historical Review* 76, 2 (January 1982): 50–71; G.R. Kremer, *James Milton Turner and the Promise of America: The Public Life of a Post-Civil War Black Leader* (Columbia: University of Missouri Press, 1991).
7. Reproduced in 1930 from his *Autobiography of an Ex-Coloured Man* in J.W. Johnson's *Black Manhattan* (New York: Da Capo, 1991), 75.
8. J.E. Moorland, "The Young Men's Christian Association among Negroes," *Journal of Negro History* 9, 2 (April 1924): 127–138; C.H. Tobias, "The Work of the Young Men's and Young Women's Christian Association with Negro Youth," *Annals of the American Academy of Political and Social Science* 140: "The American Negro," 1928, 283–286; M.H. Little, "The Extracurricular activities of Black college students, 1868–1940," *Journal of African American History* 87 (Winter 2002): 43–55.
9. J.W. Johnson, *Along This Way: The Autobiography of James Weldon Johnson* (New York: Viking Press, 1934), 208: C.M. Bernier, "'Emblems of barbarism:' black masculinity and representations of Toussaint L'Ouverture in Frederick Douglass's unpublished manuscripts," *American Nineteenth Century History* 4, 3 (Fall 2003): 97–120.
10. Van Court, *Making of Champions*, 42.
11. W. Bonnett, *Victorian San Francisco: The 1895 Illustrated Directory* (Sausalito: Windgate, 1996), 63.
12. *The Wasp* was quoted in the (Sydney) *Dead Bird*. See R.S. West, *The San Francisco Wasp: An Illustrated History* (Easthampton, MA: Periodyssey, 2004).

Chapter 6

1. *Referee*, 12/4/1918.
2. N. Fleischer, *Young Griffo: The Will o' the Wisp of the Roped Square* (New York: Fleischer, 1928); R. Drane, *Fighters By Trade: Highlights of Australian Boxing* (Sydney: ABC, 2008) has a section on Griffo. Both authors downplay Griffo's psychological problems.

3. *Referee*, 9/8/1916, 1.

4. W.H. Grimshaw, *Official History of Freemasonry Among the Colored People in North America* (Freeport, NY: Books for Libraries, 1971 [1903]).

5. H. Voorhuis, *Negro Masonry in the United States* (Whitefish, MT: Kessinger, 1995).

6. These unpublished details were kindly supplied me by the Masonic Library in Sydney.

7. *Maitland Mercury*, 11/1/1890. Gillies's reference to buffaloes could mean he knew Peter to be a member of the Royal Antediluvian Order of Buffaloes, or merely that Peter had been drinking with Martin "Buffalo" Costello.

8. L. Fink, "Byron hot springs: the Carlsbad of America," in *Contra Costa Chronicles* 1, 2 (Fall 1965): 27–34.

9. M. Powers, *Faces Along the Bar: Lore and Order in the Workingman's Saloon, 1870–1920* (Chicago: University of Chicago Press, 1998), shows opposite page 156 the 1900 plan of one South-of-Market block containing over a hundred bars.

10. R. Erdoes, *Saloons of the Old West* (New York: Gramercy, 1979): M.E. Lender and J.K. Martin, *Drinking in America: A History*, 2nd ed., (New York: Free, 1987); K. Christmon, "Historical overview of alcohol in the African American community," *Journal of Black Studies* 25, 3 (1995): 318–330; *The Sydney Slang Dictionary* (Sydney: H.J. Franklin, 1882).

11. G. Hendricks, *Eadweard Muybridge: The Father of the Motion Pictures* (London: Secker & Warburg, 1975), figures 109–110.

12. M. Oriard, *Reading Football: How the Popular Press Created an American Spectacle* (Chapel Hill: University of North Carolina Press, 1993); G. Whannel, *Media Sport Stars: Masculinities and Moralities* (London: Routledge, 2002), especially chapter 7.

13. J. Walvin, *Black and White: The Negro and English Society 1555–1945* (London: Allen Lane the Penguin Press, 1973), Chapter 12.

14. *Famous Fights Past and Present* 7, 61 (1903): 194–200.

15. A.F. Bettinson and W.O. Tristram, *The National Sporting Club Past and Present* (London: Sands, 1901), 34. The anecdote was repeated in *Referee*, 3/5/1919, and in G. Deghy, *Noble and Manly*, 108.

16. Will Lawless reproduced the photograph in the *Referee*, April 21, 1915, 8.

17. *The Ring*, December 1929, 12.

Chapter 7

1. *Examiner*, 1/22/1893.

2. S.F. Clark, "Up against the ropes : Peter Jackson as 'Uncle Tom' in America," *The Drama Review* 44, 1 (Spring 2000): 157–182

3. On Stockwell, see W.B. Durham, *American Theatre Companies, 1888–1930* (Westport, CT: Greenwood, 1987), and E.M. Gagey, *The San Francisco Stage: A History* (New York: Columbia University Press, 1950).

4. Liliuokalani, *Hawaii's Story by Hawaii's Queen* (Rutland, VT: Tuttle, 1964 [1898]), is silent on the matter.

5. G.C.D. Odell, *Annals of the New York Stage* (New York: Columbia University Press, 15 vols., 1927–1949) is useful for all performances at all theaters until 1894; supplemented for later years by T.A. Brown, *A History of the New York Stage: From the First Performance in 1732 to 1901* (New York: Benjamin Bloom, 3 vols., 1964 [1903]).

6. G. Aiken, "Uncle Tom's Cabin," in D.C. Gerould (ed.), *American Melodrama* (New York: Performing Arts Journal, 1983), end of Act VI.

7. S.F. Clark, "Up against the ropes," 157–182, makes out that Peter lost face and reputation by playing Tom.

8. W.S. Watson's *Diseases of the Nose and Its Accessory Cavities* (London: Lewis, 1875), 46–59 and the 1890 edition, 93–103.

9. A. Fields, *James J. Corbett: A Biography of the Heavyweight Boxing Champion and Popular Theater Headliner* (Jefferson, NC: McFarland, 2001), chapter 5; P. Myler, *Gentleman Jim Corbett: The Truth Behind a Boxing Legend* (London: Robson, 1998), chapters 10–13.

10. C.B. Glasscock, *Lucky Baldwin: The Story of an Unconventional Success* (Indianapolis: Bobbs-Merrill, 1933) respects all libel laws.

11. A fuller account of these incidents is R.C. Petersen, "Peter Jackson Perfect Man," *Journal of Interdisciplinary Gender Studies* 6, 2 (2001): 36–46; D.L. Chapman, *Sandow the Magnificent: Eugen Sandow and the Beginnings of Bodybuilding*, 2nd ed. (Urbana: University of Illinois Press, 1994), 77–91. B. Hjalmarson, *Artful Players: Artistic Life in Early San Francisco* (Los Angeles: Balcony, 1999), 129–131 manages to discuss Sandow as the perfect man without mentioning Peter. W. Lipsky, *San Francisco's Midwinter Exposition* (Chicago: Arcadia, 2002), portrays the celebration that brought Sandow to California.

12. H.D. Northrop, J.R. Gay, and I.G. Penn, *The College of Life: or, Practical Self-Educator, a manual of self-improvement for the colored race forming an educational emancipator and a guide to success* (Chicago: Chicago Publication and Lithograph Company, 1895).

13. The poster was in full color on eBay in October 2000 as item #451885767, and from this I derive my details.

14. J. Wood, *Hidden Talents: A Dictionary of Neglected Artists Working 1880–1950* (Billingshurst Sussex: Jeremy Wood Fine Art, 1994).

15. G. Hendricks, *Origins of the American Film* (New York: Arno Press, 1972); R. Phillips, *Edison's Kinetoscope and Its Films: a history to 1896* (Westport (CT): Greenwood, 1997), 136–137.

16. A. Fields, *James J. Corbett*, 84–86; D. Streible, "A History of the boxing film 1894–1915: social control and social reform in the progressive era," *Film History* 3 (1989): 233–257; D. Streible, *Fight Pictures: A History of Boxing and Early Cinema* (Berkeley: University of California Press, 2008).

17. P. Myler, *Gentleman Jim Corbett*, 95–96.
18. Conclusions drawn from scrutinizing D. Gifford, ed., *The British Film Catalog*, vol. 2: *Nonfiction Film 1888–1994* (London: Fitzroy Dearborn, 2001), and E. Savada, ed., *The American Film Institute Catalog of Motion Pictures Produced in the United States: Film Beginnings 1893–1910*, 2 vols. (Metuchen, NJ: Scarecrow, 1995).
19. Phillips, *Edison's Kinetoscope*, 125; *New York Sun*, 2/22/1894, 8; *Chaffee County (CO) Republican*, 6/10/1896, 4.
20. J.W. Johnson, *Along This Way*, 204–205. R.W. Logan, *The Betrayal of the Negro from Rutherford B. Hayes to Woodrow Wilson* (New York: Da Capo, 1997 [1965]) documents the process which throws shadows across W.E.B. Dubois, *Black Reconstruction in America 1860–1880* (New York: Atheneum, 1992 [1935]).

Chapter 8

1. *St. Croix Avis*, 9/23/1894, 10/16/1894.
2. *Sportsman* (London), 11/2/1894, 4.
3. Cotton, *Calcutta Old and New*, 925–930.
4. M.H. Hayes, *Among Men and Horses* (London: Fisher Unwin, 1894).
5. J.D. Astley, *Fifty Years of My Life in the world of sport at home and abroad* (London: Hurst & Blackett, 1895), 212, 348.
6. J. Thorpe, *Phil May: Master-Draughtsman & Humorist 1864–1903* (London: Harrap, 1932).
7. C. Castle, *The Folies Bergère* (London: Methuen, 1982); C. Rearick, *Pleasures of the Belle Epoque: Entertainment & Festivity in Turn-of-the-Century France* (New Haven: Yale University Press, 1985); J. Kinsman et al., *Paris in the Late 19th Century* (Canberra: National Gallery of Australia, 1997); P. Archer-Straw, *Negrophilia: Avant-Garde Paris and Black Culture in the 1920s* (London: Thames & Hudson, 2000).
8. *Le Figaro*, 12/5/1894, 6.
9. B.J. Angle, *My Sporting Memories* (London: Robert Holden, 1925), 198.
10. C.D. Stuart and A.J. Park, *The Variety Stage* (London: Fisher Unwin, 1895) is informative, and see A. Horrall, *Popular Culture in London c. 1890–1918: The Transformation of Entertainment* (Manchester: Manchester University Press, 2001).
11. According to the Cyberboxingzone entry, they boxed; but the reports in the *South Wales Daily News* for 7/14/1896 are silent on that, as is Pollack.
12. W.A. Brady, *The Fighting Man*, 61.
13. W. Bonnett, *Victorian San Francisco*, 63.
14. S.A. Riess, "Sports and machine politics in New York City 1870–1920," in D.K. Wiggins, ed., *Sport in America: From Wicked Amusement to National Obsession* (Champaign, IL: 1995), 163–184.
15. G. Brechin, *Imperial San Francisco: Urban Power, Earthly Ruin* (Berkeley: University of California Press, 1999), 263–264.
16. H. Igoe, "Peter Jackson and Jim Corbett fight," *Boxer and Wrestler*, 4/25/1935, 8.

17. J. Jeffries, "King of the Ring: Jim Jeffries' autobiography," *Sydney Sportsman*, 29/6/1910–18/1/1911 [a.k.a. *My Life and Battles*], 8.
18. "James J. Jeffries' Life and Fights: colorful story told by himself for 'The Referee': Chapter 7," *Referee*, 8/16/1927; K.R. Nicholson, *A Man Among Men: The Life and Ring Battles of Jim Jeffries* (Draper, Utah: Homeward Bound Publishing, 2002), 39–41.
19. *Vandover and the Brute*, in F. Norris, *Novels and Essays* (New York: Library of America No. 33, 1986), 236; Chapter 10 in *Faces Along the Bar* by Powers, titled "The Free Lunch," suggests that San Francisco was a capital of the phenomenon.
20. L.J.R. Wilson, "Medicine Hat—'the sporting town' 1883–1905," *Canadian Journal of History of Sport* 16, 2 (1985): 15–32.
21. R.W. Winks, *The Blacks in Canada: A History* (Montreal: McGill-Queens University Press, 2nd. ed., 1997), 272–287.
22. These details are all from R.T. Williams, ed., *The Williams Official British Columbia Directory 1899* (Victoria: Williams, 1899) and from the *Vancouver City Directory, June 1899–1900* (Vancouver: 1899).
23. R.C. Kirk, *Twelve Months in Klondike* (London: Heinemann, 1899); C. Porsild, *Gamblers and Dreamers: Women, Men, and Community in the Klondike* (Vancouver: University of British Columbia Press, 1998); M.K. Heine and K.B. Wamsley, "'Kickfest at Dawson City': native peoples and the sports of the Klondike gold rush," *Sports History Review* 27 (1996): 72–86.
24. Craddock, *City of Plagues*, Chapter 4; N. Shah, *Contagious Divides: Epidemics and Race in San Francisco's Chinatown* (Berkeley: University of California Press, 2001), Chapter 5.

Chapter 9

1. On Hogan see H.T. Sampson, *Blacks in Blackface: A Source Book on Early Black Musical Shows* (Metuchen, NJ: Scarecrow, 1980), 375–377; D.A. Jasen and G. Jones, *Spreadin' Rhythm Around: Black Popular Songwriters 1880–1930* (New York: Schirmer, 1998), 86–97; and (on McLain, too) E.G. Hill and J.V. Hatch, *A History of African American Theater* (New York: Cambridge University Press, 2003), 130–134, 140–142.
2. H. Igoe, "Peter Jackson and Jim Corbett fight," *Boxer and Wrestler*, 4/25/1935, 8.
3. Doherty, *In the Days of the Giants*, 231.
4. P. Curson and K. McCracken, *Plague in Sydney: The Anatomy of an Epidemic* (Sydney: University of New South Wales Press, n.d. [1989]).
5. See his obituaries in *Australasian Medical Gazette*, September 20, 1904, 483–4 and *The Lancet*, October 29, 1904, 1196.
6. Doherty, *In the Days of the Giants*, 205–207 and 229–230; obituary of Peter Felix, *Referee*, 11/17/1926.
7. Doherty, *In the Days of the Giants*, 231.

8. M. St. Leon, *Spangles & Sawdust: The Circus in Australia* (Melbourne: Greenhouse, 1983), Chapter 10.

9. The half-page advertisement in the *Sportsman*, 11/5/1900.

10. T. Wolf, "'A Grand assault-at-arms': tournaments and combative exhibitions in Victorian England," *Journal of Manly Arts* (August 2001) analyzes the phenomenon.

11. K. McConnel, ed., *Our Federation: Brisbane through the news 1901* (Brisbane: Brisbane History Group, "Sources No. 10," 2002).

12. W.R.F. Love, *A History of St. Helen's Methodist Hospital,* (Brisbane: Queensland Historical Society, 1975).

13. N. Parker and J. Pearn, eds. *Ernest Sandford Jackson: The Life and Times of a Pioneer Australian Surgeon* (Brisbane: Australian Medical Association Queensland, 1987).

14. D. Streible, "Fake fight films," in C.D. La Tour, A. Gaudreault, R. Pearson (eds.), *Le Cinéma au tournant du siècle/Cinema at the Turn of the Century* (Quebec: Nota Bene, 1999), 63–79

15. *Y.M.C.A. (The Journal of the Brisbane YMCA)* 42 (6/1/1903): 7; D. Hardie, "A Few notes on the climatic treatment of consumption in southern Queensland," *Australasian Medical Gazette* 16, 113 (1897): 113–116; J.A. Lindsay, *The Climatic Treatment of Consumption: A Contribution to Medical Climatology* (London: Macmillan, 1887), 102–138.

16. *Referee*, 12/18/190, 7.

17. *Roma Western Star*, 5/25/1903.

18. Queensland State Archives Series PRV8723 (previously COL/237) "Sanatoria at Roma 1897–1902: L'Estrange to Chief Secretary's Department. The regular treatment can be studied in M.C. Lidwill, *Patients' Guide to the Open Air Treatment of Consumption* (Sydney: Angus & Robertson, 1908).

19. Letter from L'Estrange to Mooney in *Referee*, 7/17/1901, 6.

20. B.E. Roy, *The Presbyterians' First One Hundred Years in Roma: special centenary edition (1866–1966),* (Roma: Maranoa Presbyterian, 1966).

21. *Examiner*, 11/16/1891 and 11/21/1891.

22. "A Clergyman on the famous fighter," *Referee*, 8/7/1901, 6.

23. G.M. Griffin and D. Tobin, *In the Midst of Life: The Australian Response to Death* (Melbourne: Melbourne University Press, 2nd ed., 1997); P. Jalland, *Australian Ways of Death: A Social and Cultural History 1840–1918* (Melbourne: Oxford University Press, 2002).

24. The *Maranoa Advocate* of Roma is not extant, but the *Referee* on 7/24/1901 reprinted its account of the "weird, impressive obsequies" in Roma, which was much fuller than the account given on July 17 in the *Western Star*.

25. Facts from the Day Book held in the offices of K.M. Smith at Bowen Hills (funeral directors since 1877). Page 108 headed July 1901 was photocopied for me by Mr. Shane Steedman.

26. *The Indian Planters' Gazette and Sporting News*, 8/17/1901, 62–63.

27. "Newcastle's tribute," in *Referee*, 7/17/1901, 6.

28. K. Savage, *Standing Soldiers, Kneeling Slaves: Race, War, and Monument in Nineteenth-Century America* (Princeton, NJ: Princeton University Press, 1997).

29. I examined the tomb in 2000, in 2003, and again in 2006. A longer account is B. Petersen, "The Peter Jackson memorial," in B. Whimpress, ed., *The Imaginary Grandstand: Identity and Narrative in Australian Sport* (Adelaide: ASSH, 2002), 141–149.

30. A.F. Bettinson and B. Bennison, *The Home of Boxing* (London: Odhams, n.d. [1924], 212.

31. J.M. Houstone, "A Pugilistic antique: researching a rare piece of Australian silver," *Australasian Antique Collector* 19 (1979): 86–89.

Bibliography

Books and Articles

Adams, R. *Sideshow U.S.A.: Freaks and the American Cultural Imagination*. Chicago: University of Chicago Press, 2001.

Aiken, G. "Uncle Tom's Cabin," in D.C. Gerould (ed.), *American Melodrama*. New York: Performing Arts Journal, 1983.

Angle, B.J. *My Sporting Memories*. London: Robert Holden, 1925.

Archer-Straw, P. *Negrophilia: Avant-Garde Paris and Black Culture in the 1920s*. London: Thames & Hudson, 2000.

Asbury, H. *The Gangs of New York: An Informal History of the Underworld*. London: Arrow, 2003 [1927].

Astley, J.D. *Fifty Years of My Life in the World of Sport at Home and Abroad*. London: Hurst & Blackett, 1895.

Aycock, C., and Scott, M. *The First Black Boxing Champions: Essays on Fighters of the 1800s to the 1920s*. Jefferson, NC: McFarland, 2010.

Bascom, W. *Shango in the New World*. Austin: University of Texas Press, African and Afro-American Research Institute, 1972.

Bayley, A. *Blue Haven: History of Kiama Municipality, New South Wales*. Kiama: Kiama Municipal Council, 2nd ed., 1976.

Beasley, D.L. *The Negro Trail Blazers of California*. Los Angeles: self-published, 1919.

Bellanta, M. "Leary kin: Australian larrikins and the blackface minstrel dandy." *Journal of Social History* (March 2009): 677–95.

Bernier, C.M. "'Emblems of barbarism': black masculinity and representations of Toussaint L'Ouverture in Frederick Douglass's unpublished manuscripts." *American Nineteenth Century History* 4, 3 (Fall 2003): 97–120.

Bettinson, A.F., and B. Bennison. *The Home of Boxing*. London: Odhams, n.d. [1924].

Bettinson, A.F., and W.O. Tristram. *The National Sporting Club Past and Present*. London: Sands, 1901.

Birchenough, C. *History of Elementary Education in England and Wales from 1800 to the Present Day*. London: University Tutorial, 1914.

Boddy, K. *Boxing: A Cultural History*. London: Reaktion, 2008.

Bogdan, R. *Freak Show: Presenting Human Oddities for Amusement and Profit*. Chicago: University of Chicago Press, 1988.

Bolster, W.J. *Black Jacks: African American Seamen in the Age of Sail*. Cambridge: Harvard University Press, 1997.

Bonnett, W. *Victorian San Francisco: The 1895 Illustrated Directory*. Sausalito, CA: Windgate, 1996.

Brady, W.A. *The Fighting Man*. Indianapolis: Bobbs-Merrill, 1916.

Brechin, G. *Imperial San Francisco: Urban Power, Earthly Ruin*. Berkeley: University of California Press, 1999.

Broome, R. "The Australian reaction to Jack Johnson, black pugilist, 1907–9," in R. Cashman and M. McKernan, *Sport in History: The Making of Modern Sporting History*. Brisbane: Queensland University Press, 1979, 343–363.

Brown, S. *Victorian Frederiksted: Details of 19th Century Caribbean Architecture of Frederiksted, St. Croix*. Christiansted: St. Croix Landmarks Society, 1981.

Brown, T.A. *A History of the New York Stage: From the First Performance in 1732 to 1901*. 3 vols. New York: Benjamin Bloom, 1964 [1903]

Buckley, R.N. "The Destruction of the British army in the West Indies 1793–1815: a medical history." *Journal of the Society for Army Historical Research* 56, 226 (Summer 1978): 79- 92.

Buddingh, S.A. *Neêrlands-Oost-Indië: Reizen 1852–1857*. Rotterdam: Wijt & Zonen, 1859.

Bullen, F.T. *The Men of the Merchant Service: Being the Polity of the Mercantile Marine for 'Longshore Readers*. London: Smith Elder, 1900.

Cahn, J. *Julius Cahn's Official Theatrical Guide, Containing Information of the Leading Theatres and Attractions in America*. New York: Empire Theatre, 1896.

Campbell, G.M. *Extant Collections of Early Black Newspapers: A Research Guide to the Black Press 1880–1915*. Troy, NY: Whitston, 1981.

Carby, H.V. *Race Men*. Cambridge: Harvard University Press, 1998.

Cashman, R. *Sport in the National Imagination: Aus-

tralian Sport in the Federation Decades. Sydney: Walla Walla, 2002.
Castle, C. *The Folies Bergère.* London: Methuen, 1982.
Chapman, D.L. *Sandow the Magnificent: Eugen Sandow and the Beginnings of Bodybuilding.* 2nd ed. Urbana: University of Illinois Press, 1994.
Chapman, M., and G. Hendler, *Sentimental Men: Masculinity and the Politics of Affect in American Culture.* Berkeley: University of California Press, 1999.
Chapman, W. "Irreconcilable differences: urban residences in the Danish West Indies, 1700–1900." *Winterthur Portfolio* 30, 2/3 (1995): 129–172.
_____. "Slave villages in the Danish West Indies," in T. Carter and B.L. Herman, *Perspectives in Vernacular Architecture*, vol. 4. Columbia, MO: University of Missouri Press, 1991, 108–120, 223- 226.
Christmon, K. "Historical overview of alcohol in the African American community." *Journal of Black Studies* 25, 3 (1995): 318–330.
Clark, L.A. *North of the Harbour: A Brief History of Transport To and On the North Shore.* Newcastle: Newey & Beath, 1976.
Clark, S.F. "Up against the ropes : Peter Jackson as 'Uncle Tom' in America." *The Drama Review* 44, 1 (Spring 2000): 157–182.
Cook, A. *Prince Eddy: The King Britain Never Had.* Stroud, UK: Tempus, 2006.
Corbett, W. "The Life and Reminiscences of Peter Jackson," in *Referee*, I: 3/27/1901, 1; II: 4/10/1901, 1; III: 5/1/1901, 1; IV: 5/29/1901, 1; V: 7/10/1901, 1; VI: 8/21/1901, 1; VII: 12/24/1901, 1.
Corbett, W.W. "Life and Boxing Skill of Peter Jackson," in *Referee*, 71 weekly numbers, 2/20/1918–6/25/1919.
Corris, P. *Lords of the Ring: A History of Prize-fighting in Australia.* Sydney: Cassell Australia, 1980.
Cotton, H.E.A. *Calcutta Old and New: A Historical and Descriptive Handbook to the City.* Calcutta: Newman, 1907.
Craddock, S. *City of Plagues: Disease, Poverty, and Deviance in San Francisco.* Minneapolis: University of Minnesota Press, 2000.
Cunneen, C. "Elevating and recording the people's pastimes: Sydney sporting journalism 1886–1939," in R. Cashman and M. McKernan, *Sport: Money, Morality and the Media.* Sydney: University of New South Wales Press, n.d. [1980], 162–176.
Curson, P., and K. McCracken. *Plague in Sydney: The Anatomy of an Epidemic.* Sydney: University of New South Wales Press, n.d. [1989].
D'Amico, S., ed. *Enciclopedia dello Spettacolo.* Rome: Le Maschere, 1956.
Daniels, D.H. *Pioneer Urbanites: A Social and Cultural History of Black San Francisco.* Philadelphia: Temple University Press, 1980.
Dawson, K. "Swimming, surfing and underwater diving in early modern Atlantic Africa and the African Diaspora," in C.E. Ray and J. Rich, *Navigating African Maritime History. Research in Maritime History* No. 41. St. John's, Newfoundland: International Maritime Economic History Association, 2009, 81–116.
Dawson, L. *Lonsdale: The Authorised Life of Hugh Lowther, Fifth Earl of Lonsdale.* London: Odhams, 1946.
De Booy, T., and J.T. Faris. *The Virgin Islands: Our New Possessions and the British Islands.* Philadelphia: Lippincott, 1918.
Degenkolv, H., ed. *Oplysninger Vedrørende den Danske Flaades Skibe i Sidste Aarhundrede.* Copenhagen: Lehmann & Stage, 1906.
Deghy, G. *Noble and Manly: The History of the National Sporting Club.* London: Hutchinson, 1956.
Deitcher, D. *Dear Friends: American Photographs of Men Together 1840–1918.* New York: Abrams, 2001.
Dignam, J. *The Dublin Guide.* Dublin: Eason, 1891.
Dillard, J.L. *Black Names.* The Hague: Mouton, 1974.
Doherty, W.J. *In the Days of the Giants: Memories of a Champion of the Prize-Ring.* London: Harrap, 1931.
Donnellon, M. *The Irish Champion Peter Maher.* Vancouver: Trafford, 2008.
Donnelly, N. *Self-Defence; or, The Art of Boxing.* London: Weldon, n.d. [1879].
Dookhan, I. *A History of the Virgin Islands of the United States.* Epping, Essex: Caribbean University Press, 1974.
Dormon, J.A. "Shaping the popular image of postreconstruction American Blacks: the 'coon song' phenomenon of the gilded age." *American Quarterly* 40, 4 (1988): 450–471.
Drane, R. *Fighters by Trade: Highlights of Australian Boxing.* Sydney: ABC, 2008.
Dubois, W.E.B. *Black Reconstruction in America 1860–1880.* New York: Atheneum, 1992 [1935].
Durham, W.B. *American Theatre Companies, 1888–1930.* Westport, CT: Greenwood, 1987.
Edwards, B. *Gladiators of the Prize Ring, or Pugilists of America and Their Contemporaries from James J. Corbett to Tom Hyer.* Chicago: Athletic Publishing, n.d. [1895].
Ellicott, J. *Waterhouse and Smith: The Rise to Power of Two Racing Dynasties.* Melbourne: Hardie Grant, 2008.
Erdoes, R. *Saloons of the Old West.* New York: Gramercy, 1979.
Famous Fights Past and Present 7, 61 (1903): 194–200.
Fields, A. *James J. Corbett: A Biography of the Heavyweight Boxing Champion and Popular Theater Headliner.* Jefferson, NC: McFarland, 2001.
Fink, L. "Byron hot springs: the Carlsbad of America." *Contra Costa Chronicles* 1, 2 (Fall 1965): 27–34.
Fleischer, N. *Young Griffo: The Will o' the Wisp of the Roped Square.* New York: Fleischer, 1928.
Gagey, E.M. *The San Francisco Stage: A History.* New York: Columbia University Press, 1950.
Gee, T. *John L. Sullivan: Cradle to Grave.* Romford (Essex): Sporting Profiles, 1998.
Gifford, D., ed. *The British Film Catalog,* vol. 2: *Nonfiction Film 1888–1994.* London: Fitzroy Dearborn, 2001.

Gilbert, E.W. *Brighton: Old Ocean's Bauble.* London: Methuen, 1954.

Gilfoyle, T.J. *City of Eros: New York City, Prostitution, and the Commercialization of Sex, 1790–1920.* New York: Norton, 1992.

Glasscock, C.B. *Lucky Baldwin: The Story of an Unconventional Success* (Indianapolis: Bobbs-Merrill, 1933.

Gordon, G. *Master of the Ring: The Extraordinary Life of Jem Mace.* Wrea Green, UK: Milo, 2007.

Gorn, E.J. *The Manly Art: Bare-Knuckle Prize Fighting in America.* Ithaca, NY: Cornell University Press, 1986.

Grieg, M. *Goin' the Distance: Canada's Boxing Heritage.* Toronto: Macmillan Canada, 1996.

Griffin, G.M., and D. Tobin. *In the Midst of Life: The Australian Response to Death.* 2nd ed. Melbourne: Melbourne University Press, 1997.

Grimshaw, W.H. *Official History of Freemasonry Among the Colored People in North America.* Freeport, NY: Books for Libraries, 1971 [1903].

Growden, G. *The Snowy Baker Story.* Sydney: Random House Australia, 2003.

Hales, A.G. *Romantic Career of Peter Jackson, His Fights Re-told* (running title: *Peter the Black Prince, A Tale of Love and Sport*). Manchester: Umpire Publishing, n.d. [1910].

Hall, N.T. *Slave Society in the Danish West Indies: St. Thomas, St. John, and St. Croix.* Baltimore: Johns Hopkins University Press, 1992.

Hardie, D. "A Few notes on the climatic treatment of consumption in southern Queensland." *Australasian Medical Gazette* 16, 113 (1897): 113–116.

Harris, D. *Eadweard Muybridge and the Photographic Panorama of San Francisco 1850–1880.* Montreal: Centre Canadien d'Architecture, 1993.

Hayes, M.H. *Among Men and Horses.* London: Fisher Unwin, 1894.

Headon, D. "'World's fistanic history,' Sydney 1908: 'Flash Jack Johnson vs. Sinking Tommy Burns.'" *Sporting Traditions* 26, 2 (2009): 1–14.

Heering, P.N. *Familiebogen: optegnelser om min slægt af Peter N. Heering, Christianshavn 19 Februar 1912.* Copenhagen: H.H. Thiels Bogtrykkeri, 1912.

Heine, M.K., and K.B. Wamsley. "'Kickfest at Dawson City': native peoples and the sports of the Klondike gold rush." *Sports History Review* 27 (1996): 72–86.

Hendricks, G. *Eadweard Muybridge: The Father of the Motion Pictures.* London: Secker & Warburg, 1975.

_____. *Origins of the American Film.* New York: Arno, 1972.

Hill, E.G., and J.V. Hatch. *A History of African American Theater.* New York: Cambridge University Press, 2003.

Hjalmarson, B. *Artful Players: Artistic Life in Early San Francisco.* Los Angeles: Balcony, 1999.

Horrall, A. *Popular Culture in London c. 1890–1918: The Transformation of Entertainment.* Manchester: Manchester University Press, 2001.

Houstone, J.M. "A Pugilistic antique: researching a rare piece of Australian silver." *Australasian Antique Collector* No. 19 (1979): 86–89.

"The ice trade between America and India." *The Mechanic's Magazine,* 4/9/1836.

Isenberg, M.T. *John L. Sullivan and His America.* Urbana: University of Illinois Press, 1988.

Jalland, P. *Australian Ways of Death: A Social and Cultural History 1840–1918.* Melbourne: Oxford University Press, 2002.

Jarvis, J.A. *The Virgin Islands and Their People.* Philadelphia: Dorrance, 1944.

Jasen, D.A. and G. Jones, G. *Spreadin' Rhythm Around: Black Popular Songwriters 1880–1930.* New York: Schirmer, 1998.

Jensen, N.T. "Safeguarding slaves: smallpox, vaccination, and governmental health policies among the enslaved population in the Danish West Indies." *Bulletin of the History of Medicine* 83, 1 (2009): 95–125.

Jensen, P.H. *From Serfdom to Fireburn and Strike: The History of Black Labor in the Danish West Indies 1848–1916.* Christiansted: Antilles, 1998.

Johnson, J. *Jack Johnson Is a Dandy: An Autobiography.* New York: Signet, 1969 [originally titled *Jack Johnson In the Ring and Out,* 1927].

_____. *My Life and Battles,* translated from *Ma Vie et mes combats* [1914] by C. Rivers. Westport, CT: Praeger, 2007.

Johnson, J.W. *Along This Way: The Autobiography of James Weldon Johnson.* New York: Viking, 1934.

_____. *Black Manhattan.* New York: Da Capo, 1991.

Katz, J.N. *Love Stories: Sex Between Men Before Homosexuality.* Chicago: University of Chicago Press, 2001.

Kinsman, J., M. Bascou, T. Gott, F. Heilbrun, and C. Mathieu. *Paris in the Late 19th Century.* Canberra: National Gallery of Australia, 1997.

Kirk, R.C. *Twelve Months in Klondike.* London: Heinemann, 1899.

Kremer, G.R. *James Milton Turner and the Promise of America: The Public Life of a Post-Civil War Black Leader.* Columbia, MO: University of Missouri Press, 1991.

_____. "The World of make-believe: James Milton Turner and black masonry." *Missouri Historical Review* 76, 2 (1982): 50–71.

Kuyk, B.M. *African Voices in the African American Heritage.* Bloomington: Indiana University Press, 2003.

Lender, M.E., and J.K. Martin. *Drinking in America: A History.* 2nd ed. New York: Free, 1987.

Lidwill, M.C. *Patients' Guide to the Open Air Treatment of Consumption.* Sydney: Angus & Robertson, 1908.

Liliuokalani. *Hawaii's Story by Hawaii's Queen.* Rutland, VT: Tuttle, 1964 [1898].

Lindsay, J.A. *The Climatic Treatment of Consumption: A Contribution to Medical Climatology.* London: Macmillan, 1887.

Lipsky, W. *San Francisco's Midwinter Exposition.* Chicago: Arcadia, 2002.

Little, M.H. "The extra-curricular activities of black college students, 1868–1940," *Journal of African American History* 87 (Winter 2002): 43–55.

Logan, R.W. *The Betrayal of the Negro from Rutherford B. Hayes to Woodrow Wilson*. New York: Da Capo, 1997 [1965].

Lomax, M.E. *Black Baseball Entrepreneurs 1860–1901: Operating by Any Means Necessary*. Syracuse: Syracuse University Press, 2003.

Love, W.R.F. *A History of St. Helen's Methodist Hospital*. Brisbane: Queensland Historical Society, 1975.

Lubbock, B. *The Blackwall Frigates*. Glasgow: Brown Son Ferguson, 1924.

_____. *The Down Easters: American Deep-Water Sailing Ships 1869–1929*. Glasgow: Brown Son Ferguson, 1929.

_____. *The Last of the Windjammers*. Glasgow: Brown Son Ferguson, 1929.

Mander, R., and J. Mitchenson. *The Lost Theatres of London*. London: Hart-Davis, 1968; 2nd ed., London: New English Library, 1976.

Massey, M. *Recollections of Calcutta for Over Half a Century*. Calcutta: Bibhash Gupta, 1986 [1916].

McConnel, K., ed. *Our Federation: Brisbane Through the News 1901*. Brisbane: Brisbane History Group, "Sources No. 10," 2002.

McInnes, P., ed. *Bob Fitzsimmons: A Pugilistic Biography*. London: Caestus, 1998.

_____, ed. *Fifty Years a Fighter: The Life Story of Jem Mace (Retired Champion of the World) Told by Himself*. London: Caestus, 1998 [1908].

Michaels, B.L. "New light on F. Holland Day's photographs of African Americans." *History of Photography* 18, 4 (1994): 334–347.

Moorland, J.E. "The Young Men's Christian Association among Negroes." *Journal of Negro History* 9, 2 (1924): 127–138.

Myler, P. *The Fighting Irish*. Kerry: Brandon, 1987.

_____. *Gentleman Jim Corbett: The Truth Behind a Boxing Legend*. London: Robson, 1998.

Naughton, W.W. *Heavy-Weight Champions*. San Francisco: John Kitchen, 1910.

_____. *Kings of the Queensberry Realm*. Chicago: Continental, 1902.

Nichols, K.D. "Memoirs of W.H. Baker." *The Historian* 7, 1 (March 1978): 5–11; 9, 2 (June 1980): 11–14.

Nicholson, K.R. *A Man Among Men: The Life and Ring Battles of Jim Jeffries*. Draper, UT: Homeward Bound, 2002.

Norris, F. *Vandover and the Brute*, in F. Norris, *Novels and Essays*. New York: Library of America, 1986.

Northrop, H.D., J.R. Gay, and I.G. Penn. *The College of Life: or, Practical Self-Educator, A Manual of Self-Improvement for the Colored Race Forming an Educational Emancipator and a Guide to Success*. Chicago: Chicago Publication and Lithograph Company, 1895.

Obi, T.J.D. "Black terror: Bill Richmond's revolutionary boxing." *Journal of Sport History* 36, 1 (Spring 2009): 99–114.

Odell, G.C.D. *Annals of the New York Stage*. 15 vols. New York: Columbia University Press, 1927–1949.

Oriard, M. *Reading Football: How the Popular Press Created an American Spectacle*. Chapel Hill: University of North Carolina Press, 1993.

Osofsky, G. *Harlem, the Making of a Ghetto: Negro New York 1890–1930*. New York: Harper & Row, Harper Torchbooks, 1971.

Parker, N., and J. Pearn, eds. *Ernest Sandford Jackson: The Life and Times of a Pioneer Australian Surgeon*. Brisbane: Australian Medical Association Queensland, 1987.

Parsons, E.C., *Folk-Lore of the Antilles, French and English*. New York: American Folk Lore Society, 3 volumes, 1933, 1936, 1943.

Pendleton, L.A. "Our new possessions — the Danish West Indies." *Journal of Negro History* 2, 3 (1917): 267–324.

Petersen, B. *Gentleman Bruiser: A Life of the Boxer Peter Jackson, 1860–1901*. Sydney: Croydon, 2005.

_____. "Peter Jackson at Lane Cove." *Lane Cove Historical Society Newsletter*, No.163, 2001, 1–5.

Petersen, E.H. *Peter F. Heering: The History of a Danish Firm During 125 Years*. Copenhagen: n.p., 1943.

Petersen, R.C. "Peter Jackson Perfect Man." *Journal of Interdisciplinary Gender Studies* 6, 2 (2001): 26–46.

Phillips, R. *Edison's Kinetoscope and Its Films: A History to 1896*. Westport, CT: Greenwood, 1997.

Pickering, M. "Eugene Stratton and early ragtime in Britain." *Black Music Research Journal* 20, 2 (2000): 151–180.

Poignant, R. *Professional Savages: Captive Lives and Western Spectacle*. Sydney: University of New South Wales Press, 2004.

Pollack, A.J. *In the Ring with Bob Fitzsimmons*. New York: WinByKO, 2007.

_____. *John L. Sullivan: The Career of the First Gloved Heavyweight Champion*. Jefferson, NC: McFarland, 2006.

Ponce de Leon, C.L. *Self-Exposure: Human-Interest Journalism and the Emergence of Celebrity in America, 1890–1940*. Chapel Hill: University of North Carolina Press, 2002.

Porsild, C. *Gamblers and Dreamers: Women, Men, and Community in the Klondike*. Vancouver: University of British Columbia Press, 1998.

Powers, M. *Faces Along the Bar: Lore and Order in the Workingman's Saloon, 1870–1920*. Chicago: University of Chicago Press, 1998.

Rearick, C. *Pleasures of the Belle Epoque: Entertainment & Festivity in Turn-of-the-Century France*. New Haven: Yale University Press, 1985.

Reel, G. *The "National Police Gazette" and the Making of the Modern American Man 1879–1906*. New York: Palgrave Macmillan, 2006.

Riess, S.A. "Sports and machine politics in New York City 1870–1920," in D.K. Wiggins, ed., *Sport in America: From Wicked Amusement to National Obsession*. Champaign, IL: Human Kinetics, 1995, 163–184.

Roberts, K. *Captain of the Push*. Melbourne: Lansdowne, 1963.
Rout, L.B. *The African Experience in Spanish America, 1502 to the Present Day*. Cambridge: Cambridge University Press, 1976.
Roy, B.E. *The Presbyterians' First One Hundred Years in Roma: Special Centenary Edition (1866–1966)*. Roma: Maranoa Presbyterian, 1966.
St. Leon, M. *Spangles & Sawdust: The Circus in Australia*. Melbourne: Greenhouse, 1983.
Salmon, D., ed. *The Practical Parts of Lancaster's Improvements and Bell's Experiment*. Cambridge: Cambridge University Press, 1932.
Sampson, H.T. *Blacks in Blackface: A Source Book on Early Black Musical Shows*. Metuchen, NJ: Scarecrow Press, 1980.
Sante, L. *Low Life: Lures and Snares of Old New York*. New York: Vintage, 1992.
Savada, E. *The American Film Institute Catalog of Motion Pictures Produced in the United States: Film Beginnings 1893–1910*. Metuchen, NJ: Scarecrow, 1995.
Savage, K., *Standing Soldiers, Kneeling Slaves: Race, War, and Monument in Nineteenth-Century America*. Princeton, NJ: Princeton University Press, 1997.
Shah, N. *Contagious Divides: Epidemics and Race in San Francisco's Chinatown*. Berkeley: University of California Press, 2001.
Shaw, G.B. *Cashel Byron's Profession*. London: Constable, 1932 [1881].
Sinclair, A., and W. Henry. *Swimming*. 3rd ed. *Badminton Library of Sports*. London: Longmans Green, 1903.
Slægten Heering: personalhistoriske optegnelser. Copenhagen: n.p., 1900.
Smalls, J. *The Homoerotic Photography of Carl Van Vechten: Public Face, Private Thoughts*. Philadelphia: Temple University Press, 2006.
Snorgrass, J.W. "The black press in the San Francisco Bay area 1856–1900." *California History* 60, 4 (1981/82): 306–317.
Somrack, F.D. *Boxing in San Francisco*. Charleston: Arcadia, "Images of Sports," 2005.
Streible, D. "Fake fight films," in C.D. La Tour, A. Gaudreault, and R. Pearson, eds., *Le Cinéma au tournant du siècle/Cinema at the Turn of the Century*. Quebec: Nota Bene, 1999.
_____. *Fight Pictures: A History of Boxing and Early Cinema*. Berkeley: University of California Press, 2008.
_____. "A History of the boxing film 1894–1915: social control and social reform in the progressive era." *Film History* 3 (1989): 233–257.
Stuart, C.D., and A.J. Park. *The Variety Stage*. London: Fisher Unwin, 1895.
Sutherland, D. *The Yellow Earl: The Life of Hugh Lowther, 5th Earl of Lonsdale*. New York: Coward-McCann, 1966.
The Sydney Slang Dictionary. Sydney: H.J. Franklin, n.d. [1882].
Tansill, C.C. *The Purchase of the Danish West Indies*. New York: Greenwood, 1968 [1932].

Taylor, C.E. *Leaflets from the Danish West Indies: Descriptive of the Social, Political, and Commercial Condition of These Islands*. London: Dawson, 1888.
Thornton, I. *Krakatau: The Destruction and Reassembly of an Island Ecosystem*. Cambridge: Harvard University Press, 1996.
Thorpe, J. *Phil May: Master-Draughtsman & Humorist 1864–1903*. London: Harrap, 1932.
Tobias, C.H. "The Work of the Young Men's and Young Women's Christian Association with Negro Youth." *Annals of the American Academy of Political and Social Science* 140: "The American Negro," 1928.
Van Court, D. *The Making of Champions in California*. Los Angeles, Premier Printing, 1926.
Vancouver City Directory, June 1899–1900. Vancouver: 1899.
Vincent, J.E. *His Royal Highness Duke of Clarence and Avondale: A Memoir*. London: John Murray, 1893.
Voorhuis, H. *Negro Masonry in the United States*. Whitefish, MT: Kessinger, 1995.
Walvin, J. *Black and White: The Negro and English Society 1555–1945*. London: Allen Lane the Penguin Press, 1973.
Ward, G.C. *Unforgivable Blackness: The Rise and Fall of Jack Johnson*. New York: Knopf, 2004.
Warne, C. *Pictorial History: Lower North Shore*. Sydney: Kingsclear, 1995.
Waterhouse, R. *From Minstrel Show to Vaudeville: The Australian Popular Stage 1788–1914*. Sydney: University of New South Wales Press, 1990.
Watlington, R.A., and S.H. Lincoln, eds. *Disaster and Disruption in 1867: Hurricane, Earthquake and Tsunami in the Danish West Indies, A Collection of Accounts and Reports*. St. Thomas: University of the Virgin Islands, 1997.
Watson, W.S. *Diseases of the Nose and Its Accessory Cavities*. London: Lewis, 1875, 1890.
Weaver, G. *The History of Trinity College*, vol. 1. Hartford, CT: Trinity College Press, 1967.
Webb, D. *Prize Fighter: The Life and Times of Bob Fitzsimmons*. Edinburgh: Mainstream, 2000.
Weightman, G. *The Frozen Water Trade: How Ice from New England Kept the World Cool*. London: HarperCollins, 2001.
Welky, D.B. "Culture, media and sport: the *National Police Gazette* and the creation of an American working-class world." *Culture Sport Society* 1, 1 (1998): 78–100.
Wells, J. *Boxing Day: The Fight that Changed the World*. Sydney: HarperSports, 1998.
West, R.S. *The San Francisco Wasp: An Illustrated History*. Easthampton, MA: Periodyssey, 2004.
Whannel, G. *Media Sport Stars: Masculinities and Moralities*. London: Routledge, 2002.
Whimpress, B., ed. *The Imaginary Grandstand: Identity and Narrative in Australian Sport*. Adelaide: ASSH, 2002.
Whitehead, H.S. "Negro dialect of the Virgin Islands." *American Speech* 7, 3 (February 1932): 175–179.
Wiggins, D.K. *Glory Bound: Black Athletes in a White*

America. Syracuse, NY: Syracuse University Press, 1997.

_____. "Peter Jackson and the elusive heavyweight championship: a black athlete's struggle against the late nineteenth century color-line." *Journal of Sport History*, 12 (1985): 143–168.

Williams, R.T., ed. *The Williams Official British Columbia Directory 1899*. Victoria: Williams, 1899.

Williams, W.H.A. *'Twas Only an Irishman's Dream: The Image of Ireland and the Irish in American Popular Song Lyrics 1800–1920*. Urbana: University of Illinois Press, 1996.

Wilson, L.J.R. "Medicine Hat—'the sporting town' 1883–1905." *Canadian Journal of History of Sport* 16, 2 (1985): 15–32.

Winchester, S. *Krakatoa: The Day the World Exploded, 27 August 1883*. Bath: Chivers, 2003.

Winks, R.W. *The Blacks in Canada: A History*. 2nd.ed. Montreal: McGill-Queens University Press, 1997.

Wolf, T. "'A Grand assault-at-arms': tournaments and combative exhibitions in Victorian England." *Journal of Manly Arts* (August 2001).

Wood, J. *Hidden Talents: A Dictionary of Neglected Artists Working 1880–1950*. Billingshurst Sussex: Jeremy Wood Fine Art, 1994

Wright, C. "Of public houses and private lives: female hotelkeepers as domestic entrepreneurs." *Australian Historical Studies*, 116 (April 2001): 57–75.

Y.M.C.A. *(The Journal of the Brisbane YMCA)* 42 (6/1/1903): 7.

Zabriskie, L.K. *The Virgin Islands of the United States of America: Historical and Descriptive Commercial and Industrial Facts, Figures, and Resources*. New York: Putnam, 1918.

Web Sites

BoxRec boxing records
British Library online newspaper archive
Brooklyn Daily Eagle
California digital newspaper collection
Colorado digital newspapers
Cyberboxingzone
Gallica Consultation *Le Figaro*
Iron Game History
Library of Congress (American Memory)
Library of Congress (Chronicling America: historic American newspapers)
New York digital state newspapers (Fulton)
NLA Australian newspapers
Papers Past (digital New Zealand newspapers)
www.cruciandictionary.com,

Newspapers

Aberdare Times, 1894.
Adelaide Express and Telegraph, 1890.
American Churchman, 1878.
Baltimore Afro-American, 1901.
Bell's Life in Sydney, 1860–1870.
Bell's Life in Victoria (Melbourne), 1860–1868.
Bird O' Freedom (Sydney), 1891–1896.
Boston Globe, 1888–1901.
Boxer and Wrestler (Sydney), 1933–1935.
Boxing and Sporting Judge (Sydney), 1917.
Bridgetown Barbados Globe, 1894.
Brisbane Courier, 1887–1903.
Brisbane Daily Mail, 1903, 1909.
Brisbane Evening Observer, 1900–1909.
Buffalo Express, 1889–1890.
Calcutta Englishman, 1894.
Chicago Herald, 1894.
Chicago Tribune, 1889–1901.
Cincinnati Commercial Gazette, 1889–1890.
Cincinnati Enquirer, 1889–1890.
Cincinnati Evening Post, 1889–1890.
Cincinnati Times-Star, 1889–1890.
Cleveland Gazette, 1889–1901.
Dead Bird (Sydney), 1889–1891.
Decatur Daily Review, 1894.
Decatur Morning Herald, 1894.
Denver Colorado Sun, 1892.
Detroit Evening News, 1889.
Detroit Free Press, 1889.
Detroit Journal, 1889.
Dublin Freeman's Journal, 1889.
Dublin Irish Times, 1889.
Geelong Advertiser. 1890, 1900.
Geelong Times. 1890, 1900.
Honolulu Daily Bulletin, 1890–1900.
Honolulu Evening Bulletin, 1890–1899.
Illawarra Mercury, 1886.
Indian Planters' Gazette and Sporting News (Calcutta), 1893–1894, 1901.
Indianapolis Freeman, 1888–1901.
Juneau Daily Alaska Dispatch, 1900.
Kansas City American Citizen, 1889–1901.
Kansas City Star, 1893.
Kingston Daily Gleaner, 1893, 1901.
Le Figaro (Paris), 1894.
Licensed Victuallers Gazette (London), 1889.
Lloyd's List and Commercial Daily Chronicle (London), 1872.
London Graphic, 1888–1900.
London Times, 1889–1901.
Los Angeles Daily Times, 1893, 1898.
Louisville Commercial, 1890.
Louisville Courier Journal, 1890.
Maitland Mercury, 1885–1892.
Marysville Daily Appeal, 1890.
Nanaimo Free Press, 1899.
National Police Gazette (New York City), 1880–1901.
New York Age, 1887–1892.
New York Dramatic Mirror, 1893–1894, 1901.
New York Times, 1870–1901.
New York World, 1889–1897.
New Zealand Truth, 1913.
Newcastle Morning Herald and Miners' Advocate, 1887–1901.
North British Daily Mail (Glasgow), 1895.

Oakland Tribune, 1893.
Ogden Standard, 1891.
Portland Oregonian, 1888.
Penny Illustrated Paper (London), 1888–1900.
People (London), 1936–1937.
Philadelphia Inquirer, 1889–1894.
Rocky Mountain News (Denver), 1889–1894.
Roma Western Star, 1901.
St. Croix Avis (Christiansted), 1870–1895.
Saint Louis Post-Dispatch, 1889–1894.
San Francisco Alta California, 1888–1901.
San Francisco Bulletin, 1888–1901.
San Francisco Call, 1888–1899.
San Francisco Chronicle, 1887–1901.
San Francisco Evening Post, 1888–1901.
San Francisco Examiner, 1887–1901.
Seattle Daily Time, 1900.
Sport (London), 1889.
Sporting Echo (Melbourne), 1889–1890.
Sporting Judge (Melbourne), 1892–1901.
Sporting Life (London), 1889–1892.
Sporting Review, 1889.
Sporting Standard (Melbourne), 1890–1893.
Sportsman (London), 1882–1901.
Sportsman (Melbourne), 1882–1901.
Sydney Arrow, 1896–1923.
Sydney Australian Sportsman, 1880–1886.
Sydney Bulletin, 1880–1901.
Sydney Evening News, 1889–1901.
Sydney Field, 1891–1892.
Sydney Mail, 1879–1890.
Sydney Morning Herald, 1880–1901
Sydney Referee, 1886–1939.
Sydney Sportsman, 1901–1903.
Toronto Globe, 1889.
Town and Country Journal, 1880–1890.
Town Topics (London), 1914.
Vancouver Daily News-Advertiser, 1899–1900.
Vancouver Daily World, 1899–1900.
Vancouver Province, 1899–1900.
Victoria (B.C.) Daily Colonist, 1899.
Virginia Daily Territorial Enterprise, 1889.

Index

Acanthus Club (Washington DC) 115
Achilles statue (London) 102
Adelaide (S.A.) 130
Adriatic (ship) 113
Agar, Alex 40
Alameda (ship) 53, 203
Alameda, CA 199, 205
Alcazar Theater (SF) 167, 169
Alhambra (Brighton, UK) 104–105
Allen, Tom 107
Allen & Ginter cigarettes 178
Allnutt, Harry 160
Alpine Club (SF) 195
Angle, Bernard J. 101
Argyle Cottage (Roma) 220
Armory (Battery D), Chicago 87, 123
Armstrong, Bob 189, 205, 209
Arrow 34
Ashton, Jack 114
Assault-at-Arms 218
Astley, Sir John 96, 102, 185

Bacchante (ship) 106
Bacigalupi, Peter 181
Baker, Reg "Snowy" 53
Baldwin, Elias "Lucky" 176, 180, 196
Baldwin Hotel 176, 180, 195–196
Banjoewangie, Java 22, 103
Barbados 50, 184
Barbecue 137
Barleythorpe, Rutland 96
Bastin, Alfred 179
Beans, George 137
Belmont, Battle of 210
Berlin, Germany 161
Bettinson, Arthur F. "Peggy" 101, 111, 155, 159, 228
Bishop, Biddy 207, 208, 209
Blarney Castle (Ireland) 108
Bond, Ward 230
Bondi, New South Wales 47–48

Boon, Fred 186
Boston MA 114
Boyer, Georges 186–187
Brand, O. 129
Brighton, England 97, 99, 179
Brighton Hotel (Botany Bay, New South Wales) 215
Brisbane General Cemetery (Toowong, Qld) 224
Brisbane Gymnasium Club 224
Britannic (ship) 154
Brodie, Steve 174
Broomfield, Sid 128
Bruges, Belgium 109–110, 154, 190
Bubonic plague 212, 213, 214
Bucknam, Capt. Charles Henry 18, 19
Bucknam, Mate Henry W. 18, 19
Burke, Jack "Irish Lad" 49, 52, 123, 178
Byron Springs, CA 138

Calcutta, India 20, 185, 219, 224
California Athletic Club 59–60, 176
Calvert, Samuel 45
Cardiff, Wales 98, 189
Cardiff, Patrick "Patsy" 56, 75
Caribbee (ship) 183–184
Chambers, Arthur 56, 66
Chiarini, Giuseppe 43
Chicago, IL 85, 122, 168
Childs, Frank 205
Choynski, Joe 13, 76 153, 155, 165, 230
Christiansted, Virgin Islands 5, 6, 8, 9, 23
Cincinnati, OH 88–89, 119–120
City of Rome (ship) 93, 162
City of Seattle (ship) 209
Clampett, Arthur 37
Cleveland OH 89
Cliff House (San Francisco) 48
Cliff House (Sydney) 48

Conroy, Charles 220, 221
Considine, John 93
Cook, Hiram 60, 68
Corbett, Harry 197
Corbett, James J. 60, 162, 165, 174–175, 181, 189, 193, 210
Corbett, William "Will" 4, 47, 125, 127, 192, 203, 210, 217, 218, 221, 223, 225, 229, 230, 231
Corri, Eugene 13, 159
Costello, Martin "Buffalo" 47, 129
Courtney, Peter 181
Craig, Frank "Coffee Cooler" 187–188, 190, 224
Creedon, Dan 193
Cruso, Charles A. 26, 117
Cuban Giants 8, 122

Dagmar (ship) 15, 16
Dannebrog (Danish flag) 11
Davies, Charles "Parson" 85–87, 97, 106, 155, 171, 180, 215, 229
Davis, Jim "Soldier" 222
Dawson, George 51, 129
Day, F. Holland 79
The Dead Bird 77–79
Decatur IL 42, 171
Delaney, Billy 174, 175, 181, 199, 200
Dempsey, Jack "Nonpareil" 37, 68, 107, 138
Denmark 14
Detroit, MI 89
Diamond, Frederick Egerton 34, 35, 132
Dieves, Joseph 60, 125, 126, 190, 199, 216
Disraeli, Coningsby 101
Dixon, George 117, 118, 162, 180, 197
Doherty, Bill 36, 214, 215, 216
Donnelly, Ned 27–28, 39, 98
Donovan, Mike 56, 124, 194

249

Dooley, Mick 27, 50, 52, 132
Douglass, Frederic Montague 217
Douglass, Frederick 122, 173
Douglass, Lottie 203
Dowridge, Jack 3, 41, 50–51, 183, 217, 218, 223, 225, 229,
Dresser, Paul 112
Dublin, Ireland 107–109
DuBois, John Clarkson 6, 12, 17–18, 105
Du Bois, W.E.B. 121
Dunlop, John C. 41, 160

Eddie, Prince 105–106, 173
Edison, Thomas Alva 180
Edwards, Billy 56, 160, 178
Ellis, Edward 33
Elmer, Billy 198
Epsom, the Derby 160
Estate Orange Grove, Virgin Islands 184

Falk, Benjamin 114
Fallon, Jack 92, 93, 97, 103
Fallows, Joe 184
Farallones 55, 212
Farnan, Billy 35–36, 43, 200, 222
Felix, Peter 215, 216
Feneley, John 27, 127
Fields, Billy 141
Fitzgerald, Dan 216, 217
Fitzgerald, Tom 216
Fitzpatrick (Fitch), Sam 3, 49, 57, 59, 60, 118, 121, 152, 165, 190, 218, 230
Fitzsimmons, Robert 38, 138, 189, 193, 195, 196, 229
Fleischer, Nat 35, 230
Fleming, John 97, 109
Flynn, Errol 230
Foley, Larry 11, 30, 103, 170, 214, 225, 229
Folies Bergère 186
Forder, E. Neville 13, 26, 45, 66–67, 220
Fox, Richard K. 31
Frederiksted, Virgin Islands 6, 8–9, 12, 15, 17, 184
Freemasonry 106, 121, 131–132, 224, 226
Fulda, Lamartine R. 56, 59, 69, 103, 113, 150–151
Furniss, Harold 156, 159

Gable, Clark 77
Gallagher, Reddy 152
Geelong (Vic) 217
Gibbs, Dr John Wilson 171–172
Gillies, John 42, 44, 54, 128–129, 132, 153

Goddard, Joe 132, 169, 195, 197
Godfrey, George 13, 48, 58–58, 67, 92, 118, 139, 161
Goode, Bill "Chesterfield" 99
Gorman, Paddy 54, 229
Govern, S.K. 8
Graves, "Professor" Joe 66
Gredden, Jim 222, 225–226
Greengate Hotel 24–26
Greggains, Alex 206
Grenadier Guards 190
Griffiths, Albert "(Young) Griffo" 50, 129, 229
Grimshaw, Atkinson 109
Gunst, Mose 85, 198

Hales, A.G. "Smiler" 9, 131, 156, 159, 189, 229
Hall, Dr. Frank W. 209–210
Hallinan, Jack 85
Hanlan, Ned 91–92
Harlem Unique Club 117
Harmony Club (London) 193, 204
Harris, Rev. Samuel C. 224
Harting, George 55, 67, 173
Havana (Cuba) 218
Heering, Capt. Herluf 15–16, 28, 211
Herget, John "Young Mitchell" 47, 57, 60, 85, 152, 174, 180, 184, 195, 196, 206, 211, 230
Heyliger, Cherra 228
Hickey, Dan 38, 53
Hildebrandt, Jake 190
Hill, George 11, 30, 32, 41, 46
H.J. Libby (ship) 19, 20, 21
Hogan, Ernest 213–214
Hogan, Patsy 75
Holst family 6, 7
Honolulu, HI 127, 138, 197, 213
Hornibrook, Frederick 230
Horse "Careless Boy" 125
Hough, George 44

Igoe, Herbert "Hype" 200, 214

Jackson, Dr. E. Sandford 219
Jackson, Felix (brother) 7, 16, 183–184
Jackson, James (brother) 7, 16, 42, 171, 180, 183, 228–229
Jackson, Joseph (father) 6–7
Jackson, Julia (mother) 6–7, 10, 182, 183
Jackson, Peter: to Australia 20–22, 126; baptism 6; birth 5–6, 23; boyhood play 5, 12; and brawling Germans 126; champion of Australia 30, 44–45, 49; death of 223; earnings 173, 188, 202; fighting colors 101, 156; freemason 131–132; and French 106–107; funeral of 223–224; grave of 226–228; illnesses 161, 214 (*see also* nosebleeds, tuberculosis); jumps ship 24; learns to box 25–26; and marriage 39–40, 99, 101, 125, 191, 203, 231; to New York 17; nosebleeds 107, 171–172; and Othello 6, 166; parentage 4, 6–7, 222; to Pernambuco 16; physique of 172, 200; and religion 15, 221–222; St. John, David 185–189; as saloon keeper 139; schooling 12–13; siblings 5, 7, 184; as singer 112; speech 10–11, 13, 221–222; as swimmer 53, 67, 111; and tuberculosis 15, 204, 205, 215, 217, 219–220; vs. Ashton, Jack 124; vs. Baker, Billy 89, 92; vs. Ball, Alf 98; vs. Bendoff, Wolf 104; vs. Brennan, Paddy 91; vs. Britten, Sam 33; vs. Brown, Charles "Sailor" 87; vs. Butler, Joe 165; vs. Cardiff, Patsy 79–82; vs. Cave, George 34; vs. Chandler, Tom 166; vs. Childs, Frank 167; vs. Choynski, Joe 169, 171; vs. Corbett, James J. 140–149; vs. Cosnett, Josh "Brum" 192; vs. Costello, Martin "Buffalo" 130; vs. Dalton, John 154; vs. Devine, "Sailor" 127; vs. Dooley, Mick 34, 50, 52; vs. Douglass, Jim 166; vs. Dubbo 31, 33; vs. Fallon, Jack 92–93, 116; vs. Farnan, Billy 36; vs. Farrell, Jack 129; vs. Flowers, Jerry 84; vs. Goddard, Joe 133–137; vs. Godfrey, George 60–66; vs. Greggains, Alex 206; vs. Gregory, Jack "Cigarette Kelly" 27; vs. Gunn, "Scotchy" Bill 104; vs. "Guy the Gipsy" 115; vs. Hallinan, Jack 56; vs. Hayes, Jack 33; vs. Healy, Hugh 50; vs. Hook, Jem 98; vs. Jackson, Alfred "Stonewall" 31, 51; vs. Jeffers, Jim 206–208; vs. Jeffries, James 200–202; vs. Johnson, Tom C. 126; vs. Kaufman, Fred 84; vs. Keating, Dick 119; vs. Kelliher, Denis 165; vs. King, Jack 154; vs. Lambert, Gus 116; vs. Leedom, Billy 165; vs. Lees, Tom 35, 43–45; vs. Lynch, Tom

89–90; vs. Maher, Peter 108; vs. Matthews, Dick 42; vs. McAuliffe, Joe 68–74, 75; vs. McCormick, Jim "Ginger" 92; vs. McLean, "Professor" Billy 165; vs. McVey, John 164; vs. Meddings, William "Coddy" 98, 191; vs. Miller, "Professor" William 43, 50; vs. Mitchell, Alf 98; vs. Nolan, Jim 50; vs. O'Brien, Mick 50; vs. Partridge, Jack "Bully" 98; vs. Peters, George C. 89; vs. Power, Billy 131; vs. Riordan, Cornelius "Con" 56; vs. "Shorty Kinkaid" *see* Kaufman, Fred; vs. "Siwash Wonder" 124; vs. Slavin, Bill 192; vs. Slavin, Paddy 156–161; vs. Smith, "Denver" Ed 122–124; vs. Smith, Jem 102–103, 104; vs. Smith, Stormo 50; vs. Sullivan, Mike 58; vs. Sullivan, Owen 190; vs. Swarzas, George 26; vs. Sykes, George 187; vs. Taylor, Tom 53; vs. Walker, "Soldier" James 115; vs. Watson, Jack 98; vs. White, "Sailor" 104; vs. Woodham, W. 104; vs. Young, Jem 104, 107; works for Foley 31
Jackson, Samuel (brother) 7, 16
Jamaica 6, 172, 174
Java 22
Jeffords, Jim 160, 206–207, 230
Jeffries, Jim 160, 165, 197, 230
Johnson, Jack 3–4, 131, 209
Johnson, James Weldon 122
Johnson, McHenry "Black Star" 59
The Judge (play) 164

Kiama, New South Wales 45–46
Kilrain, Jake 52, 75, 139, 205
kinetoscope 180–181

Lane Cove, New South Wales 24–26
Laurie, Annie 125, 131
Lawless, Will 37
Lawson, James 34, 40–41, 45
Lees, Tom 43, 45, 84, 85, 89, 101, 230
Leinster Hall (Dublin) 108, 220
L'Estrange, Dr. Guy 205, 220, 221, 230–231
Liliuokalani, Queen of Hawaii 168
Lloyd, Albert 228
Lodge Gen. Gordon 132
Long, Charley 206

Lonsdale *see* Lowther, Hugh
Lotus Club (SF) 57–57, 150, 167
Louisville, KY 118–119
L'Ouverture, Toussaint 225
Lowther, Hugh (Lord Lonsdale) 83, 96, 153, 173, 230
Lubin, Siegmund 219
Lucas, Dan 154

Mace, Jem 30–31, 32, 45, 98, 102, 194
Macintosh, Harry 223
Maher, Peter 108, 181, 188, 192, 198
Mariposa (ship) 126, 127, 211
Marshall, Annie 219
Marshall, Con 56
Marysville CA 126
Masterson, Bat 101, 123, 140, 149, 152, 154, 172
Matthews, Dick 27, 42
Matthews, Sam 129
May, Phil 185, 193–194
Maynard, Harry 27, 56
McAnally, Mary "Minnie" 220, 223, 225
McAuliffe, Joe 66, 68, 180, 196
McCarthy, Billy 37, 53
McCullum, Donald 220
McLain, Billy 215, 225
McLaughlin, George 130
McMahon, Jim 26, 197
McNab, Gavin 198
McVey, Connie 115
Meadows, Tom 38, 54, 222
Mecca cigarettes 229
Miller, Louise Anderson 168, 169
Miller, "Professor" William 35, 43, 51, 56, 60, 131, 134, 225
Missoula, MT 84
Mitchell, Charley 52, 97, 101, 154, 181, 189
Money, Dr Angel 215, 216, 217, 218
Monongahela (ship) 8
Morse, Capt. Charles 53, 56
Mount Clemens, MI 122, 174
Moyle, James Richard 94, 96
Murphy, Billy "Torpedo" 125, 129
Murphy, Dan 172

Nail, Fred 93, 184
Nail, John B. 93, 121, 195
Nanaimo, British Columbia 207
Nassau, Bahamas 6, 18, 57
National Sporting Club (UK) 96, 153, 160, 176
Naughton, W.W. "Bill" 13, 17, 35, 54, 79, 121, 140, 159–160, 166, 175–176, 192, 211, 229

Nelson's Pillar (Dublin) 108
New Orleans 138, 162
New York 18–19, 92–93, 168, 169, 181
Newcastle, New South Wales 24, 53, 128, 218, 224–225
Newsboy Plug tobacco 178
Nordrach treatment 220
Norris, Frank 204

Oakland CA 167, 195
Occidental Club (SF) 195, 198, 199
O'Connor, Eugene "Maranoa" 220, 221, 231
O'Donnell, Steve 37, 53, 190
Ogden, UT 124
Olympic Athletic Club (SF) 57, 59, 60, 194
Orinoco (ship) 184
O'Rourke, Tom 164, 180, 181, 192, 205, 209

Pages, Lewis 226–227
Palace Hotel (SF) 66, 82, 196
Parent, Dr Charles E. 199–200, 202, 205
Paris, France 106–107, 186–187
Pelican Club 116, 153
Peregrine (ship) 218
Perry, Harry C. 3, 223
Piess, George C. "Rats" 48, 52
Poniatowski, Prince André 200, 230
Portland ME 19
Powell, Ned 45
Preece, Ambrose 111, 112, 160, 173
Prince Eddie 105–106, 173

Queensberry, Marquis of 30, 52, 56, 96, 98
Queenstown, Ireland 93, 113

Reed, Mr. and Mrs. Griffin 118
Referee 34
Reid, Ike 44
Relph, Harry "Little Tich" 188, 214
Richards, Michael 11
Riordan, Cornelius "Con" 56, 154, 155
Rollins, Edward "Starlight" 51
Roma, Queensland 214, 220
Royal Aquarium Theatre 97
Royal Jubilee Hospital, British Columbia 209–210
Royal Westminster Aquarium 97, 103, 104

St. Helen's Hospital (Brisbane) 219

St. John, David (Dai) 185–186, 187, 190, 210
Sallars, Harry 28–30, 51, 167
Salt Lake City 121
Sandow, Eugen 99, 176–178, 181
San Francisco 20, 55, 57
San Francisco Wasp 125–126
Santa Cruz (Saint Croix, Virgin Islands) 7–8, 180, 182
Santa Rosa, CA 167
Sarony, Napoleon 93
Sausalito, CA 59, 140
Sayers, Tom 226, 227
Servia (ship) 194
Shango 11, 12, 132, 141
Sharkey, Tom 127, 195, 197, 206, 230
Sheadon & Flynn 114
Simpson, John B. 206
Skagway, AK 209
Slater, Edith (Slavin) 112, 206
Slaughter, Harry 18, 24–25
Slavin, Bill 51, 53, 140, 192, 193
Slavin, Francis Patrick "Paddy" 31–32, 46–47, 48, 99, 109, 111–112, 139, 154, 182, 186, 188, 192, 193, 206, 211, 230
Slavin, Jack 140, 155, 156, 192
Smith, Billy 38, 51, 60, 155, 156
Smith, "Denver" Ed 210–211
Smith, Elijah "Lige" 210, 211
Smith, George 185

Smith, Jem 54, 96–97, 154, 190
Smith, John 223, 224, 226–227
South Africa 190
Stanton, John 178
Stewart, Rev. James 17, 221–222
Stewart, Jem 50, 189
Stockwell, Lincoln R. 167, 168, 198
Stratton, Eugene 98
Sullivan, John L. 9–10, 35–36, 7, 40, 52, 58, 87, 88, 109, 113, 119, 151, 152, 153, 225
Sykes, George 187

Taber, Isaiah 67, 77, 178
Taplin, Capt. 26–27, 225
Tarbeaux, Frank 112
Taylor, Tom 38, 53
Teutonic (ship) 163, 172
Thompson, Barney 101
Thompson, Jack 39, 44
Toledo, OH 169
Toronto, Ontario 91–92
Tremayne Rodd, E.S. 193
Troy, NY 116
Trudgen stroke 37
tuberculosis 55, 107, 214
Turner, James Milton 121, 132
Tweedie, Edward "Cocker" 205, 217

Umslopogaas 166, 195
Uncle Tom's Cabin 166–171

Vancouver BC 207–208
Victoria, British Columbia 207, 209
Virginia City, NE 84
Vize, George 101, 102

Wagga Wagga, New South Wales 129
Walcott, Joe 180, 197
Walla-Walla (ship) 211
Walton, "Professor"'s cats 181
Ward, Wag 186, 190
Warren, Tommy 81
Waterhouse family 24–25
Watson, "Professor" Walter 124–125
Watson, Robert "Paul Pry" 93, 96, 106
Watson, Tom 24, 25
Welsh, James 127
Williams, Bert 55
Williams, Billy 49
Winter, Isaac 18, 19, 21
Wirth's Circus 224
Wood, John 93
Woods, Billy 151

Young, Jem 155

Zulus 26, 166, 177

www.ingramcontent.com/pod-product-compliance
Ingram Content Group UK Ltd.
Pitfield, Milton Keynes, MK11 3LW, UK
UKHW050536150426
5217IPUK00026B/1959